Marketing Communications

With the proliferation of digital and social media, there has never been a more dynamic time to engage with marketing communications – and never has the integration of marketing communications (marcoms) principles into a strategic marketing plan been more challenging. Even the best product in the world won't sell without the right reach to your potential customers and the right message to engage them.

This textbook applies a uniquely practical approach to the topic so that, whilst a structured overview of planning, development, implementation and evaluation of marketing communications is in place, the detailed cases made available by the Institute for Practitioners in Advertising (IPA) show how actual challenges faced by professionals in the field were addressed. This book will help you to develop the skills you need to turn theory into the right integrated communication plan, in order to succeed in an increasingly competitive environment.

Aided by a veritable wealth of pedagogical features, *Marketing Communications* will be essential reading for both students and professionals in marketing, communications and public relations. This textbook also benefits from a companion website which includes: a comprehensive instructor's guide, PowerPoint slides, testbank questions and answer checklists.

Lynne Eagle holds a PhD from the University of Auckland in her native New Zealand. She is currently Professor of Marketing and Associate Dean – Research for the Faculty at James Cook University in Australia.

Stephan Dahl holds a PhD in Cross-Cultural Psychology (University of Luton, UK). He is currently Senior Lecturer in Marketing at Hull University Business School, UK.

Barbara Czarnecka holds a PhD in Marketing (Middlesex University, London, UK) and currently she is Senior Lecturer of Marketing at the University of Bedfordshire, UK.

Jenny Lloyd holds a PhD from the University of the West of England, UK where she currently holds the post of Associate Head of the Department for Undergraduate Marketing.

Marketing Communications contributes to a wider understanding of how digital and social media is now a crucial basis for any successful marketing plan. Students and industry professionals can benefit from the practical approach of the book, and its supporting real-life industry case studies, while also facing the ethical issues that surround social media.

Jo Bates, Lecturer, University College Birmingham, UK

This text is a truly holistic approach to marketing communications learning, with the provision of unique opportunities to implement the presented concepts and frameworks in practice.

Natalia Yannopoulou, Senior Lecturer, Newcastle University Business School, UK

Marketing Communications

**Lynne Eagle, Stephan Dahl,
Barbara Czarnecka and Jenny Lloyd**

Routledge
Taylor & Francis Group

LONDON AND NEW YORK

First published 2015
by Routledge
2 Park Square, Milton Park, Abingdon, Oxon OX14 4RN

and by Routledge
711 Third Avenue, New York, NY 10017

Routledge is an imprint of the Taylor & Francis Group, an informa business

© 2015 Lynne Eagle, Stephan Dahl, Barbara Czarnecka and Jenny Lloyd

British Library Cataloguing in Publication Data
A catalogue record for this book is available from the British Library

Library of Congress Cataloging in Publication Data
Eagle, Lynne.
Marketing communications/Lynne Eagle, Stephan Dahl,
Barbara Czarnecka, Jenny Lloyd. – First Edition.
    pages cm
    Includes bibliographical references and index.
    1. Communication in marketing. 2. Advertising. I. Title.
    HF5415.123.E24 2014
    658.8′02–dc23   2014002230

ISBN: 978-0-415-50770-7 (hbk)
ISBN: 978-0-415-50771-4 (pbk)
ISBN: 978-1-315-77886-0 (ebk)

Typeset in Times New Roman and Helvetica
by Florence Production Ltd, Stoodleigh, Devon, UK

Contents

Visit the companion website at www.routledge.com/cw/eagle for instructor resources including: PowerPoint slides, multiple choice questions and answer checklists for the case studies, think boxes and review questions.

Figures

Tables

About the authors

Barbara Czarnecka holds a PhD in Marketing (Middlesex University, London, UK). Currently, she is Senior Lecturer of Marketing at the University of Bedfordshire, UK. Her field of interest is in cross-cultural consumer behaviour, marketing communications and ethics, and marketing research techniques. She has written articles and presented at various international conferences on a range of topics related to cross-cultural issues in marketing communications.

Stephan Dahl holds a PhD in Cross-Cultural Psychology (University of Luton, UK). He is currently Senior Lecturer in Marketing at the University of Hull, UK and Adjunct Associate Professor, James Cook University, Australia. His research interests are: health and social marketing, emancipated marketing theory and cross-cultural marketing. He has published in a range of academic journals and presented numerous research papers at international conferences.

Lynne Eagle holds a PhD from the University of Auckland in her native New Zealand. She is currently Professor of Marketing at James Cook University in Australia. Her research interests centre on: marketing communication effects and effectiveness, including the impact of persuasive communication; the impact of new, emerging and hybrid media forms and preferences for/use of formal and informal communications channels; trans-disciplinary approaches to sustained behaviour change in social marketing/health promotion/environmental protection campaigns. She has published in a wide range of academic journals, led the development of texts and contributed several book chapters for other texts, as well as writing commissioned expert papers and presenting numerous research papers at international conferences.

Jenny Lloyd holds a PhD from the University of the West of England, UK where she currently holds the post of Associate Head of Department for Undergraduate Marketing. Jenny's research focusses largely upon the role of marketing within a political context and she has particular interests in voter insight, political engagement, political branding and the impact of political marketing communications. She has contributed papers and chapters to a variety of non-profit marketing, marketing and political science anthologies and journals, and has presented papers at national and international conferences in the fields of both marketing and political science.

Acknowledgements

While the authors assume the full responsibility for the content of this book, important parts of it could not have been written without the help and support of the following people and organizations.

For providing the case studies for this textbook, we would like to thank:

- World Advertising Research Centre (WARC)
- Institute of Practitioners of Advertising (IPA)
- Design Business Association (DBA)
- Account Planning Group (APG)
- Meg Carter (www.megcarter.com).

We would also like to thank Michal Czarnecki for his volunteering work with requesting permissions to reproduce the images and figures for this book.

1 Marketing communications as a strategic marketing tool

LEARNING OUTCOMES

After studying this chapter, you will be able to:

- Provide an overview of the role of marketing communications within the overall marketing mix

- Provide a brief overview of the development of, and controversy surrounding, the concept of integrated marketing communications (IMC)

- Review the major barriers to successful integration of marketing communications

- Discuss the marketing communications challenges presented by services and social marketing compared to tangible products

- Debate the impact of new and emerging media forms on traditional marketing communications activity

Introduction

Marketing communications does not occur in isolation, but rather is part of a wider overall **marketing mix**.[1] It has traditionally been portrayed under the term **promotion** as a part of the '4Ps of marketing management', as shown in Figure 1.1.

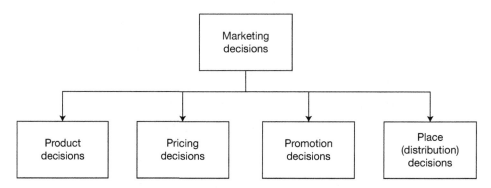

Figure 1.1 Traditional marketing management decisions[2]

Promotion in its turn is usually shown as in Figure 1.2, with separate functions that reflect the reality of distinct, independent organizations performing specialist functions without significant coordination of their activity. Thus it is possible for **advertising** to attempt to project an exclusive, **quality-based image** while at the same time **price-based sales promotions** could be used; the two communication activities projecting very different images to consumers and often occurring without linkages to other marketing activity, including packaging.[3] This separation of function and activity ignores the fact that consumers integrate information, including **marketing communications** and information from other sources including the media and via retail outlets where a manufacturer may have limited control over marketing communications. This will occur whether the marketing or advertising organization makes a conscious effort to integrate **messages** from sources under their direct control or not, with the result that messages can be put together in unexpected ways – which may even be harmful to the brand.[4]

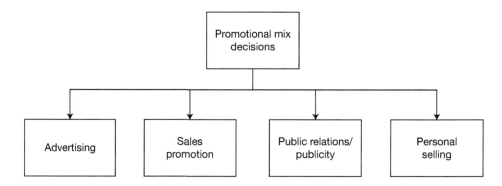

Figure 1.2 Traditional promotional mix decisions[2]

To be fully effective, **integration** starts at the initial strategic planning level and is far more than just ensuring a common look or feel to messages sent via different **channels**. Figures 1.1 and 1.2, however, are overly simplistic in that they do not reflect the complexities of the processes involved. Even within the promotional mix decision process, Figure 1.2 implies that each of the four subsets are separate activities and does not capture instances where there may be considerable overlap between the functions, such as when advertising may be the vehicle by which sales promotion activity is communicated, or the use of the **Internet** for far more than just advertising messages.

THINK BOX

Marketing communications and product types

Using Figures 1.1. and 1.2, map out the marketing communications activity of:

1. a 'fast moving consumer good' (FMCG) **product** such as bread;
2. a soft drink such as Coca-Cola or Pepsi against bottled water and energy drinks;
3. a durable product such as a refrigerator;
4. a service provider such as an airline or an organization offering packaged holidays.

In what ways are their marketing communications strategies likely to be similar and in what ways are they likely to be different – and why?

Environmental turbulence: the effect of new media forms

Most importantly, the functions shown in Figure 1.2 do not reflect the reality of communication vehicles today, particularly interactive media forms. Among these are **hybrid media** forms such as **advergames** that reflect a blurring between entertainment and persuasion in which branded products or services are frequently an integral component of a (usually) Internet-based game.[5] The aim is to offer entertainment, interaction and emotional connection between the game and the brand featured within it in a way that traditional **mass media** cannot do.[6] Figure 1.2 also does not capture the way **social media** function (see Chapter 9 for a detailed discussion). In addition, the effects and effectiveness of the growing use of **product placements** in television programmes and in movies (see Chapter 10 for a discussion of hybrid media forms) have yet to be determined across product and service categories.

The **promotional mix** shown in Figure 1.2 needs to be re-conceptualized to show the changing nature of the marketing communications vehicles that may be considered. Direct and database communication methods need to be considered as a distinct form of communication, as do Internet-based and **interactive media** forms. New communication forms will continue to evolve and any diagrammatic presentation of the promotional mix options is likely to be subject to regular revision. However, with this must come a greater understanding of what the message receiver does with the various messages received; this area remains significantly under researched.[7]

Successful **campaigns** are not always dependent on large advertising **budgets** and the use of mass media such as television, as the following example shows. This case won the best small budget category and an overall silver award at the 2008 IPA Effectiveness Awards.

MINI CASE: RADLEY

Source: Institute of Practitioners in Advertising: Best Small Budget & Silver, IPA Effectiveness Awards 2008. Case material provided by the World Advertising Research Centre (WARC) www.warc.com.

Radley is a relatively small brand of handbags with a small advertising budget in a fragmented and fickle fashion market. It has a small base of loyal purchasers but faced major challenges in increasing **market share**, particularly given the **perceptions** of their bags being functional and good quality but not stylish.

Share of voice was unlikely to be more than 3 per cent, so a truly original idea was needed to help the brand stand out from its much larger competitors such as Dolce & Gabbana and Gucci. The focus of the creative activity from 2007 onwards was chosen as:

"Truly Radley Deeply"

Distinctive advertisements such as those shown on page 5 ran in colour newspaper supplements, weekly women's magazines such as *Grazia* and fashion magazines such as *Vogue.*

As new designs were introduced, they were supported by distinctive advertisements, all linked by the common "Truly Radley Deeply" line. Two examples are shown on page 6.

A major initiative was the development of a feature window display in branches of the John Lewis department store chain, the first time such a campaign had been approved by the chain.

Sales increased three times faster than the overall handbag market and the value of the company itself tripled.

The total advertising budget was £800,000, with the advertising directly credited with increasing the value of the company by at least £3.75 million. The campaign paid for itself 5.7 times, one of the highest returns on marketing investment achieved.

Questions to consider

Try to evaluate this case using the material covered in this chapter, particularly Figures 1.1 and 1.2. Also think about how Radley might change their marketing mix in the future, including how they might use electronic media.

Specifically focus on the following questions:

1. Discuss the arguments for and against continuing to run this style of advertising.
2. Assume you are one of Radley's major competitors:

    a. how would you counter their marketing communications?
    b. what are the arguments for and against undertaking a similar store promotion with another **retailer** (e.g. Harvey Nichols, Debenhams, House of Fraser)?

3. If you were the marketing manager of one of these department stores, what would you recommend be done regarding promoting Radley and/or its competitors in store?

Justify each of your answers.

Photo 1.1a

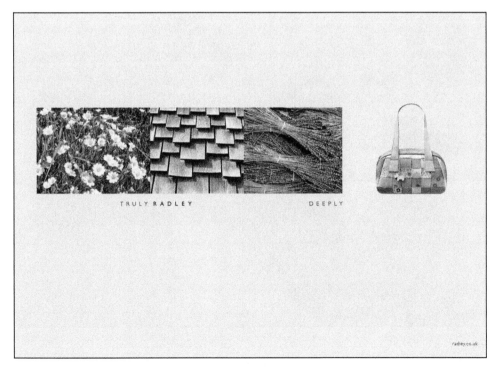

Photo 1.1b

Photo 1.2a

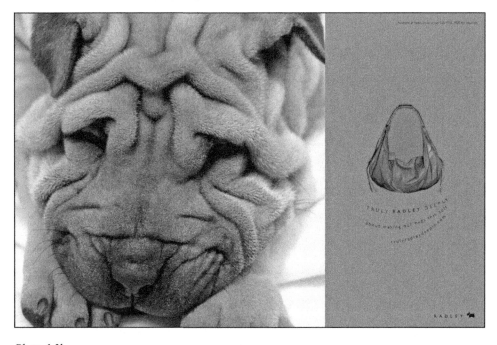

Photo 1.2b

Changes to marketing communications over time

As the academic literature shows, much of the emphasis up to the early 1980s was on how individual communications forms worked, with emphasis on mass media communication, particularly television advertising, which was seen as being somewhat passively received by consumers. A re-examination of the role and effectiveness of advertising as a marketing communications tool began in the late 1980s, and accelerated through the early 1990s. Long standing assumptions about 'what advertising does' were questioned and rephrased as what people did with the advertising to which they chose to pay attention.[8] Mass media began to **fragment**, with increasing numbers of television channels, radio stations and print media competing for a share of advertising alongside less prominent media such as cinema and a range of **outdoor** advertising options.

This was followed by the emergence, and growth, of new media forms, particularly those using **electronic technology** such as the Internet.[9] These new media changed consumers' access to, and control over, marketing communications in major markets. At the same time, there was an increasing awareness that most markets were not homogeneous, but rather made up of distinct segments with diverse interests, **attitudes** and media usage habits.[10]

Concerns were raised regarding the **impact** of clutter within mass media, i.e., many advertisements competing for a share of attention[11] and attempts to stand out from competitors and rise above the clutter which, to some observers, seemed to lead to less emphasis on product or service attributes, and more on providing entertainment, at the risk of being different rather than relevant to the consumer.[12] Unsurprisingly, a greater emphasis on determining the **return on investment** from marketing activity also occurred, leading to a focus on the measurement of the impact of marketing communications activity which continues in the current era.[13]

These pressures lead to considerable interest in the way in which marketing communications activity occurred and the way in which synergies could maximise their individual and combined efforts under the banner of **integrated marketing communications (IMC)**. This inevitably led to considerable debate as to whether IMC was merely a management fad,[14] whether it offered anything new or merely reflected best practice and calls for a precise definition as to what IMC actually was.[15]

One of the most widespread definitions is:

> a concept of marketing communications planning that recognizes the added value of a comprehensive plan that evaluates the strategic roles of a variety of communications disciplines, e.g. general advertising, direct response, sales promotion and public relations – and combines these disciplines to provide clarity, consistency and maximum communication impact.
>
> (American Association of Advertising Agencies quoted in Duncan and Everett)[15] (p. 31)

It is also suggested that a key addition to the above definition is **synergy**,

> meaning the individual efforts are mutually reinforcing with the resulting effect being greater than if each functional area had selected its own targets, chosen its own message strategy, and set its own media schedule.[15]
>
> (p. 32)

Brands are rarely created by marketing communications alone, however it is recognized that marketing communications, which primarily centred around conventional advertising in the past but now functions through an increasingly diverse range of channel options, is important in positioning the brand in consumers' minds.[16]

The question implied but rarely explicitly stated in the advertising/marketing communications literature is as follows. Marketing communications can be considered to have a positive effect on brand equity/evaluation *if* the brand's value and changes in that value over time are measurable and *if* marketing communications can be shown to be a major contributor to that change.

While a significant role for integrated communication in influencing brand equity is claimed by several authors, usually on the logical grounds of ensuring consistency of messages to customers and synergy of efforts,[17] actual evidence of a cause–effect relationship appears to be somewhat elusive. The influence of IMC on brands and branding is discussed in more detail in Chapter 7.

THINK BOX

Sales promotion

Assume you are the marketing manager for an electronics company. Your marketing communications has historically been centred on high quality and technical **innovation**. Your sales are now sluggish and your advertising **agency** has recommended a major price discount-based sales promotion.

Discuss the positives and negatives of this move, the likely impact on sales and on the way consumers perceive your brand.

What action might your competitors take if you maintain your current marketing communications approach OR if you change to a price discount-based **strategy**? Use Figures 1.1 and 1.2 to map out what information you would need to determine which option is likely to be the better choice. Justify your decisions.

While it would appear self-evident that no-one would argue against integrating communication,[18] there is clear evidence not only that integration was rarely operationalized in the past,[19] but there is evidence that some sectors of the communications industry, most notably public relations, actively opposed integration on several grounds, including that some public relations activity focussed on corporate rather than specific brand issues.[20] The move by traditional advertising agencies to embrace IMC principles appears to have originated from the recognition that communication agencies were losing budget share as funds were increasingly moved from traditional marketing communication activities to a range of newer forms and competition increased among potential providers of expertise for these new activities.[21] Expenditure allocations across media have changed significantly over time as shown in Table 1.1.

MINI CASE: ADVERTISING RIP?

In 1994, the 'death of advertising' was predicted,[22] with claims that direct marketing, sales promotions and new media would draw advertising budgets away from **traditional media**. As Table 1.1 shows, there has been a reallocation of budgets across media, but traditional media remain strong communications vehicles.

Table 1.1 United Kingdom: advertising expenditure currency: £, million

Year	Total	News-papers	Magazines	Tele-vision	Radio	Cinema	Outdoor	Internet
1999	11302	4474	1922	3672	464	123	595	51
2000	12495	5014	2020	3950	534	128	697	153
2001	11896	4896	1980	3525	487	164	678	166
2002	11941	4808	1873	3690	492	180	702	197
2003	12374	4864	1832	3722	526	180	786	465
2004	13372	5107	1901	3955	545	192	848	825
2005	13866	4906	1892	4097	521	188	897	1366
2006	14045	4695	1828	3905	480	188	933	2016
2007	14947	4680	1758	4016	497	207	976	2813
2008	14420	4118	1584	3819	454	205	939	3300
Change: 08–07	**–3.5%**	**–12.0%**	**–9.9%**	**–4.9%**	**–8.5%**	**–0.9%**	**–3.8%**	**17.3%**

Source: The Advertising Association, World Advertising Research Centre (WARC). Reproduced with permission.

1. Why might the 1994 prediction have been overly pessimistic about traditional media?
2. Why have some traditional media continued to increase advertising revenue while others have declined?
3. What do you believe the likely pattern of advertising spend might be in the next 5 years and the next 10 years?
4. Do you believe that advertising as we currently know it will eventually die?

Justify your responses to each question.

Barriers to successful integration of marketing communications elements

It was evident from the early 1990s that a focus on integrating communication activity would change the roles and accountability relationships between marketers and their specialist communication suppliers,[10] with a number of barriers to effective and efficient integration evident. These included organizational structures, the need for functional specialists to broaden their appreciation of other communication roles and of emerging technologies, turf battles, and issues surrounding who should ultimately coordinate or control activity.[23]

Several studies have focussed on attempting to prove how a specific discipline, such as public relations, exhibit marketing or **trade shows** added value,[24,25,26] or on attempting to challenge perceptions regarding the strategic versus tactical use of activities such as sales promotions.[27] A number of more macro-focussed studies have shown managerial support for the principles of IMC.[28] There is also evidence that there is a correlation between levels of integration and sales, market share and profitability, however the direction of the relationship and the factors underpinning it remain unclear.[29]

There is a need to revisit traditional ways of measuring return on investment (ROI) from individual IMC components and their combined influence; this has been seen as a major problem since IMC began to receive major focus from both practitioners and academics.[30] This is not necessarily due to unwillingness to engage in research, but rather the complexities of determining the effects of any individual marketing communications device, such as advertising or public relations, and of then identifying the synergistic impact of all communication forms used.

These effects are likely to vary according to the specific market conditions, making generalized principles difficult. In addition, external and largely uncontrollable factors such as relevant news media coverage may also impact on communication effectiveness.[31] Further, there may be time lags between exposure to marketing communications and purchase initiation.[32] Current techniques for evaluating ROI are discussed in more detail in Chapter 16.

Linking communication data to actual purchases, or other measurable behavioural outcomes such as reduced dangerous alcohol consumption or reductions in road traffic accidents as would be expected from **social marketing** activity (see p. 12 for a discussion of the latter) is also problematic. Historically, primarily transactional data (e.g. sales) has been collected, emphasizing a product rather than consumer focus; while there is a growing awareness of the importance of developing and maintaining long-term customer relationships, the ways in which that relationship might be measured requires further investigation.[33]

This is particularly acute in relation to new media forms and to the overall issue of the contribution of marketing communications to brand equity[34] and to performance-based remuneration, which has become a common component of **client**–communication agency supplier relationships.[35]

An added problem is that of determining exactly what contribution was made by each marketing communications element. For example, a purchase decision may be made in store, or the purchaser may take leaflets away to read before returning to the store, visiting other stores – or making the final purchase **online**. What was the individual or collective contribution of each piece of marketing communications? How to measure return on investment from marketing communications investments remains one of the major challenges facing marketers.

THINK BOX

Measuring the impact of marketing communications

A person may see an advertisement for a package holiday on television, hear part of the sound track on the radio, seek more information on the Internet, but then go to a conventional retail outlet such as a travel agency (where they will see point-of-sale material such as posters, DVDs and brochures) to examine and compare different options. For products such as electronic goods, a similar process may be followed, with the added option of being able to possibly trial the product in store and compare it to competing brands on offer.

How do you then measure the impact each of these communication elements had on final purchase decisions?

In relation to the previous Think Box, it is common practice to use the same or similar images across media so that the main message is consistent across different communication elements ('imagery transfer').

Retailer influence, product, services, business-to-business and social marketing

The IMC literature has tended to focus on products, particularly those in the **fast moving consumer goods (FMCG)** sector, yet there are a number of significant sectors that warrant more detailed examination as their characteristics are substantially different from FMCG goods and thus the decision processes (and thus the communication needs) of the **target markets** may also be different.

Retailer influence

The growth in retailer-owned **house brands** that compete alongside **manufacturer brands** also warrants consideration as these brands may hold up to 20 per cent of overall retail sales and are often in the top three brands of 70 per cent of supermarket product categories.[36] There is no data on how market share or house **brand strength** varies across product categories. The strength of house brands varies across countries; 2002 data suggests that house brands accounted for almost 20 per cent of retail grocery revenue in the UK, 27 per cent in Belgium, 24 per cent in Germany and between 16 and 21 per cent in the US retail grocery market,[37] with steady growth reported.[38] Within the UK's three largest supermarkets, it is suggested that retailer house brands may account for 50–60 per cent of sales.[39] In terms of specific product categories, data from the mid-1990s indicates that house brands accounted for 61 per cent of supermarket wine sales, 51 per cent of dry pasta, 47 per cent of jam and 41 per cent of potato chips.[40] More recent data from the UK indicates that nearly 40 per cent of total retail sales in 2012 were represented by sales of house brands.[41]

House brands tend to receive little promotional support and what is provided is generally price-based; the impact of this on manufacturer-brand promotional activity has not been researched.[42] Indeed, the impact of the retailer environment and promotional activity on manufacturer-originated IMC programmes, irrespective of the presence or otherwise of house brands remains yet another area in need of research investment.

MINI CASE: HOUSE BRANDS

Imagine you are the **Brand Manager** of a large multi-national fast moving consumer goods company. You have been asked to write a report on the potential threat house brands present to your own brands across various countries.

1. What may account for the difference in popularity of house brands across countries? What are the implications for manufacturers whose brands are sold in these countries?
2. What are the pros and cons of your own company producing house brands for a major retailer? This house brand would be priced lower than your brands and sold alongside them.
3. What marketing communications strategy do you recommend if your major competitor produces the retailer's house brand instead of you?

Services

The IMC literature has tended to over-emphasise tangible products rather than **services**, in spite of the fact that service provision now dominates most developed economies[43] and the significant differences between service and products which may make it difficult to project and maintain a consistent image. Services are intangible, less readily standardized than products, perishable (airline seats cannot be stockpiled for future use) and often depend on the customer or end-user as part of the production process (the benefits of belonging to a fitness centre are not dependent just on the provision of facilities, but also on the effort of the client). There is a need for further research into IMC in this area.

Business-to-business

Also under-researched is the role of IMC in the business-to-business sector which tends to rely on more rational/ less emotional buying processes and longer-term relationships between buyer and seller, together with a greater complexity in product or service characteristics and group rather than individual decision making,[44] yet there are few studies comparing the marketing communications tools and processes that may be effective for this sector.

Social marketing

A key area in which there needs to be a review of the role of marketing communications is social marketing, a **concept** that has existed since the early 1970s[45] but which has received renewed focus internationally in the last few years.[46,47] Social marketing is not a specific **theory** per se, but rather a process, that draws on the theories and concepts of commercial marketing (such as market segmentation and exchange theory) to develop interventions aimed at improving health and well-being of entire populations[48] (such as encouraging physical activity) or specific segments within populations (such as anti-smoking interventions). While health-related issues are a major focus, social marketing also encompasses activity such as environmental protection, disaster preparedness, sustainable transport, recycling and energy conservation.

Thus, there is no specific 'sales' point as for tangible goods and services. Additionally, the factors such as attitudes and beliefs underlying **behaviours** are complex and may be resistant to change, particularly in relation to addictive behaviours such as smoking. There are few studies[49] that have specifically examined the use of IMC principles within social marketing and this remains yet another area in need of research investment. Interestingly, one study into advertising for environmental issues suggests that there is a lack of integration in this area.[50]

The current focus on health-related issues is due to recognition of three major factors. Firstly, the high cost of preventable illnesses to the economy (estimated at 19 per cent of GDP (gross domestic product) for England)[51] approximately 1 million deaths per annum in the USA are claimed to be caused by **lifestyle** and **environmental factors**.[52] Secondly, many governments have specifically advocated the adoption of the principles underpinning social marketing in order to more effectively promote public health issues, acknowledging that existing information-based communication strategies in the expectation of consumers then making informed and rational choices has been ineffective.[53] The third factor is the recognition that there is a limit to the amount of **legislation** that can be introduced to enforce behaviour change.[54]

MINI CASE: CHANGING BEHAVIOUR

There are numerous examples of people being aware of health risks from their behaviours (such as unprotected sex, excessive sunbed use and unwise alcohol consumption). Attempts to address these problems have often resulted in increased awareness levels – but not in behaviour change.

1. Explain why this problem might occur.
2. Select a health-based marketing communications campaign and critique it.
3. Outline what research might be needed to understand the problem and to identify strategies that might be successful in changing behaviour.

ETHICAL ISSUE TO CONSIDER

Considerable effort and expenditure is needed to treat health problems brought about by unwise lifestyle and behaviour choices made by individuals. For example, an unhealthy diet, lack of physical exercise, smoking or excess alcohol consumption have all been shown to link to potentially serious health problems.

1. What role do marketers play in reinforcing consumption decisions that might not be in the best interest of people's long-term health?
2. What actions should marketers take to minimise any harm that may result from their activity?
3. What role is there for legislation versus personal choice?
4. How would you respond to the suggestion that people whose health is affected by poor consumption or lifestyle decisions should not expect others to pay for their treatment?
5. How would you respond to the suggestion that there should be increased taxes on products such as alcohol or foods deemed to be of low nutritional value in order to treat those whose health has been affected, even if it was their personal choice that led to their subsequent health problems?

A number of these issues are discussed in more detail in Chapter 3.

Summary

As we have shown, IMC offers considerable promise, but there are a number of areas in which there is inadequate research to fully understand the concepts and processes involved in a rapidly changing environment. Further, the communication theories that are commonly used to underpin the development of marketing communications campaigns have been developed using traditional mass media as part of a four-sector promotion mix as shown in Figure 1.2. Their relevance to the complex range of new media forms is open to question and there is a clear need to revisit many long-standing assumptions and question their application to these new media forms. This is the subject of Chapter 2.

Review questions

1. Define what is meant by 'integrated marketing communications' (IMC).
2. What are the advantages of employing an integrated approach to a marketing campaign?
3. Is integrated marketing communications as simple as ensuring that there is a common 'look' to all forms of communication? Justify your response.
4. What are the potential barriers faced by marketers when seeking to implement an integrated approach to their marketing communications campaigns?
5. Could it ever be argued that all aspects of marketing communications should not be integrated?
6. Assume you are the Marketing Director for a FMCG company with multiple divisions and products that carry several different brand names. How can you ensure that all marketing communications activity is coordinated?
7. Cornelissen and Locke, suggested in 2000[14] that integrated marketing communications is merely a management fad. Critically evaluate this view.
8. Critique the suggestion that the Internet is just another media tool.
9. Many social marketing texts suggest that planning social marketing communications campaigns should use the 4Ps in the same way as planning product marketing communications campaigns. Critique this suggestion, using examples to illustrate your answer.
10. 'Brands are rarely created by marketing communications alone.' Discuss this statement with special reference to the role that IMC might play in the communication of brand values.

Recommended reading

Caalin, G. (2008). Integrated online marketing communication: implementation and management. *Journal of Communication Management*, 12(2), 169–84.

Danaher, P.J., and Rossiter, J.R. (2011). Comparing perceptions of marketing communication channels. *European Journal of Marketing*, 45(1–2), 6–42.

Finne, A., and Gronroos, C. (2009). Rethinking marketing communication: from integrated marketing communication to relationship communication. *Journal of Marketing Communications*, 15(2–3), 179–95.

Jiang, P., and Chia, S.-L. (2010). Developing integrated marketing communication (IMC) in online communities: a conceptual perspective from search, experience and credence segmentation. *International Journal of Internet Marketing and Advertising*, 6(1), 22–40.

Reinold, T., and Tropp, J. (2012). Integrated marketing communications: how can we measure its effectiveness? *Journal of Marketing Communications*, 18(2), 113–32.

Smith, B.G. (2013). The internal forces on communication integration: co-created meaning, interaction, and postmodernism in strategic integrated communication. *International Journal of Strategic Communication*, 7(1), 65–79.

CASE STUDY 1.1

Graduates Yorkshire recruitment

Campaign designed by Honey Creative

Source: Design Business Association, www.dba.org.uk. The case won a bronze medal in the 2009 Design Effectiveness Awards. Case material provided by the World Advertising Research Centre (WARC) www.warc.com.

As the following case shows, successful marketing communications does not depend on large budgets. This case illustrates how an integrated marketing communications approach led to very successful outcomes for a regional recruitment organization.

Introduction

Graduates Yorkshire (GY) is the leading recruitment brand primarily aimed at graduate employers in the Yorkshire and Humber region. GY's parent company is Yorkshire Universities, a membership organization owned by all ten Higher Education Institutions (HEI) in the Yorkshire region. Working in partnership with the university careers services, GY operates an online recruitment service matching primarily but not exclusively graduates from Yorkshire universities with Yorkshire employers. Previously known as Graduate Link, it's a web-driven service managed out of Sheffield, Leeds and York.

The brief incorporated five strands:

- Create a brand that is capable of smoothly transitioning the service from a free one to a service that levies a fee on what it does. In other words, the resulting brand had to reflect a professionalism and gravitas that would set it apart from the competition and that establishes the business as the authority on graduate recruitment in the region.
- Provide strategic and commercial consultancy to help facilitate the brand's migration from a university 'internal service' to a stand-alone social enterprise model.
- Formulate a communications strategy that is flexible enough to enable GY to engage with a wide range of stakeholders: for example, business leaders to graduates; universities to local enterprises.
- Validate or generate a new name (formerly known as 'Graduate Link').
- Apply new branding across all touch points including: website, marketing communications (including new digital platform), advertising, **exhibitions** and recruitment tools.

Overview of market

Each year in Yorkshire, around 40,000 new undergraduates leave the region's HEIs rising to around 55,000 when postgraduate qualifications are included. Many of these graduates leave the area to return home or to work but, three years after graduation, research shows around half of all graduates from Yorkshire universities are settled in the region. The area also sees an influx of graduates from other regions each year as many return home after studying away.

In Yorkshire, the majority of graduate employers are SMEs and Public Sector Organizations. Nationally, prior to the recession, the graduate recruitment market has seen a steady year-on-year growth; however, various agencies are reporting between a 5 per cent and a 12 per cent decline in the availability of graduate jobs since the beginning of 2009.

In terms of competitors, GY is unique as there are no major commercial graduate-specific services operating solely to serve the Yorkshire region. The national competitors to GY – such as Prospects – offer very few vacancies within the region. For local recruiters, the nearest competitors include agencies who cannot match GY on price and the 'MyJobs' group which is a generic job site with regional variations that tends to host a lot of agency vacancies.

Outline of design solutions

All of GY stakeholders had a strong affinity for the existing Graduate Link brand, so any change had to be done well and managed effectively. Therefore Honey used the re-branding process to enable GY to engage key stakeholders in the **design** process to build ownership and buy-in.

Working closely with the client, Honey helped develop the business and marketing strategy, starting with a robust process for change. With these in place, we were able to create a unique and flexible brand identity that reflects the business and which enables GY to communicate clearly with a broad range of very different audiences from graduates to employers and local development agencies and Government.

Clearly with a name like 'Graduates Yorkshire', the resulting brand identity had to have a regional 'edge' that was achieved by basing the logo on the shape of Yorkshire itself, with dots representing graduates and businesses being drawn together on their respective journeys. For the graduate, that journey begins as a student, moving through graduation through to prospective employee. The service has been designed to follow this journey and offer benefit at each touch point. The role of design was to communicate the brand's offering across this life cycle.

However, at the outset it was clear that the business model could eventually be taken into new regions, both in the UK and overseas, so it was important that the identity was sufficiently flexible to allow for expansion into new areas without compromising on its integrity.

Honey developed the brand's multi-channel marketing campaign that could last for several years with a 'Put Yourself in the Picture' theme, this enables graduates to picture themselves in their dream job and employers to picture the ideal candidate for their graduate position.

The identity has now been rolled out across all marketing communications, including corporate literature, website, exhibition materials, direct mail and advertising.

In respect of the website, as this is central to all GY activities, it was particularly important to get this right both visually and technically. In this respect, Honey developed the site to engage with the different users from the start, the home page directs employers and graduates to different areas of the site with tailored information for each. All this whilst maintaining the consistent brand message.

This exercise culminated in a launch **event** that saw every member of careers staff gathered at an event in Leeds. This event was a watershed moment, and culminated in the 'reveal' of the new brand on a large exhibition stand. Delegates were given bags full of GY branded gifts that continue to be prominent in offices around the region today. Honey also ran a workshop at this event explaining design rationale, and further helping to root the new brand in the consciousness of this key group of stakeholders.

Increase in sales

The period immediately following the re-brand, April to September 2008, saw impressive trading results, in terms of client wins, incoming revenue and growth in the customer base:

- From a standing start, GY enjoyed total growth in sales from zero to **£1,036,000** in the two years since its launch and a **210 per cent** growth in sales from year one to year two.

Photo 1.3a

Photo 1.3b

- Forecasted sales for year three (2009/10) is up **44 per cent**.
- A revenue was achieved against the soft launch in October 2007 when the new brand identity was applied to the existing web technology and original copy.
- In April 2008, an **88 per cent** uplift in sales was achieved in the six months following the full re-branding of the website, working with a new technology and enhanced web 'look and feel' design by Honey.
- A revenue has been delivered through the creation and delivery of internship programmes designed for third parties such as local governmental bodies and businesses

– the reason GY was awarded the contract was because they, clients such as local governments, were so impressed with the quality of the overall branding and the design of marketing and web materials.

- A further income has been generated this year through the provision of consultancy services in the year 2008/09. The reason behind the decision to diversify in this way was the prediction that the recruitment market would be adversely affected by the downturn – so additional revenue streams would need to be found – and the realization that GY's intelligence on the youth market could be translated into a valuable resource for local employers. Building on the now trusted GY brand, Honey created a set of sales tools that clearly articulated GY's insights into the youth market. Their first target was the Government Office for Yorkshire & The Humber (GOYH) who immediately commissioned GY to undertake a research programme to establish what perceptions graduates and the younger employment market had in respect of working for local governmental offices. Local students were recruited to undertake the research, the results of which were tremendously illuminating in respect of GOYH's need to undertake a recruitment campaign to replace its ageing workforce with fresh young recruits with a contemporary outlook and specialist training.

- Following the research GOYH commissioned GY to write a strategy paper on the recruitment campaign itself, and Honey is now working with them on the development of a business plan that will lead to the creation of a new brand, e-channel and marketing communications.

- What is particularly rewarding about this initiative is that the very first client that GY targeted with the consultancy offering, has already returned a significant ROI.

- Meanwhile, plans to franchise the business to other regions in the UK are already being received positively with a contract about to be signed. This particular opportunity was recognized in the early planning stages of the business which means that the branding and web technology that GY and Honey developed together has been designed to enable expansion into new regions without compromising the brand 'look and feel' and integrity.

- As a result of the exceptional success of the relationship between Honey and GY, they are now seen to be the experts in their field which has lead to a number of interesting brand extensions:

  o   further franchising opportunities both in the UK and overseas;
  o   delivery of under/post-graduate programmes such as 'Careers Guidance', 'Graduate Enterprise' (providing advice on setting up a business) and, most recently, an internship proposition that will support graduates and businesses. This latest initiative is expected to drive a revenue over the next three years.

This was all achieved thanks to the smart and powerful design and multi channel branding created by Honey.

Martin Edmondson, CEO,
Graduates Yorkshire

In summary, GY has gone from a standing start with an original database of 5,000 graduates that took eight years to build, to a database of 23,500, demonstrating a 370 per cent increase. The website is now getting 400,000 hits per month and GY has converted four new clients.

On a lighter note, £480 has been made from sales of GY branded 'Made in Yorkshire' t-shirts that have become a bit of a legend in the region! (40 × £12 t-shirts sold and a new order of 100 t-shirts has been placed.)

This period saw a number of unprecedented achievements for GY. Historically the client base had been SMEs and some public sector, with minimal blue chip business. In this period GY won large contracts with HBOS, Asda and signed a deal with NHS Yorkshire and Humber to advertise all their graduate level roles (up to 2,000 jobs). This was down to the improved brand kudos and credibility. These relationships have continued to develop and GY is now seeing repeat business from them.

Improvements in staff morale and changes in staff behaviour productivity

As the business goes from strength to strength, employees are becoming increasingly aware of the power of their brand and are looking for every opportunity to bring it to the forefront of everyone's mind:

> The new brand gives me the confidence to approach HR Directors from some of the region's biggest companies such as PWC, the UK's largest graduate employer, and succeed. We are no longer just another place to advertise roles but the place graduate employers in Yorkshire need to be seen.
>
> John Cusworth, Business Development Manager

> I have always been really proud of the work we do. Now I'm really proud of the brand we've created too, and love to show it off whenever possible!
>
> Natalie Emmanual, Client Services and Operations Manager

> Graduates Yorkshire is a brand with a real personality. I spend a lot of my time on the road taking our 6ft long stand (or the 'beast', as it's affectionately known) to universities and events across Yorkshire. I get to see first-hand how people react to us, how we've gone from being a well kept secret to a company identifiable by our green trade mark, and how our new branding seems to warm people to us and encourage them to approach us more easily.
>
> Imogen Hesp, Marketing Officer

Changes in perception

When GY moved from a free service to a business that levied a fee on what it did, it managed to retain most of its original clients. This was because although GY was now being perceived as a commercial entity, it was still regarded as part of the 'university family'. It is fair to say that Honey's design played a large part in this by delivering a brand identity that was immediately engaging and approachable.

> Graduates Yorkshire is a fantastic, reliable and efficient way for local employers to meet their recruitment needs in the most effective manner. I would have no hesitation recommending this site to other employers, keep up the good work.
>
> Faresh Misuri, Graduate Employer, Blueberry, Leeds

GY is now perceived as the market leader – and leading voice – in regional graduate recruitment by other regions and other Regional Development Agencies (RDAs) and there has been recent interest from two other UK regions for the provision of similar services – which will probably be delivered in a franchise form managed by GY.

Post re-brand, GY's standing with Yorkshire Forward – the local RDA – is such that GY tendered and won an innovative, high profile Internship Programme in 2009.

Finally, the re-brand has given GY and its stakeholders the confidence to launch a focussed NPD programme, with a view to launching GY Consulting and a Graduate Placement scheme in 2009/10 all designed by Honey.

Research resources

The project team used:

- published data
- quantitative and qualitative research
- focus groups.

Other influencing factors

The service existed in exactly the same format as it is now before the re-branding programme – the only real change being that the services provided are no longer free.

Immediately following the re-branding, the spend on advertising was reduced by 35 per cent so the successes have been almost entirely as a result of the re-branding and the optimization of the web technology developed in conjunction with Honey.

CASE STUDY QUESTIONS

Drawing on the material in the chapter, discuss the following questions:

1. Critique this case. What were the challenges faced by the campaign and how well do you believe that campaign addressed them?
2. Use Figures 1.1. and 1.2 to review the activity. Are there elements of the marketing communications mix you believe should have been used differently? What changes to the combination of communications forms do you recommend be considered for the future? Justify your answers.
3. Specifically focus on the brand identity created – how would you recommend that this be maintained or reinforced in the future? Justify your response.
4. What factors may impact on the future success of the GY organization? What **contingency** plans should be put in place and why?
5. How would you expect their competitors to respond? How should GY prepare to respond to competitor activity?
6. Could the same principles be used in other regions within the UK, either by GY or other organizations? Justify your response and develop guidelines for organizations in other regions that might consider this approach.

Notes

1   Borden, N. (1962). 'The Concept of the Marketing Mix'. In George Schwartz (ed.) *Science in Marketing*, New York: Wiley and Sons, 386–97.
2   McCarthy, E.J. (1964). *Basic Marketing: A Managerial Approach*, Illinois: Richard D. Irwin Homewood.

3   Englis, B.G., and Solomon, M.R. (1996). Using consumption constellations to develop integrated communications strategies. *Journal of Business Research*, 37(3), 183–91.
4   Schultz, D.E. (1996). The inevitability of integrated communications. *Journal of Business Research*, 37(3), 139–46.
5   Grigorovici, D.M., and Constantin, C.D. (2004). Experiencing interactive advertising beyond rich media. Impacts of ad type and presence on brand effectiveness in 3D gaming immersive virtual environments. *Journal of Interactive Advertising*, 4(3), 1–26.
6   Arnold, C. (2004). Just press play. *Marketing News*, 38(9), 1–15.
7   McAllister, M.P., and Turow, J. (2002). New media and the commercial sphere: two intersecting trends, five categories of concern. *Journal of Broadcasting & Electronic Media*, 46(4), 505.
8   Lannon, J. (1996). Integrated communications: advertising and the wider communication mix. *Admap*, 31(3), 83–6.
9   Gronstedt, A., and Thorsen, E. (1996). Five approaches to organise an integrated marketing communications agency. *Journal of Advertising Research*, March/April, 48–58.
10 Beard, F. (1996). Integrated marketing communications: new role expectations and performance issues in the client–ad agency relationship? *Journal of Business Research*, 37(3), 207–15.
11 Dilenschneider, R.L. (1991). Marketing communications in the post-advertising era. *Public Relations Review*, 17(3), 227–36.
12 Dornfield, S. (1997). What's wrong with this ad? The disease of 'creatosis'. *The Florida Business Journal*. Online. Available HTTP: <http://www.bizjournals.com/southflorida/stories/1997/07/21focus3.html?page=all>.
13 Briggs, R. (2006). Marketers who measure the wrong thing get faulty answers. *Journal of Advertising Research*, 46(4), 462–8.
14 Cornelissen, J.P., and Lock, A.R. (2000). Theoretical concept or management fashion? Examining the significance of IMC. *Journal of Advertising Research*, 40(5), 7–15.
15 Duncan, T.R., and Everett, S.E. (1993). Client perceptions of integrated marketing communications. *Journal of Advertising Research*, May/June, 30–9.
16 Aaker, D.A. (1997). Should you take your brand to where the action is? *Harvard Business Review*, 75(5), 135–43.
17 Madhavaram, S., Badrinarayanan, V., and McDonald, R.E. (2005). Integrated marketing communication (IMC) and brand identity as critical components of brand equity strategy. *Journal of Advertising*, 34(4), 69–80.
18 Hutton, J.G. (1996). Integrated marketing communications and the evolution of marketing thought. *Journal of Business Research*, 37(3), 155–62.
19 De Pelsmacker, P., Geuens, M., and Van den Bergh, J. (2001). *Marketing Communications*, Harlow: Pearson Education.
20 Grunig, J.E., and Grunig, L.A. (1998). The relationship between public relations and marketing in excellent organizations: evidence from the IABC study. *Journal of Marketing Communications*, 4, 141–62.
21 Miller, D.A., and Rose, P.B. (1994). Integrated communications: a look at reality instead of theory. *Public Relations Quarterly*, 39(1), 13–16.
22 Rust, R.T., and Oliver, R.W. (1994). The death of advertising. *Journal of Advertising*, 23(4), 71–7.
23 Hartley, B., and Pickton, D. (1999). Integrated marketing communications requires a new way of thinking. *Journal of Marketing Communications*, 5(2), 97–106.
24 Harris, T.L. (1993). How MPR adds value to integrated marketing communications. *Public Relations Quarterly*, 38(2), 13–18.
25 Pitta, D.A., Weisgal, M., and Lynagh, P. (2006). Integrating exhibit marketing into integrated marketing communications. *Journal of Consumer Marketing*, 23(3), 156–66.
26 Smith, T.M., Gopalakrishna, S., and Smith, P.M. (2004). The complementary effect of trade shows on personal selling. *International Journal of Research in Marketing*, 21(1), 61.
27 Brito, P.Q., and Hammond, K. (2007). Strategic versus tactical nature of sales promotions. *Journal of Marketing Communications*, 13(2), 131–48.

28 Farrelly, F., Luxton, S., and Brace-Govan, J. (2001). Critical issues to understanding IMC in the future – an academic and practitioner developed integrated marketing communications curriculum for the 21st century. *Marketing Bulletin*, 12, 1–16.

29 Reid, M., Luxton, S., and Mavondo, F. (2005). The relationship between integrated marketing communication, market orientation, and brand orientation. *Journal of Advertising*, 34(4), 11–23.

30 Eagle, L.C., and Kitchen, P.J. (2000). IMC, brand communications and corporate cultures: client/ advertising agency coordination and cohesion. *European Journal of Marketing*, 34(5/6), 667–704.

31 Stammerjohan, C., Wood, C.M., Chang, Y., and Thorson, E. (2005). An empirical investigation of the interaction between publicity, advertising, and previous brand attitudes and knowledge. *Journal of Advertising*, 34(4), 55–67.

32 Smith, T.M., Gopalakrishna, S., and Chatterjee, R. (2006). A three-stage model of integrated marketing communications at the marketing–sales interface. *Journal of Marketing Research (JMR)*, 43(4), 564–79.

33 Zahay, D., Peltier, J., Schultz, D.E., and Griffin, A. (2004). The role of transactional versus relational data in IMC programs: bringing customer data together. *Journal of Advertising Research*, March, 3–18.

34 Eagle, L.C., Kitchen, P.J., Rose, L.C., and Moyle, B.M. (2003). Shades of grey: the impact of parallel importing on brand equity and values. *European Journal of Marketing*, 37(10), 1332–49.

35 Swain, W.N. (2004). Perceptions of IMC after a decade of development: who's at the wheel, and how can we measure success? *Journal of Advertising Research*, 44(1), 46–65.

36 Sayman, S., and Raju, J.S. (2004). Investigating the cross-category effects of store brands. *Review of Industrial Organization*, 24(2), 129–41.

37 Field, A.M. (2006). Store brands take over. *Journal of Commerce*, 7(8), 18–22.

38 Olbrich, R., and Buhr, C.-C. (2004). Impact of private labels on competition: why European competition law should permit resale price maintenance. *European Retail Digest*, 41(Spring), 1–6.

39 Hankinson, G., and Cowking, P. (1997). Branding in practice: the profile and role of brand managers in the UK. *Journal of Marketing Management*, 13(4), 239–64.

40 Dick, A., Jain, A., and Richardson, P. (1996). How consumers evaluate store brands. *Journal of Product & Brand Management*, 5(2), 19–28.

41 Key Note Reports. (2012). *Own Brands Market Report 2012*. Middlesex.

42 Olbrich, R., and Buhr, C.-C. (2005). Unidentifiable private labels in retailing and their impact on competition and consumers. *European Retail Digest*, 47(Autumn), 51–7.

43 Carlson, L., Grove, S.J., and Dorsch, M.J. (2003). Services advertising and integrated marketing communications: an empirical examination. *Journal of Current Issues & Research in Advertising*, 25(2), 69–82.

44 Garber, L.L.J., and Dotson, M.J. (2002). A method for the selection of appropriate business-to-business integrated marketing communications mixes. *Journal of Marketing Communications*, 8(1), 1–17.

45 Kotler, P., and Zaltman, G. (1971). Social marketing: an approach to planned social change. *Journal of Marketing*, 35(3), 3–12.

46 Bernhardt, J.M. (2004). Communication at the core of effective public health. *American Journal of Public Health*, 94(12), 2051–3.

47 Department of Health (2004). *Choosing Health: Making Healthy Choices Easier* (White Paper). London: Department of Health.

48 Andreasen, A.R. (2002). Marketing social marketing in the social change marketplace. *Journal of Public Policy and Marketing*, 21(1), 3–13.

49 Dresler-Hawke, E., and Veer, E. (2006). Making healthy eating messages more effective: combining integrated marketing communication with the behaviour ecological model. *International Journal of Consumer Studies*, 30(4), 318–26.

50 Carlson, L., Grove, S.J., Laczniak, R.N., and Kangun, N. (1996). Does environmental advertising reflect integrated marketing communications? An empirical investigation. *Journal of Business Research*, 37, 225–32.

51   National Social Marketing Centre (2006). *It's Our Health! Realising the Potential of Effective Social Marketing*. London: National Social Marketing Centre.

52   Rothschild, M.L. (1999). Carrots, sticks, and promises: a conceptual framework for the management of public health and social issue behaviors. *Journal of Marketing*, 63(4), 24–37.

53   Schneider, T.R. (2006). Getting the biggest bang for your health education buck. Message framing and reducing health disparities. *American Behavioral Scientist*, 49(6), 812–22.

54   Gostin, L.O. (2007). Law as a tool to facilitate healthier lifestyles and prevent obesity. *Journal of the American Medical Association*, 297(1), 87–90.

2   Introducing communication

LEARNING OUTCOMES

After studying this chapter, you will be able to:

- Discuss the concept and process of communication
- Identify the way that marketing communications function within a modern media society
- Discuss the variety of ways in which messages are encoded within marketing communications
- Understand how consumers decode and understand marketing communications
- Identify the main disruptors of marketing communications

Introduction

The word 'communication' is one of those ordinary terms used by people everyday in conversation. However, when we use it, do we really know exactly what it means? And when we think of 'communication' in the marketing context, is it *really* the same as communication in a social context, for example, texting to friends or talking to someone on the phone? Certainly, when it comes to academic texts, there appears to be little agreement. At the outset, most texts start with a definition. However whilst some texts offer definitions that relate specifically to the process[1] of communication (i.e. how messages move from their source to their final destination) there are others that focus upon the outcome[2] (i.e. the impact of the communication); both of which have major implications for marketers.

Over the course of this chapter we will define the concept of communication in a way that encompasses both process and outcome and consider its role within the context of marketing. Key **communication models** are identified and their relevance to modern day products and markets will be discussed. Finally, we examine the factors that either aid or inhibit the effectiveness of a piece of marketing communication and explore the reasons why this might be the case.

What is communication?

Schramm's characterization of **communication** as '[t]he process of establishing a commonness or oneness of thought between a sender and receiver'[3] is typical of one that focusses upon the outcome rather than the process. In this case, whilst the term 'process' is mentioned, the primary focus is on the 'outcome'; in this instance, mutual agreement and understanding between the 'sender' and 'receiver'. The logistical processes associated with the action or movement of communication between the two parties is not considered. This does not mean, however, that the process does not exist or is not important – it is just that, from Schramm's perspective, a successful outcome from a piece of communication appears the primary indicator of its success.

Definitions of communication such as the one offered by Schramm not only hold relevance for marketers, but also highlight the challenges and contradictions they face. Its relevance stems from the recognition that effective communication of a desired message between a 'sender' and a 'receiver' is the primary objective of the marketer's role. Yet taken literally, the Schramm definition suggests that a piece of marketing communication can only be deemed to have taken place if the message content is understood by the receiver in exactly the way originally intended by the sender. Patently, this is not always the case. No matter how clearly stated a piece of communication may appear to be, there is usually potential for it to be interpreted in different ways by different consumers. To illustrate this point, consider the following phrase:

"Tourists think that Ibiza is hot"

Depending upon who the intended 'receiver' is, this might be understood in a couple of different ways. For some consumer groups, the word 'hot' is sometimes used in place of terms such as 'popular', 'busy', or 'fashionable'. In contrast, there are other groups of potential consumers who might interpret such a communication in a literal way and read it as a comment on Ibiza's weather. It is for this reason that Schramm's concept of 'oneness' is more of an 'ideal' than a regularly achieved reality. This is because it fails to take into account the uniqueness of individuals' life experiences that act to shape their understanding of the world around them and also assumes that the sender and the receiver are of exactly the same intellectual level and thus possess an identical grasp of language and cultural understanding.

Yet whilst Schramm's definition of communication may have its flaws, alternative definitions that focus purely upon the 'process' of communication can also be seen to have strengths and weaknesses. For example, according to Fiske,[4] communication is a form of 'social interaction through messages' (p. 2), thereby identifying 'communication' in the catalyst within the wider spectrum of social activity. As such, a strength of this definition is that it closely reflects the modern day interactivity of the communications process with its use of multiple media and the existence of multiple audiences. It also recognizes that consumers are not necessarily passive recipients of marketing communications but have the potential to use them to achieve their own communication objectives. In this way, 'communications' can be seen as a form of cultural artefact. However, such a definition offers little indication as to the purpose of the process and, unlike Schramm, offers no benchmark as to whether it can ever be successfully achieved.

From a marketing perspective, whilst such a definition suggests a number of opportunities for marketers, it is also problematic. The use of marketing communications by consumers as the basis of some form of social interaction is potentially exciting in that it suggests high levels of engagement with brands and brand messages. However, in situations in which consumers get involved in the co-creation of meaning, there is the chance that marketers lose control of message content.

A factor to be considered when reflecting upon the value of individual definitions such as those offered by both Schramm and Fiske is that, by their very nature, definitions are an overt simplification of the entity they represent. As such, in seeking to offer a distilled and easily understood representation of a construct or a theory, complexities are necessarily glossed over. The result is that there are a number of unintended consequences, for example, they can appear shallow, narrow and limited or potentially out of date. For instance, Schramm's apparently narrow focus upon a single 'sender' and a single 'receiver' bears little resemblance to today's fragmented media landscape. In the early to mid-twentieth century, channels of marketing communications were much simpler and, as a consequence, the marketing industry structure was less complicated. Individual agencies tended to specialize in the provision of broad marketing services such as advertising or public relations. Further, the number and variety of media available for use by marketers was much smaller and the face-to-face selling techniques classically employed by 'door-to-door' salesmen were much more commonly employed. As a result, communication between the 'sender' and the 'receiver' was generally much more direct.

It is the nature of modern day marketing communications that only a very small proportion takes place on a 'one-to-one' basis. The majority of communication involves multiple parties either in the form of intermediaries or multiple audiences. Take, for instance, the launch of a new brand of coffee. The manufacturer may try to communicate its arrival through a combination of media such as posters, direct mail, in-store tastings, radio and television advertisements. Further, it is likely that they will also have employed a public relations agency to prepare press packs and organize press briefings to send to magazine editors and supermarket buyers who in turn might decide to communicate a message about the launch to their consumers. Ultimately, when the consumer finally receives the message about the new brand of coffee, it is likely that it will have passed through a number of different media to get to them.

From a marketer's perspective, it is clear that 'communication' should be considered from the perspective of both the process and the outcome. Anecdotal evidence from marketing professionals suggests that the two elements are inextricably linked: a successful outcome is usually the result of a clearly understood and executed process. Therefore, the ideal definition is one that combines both process and outcome. To this end, and drawing from the models of both Schramm and Fiske, a compound definition of communication may be derived. Therefore, for the purposes of this text, 'communication' may be defined as a process of social interaction undertaken with the aim of achieving an ideal end state in which all parties involved arrive at a consensus of meaning.

How does communication work?

Over the past 60 years, a number of communication models depicting the process of communication have been proposed. One of the most enduring and frequently cited is that of Shannon and Weaver[5] (see Figure 2.1). Whilst this model was formulated during the heyday of the radio, it still holds significant relevance for today's communication environment.

According to Shannon and Weaver, a message is produced by the 'Information Source' and encoded with meaning. This encoding can take a number of forms, from simple sounds and visual images to complex multi-component messages that appeal to one or more of the human senses.

In this form, the message is then passed through a 'Transmitter' to be picked up by a 'Receiver'. Originally, when this model was developed, the 'transmitter' element of the model was literally a radio transmitter and the 'receiver' the radio used by listeners to receive the message. The 'receiver' then passed the message on to the 'Destination', the radio listener. In order to maintain its relevance to today's communication landscape, more recent interpretations of this model broaden the concept of the 'transmitter' and 'receiver' to include the much wider variety of media that is used in today's communication mix. Modern day 'transmitters' and 'receivers' go far beyond the basic communication technologies envisioned by Shannon and Weaver and now include television, Internet and digital media.

One element of the Shannon and Weaver model that has increased in relevance with time is that of the concept of 'noise'. 'Noise' may be described as anything that might distort or detract from the original meaning of a message between the point of transmission to the point of reception – its final destination. 'Noise', in the original model, took the form of 'crackle'; the static or interference that occurred during the course of transmission and affected the quality of radio reception. However, in the modern day communication environment, messages are subject to distortion from a number of other sources and these are considered in more detail in the next section.

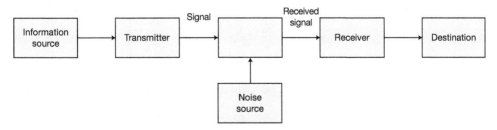

Figure 2.1 Shannon and Weaver's Model of Communication[5]

Communication in a mass market

One of the reasons that Shannon and Weaver's model is still cited so frequently is that it offers a simple and easily understood depiction of the communications process. However, in order to reflect today's marketing communication environment, three additional characteristics need to be added to increase its relevance:

1. A recognition that the final 'destination' of a marketing message, the consumer, rarely obtains information about a product or service from a single source. Even in the case of the most basic consumer products, for example, baked beans, consumers might well have obtained information in one form or another from a combination of television, radio, press and magazines and word of mouth. Consumers then process the information in their own minds to derive some form of meaning.
2. The chain of communication media is multi-layered. It is often the case that a message will pass through multiple media, each acting as a 'transmitter' before it reaches its final destination. Each **medium** of transmission is likely to have its own priorities and agenda and has the potential to transform a message by imposing its own interpretation of its contents.
3. Whilst the subject matter of each of the transmitter's messages may be the same, because individual transmitters may gather their information from different sources, the content they transmit is likely to vary in some way.

However, whilst Shannon and Weaver's model might be found lacking on these counts, a model that reflects these characteristics is depicted in Figure 2.2. This model is an adapted version of Westley and MacLean's Model of Mass Communication.[6] It retains the basic processes associated with the Shannon and Weaver model with the additional facet that it assumes that the 'Receiver' and the 'Destination' are one and the same. In addition, it responds to the apparent shortfalls of the classic model with its recognition that the receiver of the message (B) rarely obtains its communications from a single source; it illustrates how information on a specific subject may be obtained from a variety of sources (C1–3)

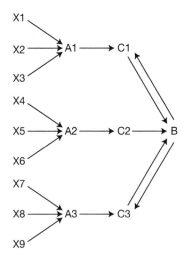

Figure 2.2 An amended version of the Westley and MacLean (1957) Model of Mass
        Communication[6]

and that, on receipt of the messages, it is the role of the receiver to merge the messages to derive some form of combined meaning.

Further, this model illustrates the potential for multiple transmitters (A1–3 and C1–3), and highlights the fact that messages are often the product of information derived from multiple sources (X1–9). Finally, unlike the Shannon and Weaver model, it recognizes that communication is not totally a one-way process, and that, on receipt of a communication, there is scope for the existence of feedback.

A good illustration of the way that this model works is a situation in which a political party seeks to publicize a new policy initiative on taxation. It would be unusual for this sort of activity to be undertaken face to face with the electorate so a more likely course of events is the organization of a press conference with the aim of encouraging the news media to 'transmit' their story for them. However, journalists rarely report such occasions verbatim. Rather, they tend to contextualize the stories they produce using a number of sources (X1–9) such as taxation experts, opposition politicians and historical accounts of the party's past activities. Based upon the **synthesis** of their respective sources, the journalists then produce their stories on the taxation initiative (A1–3), which are subject to the **editorial** policy in their respective media. This being done, there is also scope for the taxation story to be picked up by other media (C1–3) and re-reported, again subject to editorial, before it arrives at its final receiver: the voter (B). The voter, having seen news of the tax initiative on the television news, heard about it on the radio and read about it in the newspaper, then synthesizes the information into a personal understanding as to what the message means. The voter is then in a position to give feedback on the message either through a vote for that political party, a vote against them or possibly even via the act of abstention.

MINI CASE: THE PROBLEM OF POLITICAL COMMUNICATION

Every month, the polling organization IpsosMORI (www.ipsosmori.com) undertakes a poll to ascertain the relative position and popularity of political parties in the UK. Whilst political parties do their utmost to communicate the positive aspects of their policies to their 'target market' – the voters – inevitably their communications vary in their success. Some voters are persuaded to cast their vote for one party over another whilst others remain unpersuaded. Some even decide not to vote at all!

Discuss why, if voters are subject to the same communication processes and exposed to the same messages, they arrive at such different conclusions about the various parties on offer. What are the implications of this for political parties when formulating their communication strategies?

Messages, media and marketing communications: getting it right

So far in this chapter, our discussions have focussed upon the process of communication i.e. how communication takes place. However, from a marketing communications perspective, it is essential not just to make contact with the target audience, but to do so in a way that is clear and coherent. Ultimately, marketing communications provide the means by which organizations generate a dialogue with their markets that has the potential to create a commercial environment that will ultimately generate business success.

Organizations may invest tens, if not hundreds, of thousands of pounds in the construction and delivery of a piece of marketing communication. However in situations where the message is either received by the wrong audience, or received by the right audience but the content is not clearly understood, the investment of time, effort and money in the process is largely wasted. This being the case, the importance of three key areas becomes obvious: correctly identifying the target market for communication, getting the target market's attention and constructing the message in such a way that it might be clearly understood.

Identifying the right target market(s) at every level

One of the first rules of effective marketing communication is to target the right market with the right message. Target segments are generally prioritized according to:

- Size – generally, the larger the segment is, the more attractive they are to marketers as they offer a larger potential market for their product or service.
- Relative profitability – an effective marketing professional will consider the potential rate of return on money invested in a programme of marketing communications. Consumer segments that offer the potential of high rates of return are usually considered attractive targets.
- Accessibility – when seeking to target a particular consumer segment, two aspects of accessibility should be considered: consumers' ability to access the media and consumers' access to the product or service in question.

In addition, Figure 2.3 depicts four basic types of communication strategy, classified according to the degree of differentiation of media or message.

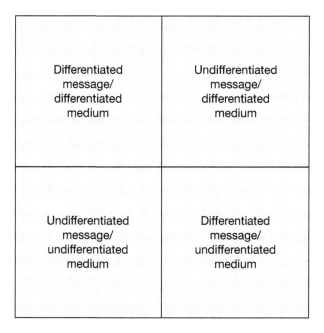

Figure 2.3 The four basic types of communication strategy

Undifferentiated message/undifferentiated medium

A communication that is undifferentiated in both its message and medium of delivery is where each target consumer is subject to the same message and media combination; no modifications are made to take into account differences between target segments or, indeed, differences inside individual target groups. Such a strategy is becoming increasingly rare as consumer sophistication is such that in order to attract their attention, marketers must clearly communicate the personal relevance of their offering to prevent it from being 'screened out' by perceptual processes such as **perceptual selectivity** and **perceptual vigilance**.

Differentiated message/undifferentiated medium

Where all of the target segments access the same medium, there are instances when multiple messages, each tailored to appeal to specific target segments, can be transmitted via the same medium. For example, the digitization of television and the development of satellite technology have resulted in an explosion of television channels now available to viewers. From the original five (BBC1, BBC2, ITV, Channel 4 and Five), viewers now have the choice of hundreds, many targeted at very clearly defined groups.

As a result, marketers can target specific groups of customers and consumers with specific messages using a single medium: television. However, whilst this approach offers the benefit of the delivery of a tightly targeted message relevant to the audience, the creation of separate **executions** catered to different groups is expensive incurring extra production costs for each additional execution.

Alternatively, the use of a single vehicle to convey messages to different target groups is also a common occurrence, particularly in television advertising. Instances such as this often happen where the customer and consumer of the product are different people, for example, children's breakfast cereals. Advertisements in such cases carry a dual message: one targeted at the customer (i.e. the parent) that emphasizes the health benefits of the product, and one targeted at the consumer (i.e. the child) communicating the 'fun' aspects of the product.

A key benefit of this approach is that the combination of multiple messages within a single advertisement can generate economies of scale in terms of production cost and, if done effectively, a synergy in the messages can actually enhance the power of the communication. However, the danger of such an approach is that conflict can arise between each of the various messages, their meaning altered and ultimately the effectiveness of the communication undermined. In the case of the breakfast cereal example, if it is the case that the message sent to the child is perceived by the parent to be too frivolous, it may detract from its healthy credentials. Conversely, the 'healthy' message may detract from the 'fun' qualities of the cereal in the eyes of the child, thereby making it less attractive. Ultimately, a balance must be achieved but, in doing so, care must be taken to ensure that the compromises made do not neuter the communication to the extent that it becomes ineffective for all target audiences.

Undifferentiated message/differentiated medium

The use of differentiated media to communicate an undifferentiated message is classically used in two situations; where a marketer is seeking to reach clear and distinct target audiences whose media preferences do not overlap or, alternatively, where the marketer seeks to reinforce a message through constant, consistent execution across multiple media. Where seeking to target multiple audiences, the marketer must ensure that a uniform message is appropriate in all aspects – content, tone and delivery – to maximize the likelihood that it will be delivered effectively. Further, marketers must recognize that the medium that carries a message has the potential to modify it in the eyes of the receiver and must make their media choices wisely.

An excellent example of a brand that reinforces a single message across multiple media is that of Heinz baked beans and their classic slogan, 'Beanz Meanz Heinz'. First introduced in the 1960s, this slogan has been a central driver of the majority of Heinz's marketing campaigns for the last 40 years. The media used has included television, radio, poster and press individually or in combination with the result that the slogan has almost become ingrained within the United Kingdom's national consciousness.

MINI CASE: RELAUNCHING WHITNEY

In 2009, following an abusive marriage and allegations of drug-taking and in an effort to relaunch her tumultuous career, singer Whitney Houston gave a long and extremely candid interview to Oprah Winfrey on her US talk show 'Oprah'. Her interview was a candid one and, whilst such an interview would have been a coup for any talk show host, it is unlikely that her choice of Oprah Winfrey was random. It is certainly the case that other shows might have been able to reach similarly large audiences and would have been willing to pay large fees for the privilege of such a high-profile interview. However, the recurring themes of integrity, honesty and redemption that are repeatedly found within the 'Oprah Winfrey' show and her magazine 'Oprah' are thought to have been more persuasive when making a choice of media vehicle in this situation.

Do you think that Whitney Houston made the right choice? In what way do you think an appearance on the Oprah Winfrey show might have added credibility to Whitney Houston's apparent desire to make a fresh start? Discuss what other media she might have used to communicate the relaunch of her career and consider their relative value.

(See: www.oprah.com/article/oprahshow/20090831-tows-whitney-houston)

Differentiated message/differentiated medium

In its essence, this is the ideal for any marketing strategy – to identify the most effective medium by which to reach individual consumers and to deliver a marketing communication that is tailored to be optimally effective on the basis of their individual needs and requirements. Whilst, for some media, this is impractical both in terms of logistical management and cost (for example, could you imagine Heinz producing an individual television advertisement for each and every one of its consumers?), for others it is a realizable objective.

Over recent decades, the development of database technology has resulted in brand owners and retailers being able to effectively track consumers' consumption habits and media preferences. They are then able to model and react to consumers' actual behaviour by contacting them with communications that they find relevant and appropriate. A good example of this is the Tesco Clubcard. The Tesco Clubcard is a 'reward card' in which the supermarket retailer, Tesco, offers consumers money-back vouchers in exchange for money spent in their stores. Consumers sign up for a Clubcard which records the details of their shopping basket using a sophisticated EPOS (Electronic Point of Sale) system every time they shop in store or online. The details are analysed and then, in addition to some generic money-off vouchers, specific offers identified on the basis of individual consumers' behaviour are generated and sent to the consumer on a quarterly basis either through the post or electronically, according to the consumer's stated wishes.

The benefit of such a system is clear for both consumer and brand owner. From the consumer's perspective, they receive information, benefits and offers that are pertinent, timely and relevant to their needs. For the brand owner, not only do they have a pool of information that allows them to target their marketing communications more effectively, but they are also able to track consumption patterns of key consumer groups. Using that information they are then able to model future behaviour and develop new products and services to respond to evolving consumer needs and then communicate those innovations to the relevant groups.

Markets: more than just consumers and customers!

Up until this point, when we have discussed markets, the focus has largely been upon the ultimate customer or consumer of products or services. However, for most organizations, the potential for long-term business success depends upon its ability to work with and work for a number of different markets and stakeholders at any given time. Of course identifying and targeting marketing communications at key consumer groups to generate sales is an essential part of business, but the importance of generating a positive brand image in other areas should not be underestimated, even if they might not offer the prospect of an immediate increase in sales. Take, for example, an organization that works in the fast-paced world of computer games. The ability to remain at the cutting edge of games technology is essential to maintain its competitive edge and the effective use of marketing communications can facilitate this. As well as being used to attract customers and consumers, marketing communications can also be used to create a positive 'buzz' around a company that will attract potential investors, suppliers and the best quality job applicants that, together, can contribute to its future success.

Marketing communications targeted at internal markets are also worthy of note. Internal markets, which include all individuals and subsidiaries that work for an organization, are identified as having an important role as part-time marketers.[7] The extent to which a product or service is delivered in line with expectations communicates something about the organization to customers and therefore even those without a formal marketing role are seen as instrumental in the marketing communication process.

A final set of markets that should not be forgotten are those that, at first glance, may not appear to have much to do with the organization in question but still have the potential to support or hinder its workings. The media, pressure groups, government (local and national) and local communities have the power to damage an organization's reputation and impede its ability to work if they feel that either their interests or those of the people they represent have been negatively affected. A process on ongoing communication is therefore essential to ensure a positive relationship is established with these groups.

This being the case, the identification of the many and varied markets associated with an organization can prove quite a challenge and indeed, Argenti[8] suggested that there might be an infinite number.[9] One way of identifying key targets for marketing communications is through the use of a 'stakeholder' perspective. Payne *et al.*[10] state that whilst there is yet to be a universally agreed definition as to what constitutes a 'stakeholder', there appear to be two schools of thought; stakeholders as those who have an interest in promoting the success of the company (i.e. shareholders) and those who are intent on

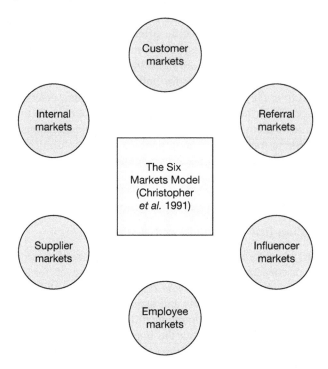

Figure 2.4 Christopher *et al.*'s Six Markets Model[11]

minimizing the negative impact of an organization's activities (i.e. pressure groups). However, Christopher *et al.*'s 'Six Markets Model'[11] (Figure 2.4) use of stakeholder theory to identify six key market areas offers a much more focussed approach.

The Six Markets Model has particular merit in that it not only acknowledges the importance of customer and consumer markets, employee markets, supplier markets and internal markets, but includes the important referral and influencer markets. 'Referral markets' are those whose positive recommendation is likely to result in additional business for an organization, for example, a mortgage advisor. By contrast, 'influencer markets' may be groups such as the financial press or the consumer group 'Which?' who possess some form of expertise or authority and whose positive or negative opinion is likely to influence potential customers or, in some cases, the organization itself. From a marketing communications perspective, this is extremely important as it recognizes the multiplicity of the market structure but it also acknowledges the social nature of communication and the role that referents play within the communication process.

MINI CASE: BETWEEN A ROCK AND A HARD PLACE

In 2007 troubles faced by the bank, Northern Rock, became one of the clearest indicators of what was to become the biggest banking crisis to hit the UK in over 50 years. The building-society-turned-bank was bailed out by taxpayers in 2007, when its model of borrowing short-term funds from wholesale markets to lend to mortgage borrowers was hit by the credit crunch. The 'supplier markets' who had previously ensured the fluidity of the markets by lending to banks stopped trading due to fears over 'toxic debt'. As a result, savers queued for hours in their efforts to withdraw savings, employees feared for their jobs and shareholders saw the value of their investments plummet. The bank was finally nationalized in February 2008 owing the Government and tax-payers £10.9bn (Source: www.bbc.co.uk).

Using the Six Markets Model, identify Northern Rock's stakeholder groups. For each of these groups discuss why effective communication strategies are important. What impact would poor communication have on each of these groups?

Getting the target market's attention

We have already noted that the simple process of making communication with a target market is not sufficient; it is essential that the message carried in that communication must be received and processed as the sender intended. The primary challenge for marketers involves cutting through the sheer volume of marketing messages received by the target audience which is often achieved through the use of a variety of **creative tactics** (see Chapter 5). Whilst concrete figures have yet to be established, anecdotal estimates suggest that an individual is subject to anything up to 4,000 branded messages every day. This being the case, not every marketing communication is going to receive the same attention. To handle this volume, the human brain appears to have developed a number of strategies to avoid overloading.

The first of these strategies involves the brain processing information at different levels of involvement, ranging in a spectrum from **high involvement** to **low involvement** (Figure 2.5).[12] High involvement processing usually occurs when the subject in question is of importance to the receiver. For example, if a consumer decides to buy a house, he or she is likely to process messages on the subject of mortgages or house prices more actively than if he or she were not looking to enter the property market at all. In situations in which high involvement processing takes place, the receiver of a message regards the subject with high levels of attention. High levels of cognitive activity take place and the content of the message is analysed, categorized and stored in relation to any prior knowledge on the subject and as fully developed attitudes, concepts and ideas.

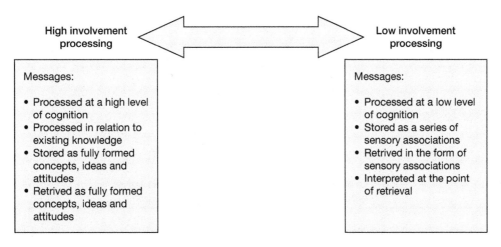

Figure 2.5 The spectrum of high and low involvement processing

At the other end of the spectrum is what is known as low involvement processing. This still involves a degree of cognitive processing but it occurs at a much lower level. Messages processed in this way are not stored as a coherent story or argument but, instead, as a series of sensory associations, for example, colours, sounds, smells or textures. The effect of different processing levels is most apparent at the point at which the message is later retrieved. In both cases the messages are retrieved in the form they were originally stored; those processed at high levels of involvement as fully developed thoughts, opinions or attitudes and those processed at low levels are retrieved in their raw, sensory state. As a result messages processed under low involvement conditions are subject to interpretation by the receiver and can vary according to the physical and emotional situation he or she is subject to at the time. Interpretation of messages under low involvement conditions therefore vary wildly from what was first intended by the sender.

The extent to which a message is processed at high or low levels of involvement may be determined by the processes of perceptual selectivity, perceptual vigilance and **perceptual defence**.[13] Perceptual selectivity relates to the filtering process employed by individuals and determines what messages will be processed and at what level of involvement. Similarly, perceptual vigilance is employed as receivers actively look out for messages that may be relevant or important to them in some way whilst perceptual defence occurs when receivers actively block messages that they do not wish to receive.

Using reference groups to gain attention

The use of **reference groups** is a common tactic employed by organizations in seeking to overcome perceptual selectivity by members of the target market and encouraging receivers to engage in high involvement levels of processing. Reference groups are defined as 'groups that are psychologically significant for one's attitudes and behaviour'[14] and according to White and Dahl[15] are typically divided into three types: **membership groups**, **aspirational groups** and **disassociative groups** (Figure 2.6).

Membership and aspirational groups are generally seen as positive as they are the ones to which one already belongs or aspires to be associated with. These groups may

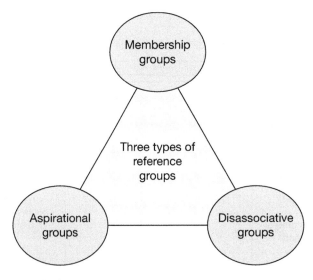

Figure 2.6 Three types of reference groups

take many forms with the key figures holding the status of **role models** and opinion leaders. Such figures are often used in marketing communications because they either possess high levels of **source credibility**, source attractiveness or both. Source credibility relates to the extent to which a source is deemed to have expertise in a particular field, for example, a paediatrician might be deemed to be a credible source of information on childhood illness whereas a professional footballer is not.[16] In contrast, source attractiveness occurs where a source is seen as particularly appealing to the receiver and is the reason why very few ugly models appear in magazines or television commercials! Interestingly, research has identified source attractiveness as an influential factor in consumers' assessment of source credibility.[17] It appears that, whilst attractive sources are not necessarily credited with greater expertise, they tend to generate more positive attitudes amongst receivers which, in turn, causes receivers to be more receptive and more positive about the message they convey.[18]

THINK BOX

Smells like Beckham

Celebrity endorsement of perfumes has become big business in recent years. A good example is the Intimately Beckham range endorsed by David and Victoria Beckham. Individually, they have enjoyed significant career success: David as ex-Captain of England's national football team and Victoria as a member of the 1990s girl-group the Spice Girls and latterly in the world of fashion.

What is it that makes celebrities such as the Beckhams such popular candidates for models/**endorsers** for perfumes?

In contrast, disassociative groups are those that a target population does not want to be associated with and in conventional marketing communications are not often employed unless as part of a 'shock' or 'teaser' campaign (see Chapter 5) because they struggle to penetrate the filters of perceptual selectivity. However, the use of dissociative groups in marketing campaigns has been seen to have real value in health and social marketing campaigns.[19] Take for instance a recent anti-smoking campaign in the UK that filmed conversations with smokers dying of lung cancer and also with the relatives of those who had lost their lives to the disease. There is no doubt that the dying and the bereaved are a group that no one wishes to join and may therefore be considered disassociative. Whilst in some cases the use of such an emotive disassociative group might cause the target market (smokers) to block out the message by ignoring it or avoiding it completely by switching channel or walking out of the room in a form of perceptual defence, the negative portrayal of their own membership group to convey such a dire warning might encourage them to re-evaluate their situation and change their behaviour.

It is important to note that the degree of positivity felt by an individual toward an organization or its brands is no indication of his or her intention to process the content of any messages received. It is true that once a message penetrates the filters of perceptual selectivity and perceptual defence, those that either reflect or reinforce the receiver's personal values, attitudes and aspirations are the ones that are more easily accepted. This is simply because they act as a form of positive reinforcement. However, if the content of a message is predictable, the receiver is likely to regard it as 'redundant' (i.e. it does not add anything to the individual's existing pool of knowledge and only serves to remind the receiver of the existence of the source).[20] This being the case, such messages are likely to be processed at very low levels of involvement.

In contrast, marketing communications that are unpredictable and '**entropic**' often prompt high levels of involvement processing as receivers question previous assumptions.[21] A good example of how this was employed can be seen in the 2009 'Change for Life' campaign. Traditionally campaigns to encourage people to adopt healthier lifestyles have been fragmented and targeted purely at adults. However, this campaign adopts a 'whole family' approach and explains the value of a healthier lifestyle, both in terms of the type of food consumed and the need for exercise, in a way that can be understood by all. The clear message is supported by bright, engaging graphics that explain not only what action consumers should take but also why they should take it. In this way, adults and children alike are encouraged to question their previous lifestyle choices and make more healthy ones.

The aim of communications such as these is to generate **cognitive dissonance** on the part of the receiver; a state of tension that is experienced when an individual feels that the status quo deviates to some degree from what they perceive to be ideal. In such cases, action is taken by the individual to resolve this tension.[22] In the case of the 'Change for Life' campaign, the aim was to make the target audience feel uncomfortable about the potential impact that an unhealthy lifestyle and poor food choices were likely to have on both them and their family. In addition, it offered simple suggestions as to how the audience might rectify the situation.

Overcoming cognitive dissonance

The state of tension felt by consumers when experiencing cognitive dissonance is one that they generally seek to resolve in some way and Newcomb's classic ABX Balance Theory[23] model (Figure 2.7) offers real insight into how they might seek to achieve this. In its simplest form, Newcomb's ABX model describes the transmission of a message from one party (A) to another (B) about object (X). A good illustration of this is the use of celebrities by cosmetic companies (A) to sell the benefits of their products (X) to consumers (B). In a situation where the receiver feels either positively or negatively on all aspects relating to both the product and the **celebrity**, the receiver is in a state of balance or '**homeostasis**'.

However, in situations where the receiver feels positive about the communicator (in this case the celebrity) and negative about the object or, alternatively, negative about the communicator and positive about the object, an imbalance is generated as he or she questions opinions previously held about the celebrity and the product. This creates 'cognitive dissonance' on the part of the receiver and he or she will seek to resolve it. According to Newcomb, cognitive dissonance can be resolved in three main ways:

1. The receivers might reduce levels of dissonance by lessening the perceived relevance or importance of the object in their own mind. ('The product isn't of any real importance to me so it doesn't matter'.)
2. The receivers might persuade themselves that the source of the message might not be as attractive or as credible as they first thought. ('Perhaps that celebrity isn't as credible/knowledgeable as I first thought'.)

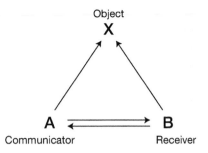

Figure 2.7 Newcomb's ABX Balance Theory (1953)[23]

3. Receivers might allow themselves to be persuaded that their original perceptions toward the object were incorrect and alter their attitude. ('Well if that celebrity likes it then I was wrong and it must be good.')

Creating messages that mean something

Having identified the appropriate target markets and developed a strategy to overcome the filters of perceptual selectivity, the next challenge in the communications process is the creation of a message that will be read and understood by the receiver in the way intended by the original source.

Within an IMC context, a useful way of conceptualizing the process is through the perspective used by those working in the fields of sociology and cultural studies. Rather than the uni-dimensional label of 'message', the term 'text' is used to describe anything that conveys meaning.[24] For students of IMC, this is particularly important as it recognizes the fact that almost anything might be considered a medium for communication. The use of 'text' as a way of conceptualizing media raises two major implications for marketers: that the vehicle that carries the communication has the potential to communicate a message in its own right and that, ultimately, marketers are reliant on consumers' ability to 'read' a message in the way that it was intended. This being the case, marketers must recognize that every aspect of the communication process has the potential to generate meaning and therefore as much care must be taken when constructing message/medium combinations.

The question then arises: how is meaning generated by a piece of marketing communication? At the most basic level, it is simply a process of encoding and **decoding**. Marketers encode a message with meaning and transmit it to the target market who, in turn, decode it to derive meaning. However, this process makes one important assumption: that the marketer and the target market are using the same 'code'.

Decoding the concept of 'codes'

A **code** is, in effect, anything that can be detected using the senses and from which an individual can derive meaning. Take, for example, a set of traffic lights, we understand that a red light communicates to drivers that they should 'stop' and a green light that they should 'go'. In effect, the coloured lights act as codes that communicate to drivers what kind of action is appropriate at that given time. The meaning of the coloured lights is based upon 'received wisdom', which, just like all other aspects of coding, is culturally driven.

The codes themselves are constructed from a series of **signs**. The study of signs, known as **semiology**, recognizes that individuals use objects or 'signs' to generate meaning, for example, pink is usually seen as a feminine colour and blue, masculine. A sign consists of two elements: a 'signifier' (the form that the sign takes), the 'signified' (what the sign represents). Therefore, using the earlier example of the traffic light, the red light is the 'signifier' of the need to stop (the signified). An understanding of semiology is particularly important for IMC practitioners seeking to formulate coherent messages that communicate brand values in a consistent fashion.

Because of the culturally driven nature of codes and the signs that are used to construct them, there is a high degree of subjectivity in the process of encoding and decoding of a message. A clear understanding of the cultural background of the target market is therefore essential for any marketer seeking to construct an effective programme of marketing communication. In particular, marketers should have a particular appreciation of the **conventions** or '**norms**' associated with consumers' **cultures** as these can vary from one culture to another. For example, in western cultures, prolonged eye contact is seen positively as a sign of engagement and attention whereas in Japan, Africa, Latin America and the Caribbean eye contact is often avoided as a sign of respect.

THINK BOX

Cultural codes and colours

Everyday we 'crack' cultural codes to gain information about the world around us. Think, for example, about the colours red, gold and green. Respectively, they are often used to represent danger, luxury and ecological friendliness; in concert they are associated with the concept of Christmas. How many other colours can you think of that have specific meanings? Think of some of your favourite brands – how have colours been used to encode meaning into the marketing communication, logos and product packaging?

Consumers as co-producers of meaning

The fact that consumers' play an active role in decoding marketing communications as they receive them means that they play an active part in production of their meaning. This co-production has the potential to yield both positive and negative benefits for brand owners. From a positive perspective, consumers not only decode a message's meaning but also have the potential to enhance its meaning and create a 'buzz' through positive word of mouth communication; the classic example of this being Cadbury's 'Gorilla' advert. It quickly became an online viral sensation[25] and its quirkiness and originality soon became a media talking point both online and in the traditional media. In addition, a number of parodies of the advertisement began to circulate online; the vast majority being endearing, respectful or humorous homages to the original piece of advertising. As a result, the 'Gorilla' campaign generated millions of pounds worth of free **publicity** as well as enhancing both the image of the Dairy Milk brand and Cadbury's corporate image.

However, in some cases, parodies are not always welcome. In situations in which consumers become offended by a brand or an organization, they can actively seek to alter the sign value of communication content in a way that distorts the signified message.[26]

A good example of this occurred when posters produced for the Mexican advertising agency TERAN/TBWA promoting the Swedish vodka brand Absolut began circulating on the Internet.[27] The posters depicted an image of California, Arizona, Texas, New Mexico and other US states being part of Mexico. The posters were part of a long-running campaign depicting 'perfect situations' with the strapline 'In an Absolut World'. The aim was to reflect Absolut's brand proposition as the perfect vodka.

Whilst there was very little dissent from Mexican consumers, unfortunately US consumers perceived it as anti-American and a number of parodies began to circulate on the Internet. Far from perceiving it as 'perfect', the parodies actively sought to demonize the product. The parodies borrowed the signifiers used in the Mexican campaign (the maps, the **typeface** and brand name and strapline) and used them in a way that signalled opposition to the brand and its perceived values. In response, Paula Eriksson, Vice President of Corporate Communications for V&S Absolut Spirits issued the following statement on its website[28]:

> In no way was the ad meant to offend or disparage, or advocate an altering of borders, lend support to any anti-American sentiment, or to reflect immigration issues.

> To ensure that we avoid future similar mistakes, we are adjusting our internal advertising approval process for ads that are developed in local markets.

Whilst it was clear that V&S Absolut had no intention of offending its US markets, unfortunately the damage was already done; in the eyes of many American consumers Absolut was less than perfect.

Noise as a disruptor of communication

Regardless of the amount of care and effort put into the production of a piece of marketing communication, there is always the chance that the delivery of the message will be disrupted by 'noise'. **Noise**, defined as any factors that have the potential to inhibit the effectiveness of the communications process,[29,30] comes in a number of forms.

In the original discussion of their model, Shannon and Weaver[31] identify three types of 'noise'. Their definitions, though rather clumsy, reflect the era in which they were first generated. The three types were:

- **technical or mechanical noise**
- **semantic noise**
- noise that detracts from the effectiveness of the communication when it is received.

Originally used in reference to static or picture interference, 'technical or mechanical noise' has been used more recently to describe any form of external distraction from the message.[32] This could include noise or distractions at the point of reception, for example, noise from family or friends.

The second form of 'noise', 'semantic noise', occurs when the meaning is distorted during the course of the communication process. An interesting facet of this type of noise is that it can occur either intentionally or unintentionally on the part of any of the members of the communication chain.[33] Unintentional semantic noise is often generated if unclear, conflicting, ambiguous or overly technical terms are used.[34] In such cases, receivers have the potential to misinterpret the content of messages because insufficient information or a lack of clarity requires them to make mental 'leaps' to make sense of the content. In contrast, semantic noise can be generated intentionally by transmitters acting as intermediaries. For example, it is acknowledged that, in the UK, individual newspapers tend to have distinct leanings toward the main two political parties. When reporting the activities of these parties it is not unknown for the press to put a particular 'spin' on their accounts in line with their political leanings.

With regard to Shannon and Weaver's third type of noise, it is generally acknowledged that their definition is rather unclear. As a contemporary alternative, Wu and Newell (2003)[35] suggest the term 'internal noise', a situation in which peoples' frame of mind affects their receptiveness to communication and is sometimes termed 'emotional noise'. This is particularly pertinent in today's market where issues of time-poverty and stress have major effects upon individuals' ability to process messages that are put in front of them by marketers.

More recently the existence of a fourth form of noise has been recognized. 'Clutter' is a form of noise that reflects modern consumers' exposure to multiple media. It is defined by Tellis[36] as the result of the 'proliferation of ads that compete for an audience's attention within a particular time period or printed space'. A classic example of 'clutter' may be seen in the 'classified' section of a newspaper. Such sections are filled with advertisements that are similar in both structure and content with little to distinguish them. The challenge in such situations is to cut through the homogeneity to create a clearly differentiated message that will permeate consumers' perceptual defences and that they will be willing and able to process at high levels of involvement.

Summary

Over the course of this chapter we have sought to explore **communication theory** and the implications that it holds for the process of integrated marketing communications. It is clear that it is not simply a question of sending a message to the market, but communicating the *right* set of messages, using the *right* combination of media to the *right* set of markets. Yet even if this is achieved, there can be no guarantee that the target consumers are in the right frame of mind to receive and decode individual messages correctly. Consistency in the application of integrated marketing principles are therefore essential to maximize the chance that a marketing message will be communicated effectively and these will be explored more fully in the following chapters.

Review questions

1. What do we mean by 'communication'?
2. Outline the process and key components of the Shannon and Weaver's (1949) seminal Model of Communication. To what extent do you feel that it has relevance today?
3. What are the main impediments to effective communication? Explain the term 'semiology'.
4. What is meant by the term 'target market' and what is its relevance for integrated marketing communications?
5. What is meant by the term 'involvement' and how might it be used to improve the effectiveness of a piece of marketing communication?
6. What are 'reference groups' and what influence might they hold over the way a consumer interprets a piece of marketing communication?

7. Distinguish between perceptual selectivity, perceptual vigilance and perceptual defence and explain how each might affect a consumer's willingness to receive and decode a piece of marketing communication.
8. 'Effectively communicating a marketing message in such a fragmented media market is impossible.' Discuss.
9. Choose one of the models of communication outlined in this chapter and discuss its relevance in today's market place.

Recommended reading

Littlejohn, S.W. (2007). *Theories of Human Communication*, Belmont, CA: Wadsworth.
Windahl, S., Signitzer, B., and Olson, J.T. (2008). *Using Communication Theory: An Introduction to Planned Communication*, London: Sage Publications Ltd.

CASE STUDY 2.1

Growing food glorious food

The National Trust

Source: www.thirdsector.co.uk/news/1032279/; www.forster.co.uk/case-studies/the-national-trust/. Agency: Forster, www.forster.co.uk.

The National Trust is a UK charity whose primary mission is to protect and open to the public over 360 historic houses and gardens and 49 industrial monuments and mills. They also act as guardians for a number of natural and man-made 'treasures' such as forests, woods, fens, beaches, farmland, downs, moorland, islands, archaeological remains, castles, nature reserves and villages. Their activities are funded by membership fees, donations and legacies, together with revenue raised from commercial operations.

As part of their mission to preserve the national heritage, the National Trust has expressed a commitment to sustainable food production and has launched two concurrent campaigns: 'Growing Spaces' and 'Food Glorious Food'.

The 'Growing Spaces' campaign was unveiled in 2009 when the National Trust announced new plans to create 1,000 new allotments on their land over the next three years with the aim of encouraging local people to grow their own fruit and veg. Difficult economic conditions and a growing awareness over issues of food quality had meant that the demand for allotment space was at an all time high. An estimated 100,000 people were currently on waiting lists and the release of National Trust land for use as allotments meant that there was the potential for new growing spaces on communities' doorsteps across England, Wales and Northern Ireland. According to National Trust, the new sites had the potential to produce 2.6 million lettuces per year, 50,000 sacks of potatoes or mixed produce to the value of £1.5 million and the new plots were to be registered on the Land Share website.

At the same time, the 'Food Glorious Food' campaign was launched to support families in their efforts to develop a better understanding of food and its origins. It was targeted at children between 5 and 12 years of age together with their parents, and with the objective of engaging them in the growing, purchasing, eating and the celebration of local and seasonal food. As part of the campaign, the National Trust gave away three quarters of a million packets of rocket, lettuce and pumpkin seeds, and taught children and adults how to plant, grow and cook their own food in an effort to encourage more active, healthy and sustainable lifestyles. A series of food themed events took place at National Trust properties throughout the year and included such things as family food trails, food and craft festivals, hands-on 'grow your own' workshops, tasting sessions and local farmers' markets.

The campaign was supported by a **microsite** that contained an advergame in which children could grow their own 'virtual' garden. It included useful gardening 'hints and tips', information on the events that are held at National Trust properties and advice to parents and children as to how home-grown vegetables might be used to stretch the family budget.

CASE STUDY QUESTIONS

1.   To what extent do you believe that the National Trust is an appropriate organization to support healthy eating/ lifestyle campaigns such as these?
2.   Discuss the benefits and pitfalls associated with running two campaigns at the same time.
3.   Who are the target groups for these campaigns? Justify your answer.
4.   If you were the agency in charge of these campaigns, what primary media for communication would you choose for targeting each of these campaigns?
5.   How could you measure the success campaigns like these?

Notes

1   Fiske, J. (2002). *Introduction to Communication Studies*, London: Routledge.
2   Schramm, W. (1955). *The Process and Effects of Mass Communication*, Illinois: University of Illinois Press, 17/13, pp. 3–10.
3   Schramm, W. (1955). *The Process and Effects of Mass Communication*, Illinois: University of Illinois Press, 17/13, p. 571.
4   Fiske, J. (2002). *Introduction to Communication Studies*, London: Routledge.
5   Shannon, C., and Weaver, W. (1949). *The Mathematical Theory of Communication*, Illinois: University of Illinois Press.
6   Westley, B., and MacLean, M. (1957). A conceptual model for communication research. *Journalism and Mass Communication Quarterly* (March), 34(1), 31–8.
7   Festinger, L. (1957). *A Theory of Cognitive Dissonance*, Stanford: Stanford University Press.
8   Argenti, P.A. (1997). *Strategic Corporate Communication*, India: Tata McGraw-Hill Pub Co.
9   Argenti, P.A. (1997). *Strategic Corporate Communication*, India: Tata McGraw-Hill Pub Co.
10   Payne, A., Ballantyne, D., and Christopher, M. (2005). A stakeholder approach to relationship marketing strategy. *European Journal of Marketing*, 39(7/8), 855–71.
11   Christopher, M.G., Payne, A., and Ballantyne, D. (1991). *Relationship Marketing: Bringing Quality, Customer Service, and Marketing Together*, Oxford: Butterworth Heinemann.
12   Heath, R., and Nairn, A. (2005). Measuring affective advertising: implications of low attention processing on recall, *Journal of Advertising Research*, 45(2), 269–81.
13   Solomon, M., Bamossy, G., and Askegaard, S. (2005). *Consumer Behaviour: A European Perspective*, London: Prentice Hall.
14   Turner, J.C. (1991). *Social Influence*, London: Open University Press, p. 5.
15   White, K., and Dahl, D.W. (2006). Are all outgroups created equal? The influence of consumer identity and dissociative reference groups on consumer preferences. Working paper, University of Calgary.
16   Solomon, M., Bamossy, G., and Askegaard, S. (2005). *Consumer Behaviour: A European Perspective*, London: Prentice Hall.

17 Wiener, J.L., and Mowen, J.C. (1986). Source credibility: on the independent effects of trust and expertise. *Advances in Consumer Research*, 13, 306–10.

18 Joseph, W.B. (1982). The credibility of physically attractive communicators: a review. *Journal of Advertising*, 11, 15–24.

19 White, K., and Dahl, D.W. (2006). Are all outgroups created equal? The influence of consumer identity and dissociative reference groups on consumer preferences. Working paper, University of Calgary.

20 Fiske, J. (2002). *Introduction to Communication Studies*, London: Routledge.

21 Fiske, J. (2002). *Introduction to Communication Studies*, London: Routledge.

22 Festinger, L. (1957). *A Theory of Cognitive Dissonance*, Stanford: Stanford University Press.

23 Newcomb, T. (1953). An approach to the study of communication acts. *Psychological Review*, 60, 393–440.

24 Hall, S. (1996). 'Encoding, Decoding'. In S. Hall, D. Hobson, A. Lowe, and P. Willis (eds) *Culture, Media, Language*, London: Routledge.

25 This ad can be viewed at: www.youtube.com/watch?v=TnzFRV1LwIo

26 Holt, D.B. (2002). Why do brands cause trouble? A dialectical theory of consumer culture and branding. *Journal of Consumer Research*, 29, 70–90.

27 Simons, A. (2008). The Rise of the Anti-American Brand? Online. Available HTTP: <http://brandeo.com/node/955> (accessed 6 June 2010).

28 Eriksson, P. (2008). We Apologise. Online. Available HTTP: <http://absolut.com/iaaw/blog/we-apologize> (accessed 6 June 2010).

29 Mowen, J.C. (1995). *Consumer Behaviour*, 4th edition, Englewood Cliffs, NJ: Prentice Hall.

30 Schiffman, L.G., and Kanuk, L.L. (2000). *Consumer Behaviour*, 7th edition, Englewood Cliffs, NJ: Prentice-Hall.

31 Shannon, C., and Weaver, W. (1949). *The Mathematical Theory of Communication*, Illinois: University of Illinois Press.

32 Watson, J. (2003). *Media Communication: An Introduction to Theory and Process*, Basingstoke: Palgrave Macmillan.

33 Fiske, J. (2002). *Introduction to Communication Studies*, London: Routledge.

34 Watson, J. (2003). *Media Communication: An Introduction to Theory and Process*, Basingstoke: Palgrave Macmillan.

35 Wu, B.T., and Newell, S.J. (2003). The impact of noise on recall of advertisements. *Journal of Marketing* (Spring), 56–65.

36 Tellis, G.J. (1998). *Advertising and Sales Promotion Strategy*, Reading, Massachusetts: Addison Wesley.

3 Ethical issues and current challenges*

LEARNING OUTCOMES

After studying this chapter, you will be able to:

- Critically discuss a number of major criticisms regarding the effects and effectiveness of marketing communications

- Discuss different ethical perspectives regarding marketing communications and the role of legislation and regulation

- Review the particular challenges presented by social marketing communications, together with the contentious issue of communicating with and to vulnerable groups in society, including the contentious issue of marketing communications directed at children

- Provide an overview of the largely overlooked challenge of communicating effectively with those who may struggle with poor literacy levels.

Introduction

In addition to the substantial challenges to the fundamental concepts and theories under-pinning marketing communications that were reviewed in the previous chapter, the industry itself is facing increasing criticism regarding the impact it has on society. Historically, advertising has been perceived as providing value through reduced search and information costs to consumers arising from the fact that advertising with higher sales of advertised products leads to economies of scale and also lowers prices.[1] Also the level of advertising can act as a signal of product or service quality.[2,3]

Marketing communication, particularly advertising, has received considerable criticism over a sustained period of time[4] in relation to claimed adverse effects and a perceived lack of ethical behaviour. It should be noted that other sectors of marketing communications such as public relations and sales promotions have also come in for criticism over a long period of time.[5,6]

> Advertising is in an odd position. Its extreme protagonists claim it has extraordinary powers and its severest critics believe them. Advertising is often effective. But it is not as powerful as is sometimes thought, nor is there any evidence that it actually works by any strong form of persuasion or manipulation".[7]
>
> (p. 39)

There is, however, a negative side that must be recognized, i.e. "Marketing is directly implicated in some preventative health-care issues",[8] (p. 350) being accused of contributing to a number of social problems such as smoking, misuse of alcohol and rising obesity rates.[9] As a result, the advertising industry in many countries faces calls for partial or total bans on advertising to children, advertising of liquor,[10] or advertising of tobacco. Direct links are claimed between certain advertised food types and obesity in adults and children.[11,12] Simultaneously, governments are under pressure to be seen to act on con-stituents' concerns. Therefore, either restricting or banning advertising may seem an easy way to show that governments take such issues seriously, even though these actions are unlikely to achieve the objectives set by policy makers.[13]

The link between advertising and obesity is not clear cut and there is a growing recognition that there may be a number of inter-related genetic and environmental factors that contribute to the problem;[14] the role of advertising appears to be relatively minor compared to other factors such as family dietary habits.[15] That is not to say that advertising does not have some influence and the industry's long-held assertion that if a product is legal to sell, it should be legal to advertise no longer has any credibility.[16] Many of the criticisms of advertising reflect philosophical opposition to persuasion per se, i.e. that advertising is inherently untruthful, deceptive, and manipulative, and persuades people to buy products they do not need or may ill-afford to purchase.[17]

MINI CASE: DOES ADVERTISING CAUSE OBESITY?

In the USA, several unsuccessful lawsuits were brought against McDonalds alleging that eating their products has caused individuals to become obese.[18] Advertising was cited as having encouraged people to eat more 'fast food' than was good for them.

What role does advertising actually play in decisions regarding whether to eat fast food, how much and how often?

What do you recommend fast food advertisers and regulators do to monitor public opinion?

Review advertising (including posters and displays at point of sale) for different fast food advertisers. Critique it in relationship to potential influences on dietary choices.

ETHICAL ISSUE TO CONSIDER

Do you believe that advertising manipulates people into buying goods and services that they do not really need? Give examples to justify your response.

Visit the UK advertising regulator's website (www.asa.co.uk) and review the **Codes of Practice** for advertising. How effective do you believe they are in addressing the main criticisms levelled at advertisers?

What changes do you believe should be considered for electronic media forms?

There is agreement that advertising targeting sectors of the population such as children should be restricted, both because of the concerns noted earlier and because of concerns regarding the ability of children to understand the persuasive intent of advertisements. Key aspects of this debate are reviewed in the following section.

ETHICAL ISSUE TO CONSIDER

Review the advertising contained in your top three favourite programmes from commercial channels. Draw on the ASA codes and critique these advertisements in terms of the criticisms of:

- Lack of truthfulness
- Deception
- Manipulation

What, if anything, do you recommend that marketers and regulators should do to protect consumers? Justify your responses.

Marketing communications and children

Persuasive communication is not necessarily intentionally deceptive, however children's relatively undeveloped cognitive skills, means that they are seen to be at greater risk of being misled by persuasive communication than adults.[19] **Media literacy** education and training is a tool frequently advocated to protect consumers, especially children, from the negative impact of persuasive communication and to enable children in particular to make informed choices before purchasing, or requesting, products.[20,21] Several media literacy programmes have been developed by organizations affiliated to, or with input from, the marketing industry in North America, the UK and several other EU countries.[22,23]

While such interventions are claimed to be designed to encourage children to be critical of commercial messages in general, critics of the marketing industry suggest that the motivation is simply to be seen to address a problem created by the industry itself, that is, the negative social impacts to which marketing activity has contributed.[24] Industry-sponsored media literacy programme organizers counter with claims that such programmes were developed voluntarily and have been operating for a considerable period of time. In Canada at least, media literacy interventions have operated for over 15 years – well before issues such as childhood obesity gained prominent focus.[25]

By contributing media literacy education resources, the marketing industry is positioning itself as being part of the solution to these problems and thereby seeks to avoid wide restrictions or outright bans on marketing communication, particularly for food products deemed to have little nutritional value directed at children.[26,27] The need to be seen to be taking positive action primarily in order to avert potential restrictions on advertising is openly acknowledged by some sectors of the industry itself.[28] If we accept that the existing media literacy programmes do have self-interest as a major motivating factor, does this make them necessarily wrong? If they are effective, does this mean that the intervention programmes can be offset against any potential harm done by marketing directed at children?

The implicit theoretical foundation underpinning media literacy programmes is inoculation theory, which regards media exposure as somewhat pathological in nature[29] and suggests that it is possible to immunize people against pressures generated via media content or advertising to act in particular ways or to consume products such as tobacco.[30]

As noted in the previous chapter, media usage, and advertising specifically, may play a major role in social identity formation and reinforcement through shared knowledge and interpretations.[31,32,33] This is in spite of **scepticism** towards advertising per se being well documented,[34] including among children and adolescents.[35]

The interaction between media consumer and the media itself is undoubtedly complex. Critics suggest that approaches taken by both educators and policy makers with regard to media literacy education are therefore overly simplistic and ignore the complex relationship consumers have with their chosen media.[32]

It must be recognized that, as noted earlier, children's cognitive abilities are not yet fully developed and that children are influenced by advertising in different ways to adults.[36,37] However, there is a substantial gap in the literature regarding the specific differences between children, adolescent and adult processing of persuasive communications and the impact that this communication may have on subsequent behaviour.[38,39] Further, it has long been recognized that awareness of persuasive intent does not necessarily promote the ability to resist it.[40,41,42]

No single coherent framework exists by which the way persuasive communication is perceived at different stages of children's cognitive development can be evaluated.

While Piaget's theories have provided the foundation for many prior studies, recent reviews have highlighted limitations inherent in applying the theories to activity within an increasingly complex environment and have proposed inclusion of a wider range of theories including information processing, the development of **persuasion knowledge** and theories of the mind.[21,45,43] These theories provide a more operationally useful foundation upon which to base predictions of how and when children develop an understanding of the motives and biases behind persuasive communication and are able to draw on and use prior knowledge such as that gained from media literacy programmes.

While there are wide variations in children's abilities at any specific age and also variations across **socio-economic** and cultural dimensions that have not been adequately explored, in general there appear to be relatively clear differences between two age groups. Children between the ages of 7 and 11 need to be prompted to retrieve and use information previously gained, such as through media literacy education; they are unable to link such information to current situations without some form of reminder.[44] Children under the age of 7 are unable to use prior information even when prompted; their undeveloped cognitive skills equate to a lack of effective cognitive defences.[45,21]

Even for those whose cognitive development would allow them to retrieve prior knowledge if given a reminder of it, there is little likelihood of this occurring through the intervention of parents, given that children's media consumption environment is largely unsupervized.[24] Up to 85 per cent of children's viewing in multi-set households is unsupervized, and 79 per cent of British children aged 10–15 years and 58 per cent of children aged 4–9 years have television sets in their bedrooms.[45] Thus, viewing is likely to occur without adult or even sibling presence.

A further complication in the analysis of message forms is widespread simultaneous media usage, particularly television and the Internet, as the following figures indicate: 32.7 per cent of males and 36.4 per cent of females watch television while they are online, with the two media becoming either foreground or background depending on the task and interest.[46] The way in which messages across these media may interact and reinforce each other is totally unresearched.

There are a number of issues that arise: given that media literacy initiatives are voluntarily funded by industry, there is no actual requirement for them to set specific and measurable objectives – or to make any measurement data publicly available. Indeed, the question must be asked – with whom does any burden of proof lie – with industry to prove effectiveness, or with critics to prove the reverse?

Much of the debate has centred on conventional advertising, however the variety of message forms has expanded substantially and there are specific challenges posed by new electronic media forms as opposed to traditional print or mass electronic forms such as television.[47] For example, children appear to have high levels of access to electronic media,

THINK BOX

Simultaneous media use

What strategies do you recommend to investigate the extent, nature and impact of simultaneous media use on attitudes towards, and purchase of a range of products and services? Justify your recommendations.

What impact might your findings have on current and future **regulation** of marketing communications?

THINK BOX

Social media

Given that social media content such as blogs, Facebook or Twitter sites is generated by its users, can content be effectively regulated? What do you recommend might be warranted in order to protect children?

with some 75 per cent of children aged 7–16 having access to the Internet[48]: one third of children use it each day.[49] Further, almost all of children's websites permit advertising, with advertising income being the main revenue source for two thirds of these sites.[50] There is concern that children may have the skills to access and navigate Internet sites, but may uncritically trust material encountered and also lack the critical skills to identify the underlying persuasive communication elements.[32]

Any examination of the effects of media literacy interventions needs to be considered in the context of new and evolving media forms and **media convergence**[51,52] and the blurring of the borders between advertising, information and entertainment.[53,54] In addition, a distinction should be made between overt commercials and subtle persuasive attempts embedded within programme content, such as product placements[55] and 'advergames', embedded commercial messages within online electronic games and videogames sold through a variety of retail outlets.[56,57] The level of interactivity of websites may be directly linked

---

THINK BOX

Media literacy

Visit the websites for Media Smart in the UK and Concerned Children's Advertisers in Canada.

Review and contrast the material and approaches taken by the two organizations for their respective media literacy activity.

What recommendations would you make to both organizations and to regulators regarding future activity?

ETHICAL ISSUE TO CONSIDER

Firstly, review the ASA Advertising Codes as they relate to children. Then review the advertising contained in three programmes from commercial channels that are likely to have high numbers of children viewing. Draw on the ASA codes and critique these advertisements in terms of the criticisms of:

• Lack of truthfulness
• Deception
• Manipulation

How effective do you believe that media literacy education is likely to be in protecting children from any adverse effects from the advertisements you have reviewed? Justify your response.

What specific ethical issues are raised by advergames and product placements?

Compare the codes as they relate to traditional media and to electronic media forms. What, if anything, do you recommend that marketers and regulators should do to protect children in addition to current advertising codes? Justify your responses.

to attitudes towards the site and, by implication, it is possible that this may extend towards the products featured within it.[58]

Given this, it is possible that mere exposure theory, originally introduced in the 1960s,[59] may provide a valid foundation for concerns as there is some evidence that repeated exposure to a stimulus such as an advertisement can enhance children's liking for the product featured; conversely if a product is disliked, repeated exposure is likely to increase the strength of dislike.[60] Children may play a game a hundred or more times;[61] this suggests that the effects of sustained exposure to non-overt persuasive communications offers yet another avenue for detailed future study. Indeed, there is a dearth of research examining new and evolving media from the perspective of the user. Once again, existing communication theories may not provide a complete framework for understanding the uses by, and impact on, media among all sectors of the population. Further research programmes may therefore involve testing and/or extending existing theories together with the development of new theories that encapsulate the complexities of the new – and likely future – media environment. These factors are discussed in more detail in Chapters 9 and 10.

Communication with consumers with low literacy levels

A further challenge facing the marketing communications industry is the failure to take into account the ability of people to access and comprehend communication. While almost all adults in first world countries are assumed to be able to read and write, some 20 per cent of adults have only rudimentary skills, leaving them unable to extract even simple information from printed material. A further 20–25 per cent can perform simple reading functions but cannot integrate or synthesize information in written material. While data from the 1996 International Adult Literacy Survey indicates that there is some variation in these rates across countries, with Scandinavian countries performing marginally better and countries such as Poland performing worse, the problem is a global one.[62,63] An additional, largely unidentified group, are 'alliterate', in that they are able to read but choose not to, and rely on television rather than print media for news. More importantly, they learn through trial and error rather than by reading instructions.

There are obvious serious implications in the health communication area where there is substantial evidence that a considerable amount of information material is written at a level well above that of the average person's ability to understand it.[64,65] There are potentially much wider consequences, with the impact of **literacy** problems extending to areas such as financial information, or even instructions for a product's safe use, yet this issue appears to be largely ignored, and there is no mechanism by which industry can ensure that all communication material is readily comprehendible. The main coordinating mechanisms within the industry extend only to regulating the content of communications, and this mechanism is far from being unproblematic.

The following provides an illustration of the unintended barrier caused by overly complex language: We have reproduced a section of the information provided, then the SMOG (simple measure of gobbledegook) score for the material. For the two examples provided, a reading level equating to a person having completed high school would be required. Think about the consequences, not just for health, but for the understanding of material in a wide range of everyday life.

Examples of SMOG reading grade level scores on NHS Direct website

Table 3.1 presents SMOG[66] grades and the corresponding educational level.

Table 3.1 SMOG grades

SMOG grade	Educational level
0–6	Low-literate
7–8	Primary school
9–11	Secondary school (age 11–15)
12	High school graduate (age 16+)
13–15	Some college/university (age 16–21)
16	University degree (age 21+)
17–18	Post-graduate studies
19+	Post-graduate degree

EXAMPLE 1: ASTHMA IN ADULTS – SYMPTOMS EXTRACT

The severity and duration of the symptoms of asthma are often variable and unpredictable, and are sometimes worse during the night or with exercise. The symptoms of a severe asthma attack often develop slowly, taking between 6–48 hours to become serious. You should remain alert for any signs of worsening symptoms.

SMOG Score: 11.94, which equates to age 16+

EXAMPLE 2: PASSIVE SMOKING

Passive smoking, also known as second-hand smoke, is when people other than the smoker breathe in the smoke from cigarettes, cigars and pipes. A smoker inhales only 15 per cent of the smoke from a cigarette – the rest goes into the surrounding air and other people breathe it in. Second-hand smoke contains over 4,000 toxic chemicals and 69 of these are cancer-causing chemicals. People who passively breathe in smoke are therefore at the same risk of disease and infection as actual smokers.

SMOG Score: 12.22

Ethics, regulation and communication

The advertising industry in many countries is governed by numerous consumer protection laws that apply to all sectors of society. Below the 'layer' of broad legislation, the industry is, in many countries, self-regulating,[67,68] with the various communication industry sectors, including advertisers, advertising agencies and the media have cooperated in drawing up Codes of Practice. A major regulatory body, usually accorded a title such as Advertising Standards Authority, is established to oversee the processes by which advertising conforms to both the letter and the spirit of the relevant codes. Supporting this structure, joint industry bodies may exist to maintain consistent advertising standards across specific media such as television channels. There are attempts to ensure consistency of regulatory provisions across borders, such as European Union-wide initiatives.[69]

Self-regulation has been proposed as the most efficient tool for curbing excesses and illegality in advertising.[70] These systems were introduced at a time when mass media dominated. More recent research suggests that new, electronic media forms such as advergames which comprise embedded commercial messages within the content of retail-accessible video games and online electronic games and reflect the growing blurring between entertainment and persuasion[71,72] fall outside the existing self-regulatory provisions. The majority of advergames would not comply with the regulations imposed on mass media if these regulations were to be extended.[73] The growth of new media is discussed on more detail in Chapters 9 and 10.

Further, programme content is not subject to the same level and type of regulation, and there is evidence that food portrayal in programmes would also breach advertising regulatory provisions if they were to be applied.[74] This brings into question product placements which involve the use of a recognizable branded product in traditional mass media such as movies or television programmes and in newer electronic media such as videogames. Placement can take many forms in traditional media, from passive (the product is shown as part of the setting, but is not actually used), through to active (the product is used by an actor with or without verbal acknowledgement as part of the script). Placement therefore provides an indirect form of celebrity endorsement for the product featured.[75] In newer electronic media such as video or computer games, the product is often an integral part of the game itself, such as accurately depicted cars in a motor racing game.[76]

ETHICAL ISSUE TO CONSIDER

A decision was made in 2010 to permit product placements in television programmes produced within the UK.[77] This involves the use of a recognizable branded product in movies or television programmes and in newer electronic media such as videogames. Product placements as a communications platform are discussed in more detail in Chapter 10. At this point, we want you to think of the ethical and regulatory issues that may arise through their use.

While products such as alcohol, tobacco, gambling and foods deemed to be of low nutritional value will not be permitted and the BBC will remain banned from promoting any products,[78] there is technically nothing to prevent sunbeds being featured in UK-produced programmes, in spite of legislation also introduced in 2010 banning the use of sunbeds by those aged under 18.[79]

Also largely outside the scope of existing self-regulatory provisions are home delivered promotional leaflets and flyers.[80] Little is known about the impact they have on food choices.

Tactics used to build discussion and debate ('buzz') through techniques such as viral marketing (also called **guerrilla marketing**) also cause concern[81] as does the Internet, particularly in relation to aspects of information privacy and access.[82]

The effectiveness of existing legislation, regulation and self-regulatory mechanisms on covering all facets of a rapidly changing media environment is likely to remain a topic of debate for the foreseeable future.

Special challenges of social marketing communications

As discussed in Chapter 1, social marketing seeks to improve the welfare of society. Communication used as part of social marketing interventions may lead to unintended effects, as illustrated in Table 3.2 in relation to health communication.

Table 3.2 Unintended effects of health communication campaigns**, p. 300

Effect	Definition
Obfuscation methods	Confusion and misunderstanding of health risk and risk prevention
Dissonance	Psychological discomfort and distress provoked by the incongruence between the recommended health states and the audience's actual states
Boomerang	Reaction by an audience that is the opposite to the intended response of the persuasion message
Epidemic of apprehension	Unnecessarily high consciousness and concern over health produced by the pervasiveness of risk messages over the long term
Desensitization	Repeated exposure to messages about a health risk may over the long term render the public apathetic
Culpability	The phenomenon of locating the causes of public health problems in the individual rather than in social conditions
Opportunity cost	The choice of communication campaigns as the solution for a public health problem and the selection of certain health issues over others may diminish the probability of improving public health through other choices
Social reproduction	The phenomenon in which campaigns reinforce existing social distributions of knowledge, attitudes and behaviours
Social norming	Social cohesion and control accompanying marginalization of unhealthy minorities brought about by campaigns
Enabling	Campaigns inadvertently improve the power of individuals and institution and promote the images and finances of industry
System activation	Campaigns influence various unintended sectors of society, and their actions mediate or moderate the effect of campaigns on the intended audience

Those charged with developing and implementing social marketing interventions need to be particularly aware of the potential negative impact of their activity. Unfortunately, there are no absolute rules that can be applied to every possible circumstance. There are, however, two common ethical frameworks that can be considered: one focussed on intentions (**deontology**), and the other on consequences (**teleology**, also referred to as consequentialism), with the latter being broken down further into utilitarianism and egoism.[83,84,85]

Deontology (from the Greek word for 'duty' and largely based on the work of eighteenth-century philosopher Immanuel Kant) holds that there are ethical 'absolutes' that are universally applicable, with the focus on means or intentions. Under this framework, there is an acceptance that actions intended to do good may have unintended negative consequences.

Teleology (from the Greek word for 'ends'), also known as *consequentialism*, focusses on the outcomes or effects of actions and is usually divided into:

1. Utilitarianism, in which behaviour is ethical if it results in the greatest good for the greatest number. Difficulties arise when comparing alternative courses of action with different levels of potential impact, for example, a programme that provides minor benefits to all, versus one that provides major benefits to many but no, or negative impact on others.
2. Egoism, in which the benefits to the individual undertaking action are stresses and the impact on other people is deemphasized. This latter framework is seldom used in marketing activity, as there are few situations where benefits accruing to an individual would be tolerated if there were significant negative impacts on others.

The existing self-regulatory provisions reviewed in the previous section do not provide explicit direction as to whether deontology or teleology are the preferred framework, however a review of the rulings when complaints have been made about specific marketing communication campaigns indicates that the utilitarian framework within teleology underpins the decision process.

For example, the Department of Health (DoH) fear-based smoking cessation 'fish-hook' campaign (see: http://smokefree.nhs.uk/resources/news/campaigns/2007-smokefree-campaign-hooked-office-hooked/) would be acceptable under deontological reasoning. Others would argue that it is unacceptable to knowingly cause anxiety under deontological reasoning.[86,87]

The campaign received 774 complaints and was deemed by the **Advertising Standards Authority (ASA)** in May 2007 to be in breach of advertising regulations and ordered to be amended or discontinued. The majority of complaints related to children's fear and distress upon seeing the advertisements.[88] There is, however, no explicit statement of ethical principles in the *Television Advertising Standards Code*.

THINK BOX

Advertising controversies

Advertising creates numerous controversies, some of them deliberately to stimulate interest and attention. However, there are many instances when advertisements are deemed to be unethical. Why do you believe this occurs and what, if anything, should be done to improve things?

Visit the ASA website for the Codes of Practice and review the ethical provisions they contain. Do you believe that they make the ethical standards expected of advertisers clear or not? Justify your response.

MINI CASE: PRIMARK – SEXUALIZING CHILDREN

In April 2010, the retail clothing chain Primark introduced and advertised a range of padded bikini tops for girls as young as 7.

Media headlines included the following:

Primark padded bikini row: other high street chains caught 'sexualizing children'
Daily Telegraph, 15 April, accessed from www.telegraph.co.uk

In the article, the (unnamed) *Daily Telegraph* journalist notes that:

- Tesco had been forced to remove a home pole dancing set from the toys section of their online system, which had included a pole, frilly garter and a DVD to demonstrate sexy dance moves from its toy section in 2006.
- A few years earlier, Asda had been forced to withdraw black and pink lace knickers.
- Disney withdrew a range of children's knickers with the slogan *Dive In* (part of a **joint promotion** around the movie *High School Musical 2* which had a swimming pool theme) from sale in Asda stores.
- WHSmith withdrew a range of Playboy stationery including a pencil case featuring the Playboy bunny logo in 2009.

What specific issues do these cases raise in regard to the marketing and promotion of products with an implicit or explicit sexual message when children may be the target?

Search both the academic and practitioner media for other examples of this type of problem. Why do you believe these types of problems continue to occur? What should marketers and legislators do to prevent these issues from occurring in the future?

Summary

Several ethical perspectives exist to direct marketing practitioners in their choices of communications strategies. At the minimum, communication professionals should strictly follow the legal guidelines in the countries in which they operate, and should fully cooperate with the self-regulatory bodies and procedures in place. Some groups of consumers require special protection from the influence of marketing communications, for example children are often cognitively not developed enough to recognize the persuasive nature of creative communication and therefore are protected by stricter legal regulations than adults. Marketing communications specialists should act ethically because it is in their best long-term business interest to be and to be perceived as responsible corporate citizens of the communities in which they market their products.

Review questions

1. Critique the suggestion that products that are legal to sell should be able to be advertised without restriction.
2. Evaluate the evidence for and against the impact of marketing communication on problems such as obesity. What recommendations can be made to regulators?
3. What ethical frameworks should be used to guide the development of social marketing communication programmes?
4. Assess the efficacy of advertising self-regulatory provisions in a country of your choice and across the EU.
5. Is advertising to children inherently unethical? Justify your answer.
6. How do you suggest marketing communication be adapted to meet the needs of those who have low functional literacy levels?
7. What do you believe are the major potential ethical dilemmas in **stealth marketing**, sales promotions and PR? How do you recommend these be resolved?
8. 'Advertising creates unattainable ideals.' Discuss this statement using examples to illustrate your answer.

9. Identify an advertisement that you believe to be targeted at one of the following 'vulnerable' groups:

   - children
   - individuals with special needs and/or learning difficulties
   - the elderly or infirm.

   Discuss the challenges faced by advertisers seeking to communicate with your chosen group and consider the various ways they might seek to overcome them.
10. To what extent do you believe that the Government should regulate marketing to children and other vulnerable groups? Discuss the positive and negative implications of Government regulation for both brand owners and consumers.

Recommended reading

Holbrook, M.B. (1987). Mirror, mirror, on the wall, what's unfair in the reflections of advertising? *Journal of Marketing*, 51, 95–103.

Livingstone, S. (2005). Assessing the research base for the policy debate over the effects of food advertising to children. *International Journal of Advertising*, 24(3), 273–96.

Livingstone, S., and Helsper, E.J. (2006). Does advertising literacy mediate the effects of advertising on children? A critical examination of two linked research literatures in relation to obesity and food choice. *Journal of Communication*, 56(3), 560–84.

Moses, L.J., and Baldwin, D.A. (2005). What can the study of cognitive development reveal about children's ability to appreciate and cope with advertising? *Journal of Public Policy & Marketing*, 24(2), 186–201.

Pechmann, C., Levine, L., Loughlin, S., and Leslie, F. (2005). Impulsive and self-conscious: adolescents' vulnerability to advertising and promotion. *Journal of Public Policy & Marketing*, 24(2), 202–21.

Pollay, R.W. (1986). The distorted mirror: reflections on the unintended consequences of advertising. *Journal of Marketing*, 50, 18–36.

Shrum, L.J. (Ed.) (2004). *The Psychology of Entertainment Media*, Mahwah, NJ: Lawrence Erlbaum.

CASE STUDY 3.1

SKCIN (Karen Clifford Skin Cancer Charity)

Source: Account Planning Group (UK): Silver, Creative Strategy Awards, 2009. Author: James Hamilton. Case material provided by the World Advertising Research Centre (WARC) www.warc.com.

Summary

This case study focusses on engaging an audience that didn't want to be engaged; talking to them about a subject that they didn't want to discuss and, perversely, persuading them to spread that message themselves. It's a story about a small charity with big ambitions and a strategy that enabled it to punch way above its weight.

The SKCIN campaign targeted those most at risk of developing skin cancer – the sunbed-obsessed 'tanorexics' – by using their obsession against them. The campaign created a fake, online tanning product designed to appeal to tanorexics' thirst for new tanning technology. The campaign then became self-selecting: those most at risk were most likely to suspend disbelief and visit the site. Visit the site they did – in their droves. So far, visits to computertan.com stand at 422,686 and counting.

Introduction

Karen Clifford was not a sun-worshipper, but she felt better with a suntan. Along with her husband, Richard and their daughter, Kathryn, Karen habitually visited Spain on a package holiday for two weeks every year. By the time Karen's skin cancer was diagnosed, it had already spread to her liver. She died aged 61 on New Year's Eve, 2005.

Kathryn and Richard Clifford founded the Karen Clifford Skin Cancer Charity – SKCIN – in 2006, with the ambition of being the largest skin cancer specific organization in the UK. They did so as a result of their loss, but also because rates of skin cancer are growing faster than any other form of the disease in the UK. They approached McCann-Erickson with a challenge: bring skin cancer to the forefront of UK awareness and allow SKCIN to unify and magnify the work of the numerous small charities who work to fund research into the disease.

Background – skin cancer in the UK

In the last 30 years, rates of skin cancer have more than quadrupled, from 3.4 cases per 100,000 people in 1977 to 14.7 per 100,000 in 2006. The British Association of Dermatologists reports up to 18 per cent increases of melanoma over two years in some areas of the UK, and more than 8,100 cases of malignant melanoma – the deadliest form of skin cancer – will be diagnosed this year. More than 1,700 of those sufferers will die from the disease: almost five people a day. While Government spending on skin cancer awareness messaging remains low, there have been numerous national initiatives which have sought to raise awareness of the dangers of over-exposure to the sun: Cancer Research's SunSmart campaign, Boots' Soltan range and a screening campaign among English cricketers have all increased awareness of the need for adequate protection when in strong sunlight.

Studying the skin cancer problem in the UK, another worrying trend was evident: the dangerous increase in popularity of sunbed tanning. Here was a platform upon which SKCIN could successfully campaign; a platform which focussed on the 50 weeks a year when skin cancer is not in front of mind in the public.

The sunbed problem and the rise of the tanorexic

The number of sunbeds in the UK has risen by a third in the last decade and studies estimate that as many as eight out of ten sunbeds produce levels of UVB which exceed EU recommendations. Research by Cancer Research suggests that using a sunbed just once a month can increase the risk of skin cancer by more than half, and many sunbed users – predominantly young women – are using sunbeds far more than 12 times a year; some are using sunbeds twice a week or more. Sunbeds are most popular among hardcore tanners: those most at risk of developing skin cancer.

As far back as 2004 the British Medical Association drew attention to the phenomenon of 'tanorexia' in a 2004 report. Tanorexia is an obsession with achieving the 'perfect' tan and is most prevalent in young women.

While its effects may be medical, the root cause is cultural. Coco Chanel is credited with promoting the tan back in the 1920s and the fashion and beauty industry has driven home the message that a suntan is sexy and – perversely – healthy, ever since. Sunbeds are commonly found at health spas and in gyms and today's celebrity-obsessed culture has only exacerbated the problem, with a slew of magazines and TV shows seemingly dedicated to convincing people that they need to emulate their heroes if they're to be successful in life. The stars they're emulating are rarely seen without a 'healthy' tan.

In turn, the growth and acceptance of sunbeds as part and parcel of modern grooming has led to a blasé attitude towards their effects. As a team at the Ninewells Hospital & Medical School in Dundee discovered, as many as 15 per cent of users do not believe that sunbeds carry a health risk, while of those that do acknowledge that a risk is involved, only half mention skin cancer.

The strategy

The communications strategy was a simple one – create a campaign that talks to those most at risk about the dangers of using sunbeds. As is increasingly usual with charity advertising, budget was an issue. SKCIN is not a large charity with access to the kinds of funds needed for a traditional above the line awareness campaign – they needed a campaign platform that allowed SKCIN to punch way above its weight, while simultaneously conferring credibility on the message.

The first hurdle was the at-risk target audience – not only are more than half hardcore sunbedders blind to the dangers of their obsession, very few of those addicted want to hear that their habit could put them in danger. Add to this the fact that the effects of sunbed usage might only manifest themselves 20 years down the line, and the campaign's central message – that there is no such thing as a safe sunbed – is not one that has much traction with its target audience.

This called for a disruptive approach, both strategically and creatively: they needed to target those most at risk in the full knowledge that this audience was going to be hardest to reach.

The tanorexic mindset

In order to speak to those with a sunbed addiction, the team needed to understand their tanning mindset. They visited and interviewed tens of tanning salons – from gyms to the coin-operated electric beaches where some of the most extreme sunbed-addicted behaviour manifests itself. Interviewing managers and their customers, they made a number of discoveries that chimed with the available research: a widespread belief that a tan is healthy (one salon visited combined its tan cabin with a vibrating-plate exercize machine, so users could lose weight while they tanned); a common trend of users visiting tanning salons to get a 'pre-tan' head start before they go on holiday; and a hardcore which is seemingly desperate for the perfect tan.

The team discovered that few – if any – users ask about health risks. And those that do are told, categorically, that no risks exist. And they discovered something that goes beyond desperation for a tan. They witnessed tanorexia first hand: habitual behaviour that displayed an obsession with the latest tanning technology. Tanorexics knew all about the latest innovations in tanning technology: which salons had the most powerful, fastest tubes; which products were best to use at home; even which 'accelerator' drugs and lotions to use in order to maximize the effects of UV exposure. One described the pills they took as helping them to 'tan on the train home' after a tanning session.

Thinking outside the cabin

For the tanorexics, sunbathing did not just mean a couple of weeks on the beach in the summer, or a couple of sessions a month on the sunbed, their lives revolved around accessing the latest technology in order to get the perfect tan.

Working from this insight the team realized that if they could fool these people into thinking there was an innovative piece of tanning technology that they were missing out on, they could use that technology to carry the SKCIN warning message.

Using this strategy they started to think about other ways in which tanorexics could feed their obsession. They explored in-home, but discovered a wealth of products – from lamps to self-tan sprays – that already catered for that market. So where else could they engage them?

This led to a simple brief: create a piece of brand utility to carry a sunbed warning message: there is no such thing as a safe sunbed. The creative team came back with computertan.com.

Website computertan.com

Computertan.com was brilliant both in its simplicity and its effectiveness – a self-selecting piece of communication, created to appeal to those most gullible, most willing to suspend disbelief and hence, most at risk from sunbed abuse.

To give the target audience exactly what they wanted – a new and effective way of getting a tan – the team developed a revolutionary software application, available for download from computertan.com. The application supposedly turned an everyday computer monitor into a 'tanning screen' and enabled people to tan themselves from the comfort of their desks.

To drive traffic to the site they developed an infomercial offering free online tanning sessions at computertan.com.

This was seeded on thousands of websites as well as being PR-ed across key bloggers for relevant interest groups together with an extensive national press PR campaign. 25,000 free tanning vouchers were printed, which spray-tanned volunteers distributed across the UK, and the infomercial was displayed on 50 digital cross track panels in ten London underground stations and in 1,000 London taxi screens.

In a second wave of activity, they launched an iPhone application, which was sent out to an email database and supported with online advertising.

Only when users begin their trial and are 20 seconds in to their first session does it become apparent that the technology is a hoax. Five images depicting the ravaging effects of skin cancer are projected on to the screen with the message that this is the number of people that die each day from the disease. It is at this point that the user is introduced to the real organization behind the campaign, SKCIN.

Reveal

Visitors can then visit SKCIN's website, or hoax a friend into logging on to the site. Granted, not all of the visitors were duped into believing the technology was real, but the amount of traffic to the site clearly demonstrated the message was one of real interest to a wider audience than just our tanorexics.

Results

Within 24 hours of launch, computertan.com had received over 30,000 hits. Within four weeks, the number of hits had reached over 230,000 from an incredible 180 countries. The campaign clearly engaged a wide audience. To date, computertan has had 422,686 visits and over 1.6 million page views, with an average dwell time of over two minutes. 1.7 million people were exposed to the CBS digital cross track panels, 700,000 through London

Cabvision and the media agency Universal McCann achieved over 17 million page impressions with its online bookings.

SKCIN's profile has grown immeasurably. Limelight's PR campaign delivered extensive national press coverage across titles including *The Sun*, *The Independent*, *The Daily Express*, *The Guardian* and also online with BBC News, BBC Radio One, The New Zealand Herald, Fox US and Yahoo News. Such was the interest from readers of *The Sun* that the paper has become an unofficial media partner to SKCIN.

Richard and Kathryn Clifford, Trustees of SKCIN, say of the Campaign:

> The value and success of the 'Computertan' campaign has far exceeded our expectations. There is clear evidence that the spoof was so meticulously engraved that the campaign very quickly achieved its objectives and then some. It was a bold idea that was pulled off spectacularly by a truly talented, dedicated and extremely incredible team.
>
> SKCIN's aims and objectives from the outset have been to significantly increase public awareness of skin cancer through education and resultant early diagnosis, thereby saving lives. There is no doubt that McCann Erickson has made a huge and otherwise unobtainable impact in this regard and for that the management are eternally grateful.
>
> The profile of the charity has obviously been significantly increased on a national level resulting in a wide range of public, private and media contacts, leaving us very excited about the future of the charity.
>
> (Richard Clifford)

CASE STUDY QUESTIONS

1. Critique the approach used (you may find it useful to visit the website as well). Do you agree with the use of 'hoax' communications? What ethical issues does this technique raise? Justify your response.
2. What ethical issues are raised by the abrupt revelation of skin cancer statistics and the graphic photos of actual skin cancers? How do you believe the target group would have responded to the images?
3. The campaign may have increased awareness of skin cancer dangers in the short term; how effective do you believe it will have been in the longer term in changing attitudes towards sun tanning and sunbed use? What effect do you believe it will have had on actual sun protective behaviours? Justify your responses.
4. Discuss the use of graphic images and scare tactics (also used for activity such as road safety). Do you believe that they are effective or not? Do you think that individual segments of the population may respond differently to these types of approaches? If so, what are the implications for marketers? Justify your responses.
5. The computertan.com case used a totally different approach to that used by Cancer Research UK for the SunSmart campaign (visit www.cruk.org.uk). Discuss the lack of integration of messages between the two organizations. What impact do you believe that this may have had on the effects and effectiveness of overall communications regarding skin cancer risk? What do you recommend should be done to ensure greater integration in the future?
6. Critique both the Cancer Research UK and SKCIN activity, using their websites. Provide recommendations for future activity, including ethical issues that should be considered.

CASE STUDY 3.2

Political advertising – back to the future

In the lead up to the 2010 UK elections, Labour released a poster showing the Conservative Leader, David Cameron, as a character from a popular television series *Ashes to Ashes*, Gene Hunt, seated on the bonnet of an Audi Quattro, a make of car featured prominently in the series and driven by Hunt. The character of Gene Hunt is a 'hard' police officer, with a range of sexist and politically incorrect views and a tendency to 'bend the rules' in order to make arrests. The copy suggested that the Conservatives wanted to take the country back to the 1980s (in which the TV series is set).

The series, and the character were popular and early indications were that the message intended to be sent was not what was taken from the advertisements by potential voters, who viewed the character in a positive rather than negative light.

The Conservatives were quick to capitalize on this by releasing their own version of the poster showing David Cameron in the same pose but with the copy now reading: 'Fire up the Quattro. It's time for a change'.

CASE STUDY QUESTIONS

1. Critique the approach taken by the Labour party. What ethical issues does this approach raise?
2. Critique the Conservative party response and any ethical issues that you believe their response may raise.
3. Given the approach may have backfired, how might the potential reaction to the approach have been tested before being implemented?
4. How would you measure the impact of both parties' activity on voter intentions?

CASE STUDY 3.3

Communication controversy: regarding direct-to-consumer advertising of prescription medicines

Introduction

Advertising of prescription medicines direct to consumers (DTC or DTCA) via mass media is permitted only in the USA, where a deliberate change was made to legislation in 1997, and New Zealand, where a loophole in legislation permits it – a fact not evident until the American laws changed. It represents a unique product category in that advertising may be seen by a patient, but they are unable to purchase the medication themselves – it still must be prescribed by a doctor.

DTC is extremely controversial in both countries and in countries that have considered permitting it. Much of the debate regarding DTC's impact is focussed on the perceived impact on, or views of, medical professionals.[89] Highly polarized views abound, with strong opposition[90,91] and positive perspectives.[92,93] Much of the debate is also highly emotive with little critical review or empirical evidence of DTC's actual impact.[94] There is little empirical data regarding the actual impact of DTC on consumers that offers guidance to marketers and policy makers alike regarding the way in which this market sector operates.

There is a need for considerably more research as any potential impact of DTC should be viewed in the context of wider cross-country societal changes such as aging populations.[95] In addition, the advocacy of more aggressive treatments for some medical conditions such as cholesterol will undoubtedly have a confounding effect that requires further investigation. There are undoubtedly different market segments in terms of demographics, psychographics and disease states with regard to the influence of DTC on communication between patients and medical professionals and, ultimately, on medication usage,[96] whose precise characteristics have yet to be analysed in depth.

A larger amount of debate was generated in the late 1990s and early years of the twentieth century. The key consumer-oriented debates in the literature were that DTC advertising is biased, misleading, inaccurate and unbalanced, overstating or exaggerating benefit claims and providing inadequate risk information.[97,98] Proponents of the practice countered by asserting that existing legislative and regulatory provisions ensure that information is truthful and accurate. They further contended that advertising leads to increased awareness of risks/side effects and improved compliance.[99]

While this debate continues today, it may be somewhat irrelevant as electronic technology such as websites enables patients in countries where DTC is not permitted to access the sale amount and types of information on medications as are available in the USA and New Zealand.[100]

CASE STUDY QUESTIONS

1. Critique the role of mass media advertising in promoting prescription medications. Consider the impact on patients and on their relationships with medical professionals.
2. Visit websites for prescription medicines and critique the quality of information available for patients. Look specifically for examples of DTC activity. How ethical do you believe the advertisers are?
3. Visit the ASA codes of advertising relating to medicine promotion (including over-the counter medicines etc.). Do you believe they provide adequate consumer protection? Justify your response.
4. Given the anomaly of advertising being available via websites but not through mass media, what action do you believe regulators should take in the future and why?
5. What research do you believe should be conducted to clarify understanding of the impact of DTC advertising?

Note: for specific New Zealand perspectives regarding DTC, see the following papers:

Eagle, L.C., and Chamberlain, K.C. (2002). Direct to the consumer promotion of prescription drugs. A review of the literature and the New Zealand experience. *International Journal of Medical Marketing*, 2(4), 293–310.

Eagle, L.C., and Chamberlain, K.C. (2004). Prescription medicine advertising: professional discomfort and potential patient benefits – can the two be balanced? *International Journal of Advertising*, 23(1), 69–90.

Hoek, J., and Gendall, P. (2002). Direct-to-consumer advertising down under: an alternative perspective and regulatory framework. *Journal of Public Policy and Marketing*, 21(2), 202–12.

Notes

* Part of this chapter is based on Eagle, L.C. (2007). Commercial media literacy: what does it do, to whom – and does it matter? *Journal of Advertising*, 36(2), 99–108.
** Adapted from Cho, H., and Salmon, C.T. (2007). Unintended effects of health communication campaigns. *Journal of Communication*, 57(2), 293–317.

1 Comanor, W.S., and Wilson, T.A. (1971). On advertising and profitability. *Review of Economics & Statistics*, 53(4), 408.
2 Telser, L.G. (1968). Some aspects of the economics of advertising. *Journal of Business*, 41(2), 166–73.
3 Telser, L.G. (1964). Advertising and competition. *Journal of Political Economy*, 72(537), 547–51.
4 Calfee, J.E., and Ringold, D.J. (1994). The 70% majority: enduring consumer beliefs about advertising. *Journal of Public Policy & Marketing*, 13(2), 228–38.
5 Hughes, P., and Demetrious, K. (2006). Engaging with stakeholders or constructing them? *Journal of Corporate Citizenship*, (23), 93–101.
6 Ward, J.C., and Hill, R.P. (1991). Designing effective promotional games: opportunities and problems. *Journal of Advertising*, (20), 69–81.
7 Ehrenberg, A.S.C. (2000). Repetitive advertising and the consumer. *Journal of Advertising Research*, 40(6), 39–48.
8 Goldberg, M.E. (1995). Social marketing: are we fiddling while Rome burns? *Journal of Consumer Psychology*, 4(4), 347–70.
9 Desrochers, D.M., and Holt, D.J. (2007). Children's exposure to television advertising: implications for childhood obesity. *Journal of Public Policy & Marketing*, 26(2), 182–201.
10 Nelson, J. (2005). Beer advertising and marketing update: structure, conduct, and social costs. *Review of Industrial Organization*, 26(3), 269–306.
11 Eagle, L., Bulmer, S., de Bruin, A., and Kitchen, P.J. (2005). Advertising and children: issues and policy options. *Journal of Promotion Management*, 11(2/3), 175–94.
12 Jardine, A., and Wentz, L. (2004). Markets brace for food-ad rules. *Advertising Age*, 75(37), 20.
13 Young, B.M. (2003). Does food advertising influence children's food choices? A critical review of some of the recent literature. *International Journal of Advertising*, 22(4), 441–59.
14 Ebbeling, C., Pawlak, D., and Ludwig, D.S. (2002). Childhood obesity: public health crisis, common sense cure. *The Lancet*, 360(9331), 473–82.
15 Livingstone, S. (2005). Assessing the research base for the policy debate over the effects of food advertising to children. *International Journal of Advertising*, 24(3), 273–96.
16 Casswell, S., Stewart, L.I.Z., and Duignan, P. (1989). The struggle against the broadcast of anti-health messages: regulation of alcohol advertising in New Zealand 1980–1987. *Health Promotion International*, 4(4), 287–96.
17 Shimp, T.E. (2003). *Advertising, Promotion and Supplemental Aspects of IMC*, 6th edition, Independence, KY: Thompson South-Western.
18 Duin, J. (2012). Obese people use lawsuits to get government involved, *Washington Times*, DC.
19 Moses, L.J., and Baldwin, D.A. (2005). What can the study of cognitive development reveal about children's ability to appreciate and cope with advertising? *Journal of Public Policy & Marketing*, 24(2), 186–201.
20 Rogers, D. (2002). Media Smart tells kids 'be sceptical'. *Marketing (UK)*, Nov 14, 4.
21 Armstrong, G.M., and Brucks, M. (1988). Dealing with children's advertising: public policy issues and alternatives. *Journal of Public Policy & Marketing*, 7(1), 98–113.
22 Concerned Children's Advertisers (CCA) (2004). *2004 Annual Report*. Toronto, Canada: Concerned Children's Advertisers.
23 Media Smart (2003). Media Smart Overview. Online. Available HTTP: <http://mediasmart. org.uk/media_smart/ofcom.html>.
24 Goldberg, M.E. (1995). Are we fiddling while Rome burns? *Journal of Consumer Psychology*, 4(4), 347–70.

25   Loblaw, C. (2001). The whole world is watching. *Marketing Magazine*, 106(31), 11.

26   Kleinman, M. (2003). Heinz fights food ad criticism with media smart link. *Marketing (UK)*, October 2, 1.

27   Teinowitz, I. (2001). World Ad Federation seeking consistency. *Advertising Age*, 72(15), 35.

28   Cincotta, K. (2005). Accord Gets Kids to Munchright, *B&T Magazine*, 8 April, 26. Online. Available HTTP: <www.bandt.com.au> (accessed 27 June 2005).

29   Buckingham, D. (2004). The Media Literacy of Young People. Report prepared for OFCOM. Online. Available HTTP: <www.ofcom.org.uk> (accessed 21 September 2005).

30   Considine, D.M. (2002). National developments and international origins (media literacy). *Journal of Popular Film and Television*, 30(1), 7–15.

31   Dotson, M.J., and Hyatt, E.M. (2005). Major influence factors in children's consumer socialization. *Journal of Consumer Marketing*, 22(1), 35–42.

32   Harwood, J. (1999). Age identification, social identity, gratification and television viewing. *Journal of Broadcasting and Electronic Media*, 43(1), 123–36.

33   Ritson, M., and Elliott, R. (1999). The social uses of advertising: an ethnographic study of adolescent advertising audiences. *Journal of Consumer Research*, 26(3), 260–77.

34   Calfee, J.E., and Ringold, D.J. (1994). The 70% majority: enduring consumer beliefs about advertising. *Journal of Public Policy & Marketing*, 13(2), 228–38.

35   Derbaix, C., and Pecheux, C. (2003). A new scale to assess children's attitudes towards TV advertising. *Journal of Advertising Research*, 43(4), 390–9.

36   Friestad, M., and Wright, P. (2005). The next generation: research for twenty-first century public policy on children and advertising. *Journal of Public Policy & Marketing*, 24(2), 183–5.

37   Mallalieu, L., Palan, K.M., and Laczniak, R.N. (2005). Understanding children's knowledge and beliefs about advertising: a global issue that spans generations. *Journal of Current Issues and Research in Advertising*, 27(1), 53–64.

38   Wright, P., Friestad, M., and Boush, D.M. (2005). The development of marketplace persuasion knowledge in children, adolescents, and young adults. *Journal of Public Policy & Marketing*, 24(2), 222–33.

39   Boush, D.M., Friestad, M., and Rose, G.M. (1994). Adolescent skepticism towards TV advertising and knowledge of advertiser tactics. *Journal of Consumer Research*, 21(1), 165–75.

40   O'Sullivan, T. (2005). Advertising and children: what do the kids think? *Qualitative Market Research: An International Journal*, 8(40), 371–84.

41   Brucks, M., Armstrong, G.M., and Goldberg, M.E. (1988). Children's use of cognitive defences against television advertising: a cognitive response approach. *Journal of Consumer Research*, 14(4), 471–82.

42   John, D.R. (1999). Consumer socialization of children: a retrospective look at twenty-five years of research. *Journal of Consumer Research*, 26(3), 183–213.

43   Friestad, M., and Wright, P. (1994). The persuasion knowledge model: how people cope with persuasion attempts, *Journal of Consumer Research*, 21(1), 1–30.

44   Neeley, S.M., and Schumann, D.W. (2004). Using animated spokes-characters in advertising to young children. *Journal of Advertising*, 33(3), 7–23.

45   Muto, S. (2004). Children and media. *Young Consumers*, 6(1), 37–43.

46   Pilotta, J.J., Schultz, D.E., Drenik, G., and Rist, P. (2004). Simultaneous media usage: a critical consumer orientation to media planning. *Journal of Consumer Behaviour*, 3(3), 285–92.

47   Hobbs, R., and Frost, R. (2003). Measuring the acquisition of media literacy skills, *Reading Research Quarterly*, 38(3), 330–55.

48   Clarke, B. (2002). Eating trends: adapting to kid's lifestyles. *Advertising & Marketing to Children*, 3(2), 33–7.

49   Kunkel, D. (2005). Predicting a renaissance for children and advertising research. *International Journal of Advertising*, 24(3), 401–5.

50   Moore, E.S. (2004). Children and the changing world of advertising. *Journal of Business Ethics*, 52(2), 161–7.

51   Livingstone, S. (2004). Media literacy and the challenge of new information and communication technologies. *The Communication Review*, 7(1), 3–14.

52 Silverstone, R. (2004). Regulation, media literacy and media civics. *Media, Culture & Society*, 26(3), 440–9.

53 Grigorovici, D.M., and Constantin, C.D. (2004). Experiencing interactive advertising beyond rich media. Impacts of ad type and presence on brand effectiveness in 3D gaming immersive virtual environments. *Journal of Interactive Advertising*, 5(1), 1–26.

54 Shrum, L.J. (ed.) (2004). *The Psychology of Entertainment Media. Blurring the Lines Between Entertainment and Persuasion*, Mahwah, NJ: Lawrence Erlbaum.

55 Kretchmer, S.B. (2004). 'Advertainment: The Evolution of Product Placement as a Mass Media Marketing Strategy'. In Mary-Lou Galician (ed.) *Handbook of Product Placement in the Mass Media: New Strategies in Marketing Theory, Practice, Trends and Ethics*, Bighampton, NY: Best Business Books/The Haworth Press, pp. 37–54.

56 Lindstrom, M. (2005). Get a jump-start on playing the new brand game. *Media Asia*, 28 June, 21.

57 Arnold, C. (2004). Just press play. *Marketing News*, 38(9), 1 and 15.

58 Kiousis, S. (2002). Interactivity: a concept explication. *New Media & Society*, 4(3), 355–83.

59 Zajonc, R.B. (1968). Attitudinal effects of mere exposure. *Journal of Personality and Social Psychology*, 9(1), 1–27.

60 Mizerski, D. (2005). Issues concerning the effects of advertising on children. *International Journal of Advertising*, 24(3), 399–401.

61 Gunn, E. (2001). Product placement prize, *Advertising Age*, 72(7), 10.

62 Wallendorf, M. (2001). Literally literacy. *Journal of Consumer Research*, 27(4), 505–11.

63 Ministry of Education. (2004). *Tertiary Education Strategy 2002–2007 Baseline Monitoring Report*, Wellington, NZ: Ministry of Education.

64 Hoffman, T., McKenna, K., Worrall, L., and Read, S. (2004). Evaluating current practice in the provision of written information to stroke patients and their carers. *International Journal of Therapy and Rehabilitation*, 11(7), 303–9.

65 Wallace, L., and Lemon, E. (2004). American academy of family physicians patient education materials: can patients read them? *Family Medicine Journal*, 36(8), 571–5.

66 McLaughlin, G.H. (1969). SMOG grading: a new readability formula. *Journal of Reading*, 12(8), 639–46.

67 Boddewyn, J.J. (1989). Advertising self-regulation: true purpose and limits. *Journal of Advertising*, 18(2), 19–27.

68 Le Guay, P. (2003). The regulation of advertising to children in Australia. *International Journal of Advertising & Marketing to Children*, 4(2), 63.

69 Garde, A. (2008). Food advertising and obesity prevention: what role for the European Union? *Journal of Consumer Policy*, 31(1), 25–44.

70 Abernethy, A., and Wicks, J.L. (2001). Self-regulation and television advertising: a replication and extension. *Journal of Advertising Research*, 41(3), 31–7.

71 Grigorovici, D.M., and Constantin, C.D. (2004). Experiencing interactive advertising beyond rich media. Impacts of ad type and presence on brand effectiveness in 3D gaming immersive virtual environments. *Journal of Interactive Advertising*, 4(3), 1–26.

72 Shrum, L.J. (ed.) (2004). *The Psychology of Entertainment Media*, Mahwah, NJ: Lawrence Erlbaum.

73 Dahl, S., Eagle, L., and Baez, C. (2006). *Analyzing Advergames: Active Diversions or Actually Deception*. London: Middlesex University Business School.

74 Hawkins, J.C., Eagle, L.C., and Bulmer, S.L. (2004). Cross-cultural Comparison of Food in the Children's Media Environment in New Zealand and Japan. Paper presented at the Corporate and Marketing Communications Conference, University of Warwick.

75 Law, S., and Braun, K.A. (2000). 'I'll have what she's having.' Gauging the impact of product placements on viewers. *Psychology & Marketing*, 17(12), 1059–75.

76 Moltenbrey, K. (2004). Adver-driving. *Computer Graphics World*, 27(6), 30–1.

77 Neate, R. (2010). TV Product Placement Ban Lifted in UK. *Daily Telegraph*, 9 February. Online. Available HTTP: <www.telegraph.co.uk/finance/newsbysector/mediatechnologyandtelecoms/media/7197867/TV-product-placement-ban-lifted-in-UK.html>.

78 Department for Culture, Media and Sport (2010). Written Ministerial Statement on Television Product Placement. Online. Available HTTP: <www.culture.gov.uk/reference_library/minister_speeches/6624.aspx/>.

79 Smith, R. (2010). Children Banned from Using Sunbeds in New Law. *Daily Telegraph*, 8 April. Online. Available HTTP: <www.telegraph.co.uk/health/healthnews/7567712/Children-banned-from-using-sunbeds-in-new-law.html>.

80 Eagle, L., and Brennan, R. (2007). Beyond advertising: in-home promotion of 'fast food'. *Young Consumers*, 8(4), 278–8.

81 Milne, G.R., Bahl, S., and Rohm, A. (2008). Toward a framework for assessing covert marketing practices. *Journal of Public Policy & Marketing*, 27(1), 57–62.

82 Palmer, D.E. (2005). Pop-ups, cookies, and spam: toward a deeper analysis of the ethical significance of Internet marketing practices. *Journal of Business Ethics*, 58(1–3), 271–80.

83 Ferrell, O.C., and Fraedrich, J.B. (1994). *Business Ethics: Ethical Decision Making and Cases*, 2nd edition, Boston: Houghton Miflin.

84 Harvey, B. (ed.) (1994). *Business Ethics: A European Approach*, Hertfordshire UK: Prentice Hall International (UK).

85 Andreasen, A.R. (ed.) (2001). *Ethics in Social Marketing*, Washington, DC: Georgetown University Press.

86 Duke, C.R., Pickett, G.M., Carlson, L., and Grove, S.J. (1993). A method for evaluating the ethics of fear appeals. *Journal of Public Policy & Marketing*, 12(1), 120–9.

87 Hastings, G., Stead, M., and Webb, J. (2004). Fear appeals in social marketing strategic and ethical reasons for concern. *Psychology & Marketing*, 21(11), 961–86.

88 Advertising Standards Authority. (2007). Adjudication Department of Health. Online. Available HTTP: <www.asa.prg.uk/asa/adjudications/Public/TF_ADJ_42557.htm> (accessed 29 May 2007).

89 Wilkes, M.S., Bell, R.A., and Kravitz, R.L. (2000). Direct to consumer prescription drug advertising: trends, impacts and implications. *Health Affairs*, 19(2), 110–28.

90 Lurie, P. (2009). DTC advertising harms patients and should be tightly regulated. *Journal of Law, Medicine & Ethics*, 37(3), 444–50.

91 Wang, J.C. (1999). Beyond DTC: what to do if FDA scales back DTC advertising. *Pharmaceutical Executive*, July, 58–60.

92 Cox, A.D., and Cox, D. (2010). A defense of direct-to-consumer prescription drug advertising. *Business Horizons*, 53(2), 221–8.

93 Findlay, S.D. (2001). Direct-to-consumer promotion of prescription drugs. Economic implications for patients, payers and providers. *Pharmoeconomics*, 19(2), 109–19.

94 Lexchin, J. (2001). Lifestyle drugs: issues for debate. *Canadian Medical Association Journal*, 164(10), 1449–51.

95 Yuan, S. (2008). Public responses to direct-to-consumer advertising of prescription drugs. *Journal of Advertising Research*, 48(1), 30–41.

96 Berndt, E.R. (2001). The US pharmaceutical industry: why major growth in times of cost containment? *Health Affairs*, 20(2), 100–14.

97 Paul, D.P., Haudline, A., and Stanton, A.D. (2002). Primary care physicians' attitudes toward direct-to-consumer advertising of prescription drugs: still crazy after all these years. *Journal of Consumer Marketing*, 19(7), 564–74.

98 Bell, R.A., Kravitz, R.L., and Wilkes, M.S. (1999). Direct-to-consumer prescription drug advertising and the public. *Journal of General Internal Medicine*, 14(11), 651–7.

99 Calfee, J.E. (2002). Public policy issues in direct-to-consumer advertising of prescription drugs. *Journal of Public Policy & Marketing*, 21(2), 174–93.

100 Choi, S., and Lee, W.-N. (2007). Understanding the impact of Direct-to-Consumer (DTC) pharmaceutical advertising on patient-physician interactions: adding the web to the mix. *Journal of Advertising*, 36(3), 137–49.

4 Analysing the integrated marketing communications environment

LEARNING OUTCOMES

After studying this chapter you will be able to:

- Locate the role of IMC within the organization

- Define the concept of the IMC environment

- Identify the key elements of the IMC environment

- Explain the role and importance of an IMC environmental analysis

- Outline the process and models associated with an IMC environmental analysis

- Evaluate the benefits, pitfalls and challenges associated with an IMC environmental analysis communications activity

Introduction

The role that integrated marketing communications (IMC) plays within an organization is an often misunderstood one. The field of marketing communications – integrated or otherwise – is regularly dismissed as superficial with its potential impact upon broader issues of strategy and the 'real' day-to-day business of an organization underestimated. Yet despite this, it is clear that an effective integrated marketing communications strategy is inextricably linked to every layer of the organizational structure and process.

It has already been noted in Chapter 1 that the adoption of an integrated approach has the potential to increase the synergy of a marketing communications strategy. However, a fact that is often ill-considered is that the role of marketing communications strategies is not only to communicate externally (i.e. to customers, consumers and external stakeholders) but also internally (i.e. to employees) as well.

Alongside the emergence of the relationship paradigm within the field of marketing, there has also been recognition that, far from simple, single transactions, organizations' contact with their customers is actually multi-faceted and occurs over extended periods of time.[1] It is therefore essential that at every point of contact, a consistent and clear message is conveyed to the client. For sole traders and small enterprises, consistency of communication may be a relatively simple affair. However, the larger an organization is, the greater number of potential contacts and therefore a greater opportunity exists for the customer to receive different or even conflicting messages from each service encounter.

Therefore, where a strategy of integrated marketing communications is employed, it should ensure delivery of critical marketing messages to audiences both inside and outside of the organization. According to Kay,[2] such messages should include the following:

* corporate image, market **positioning** and corporate values information;
* brand-related differential advantages and value information;
* and product- or service-specific features, benefits and advantages over competitive offerings.

Kay also suggests that three levels of information should be transmitted through a programme of integrated **internal marketing** communications:

1. marketing information intended for training and orientation of a company's **sales force** and customer service personnel;
2. marketing information intended for receipt by customers and prospects, which is likely to be delivered by a company's sales and/or customer service personnel;
3. information intended for the general employee population to foster a company-wide understanding of the company's marketing objectives and key messages.

THINK BOX

Shopping experiences

Think of a shop that you visit on a regular basis. Is the experience exactly the same every single time? Consider what is different and discuss why this might be the case. Where variations do occur, what form of integrated internal marketing communications might rectify these variations?

On this basis, it is essential that as well as an integrated strategy targeted at customers and consumers, an internal integrated marketing communications strategy is also required to ensure that every member of staff has a uniform understanding of the organization's values, product and service offering. In effect, everyone in an organization should be 'on message'. Such an approach offers four key benefits:

1. A uniform understanding of a marketing message ensures consistency of delivery.
2. A uniform understanding has the potential to minimize internal organizational conflict and enhance use of resources. For example, in a situation where a customer receives conflicting information from different departments or members of staff, a third party may be consulted. Not only has this the potential to generate conflict between parties as to who offered the correct information, but the process of clarification will take time, effort and resource that might be better employed elsewhere in the organization.
3. Uniformity and consistency of delivery in accordance with the organization's values has the potential to enhance and reinforce a professional reputation.
4. Clear communication will encourage staff to become knowledgeable about the organization's products and services and give them confidence and a sense of empowerment, particularly when dealing with customers.

The first steps: setting clear objectives

Pivotal to the effective generation of both internally-focussed and externally-focussed integrated marketing communications programmes is a clear expression of the organizational **objectives**. Objective setting is an essential function at all levels of a successful organization. Objectives, when clearly set, offer those that work within an organization a sense of purpose and the ability to drive business in a single direction.

However, for any organization, when it comes to setting objectives, it is not simply a case of 'one size fits all'. The nature of 'objectives' may vary according to the point within the organization in which they will be executed. For example, the objectives formulated by a Board of Directors are likely to vary in level and detail from those formulated by a Marketing Manager. However, objectives at all levels should correspond and support the 'Business Mission'. Within the context of IMC, objectives are formulated at four different levels, all depicted in Figure 4.1.

The business mission

The central driving force behind all organizations: the business mission. The concept of a mission is comprehensively defined by Toftoy[3] as something like that:

> distinguishes its business from its peer firms, identifies its scope of operations, embodies its business philosophy and reflects the image that it seeks to project.

Generally, organizational missions are expressed in a 'mission statement'; a clear and unambiguous form of words that sums up the essence and direction of the organization itself. The primary aim of a 'mission' and the accompanying 'mission statement' is to ensure that stakeholders, both internal and external to the organization, are clear as to what it is doing and how it intends to achieve this.

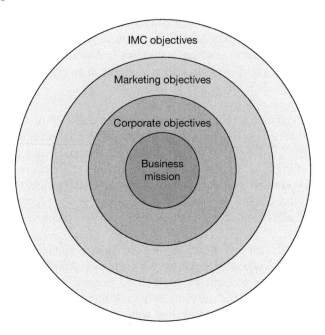

Figure 4.1 The layers of organizational objective

MINI CASE: BBC – A MISSION ACCOMPLISHED?

The British Broadcasting Corporation, now more commonly known as the BBC, was first launched on 14 November, 1922. In 1927, under the leadership of John (later Lord) Reith, the BBC became a public corporation and was awarded a Royal Charter which granted the organization the right to broadcast its radio programmes supported by the payment of a broadcast-receiving licence fee of 10 shillings a year. Since this time, the breadth and number of services offered by the BBC has grown exponentially. Today, it operates eight national TV channels plus regional programming, ten national radio stations, 40 local radio stations, an extensive website, and most recently has launched an '**on demand**' service known as 'iPlayer'. This service allows consumers to download and watch radio and television pro-grammes on their computers at their convenience (and providing that they have sufficient **broadband** speeds).

The BBC mission statement is very clear. It reads:

> To enrich people's lives with programmes and services that inform, educate and entertain.

Access the BBC website (www.bbc.co.uk) and explore the various sections within it. Discuss the extent to which it achieves its mission. How does it seek to do this both in terms of content and also presentation? Illustrate your answer with examples.

Contrast the role of the BBC with that of commercial media organizations (i.e. those that depend on advertising revenue rather than licence fee revenue). What advantages/disadvantages does each have and what are the implications for marketers?

It is also important for external stakeholders to have a clear view of what an organization is trying to achieve. An external stakeholder can be defined as any individual or organization, outside of the organization in question, that has an interest in the way it functions. External stakeholders can take many and varied forms, for example, they might provide finance, regulate the industry or simply affect consumer preference. In the case of the BBC, it is particularly important to communicate the organization's mission to its external stakeholders as they are the individuals and organizations to whom they are accountable for both the quality and value of their output.

These stakeholders, who include the Government, Ofcom (the communications regulatory authority) and consumers, determine whether the BBC is adhering to its commitment to the Charter and, ultimately, are responsible for financing the organization's work either through a 'license' scheme or Government subsidy. If the BBC's external stakeholders believe that it has departed from their stated mission, it is within their power to limit its ability to function effectively through the withdrawal of funding or the imposition of laws or other regulations.

Corporate objectives

Having established a clear mission, an organization should then establish a set of corporate objectives. Corporate objectives may be described as a set of clearly defined goals that an organization needs to achieve in order for it to satisfy its mission. Ultimately, they are the yardstick by which key stakeholders will judge the performance of the organization and may be stated in a variety of terms that include degree of market expansion, impact upon stakeholders, profit, return on investment, change in net worth, brand perception or corporate reputation. Sometimes organizations issue long lists of corporate objectives, however the most effective are often the most simply stated, for example, Marks and Spencer, one of the UK's leading retailers offers a single overriding corporate objective:

> The Group's overriding corporate objective is to maximize long-term shareholder value whilst exceeding the expectations of our customers, employees and partners.[4]

In this way, key groups of stakeholders are identified (shareholders, customers, employees, partners) together with the criteria with which the relative success of an organization might be measured (increase shareholder value, exceeding expectations).

Marketing objectives

The next stage of the structure relates to the setting of marketing objectives. Marketing objectives may be defined as goals that are specifically devised to satisfy the marketing-specific elements that are derived from the broader corporate objectives. The diversity of the objectives reflects the diversity of the field of marketing itself. Not only do marketing objectives encompass day-to-day management of the products and brands, but they can also involve new product development, market development, research and marketing analytics. Such objectives should be clearly stated, measurable, achievable and executable over a specified time period. Examples of marketing objectives can include:

- to increase market penetration by X per cent over X months/years;
- to stimulate market growth by X per cent over X months/years;
- to develop a product/service in response to a gap in the market over a given time period.

IMC objectives

Finally, integrated marketing communications objectives are formulated to support the mission, corporate and marketing objectives. Addressed to both internal and external stakeholders at brand/product-specific and corporate levels, these objectives focus upon how stakeholders perceive or understand the organization and what it is trying to achieve. IMC objectives take many forms and relate to factors that can be directly influenced by marketing communications. These factors include such things as levels of awareness, degree of positivity toward the product or service and likelihood of trial. Therefore, examples of IMC objectives might include:

- to increase awareness of Brand Y by X per cent over the course of a specified campaign;
- to increase levels of trial of the brand by a given segment by X per cent over the course of a specified campaign;
- to increase consumer positivity toward the brand relative to its rivals over the course of a specified campaign.

Having established a set of IMC objectives, the next stage is for marketers to identify the factors that might either support or hinder the ability of target stakeholders to receive, assimilate and correctly interpret the communications and their content. In order to do this, they must obtain an understanding of the IMC environment in order to identify the factors that will affect the way that the communications will be both transmitted and received.

MINI CASE: A WII CASE OF ATTRACTING NEW MARKETS

In May, 2009, Nintendo announced that the sales of Wii consoles had defied the recessionary economic conditions with an increase of 9.9 per cent, equating to 1.839 trillion yen and an 8.5 per cent profit increase to the equivalent of $2.8bn (€3.1bn, £4.2bn) against $2.5bn in 2008.

Not only has the Wii caught up with Nintendo's former best seller, the DS console, in terms of unit sales (each shipping around 26 million units in the year to March 2009), it is the fastest selling games console to date, having exceeded 50 billion units in just over two years. In addition, the supporting market of games has also proved a lucrative one for Nintendo. To date it has sold in excess of 220 million Wii games, the most popular including *Brain Age 2*, *Mario Kart Wii* and *Pokemon Platinum Version*.

However, the period between May and October 2009 saw sales slump dramatically, with business commentators suggesting that the traditional youth market, as it stood, had now reached saturation point. According to Nintendo, sales in the six months from April had fallen 34.5 per cent to ¥548bn with the result that the company was forced to lower its profit forecast for the full year from ¥300bn to ¥230bn. It sold 5.75m of the consoles between April and September, far fewer than the 10 million it shifted in the same period last year and a 20 per cent reduction in the price of a Wii console did not appear to have any significant effect.

Faced with saturated market conditions, discuss what you believe Nintendo's priorities should be when seeking to stimulate new growth. State these priorities in terms of marketing objectives. What IMC objectives should be constructed to support these marketing objectives?

Source: www.guardian.co.uk/business/2009/oct/29/nintendo-profits-plunge-wii-sales (accessed 1 November 2009).

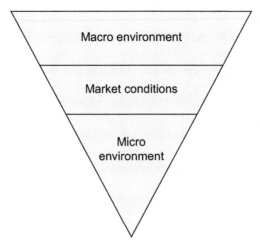

Figure 4.2 The integrated marketing communications environment

Understanding the IMC environment

The IMC environment can be divided into three basic components: the macro environment, market conditions and the micro environment (Figure 4.2).

The macro IMC environment

The macro IMC environment consists of the broad forces that exist outside of a market that affect the way that an organization, its competitors and its stakeholders are able to function. There are five main elements to the macro IMC environment: social forces, political forces, economic forces, 'natural' forces and technological forces, and these may be collectively known as the 'SPENT' factors.

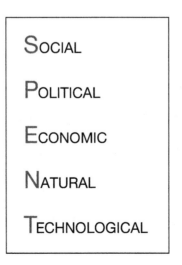

Figure 4.3 The 'SPENT' factors

Social factors

Social factors relate to social and cultural changes that affect the way a market functions and/or the way that customers and consumers view a product, organization or even market sector as a whole. Social factors can include such things as demographic changes, changes in the cultural or ethnic make-up of a given market or even attitudinal changes. A good example of one such social factor is the general change in attitude towards smoking that has happened over the last 50 years. Smoking was once considered a sophisticated and enjoyable pastime until the dangers of both actively and passively consuming the product permeated the public consciousness and it has gradually become seen as an almost anti-social habit. As a result, the proportion of men and women who smoke in the UK has fallen substantially.

Political factors

Political factors relate to the opportunities and restrictions that are in place as a result of the political environment and the legal system that applies to a given market. Countries within the western hemisphere largely operate on a free market system where countries are subject only to laws relating to health, safety and consumer protection. In the UK, for example, companies wishing to **trade** are expected to comply with such legislation as the Sale of Goods Act 1979, the Supply of Goods and Services Act 1982, the Sale and Supply of Goods Act 1994 and the Sale and Supply of Goods to Consumers Regulations 2002 which states that goods must be fit for purpose and be of a satisfactory quality given the price and description at point of sale. Similarly, products that are potentially dangerous to the consumer are either banned or regulated using the Consumer Protection Act of 1987.[5]

However, in more planned economies, government regulations can sometimes place limitations on what can be produced, where and to whom it might be distributed and with it they can limit access to certain channels of communication. This has been the case in recent years where the Chinese Government blocked its people from accessing the Internet search engine Google. To overcome this problem it agreed to produce a modified version that limited access to websites that the Chinese Government deemed inappropriate or sensitive such as those dealing with such topics as Taiwanese independence or the Tiananmen Square Massacre.[6]

Economic factors

Economic factors may be defined as forces linked to the economy that affects the way that an organization can function in any given market. These include such factors as Government monetary policy, interest rates, exchange rates and levels of taxation. From a communications perspective, economic factors have a major influence over the degree to which consumers experience the 'feel good factor' – a high level of general positivity – particularly when they are feeling secure and affluent. When consumers experience the 'feel good factor', they are more receptive to marketing communications and are more likely to feel that they have the resources to act on them.

'Natural' factors

'Natural' factors may be defined as the way that the physical environment and natural resources impact upon the way that consumers, organizations or indeed the market as a whole are able to function. When it comes to 'natural' factors, the finite nature of resources – oil, gas, land – and the impact that humans have upon the environment pose particular issues. An illustration of the potential impact that natural factors can have upon markets, organizations and consumers can be seen in the fluctuation in the cost of oil together with the perceived impact that fossil fuels have upon global warming. A whole new industry has emerged as a result of the search for carbon neutrality and the desire to reduce energy costs and consumption levels. The last 10 years have seen major growth in activities and technologies such as wind turbines, recycling and dual fuel cars that had previously been dismissed as quirky or eccentric.

'Sustainability' has become a buzzword as consumers look for products that minimize their impact upon the environment and with it, organizations are increasingly keen to develop and communicate their 'green' credentials.

Technological factors

Changes and developments in technology over the last 20 years have revolutionized the way that both organizations and consumers function within their given markets. From a communications perspective, the development of digital technology and the availability of the Internet have increased both the number and variety of communications channels available to marketers seeking to reach their target consumers. Communications are no longer restricted to press, poster and television advertising, as the use of digital computer technology has aided the growth of new channels such as direct mail, text messaging and Internet advertising.

Changes in technology have also encouraged growth in the communications potential of existing channel types. In the UK in the 1970s, consumers had only three television channels to choose from, only one of which carried advertising, and there were no officially recognized commercial stations (although a few commercial pirate stations such as Radio Caroline and Radio Luxemburg did broadcast offshore). By contrast today, developments in satellite and cable television have spawned over a hundred channels, the majority of which are commercial and many clearly targeted at distinct market segments and interest groups.

However, the digital revolution may also be seen to have empowered the consumer within the communications process on a number of levels. The Internet offers consumers access to unprecedented volumes of information so that, when seeking out a product to satisfy a specific need, they can actively search for the most appropriate solution and compare the alternatives available. As a result, numerous 'comparison' websites have emerged in response to this growing trend. Two industries where the impact has been most keenly felt are insurance and tourism. Insurance is particularly appropriate, as the product itself is perceived as generic with the primary basis for comparison being price. By contrast, there has been an increasing trend away from the use of travel agencies as consumers find that they are able to put together packages that specifically suit their needs using specialist Internet sites such as Expedia (www.expedia.com). In addition, social networking sites such as **Facebook** and **Twitter** offer consumers the capacity to offer instant feedback, both positive and negative, about companies and brands and communicate this to potentially massive audiences.

MINI CASE: SOCIAL NETWORKS BADLY HANDLED

In July 2009, a property management company in Chicago, Illinois, USA, threatened a $50,000 lawsuit when a woman called Amanda Bonnen 'Tweeted' to 22 of her 'followers' the following message about an apartment that she rented from them. It read, in part:

> Who said sleeping in a moldy apartment was bad for you? Horizon Realty thinks it's okay.

A representative of the management company, quoted in the *Chicago Sun-Times* said that: 'The statements are obviously false, and it's our intention to prove that', adding that Horizon has a good reputation to protect. It appears that Bonnen wasn't contacted before the suit was filed, nor was she asked to remove the **Tweet**. When questioned, the representative replied: 'We're a "sue first, ask questions later" kind of an organization'.

Unfortunately for the management company, this comment generated a backlash from those on Twitter that prompted an apology for the 'tongue in cheek' comment and became a topic of conversation on a number of other online sites that included the *Chicago Sun-Times* and the *Wall Street Journal* blog sites.

1. What do you think had the potential to damage the management company more: the initial Tweet or the company's response?
2. Why do you think this is the case? How might this situation have been better managed?
3. Consider the impact of this situation on the credibility of Horizon Realty – what lessons can be learned for the future?

Market conditions

Having explored all of the external, 'macro' factors that impact upon the market as a whole, the next area for scrutiny in the IMC environment is the market characteristics themselves. Each market is comprised of a unique set of characteristics that determines how easy it is to communicate with key customer/ consumer segments and how profitable it is likely to be in the short, medium and long term. These have been divided into five key dimensions, which are depicted in Figure 4.4.

Having completed their analysis of each of these dimensions, IMC professionals are in the position of making an informed judgement concerning which channel or channels

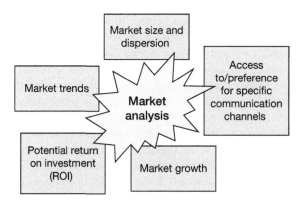

Figure 4.4 Key dimensions of an IMC market analysis

of communication might be most appropriate, most effective and most cost-effective in reaching the target market in a given situation.

Associated with each of these dimensions are questions that help to structure an IMC market analysis and these are detailed below.

Market size and dispersion

Questions of profitability are always at the forefront of minds in both client and agency organizations. To this end, market size and dispersion give a marketer a good indication as to the potential viability of the target market. Therefore the following questions will lend insight into whether a market is large enough or concentrated enough to ensure that the outcome of a communication strategy is likely to cover its costs.

- What is the size of the market in terms of volume?
- What is the market size in terms of value?
- How is the market segmented?
- What is the relative importance of each segment in terms of volume, value and relative profitability?
- How dispersed geographically are the individual segments?

Access to/preference for specific communications channels

Having identified the target segments, it is important that appropriate channel(s) of communication are selected in a way that will reach its audience both effectively and cost effectively. To this end, the following questions require consideration:

- For each of the target segments, which channels do they have access to?
- What channels do they have access to most frequently?
- Through which channels do they prefer to receive communications?

Market growth

Whilst in some cases, a programme of integrated marketing communications might have a short-term, tactical focus, most marketers recognize that any and all aspects of marketing communications can be regarded as a form of investment. Research has shown that every perceived communication leaves some form of mental trace, even at very low levels of information processing.[7] Therefore, the most attractive investments are those in markets that are likely to yield positive returns in the short, medium and long term. As such, the following factors require examination:

- What are the current levels of market growth by volume and value?
- What segments of the market are showing the greatest levels of growth?

Potential ROI from communications activity

Whilst in Chapter 16 we discuss the concept of 'return on investment' in detail, suffice to say at this stage that, ideally, marketers should be able to measure the benefit that a piece of IMC activity brings to a brand or an organization. In many cases it is a simple matter to measure consumer response in monetary terms (i.e. in uplifts in sales) but, in others, the basis of measurement becomes much more difficult. For example, how can a marketer measure the monetary value of brand awareness or an improved attitude toward the brand? Whatever the case, there should be consensus amongst marketing management that the cost of achieving the stated objectives should not outweigh the benefits. Therefore the following questions need to be considered:

- How much does it cost to reach each member of the target segment?
- What is the projected result of the communication activity by segment and by communication channel?
- Is it possible to quantify the result?
- What is the projected effect upon consumers'/customers' lifetime value?

Market trends

Every seasoned marketer knows all too well that markets are not static entities but dynamic, evolving environments. Emerging factors in both the IMC macro environment constantly generate potential opportunities for businesses who are alert enough to take advantage of them; either in terms of their product/ service offering or the way that it is communicated. Therefore it is essential for organizations to monitor market trends in order that they might exploit market changes to the fullest degree. In such circumstances, where organizations are first to exploit a new product area or technology, they are seen to gain 'first mover advantage'. Questions to consider when monitoring market trends are:

- What are the trends currently visible in the market?
- Are these changes transient or are they likely to become a more permanent feature of the market (i.e. is it a trend or is it purely a fad)?
- Are these developments likely to yield a profit?

THINK BOX

Toy brands

Every year, a few months prior to Christmas, the UK Toy Retailers Association releases what it predicts to be the 'Dream Dozen'; the top 11 toys that children in the UK are likely to want for Christmas. In 2013, the list was as follows:

1. City Coast Guard (LEGO Company)
2. Doc McStuffins Doctor's Bag Playset (Flair Leisure Products)
3. Flying Fairy by Flutterbye (Spin Master Toys UK)
4. Furby Boom! (Hasbro)
5. InnoTab 3S (VTech Electronics Europe)
6. LeapPad Ultra (Leapfrog Toys)
7. Monopoly Empire (Hasbro)
8. Monster High 13 Wishes Doll (Mattel)
9. Nerf N-Strike Elite RapidStrike CS-18 (Hasbro)
10. Robo Fishbowl (Zuru-Geemac)
11. Teksta Robotic Puppy (Character Option)

Looking at this list, how many of these toys do you recognize from your own childhood? Consider the ways in which these toys varied from the ones that you were familiar with. Why do you think this is the case? What are the implications for IMC strategists?

Source: UK Toy Retailers Association (2013)

Segmentation and targeting

As part of the market analysis, decisions are made regarding what specific segments of the population to target. Few products and services appeal equally to all people. Generally, decisions are made to focus activity on specific groups or segments of the population.

Segmentation originates from market research and is based on the principle of being able to divide the population into subgroups on the basis of similar characteristics, so that each segment contains clearly defined, and mutually exclusive groups with particular emphasis on factors that influence behaviours.[8] Identifying specific segments allows strategies to be developed that meet the specific needs of each segment.

Segmentation always involves a trade-off between trying to achieve greater communication effectiveness in terms of products, services or marketing communication material that is of the most appeal to each segment, and the costs involved in developing products or services specifically for each segment to best meet their needs. Totally different ways of communicating with each segment, including different media selection may also be identified, but the outcome when successful is effective allocation of resources/less wastage than if one standard communication is used to cover all segments.

There are many ways in which a target population may be segmented, including:

- Product/service usage (identifying heavy users of products or services).
- Demographics such as gender, age, marital status, occupation, income, socio-economic status.
- Psychological: motivations, personality, perceptions, attitudes, motives, beliefs, values.
- Psychographics, including lifestyles, knowledge, activities, family life cycles, interests and opinions (AOI).
- Usage/behaviour – usage statistics, or benefits sought.
- Geodemographics: based on assumption that people who live close to one another are likely to have similar financial means, lifestyles and consumption habits.
- Cultures or subcultures, including aspects of ethnicity and factors such as religious beliefs that may impact on products or services that are considered acceptable and extending to acceptability of forms of medical treatment.[9] For example, some religious groups oppose immunization.[10]
- Epidemiology is used widely in health promotion/social marketing activity where intervention development includes the identification of parts of a country where the highest concentration of a specific illness occurs.

Analysing the micro IMC environment

Having undertaken a macro and market analysis, the focus then shifts to the micro environment. The micro environment may be defined as a set of actors that operate close to an organization that also have a direct impact upon its ability to serve its customers/consumers effectively. Micro forces differ from those in the macro environment in that an organization has the potential to influence the behaviour and actions of the actors in the micro environment whereas they have very little influence over the forces present in the macro environment. These forces are illustrated in Figure 4.5. From an IMC perspective, 'micro' factors have real importance because they have the potential to directly affect the way that an organization and its product is viewed.

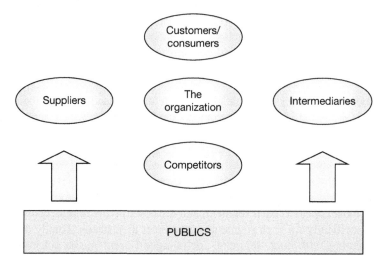

Figure 4.5 Forces in the micro environment*

The organization

Central to any micro analysis must be some consideration of an organization's ability to function in its chosen market. One of the prime issues for consideration is whether it has the financial ability or managerial expertise required to successfully achieve the marketing and organizational objectives and, ultimately, achieve its mission. From a communications perspective, questions should also be asked as to whether the mission, corporate and marketing objectives have been communicated effectively and are clearly understood by all of its stakeholders, both internal and external to the organization. A clear and uniform understanding minimizes the potential for conflict and has the potential to communicate an aura of professionalism to consumers and stakeholders.

Customers/consumers

Some consideration of customer/consumer issues should already have been undertaken at the 'market analysis' stage but this is only likely to have been done within the wider context of market conditions. However, for a micro analysis, a more specific focus should be adopted to explore the way that customers and consumers interact with the organization. It is essential to understand how consumers appreciate the function and ethos of the organization, perceive the positioning of its brands relative to competitors and view the suppliers and intermediaries as all of these factors will affect the way that they interpret marketing communications once they are received.

Competitors

Having analysed the way that consumers and customers interact with the organization and its competitors, it is then essential to analyse the nature of the competition. Competing firms should be identified in terms of organizations and entities that fulfil a specific consumer need. For instance, when seeking to identify competitors to an organization such as BMW cars, the temptation is to look directly to other car manufacturers such as

VW and Mercedes. However, depending upon what consumer need is being satisfied, the competing firms might be seen to be very different. If it is the case that the consumer 'need' in question is simply a mode of transport, then in addition to other car brands, suppliers of bus, train and air transport might also be considered competition. However, if the consumer's 'need' is for the possession of a status symbol, perhaps brands such as Rolex or Tiffany offer products that might also satisfy the need. This example illustrates the essential requirement of organizations to clearly understand the nature of the needs that their consumers are seeking to satisfy when purchasing their brands. Only then are they in a position to target them with relevant messages relating to the specific benefits their products and services offer.

Suppliers and intermediaries

The role that suppliers and intermediaries have in communicating corporate or brand messages is regularly ignored but, often at an organization's peril. Customers and consumers rarely distinguish between an organization, its suppliers and its intermediaries when considering its product offering. Therefore it is essential that suppliers and intermediaries are aware of an organization's mission and defining principles and are willing to work in conjunction with it to achieve its corporate and marketing objectives. In instances where this proves not to be the case, the impact upon the organization can be immense.

Take, for example, the recent problems experienced by Mattel who were forced to **recall** over 18 million toys worldwide originally made by a subcontractor in China over a variety of safety issues.[11] Mistakes made by companies working with or for an organization can result in consumers receiving messages from 'uncontrolled' sources about the organization i.e. those that emanate from sources other than the organization and over which that organization has no control. Uncontrolled sources such as the news media and consumer groups have the potential to transmit messages that can run counter to that of the organization and create inconsistency in the messages being transmitted. This, in turn, can create unnecessary 'noise' within the communications channel and result in consumers and customers either misunderstanding or, worse still, not believing marketing communications at all.

Publics

A 'public' may be defined as a group of people who are loosely related through a shared interest or function. If that interest is partly or wholly involved with the organization in question then that 'public' can also be regarded as 'stakeholders'. **Publics** can take many and varied forms. However, for the purpose of a micro analysis, there are three key publics that should be analysed: the 'media public' (newspapers, television, radio etc.), the 'financial public' (banks, building societies, the Stock Market) and the 'general public'. It is essential to identify these entities and ensure that good communication and a positive relationship are established with them. Negative media reports can inflict long-lasting damage to corporate and brand image whilst a poor reputation amongst the financial publics can cause problems when trying to raise capital and other finance in the money markets. One of the greatest difficulties faced by brands is when something becomes 'received knowledge' in the eyes of the 'general public'. The car manufacturer Skoda still finds it difficult to shake off its image of poor quality even though it has been bought and its cars manufactured by Volkswagen Audi, a company famed for the quality of its vehicles.

Making effective use of the environmental analysis

An IMC environmental analysis is only of any real value if it is used to drive the formulation of an effective integrated marketing communications strategy. A particularly effective model is the TOWS analysis;[12] a development upon the often-cited **SWOT (Strengths, Weaknesses, Opportunities, Threats) analysis** (Figure 4.6). This form of analytical framework is usually associated with a standard analysis of the wider business environment. However it has specific relevance to IMC because it allows them to work both reactively and proactively to ensure the effectiveness of their strategies:

*   It enables marketers to identify what changes in the environment might affect the effective working of communication process (either positively or negatively) and make appropriate alterations to their strategy according to their strengths and weaknesses if required.
*   The analysis will highlight consumers' evolving needs and allow marketers to develop communications strategies in response.
*   It enables marketers to model the changes in the marketing environment and proactively develop not only products and services but also the communication vehicles that best support them.

The TOWS analysis process offers a clear, structured way of analysing the IMC environment. There are four basic stages:

Stage 1   Using macro and market analyses, potential opportunities and potential threats to an organization's business are identified.

	Threats	Opportunities
Strengths	What strengths does the company possess that can overcome potential threats?	What strengths does the company possess that can help it exploit emerging opportunities?
Weaknesses	Do the weaknesses leave the company vulnerable to threats?	What weaknesses does the company need to address to enable it to exploit emerging opportunities?

Figure 4.6 TOWS diagram

Stage 2   In light of these opportunities and threats, the outcome of the micro analysis is used to measure the extent to which the organization has sufficient strengths to exploit the opportunities and counter the threats and identify key areas of weakness. The TOWS grid depicted in Figure 4.6 offers an ideal structure with which to break down each of these elements in turn.

Stage 3   Where opportunities are seen to emerge, IMC professionals should then reassess their existing strategies to ensure their relevance both in terms of medium and message. If areas of weakness appear to prevent an organization from exploiting an emerging opportunity, they should be addressed as a priority.

Stage 4   In light of emergent threats, IMC professionals should reassess their position to ensure that their current strategies continue to communicate the strengths of the organization effectively. Where requirements change, so should the communication strategy.

Armed with this information, marketers are able to manage their communications strategy in a way that accommodates a dynamic market environment.

The benefits and pitfalls of IMC environmental analysis

There are three key benefits to organizations undertaking an analysis of their communications environment. Firstly, it enables them to identify and understand the broad forces that affect the actors in the markets in which they function. This being the case, they are able to identify those factors that prevent target stakeholders from receiving and interpreting their marketing communications. Secondly, it places the organization in position to proactively identify emerging opportunities and maximize their chance of exploiting them successfully by communicating its strengths and ability to satisfy key consumer needs. Finally, it allows organizations to identify potential threats that they can minimize through effective communications strategies.

However, in order for environmental analysis to be a useful tool for marketing communications specialists, it must be undertaken thoroughly and regularly. Markets are dynamic entities and in order for an organization to claim real knowledge of its markets and the potential opportunities within it, they must undertake a process of environmental analysis on a continuous and on-going basis.

Summary

Over the course of this chapter we have seen that in order to effectively analyse the integrated marketing communications environment, it must be broken down into the macro and micro components. In doing this, marketing practitioners are able to identify potential opportunities and threats and formulate appropriate strategies on the basis of their organization's strengths and weaknesses. In this way, such knowledge arms an organization with the power to control their own destiny rather than being a victim of unforeseen circumstances. However, that being case, the quality and the quantity of that knowledge is an essential factor in effective decision making and therefore regular and thorough analyses must be undertaken for organizations to maximize their market potential.

Review questions

1. Define the four layers of organizational objective and explain their purpose.
2. What are the main components of a 'macro' analysis?
3. Why do you think it is important to undertake a marketing analysis?
4. What are the main components of a 'micro' analysis?
5. In your opinion, which of the following offers greatest value to marketers when seeking to analyse the marketing environment?

   - Broadsheet newspapers
   - Census statistics
   - The Internet
   - Television and radio news
   - Company reports

6. When analysing the 'micro' environment, to what extent do you think it is important to analyse the position of suppliers and intermediaries?
7. What is the value in undertaking a TOWS analysis?
8. Explain what is meant by the term 'stakeholder' and explain their potential influence within an organization's marketing environment.
9. 'Knowledge is strength'. Discuss the extent to which such a statement applies to the marketing environment.
10. What is the relative value to an organization of an ongoing and coordinated programme of market analysis?

Recommended reading

Baines, P., Fill, C., and Page, K. (2008). *Marketing*, Oxford: Oxford University Press.
Jobber, D. (2006). *Principles and Practices of Marketing*, London: McGraw-Hill.
Kotler, P., and Keller, K.L. (2006). *Marketing Management*, Englewood Cliffs, NJ: Prentice Hall.
Reinold, T., and Tropp, J. (2012). Integrated marketing communications: how can we measure its effectiveness? *Journal of Marketing Communications*, 18(2), 113–32.

CASE STUDY 4.1

Elephant Chakki Gold

Source: Institute of Practitioners in Advertising: IPA Effectiveness Awards 2009. Authors: Saad Saraf and Nithya Thyagarajan. Agency: Mediareach Advertising. Case material provided by the World Advertising Research Centre (WARC) www.warc.com.

This case illustrates what can be achieved on a limited budget when the target segment is clearly defined and their media usage understood.

Background

Atta (flour) is a staple ingredient in Asian meals. Even the most basic meal in an Asian household includes chapattis (Asian flatbread). UK South Asians are deemed to be those of Indian, Pakistani and Bangladeshi origin (some from Uganda) and there are over 3 million such people living in the UK. They started to migrate to the UK following the Second World

War, with migration peaking in the 60s and 70s. Our audience still eats curries each day, as those from the North and West of India and all of Pakistan eat chapattis as the staple cereal with curry or daal (lentils).

As they are concentrated principally in urban areas, with their own retail network and media channels, they are a relatively easy niche to access. However, as we enter the third generation of British Asians in the UK, there is far more integration, but certain touchstones remain. Chapattis carry far more cultural significance than would perhaps be anticipated. They are highly emotive, having religious symbolism, represent a sign of womanhood (maternal care and being a good housewife) and also have communal importance (to the family and to Asian identity and history). The tradition of making chapattis is passed on from generation to generation in Asian families.

Elephant is the original atta in the UK and has always been a part of this tradition and heritage. Elephant atta leads due to its texture, flavour and quality, and at the same time, is dedicated to the Asian community and the values they hold dear. The atta market offer variants based upon 'bran' content. The variants available from Elephant Atta are Medium, Fine White, Brown, Wholemeal, Self Raising and now Chakki Gold.

Elephant Chakki Gold was introduced in 2005 to capitalize on the growing market for premium atta and to cater for the changing needs of the consumer (adopting a healthier lifestyle). Elephant Chakki Gold represents 5 per cent of total Elephant Atta volume. Elephant Chakki Gold is a premium product with over 51 per cent wholemeal content. It is easy to knead, with a fine texture to make soft, white chapattis. As a whole grain food, it can help look after the heart as a part of a balanced diet and active lifestyle. The health positioning of Elephant Chakki Gold was further strengthened in 2007 by an association with the British Heart Foundation, by sponsoring their 'healthy meals, healthy heart' recipe book that targeted South Asians.

Great care was taken in the selection of the name. Chakki in Hindi means 'mill', traditionally a stone-ground mill where whole wheat is ground to flour (or atta). It therefore reinforces the purity and authenticity of the product. Gold, as in most cultures, symbolizes a premium product, as it is something precious and expensive.

The decision was made that the time was now right to promote Elephant Chakki Gold on broadcast media. The campaign objective therefore was clear: to make consumers aware that a premium product exists that offers them the best of both worlds, health and taste, without compromising either.

The team aimed to measure success in a number of ways:

- media coverage achieved on a low budget
- performance of the brand volume and growth.

Understanding the audience

The target audiences are the second or third generation working mothers or housewives from Punjabi, Pakistani and Gujarati households.

The commercial was run in the relevant ethnic languages to better relate with the different audiences. Care was taken over the cultural and religious nuances of each audience, to make a commercial that would appeal to all.

Approach to media

The budget for the year 2008–2009 for Elephant Chakki Gold was £28,000.

The South Asian community tends to be most responsive to TV as a medium, with television more popular and effective than print, radio or outdoor. The South Asian communities are avid watchers of TV, they follow soaps, competitions, music countdown shows and movies. They are huge fans of 'Bolly/Lolly-wood'. Therefore movies, music and popular serials were chosen to penetrate the audience in the most effective and direct manner.

The key ethnic channels employed were Zee, Star, Prime, Geo and DM Digital, the channels that reach out to specific communities. Also, **sponsorships** were taken for popular prime time programmes, to reach the audiences more effectively. A two-month campaign ran from May to July 2008, addressing all the three target groups simultaneously.

The creative solution

The challenge at hand was to emphasize the healthy benefits of Elephant Chakki Gold whilst complying with any communication and product guidelines.

For many people, white chapattis look and taste better, although wholemeal is a healthier choice, just like bread. As health is not associated with taste generically, it was important to establish the same through imagery in the campaign.

To summarize, the team had three key insights for developing our campaign:

- Reinforce health and taste using product imagery and the image of an active child.
- Drive a behavioural shift and convey a sense of wisdom by using the older generation – mother and grandfather.
- Align Elephant Chakki Gold to the overall brand values of Elephant Atta – heritage, tradition and Asian values.

Therefore, the creative idea was to employ a growing active child whose needs for nourishment and taste are catered for by chapattis made from Elephant Chakki Gold Atta. Health (or strength) was cleverly demonstrated by the 'muscle flexing' imagery of the growing child. The astute choice of the decision maker of the family (the mother) is further reinforced by the wise grandfather, who takes pride in his grandchild's development and activeness.

The mother is already a familiar figure associated with the brand by the target audience, as she was established in the main Elephant Atta TV commercial in 2003, where she passes down the 'secret' and tradition of making chapattis to her daughter.

What happened?

The campaign delivered successfully on all counts.

Results from Synovate's quantitative findings, 2008, are as below:

1. The campaign registered a 17 per cent increase in advertising awareness in the Indian Gujarati community subgroup.
2. 64 per cent brand awareness level for all communities, led predominantly by spontaneous awareness.
3. 20 per cent and 23 per cent increase in spontaneous awareness amongst the Punjabi and Gujarati sub-groups respectively.
4. 21 per cent increase in Asian Integrated audience brand awareness level (spontaneous) towards Chakki Gold.

5. Attitudinal shift of 5 per cent more, than in previous phases, of people who think that it's important to maintain a healthy and balanced diet.
6. Ad recognition for Chakki Gold has increased by 8 per cent from previous years.
7. Campaign reach was 63 per cent.

Strongest recognition of product values/ attributes was observed, when compared to competitor brands, in terms of brand image, as below:

*   perceived as a high quality product
*   a famous brand
*   makes light, fluffy, puffed-up chapattis
*   dough is easy to knead
*   good value for money
*   authentic brand
*   a brand that can be trusted
*   has been around for generations
*   is a part of the tradition of chapatti making
*   values Asian culture
*   uses fresh ingredients
*   worth paying more for
*   natural product
*   low price.

Conclusions

The joint strategy of targeted media and effective creative positioning led to a good response and surge in awareness and response levels.

From 2007 to 2008, Elephant Chakki Gold Atta has achieved a fantastic growth rate of **206 per cent**.The brand continues to flourish rapidly and the agency is constantly evaluating whether it needs to extend into other ethnic communities to further widen the consumer base.

CASE STUDY QUESTIONS

1. Critique the case study. What are the factors you believe led to the campaign's success? Justify your response.
2. The authors of this case note that many of the target group are third generation British Asians who have integrated into British society. How would you determine the impact of this integration versus distinct cultural identity on products and services used in homes? Discuss the implications of this for marketers.
3. Discuss the importance of understanding cultural values, norms and traditions in developing marketing communications targeting this or other cultural groups.
4. There has been some criticism of minority cultural groups for maintaining their cultural identity rather than adopting those of the dominant culture in which they now live. What role does marketing communications play in maintaining or challenging cultural values? Discuss the ethical issues that may arise from different marketing communications approaches to cultural issues.
5. The case study authors note that they are evaluating whether to extend the brand into other ethnic communities. What advice would you give them? How would you

recommend evaluating potential acceptance of the Elephant Chakki range in these communities? How would you evaluate the marketing strategies of potential competing products and what implications might there be for Elephant Chakki's future marketing communication strategies?

CASE STUDY 4.2

The ups and downs of recession

On 24 October 2009, the UK Office of National Statistics revealed that, despite optimistic predictions to the contrary, Britain was still in the grip of a major economic recession. A recession is deemed to have occurred when the gross domestic product (GDP) of a country falls for two consecutive quarters and the economy experiences what is termed 'negative growth'. However, this downturn appeared particularly grim as the fall in GDP extended to a sixth consecutive quarter; making it the longest decline since figures were first recorded quarterly in 1955.

A primary cause of the recession was a crisis that originated in the banking sector. Overly complicated products, over-development of 'sub-prime' markets and poorly regulated practices had left many banks with high levels of 'toxic' or bad debt. Shockwaves ran through markets as high profile names such as Lehman Bros. and Northern Rock filed for bankruptcy or sought assistance from government. As a result, credit markets froze. Companies whose survival relied on their ability to access credit soon found themselves struggling for survival. As for consumers, those seeking to finance high-value purchases such as cars or houses found loans difficult and expensive to obtain.

The period between September 2008 and September 2009 saw the consumer boom of the previous ten years screech to a shuddering halt. The landscape of the British High Street changed disconcertingly quickly as household names such as Woolworths, Adams, MFI, Zavvi and The Pier shut their doors for the last time. Unemployment rose to 2.5 million and dire predictions were made about the depth and the duration of the downturn.

Yet whilst some companies suffered agonies in their attempts to fend off bankruptcy, others found that their business boomed as consumers changed the way that they shopped. Increasingly looking for value, consumers sought to stretch their budgets by shopping at discount supermarkets such as Aldi, Netto and Lidl. Research by TNS Worldpanel suggested that over the course of the recession, Aldi had actually experienced 20 per cent year on year growth and Lidl, 14 per cent over the same period. Companies such as Domino's, the takeaway pizza franchise and JD Wetherspoon benefited from consumers forgoing expensive restaurant meals in favour of take away and pub meals. A trend towards holidaying in the UK saw budget hotel chain, Travelodge and Pontin's, the owner of seven holiday camps across the UK, forecast an increase in sales whilst Halfords reported strong demand for bicycles and camping equipment.

However, despite the constrained economic circumstances, consumers did not appear to totally abstain from indulgence. Cadbury's, producer of some of the UK's foremost chocolate brands, reported a 7.3 per cent rise in profits in the first half of 2009. Fashion also appears to be an item that is immune to recession with H&M reporting 14 per cent like-on-like increase in sales for the month of May, 2009, JD Sports Fashion reported a 54 per cent increase in half year profits and Burberry recorded an increase in sales in the first quarter of 25 per cent.

Whether spending or saving, from a marketing perspective, it is essential to understand who your consumers are and why they behave as they do within specific market conditions. Not only does it help you to develop products and services that will cater to their needs as the environment changes but it can also help in the formulation of effective integrated marketing communications campaigns. To this end, advertising group M&C Saatchi have published a report entitled 'Reacting to Recession' in which they have segmented consumers according to their demographic characteristics and their behaviour within difficult economic conditions. They have identified eight distinct segments:

Crash dieters Largely female, older and from the lower socio-economic groups, 'crash dieters' account for approximately 20 per cent of the population. They are pessimistic about the economy and cut expenditure wherever they can. They are 'promotionally promiscuous' in that they are always looking for special offers and are users of **coupons** and vouchers but otherwise tend to buy budget brands.

Scrimpers Scrimpers seek to maintain their lifestyle by looking for lower cost options. Predominantly young families, this group account for approximately 19 per cent of the market and are particularly strong targets for retailers such as Aldi and Lidl whose proposition of quality at low prices would be particularly attractive.

Justifiers Justifiers are particularly drawn to the idea of added value and while they may be attracted by low price, it is not necessarily the deal-maker. Instead they particularly like 'free' extras, for example, a case to go with a camera or low-cost broadband with a telephone contract. Accounting for approximately 14.5 per cent of the population, they tend to be 'empty nesters' (i.e. their children have grown up and left home) so have disposable income with which to spend – they just need to be persuaded to part with their money.

Ostriches Ostriches account for about 13 per cent of the population and tend to be single men in one of the higher socio-economic groups. They may be aware of the economic difficulties facing the nation but are in denial, still spending as if credit were not an issue. They have a tendency to 'max out' their credit cards and at some point their credit will come to a shuddering halt.

Treaters Treaters, who represent just over 12 per cent of the population, recognize the difficulties generated by the recession, but like to reward themselves with self-gifts to maintain their motivation. Self-gifts can come in many forms – from a bar of chocolate to a gym membership – and are a significant opportunity to marketers.

Abstainers Abstainers are spread relatively evenly across all of the **social groups** and account for 9 per cent of the market. They have halted their spending and, instead, browse in readiness for the time when finances improve and they are in the position to purchase.

Clothcutters Clothcutters account for a relatively small proportion of the population, just 7 per cent, but they have great potential. They tend to be well off, middle-aged and uncompromising when it comes to quality. However, in recessionary times, they will trade off one big purchase, for example, a new car, for another, a holiday.

Vultures Vultures are the smallest consumer group at only 5.5 per cent. They are likely to be amongst the highest earners and are positive about their prospects, despite the recession. Instead, they view the recession as an opportunity to grab a bargain. They are not averse to indulge in self-gifts and are happy to pay for quality.

CASE STUDY QUESTIONS

1. For each of the following brands, discuss the opportunities and threats that a recessionary economic climate poses for their business:

   - ASDA
   - Chanel
   - Sony
   - BMW.

2. Discuss why marketing communications strategies in a recession might differ from those in a booming economic climate.
3. The case study listed a number of retailers that have benefited from a recessionary climate. Discuss their relative strengths and weaknesses. How will their position change if or when the economy improves?
4. Choose a well known brand and, for each of the consumer segments identified in the M&C Saatchi report, construct a marketing proposition that you believe would entice that segment to buy your brand.

Notes

* Porter, M.E. (1980). *Competitive Strategy*, New York: Free Press.

1 Gronroos, C. (2009). Marketing as promise management: regaining customer management for marketing. *Journal of Business and Industrial Marketing*, 24(6), 351–9.
2 Kay, R.L. (1999). Internal marketing communications, *The Advertiser*, October (Accessed online via WARC 21 October 2009).
3 Toftoy, C.N., and Chatterjee, J. (2004). *Business Strategy Review*, 15(3), 41–4.
4 http://annualreport.marksandspencer.com/governance/accountability.html (accessed 24 June 2008).
5 http://berr.gov.uk/files/file22866.pdf (accessed 24 June 2008).
6 http://news.bbc.co.uk/1/hi/technology/4645596.stm (accessed 25 June 2008).
7 Heath, R. (2003). 'Low Involvement Processing'. In F. Hansen and L.B. Christensen (eds) *Branding and Advertising*, Copenhagen: Copenhagen Business School Press.
8 Moss, H.B., Kirby, S.D., and Donodeo, F. (2009). Characterizing and reaching high-risk drinkers using audience segmentation. *Alcoholism, Clinical And Experimental Research*, 33(8), 1336–45.
9 Huhman, M., Berkowitz, J.M., Wong, F.L., Prosper, E., Gray, M., Prince, D., *et al.* (2008). The VERB Campaign's strategy for reaching African-American, Hispanic, Asian, and American Indian children and parents. *American Journal of Preventive Medicine*, 34(6 suppl.), S194–209.
10 Slater, M.D., Kelly, K.J., and Thackeray, R. (2006). Segmentation on a shoestring: health audience segmentation in limited-budget and local social marketing interventions. *Health Promotion Practitioner*, 7(2), 170–3.
11 BBC News (2007). Mattel recalls millions more toys. Online. Available HTTP: <http://news.bbc.co.uk/1/hi/business/6946425.stm> (accessed 26 June 2008).
12 Weihrich, H. (1999). Analyzing the competitive advantages and disadvantages of Germany with the TOWS Matrix – an alternative to Porter's model. *European Business Review*, 99(1), 9–22.

5   Creativity and creative tactics

LEARNING OUTCOMES

After studying this chapter, you will be able to:

- Define 'creativity'

- Appreciate the important role that creativity has the potential to play in the success of an IMC campaign

- Appreciate the various creative tactics that can be employed in the construction of an IMC campaign

- Understand the challenges and pitfalls associated with the use of a 'creative' approach

Introduction

When thinking about the concept of 'creativity', the title of a classic jazz song of the 1930s springs to mind. 'T'ain't What You Do (It's the Way That You Do It)', written by Melvin 'Sy' Oliver and James 'Trummy' Young, sums up the notion that it is not enough just to undertake an IMC campaign, but that it should be undertaken in a way that makes it stand out from all the others. This chapter examines the nature of 'creativity' and discusses its potential contribution to the overall success of an IMC campaign. It then outlines some of the frequently-used creative tactics employed by marketers to communicate their marketing messages and distinguish their brands from others in the market place. Finally, it considers the challenges and difficulties associated with the concept of creativity and, in particular, considers the benefits and challenges associated with 'creativity' and suggest strategies that might be employed to manage them.

What is 'creativity'?

Creativity is one of the many terms that exist within the field of marketing that struggles to achieve a consensus of definition. A good starting point is that of Amabile[1] who suggests that creativity can be defined as the production of novel and useful ideas by an individual or by groups working in concert. Within a commercial context, it is more often viewed as a way of solving complex problems to the benefit of organizations.[2] In academic literature, discussions of creativity tend to vary widely; from the adoption of a focus upon individual components of creativity, for example, the individual notions of originality, newness[3] to a view of creativity as an entity comprised of multiple elements. Ang, Lee and Leong[4] adopt such a view, suggesting that creativity emerges from a combination of novelty, meaningfulness and 'connectedness' – the latter term relating to the degree to which the target audience can identify with the campaign.

However, for marketing professionals, it is not enough for creativity to exist in isolation, creative ideas need to be generated in a form that can be translated into solutions that address corporate and marketing objectives. Therefore, within a marketing context, a truly creative idea is one that not only possesses originality but is also appropriate to a given market situation.[5]

However, according to Kilgour and Koslow,[6] originality and appropriateness are to some extent mutually exclusive and an effective creative idea can only be achieved through a balance between two different types of creative thinking style: convergent and

---

THINK BOX

Creative advertising

Find examples of advertising campaigns you think are really creative. Use the divergence components to assess the campaign. What is it that you believe makes the campaign stand out?

Compare your findings to five of your fellow students. What conclusions can you draw from your combined evaluations?

Now repeat the same process for advertising campaigns you feel lack creativity. What advice would you give to the advertiser?

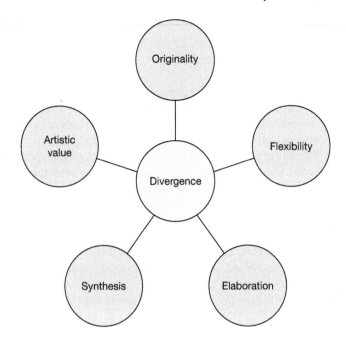

Figure 5.1 The components of 'divergence'

divergent. **Convergent thinking** involves a process in which an individual logically considers all of the concepts and ideas that currently exist within a given domain to determine their relative appropriateness when seeking to solve a particular problem. In contrast, **'divergent' thinking** occurs when previously unconnected domains or contexts are drawn together to create something that might be considered unusual, novel or different.[7]

One of the greatest challenges for those seeking to understand the nature of divergence is the difficulty in understanding what can actually make something novel or different. There appears general agreement that concept of 'divergence' is comprised of multiple components[8] and these are illustrated in Figure 5.1.

Smith *et al.* describe the components that comprise 'divergence' as follows:

Originality   Communications that contain elements that are rare, surprising or deviate from the commonplace.

Flexibility   Communications that switch from one perspective to another and/or contain multiple ideas.

Elaboration   Communications that either contain unexpected details and/or are structured in such a way that they encourage the recipient of the message to move beyond the basic message to something that is more complicated or sophisticated.

Synthesis   Communications that blend two or more otherwise unconnected ideas within a single message.

Artistic value Communications that contain attractive or striking artistic visual or auditory impressions.

The role and importance of creativity

Ultimately, creativity is a 'means to an end', which, within the context of IMC, means to successfully effect a change in either attitude or behaviour on the part of the target market.[9]

Creativity in an IMC campaign has the potential to impact upon the consumer in three key ways. Firstly, it can maximize the chance that the target consumers will actually take sufficient notice of the message for it to be effectively received. When marketing communications were in their infancy, relatively few messages were present in consumers' day-to-day lives. Therefore, when consumers did receive marketing communications, they were novel and gained attention. However over the decades, the number and variety of marketing communications consumers receive on a daily basis has increased exponentially and they have, through experience, learned to become more 'savvy' over the messages that they carry.[10] In response, consumers have built up filtering mechanisms such as perceptual selectivity and perceptual vigilance (discussed in detail in Chapter 2) that screen out all but that which is considered interesting or of relevance. As a result, creativity is seen as one of the most important weapons in the marketer's armoury when seeking to break through these barriers.

Secondly, creativity within an IMC campaign enhances the chance that, once received, the consumer will process the message in a way that will support the overall objectives of the campaign. The **elaboration likelihood model**[11] recognizes the fact that individuals process information in different ways depending upon their level of involvement with the result that there are two main routes of persuasion. Those who experience a high level of involvement with brand or product sector are subject to the **'central' route of persuasion** and tend to actively process and retain product-related information. By contrast, the **'peripheral' route of persuasion** is experienced by those who are less involved and are therefore less motivated to process messages when presented to them. In such cases, creativity can be used to increase the communication effectiveness by encouraging involvement with the vehicle that carries the message using one or more of the methods detailed in the section 'Creative tactics'. Therefore we can see that consumers can be persuaded to have a positive disposition towards a brand in two ways: through an explicit communication of the message and through the implicit messages carried through the peripheral cues.

Finally, there is significant research to suggest that the use of 'creativity' in IMC campaigns facilitates recall.[12] There is general acceptance of the fact that powerful marketing communications can have an immediate effect upon consumers' perceptions of a brand.[13] However, research has shown that a creative approach can encourage recall long after the initial impact of the message has taken place. This is an extremely important

---

THINK BOX

Media forms and creative approaches

Find an example of an integrated campaign that uses at least three different media including television and/or radio and newspapers and/or magazines, plus any other types of media.

How do the media formats influence the type of creative approaches used?

consideration for marketers as it is often the case that time delays exist between the time the communication is received and the point of consumer choice.

MINI CASE: BEAUTY IS IN THE EYE OF THE BEHOLDER

Photo 5.1

Dove is an internationally renowned toiletry brand with a broad product range that encompasses soaps, cleansers, moisturizers and hair products. With its Campaign for Real Beauty 'Big Ideal' campaign, Dove's communication strategy appears to run counter to many of the conventions associated with the beauty sector. Rejecting the idea of perfection as the ideal of beauty, they have embraced evidence that suggested that the projection of such perfect but unrealistic images of women in the media had a negative effect upon women's self esteem. As a result, their campaign-based communication programme encouraged women to aspire to a more achievable notion of beauty and thereby inspire them to take greater care of themselves. The 'Big Ideal' campaign used women of all ages, shapes, sizes and races to convey the message, primarily through TV, PR and sponsorship.

Using each of the components identified by Smith *et al.*, discuss the extent to which you believe this campaign to be creative/'divergent'.

Creative tactics

Creative tactics can be employed in two key ways within an IMC campaign: in the content of the message and in its mode of delivery. Within the content of the communication there are a variety of creative vehicles that include humour, sex and sexual representation, fear/shock, expertise/authority, and teaser campaigns.

Table 5.1 Types of humour commonly found in marketing communications

Humour type	Definition
Pun	The use of a word or phrase that is subject to two or more interpretations
Understatement	Representing something as less than would normally be perceived to be the case
Joke	Speaking or acting without seriousness
Ludicrous	A portrayal to highlight the absurd or ridiculous
Satire	The use of sarcasm to expose vice or folly
Irony	Where actual message communicated is opposite to its literal content

Source: Adapted from Toncar, M.F. (2001). The use of humour in television advertising: revisiting the us–USA comparison. *International Journal of Advertising*, 20: 521–39.

Humour

Humour can take a variety of forms; the most common forms are listed in Table 5.1.

The use of humour in marketing communications is particularly popular with marketers as, in most instances, it is a low-risk option. Effective use of humour has the potential to generate high levels of 'ad-liking' which in turn relates positively not just to levels of advertising recall[14] but also increases the likelihood of the consumer possessing a positive disposition towards the product or service at the centre of the marketing message as a result.[15] Further, in contrast to the use of sex or fear within the content of a communication, unless the subject of the humour is particularly contentious, there is little likelihood of offence.

However, whilst humour may be perceived as a relatively low risk option, its use is not totally without pitfalls. There is some evidence to suggest that whilst **humour appeals** can be highly persuasive in low involvement situations, in the case of high involvement products, humour can have the opposite effect as it can raise questions in the mind of consumers as to the performance of the product.[16] As a result, humour is only rarely used in campaigns for such high involvement products such as cars or houses. There are, however exceptions. For many years the Czechoslovakian car brand Skoda suffered from quality issues and subsequently was the butt of many jokes. However, in 2001 it became a subsidiary of the Volkswagen group who then attempted to reposition the brand. Recognizing that they could not ignore the brand's troubled history, they sought to highlight the improvements achieved by the takeover with the 'It's a Skoda, honest' campaign. In one execution, a woman buyer talks glowingly and knowledgeably to a Skoda

THINK BOX

Humour in advertising

Find examples of advertisements using each of the types of humour listed in Table 5.1. Critique them against the divergence components. How well do you believe your selected advertisements work? Justify your response.

Do you think that these types of advertisements wearout quicker than those using other creative approaches? Justify your response.

salesman and appears poised and ready to buy the car. However, at the last moment, she hesitates and sprints across the forecourt. In another execution, a male customer jumps though a hedge and sprints across a field instead of returning to the showroom to purchase the car. In the case of both ads, they finish with the strapline: 'It's a Skoda. Which, for some, is still a problem.'

In addition, care must be taken when rolling out humour-based campaigns on an international basis. The globalization of brands is a fact of life for many organizations and potential economies of scale are one of the major attractions associated with the growth of new markets. However, **standardization** of marketing communications is not always as easy as for other aspects of business practice. Humour is culturally grounded and therefore what is considered humorous in one market may not be considered at all amusing elsewhere.[17] As a result, marketers are often faced with the prospect of modifying individual campaigns to reflect local cultural sensitivities.

MINI CASE: PLEASE LOOK AFTER THIS BRAND: MARMITE'S USE OF PADDINGTON BEAR TO LAUNCH MARMITE 'SQUEEZY'

Authors: Kirsty Saddler, Sarah Carter, Les Binet and Alex Vass, Institute of Practitioners in Advertising, Bronze, IPA Effectiveness Awards 2008. Case material provided by the World Advertising Research Centre (WARC) www.warc.com.

Marmite is a concentrated food product made of brewer's yeast. Most commonly used as a spread on bread or toast, it can also be used as a stock (if diluted with hot water) or as flavouring for soups or stews. It was first launched in 1902 and, since then, has become one of Britain's most iconic brands.

In 2008, Unilever, current owner of the Marmite brand, sought to launch a 'squeezy' variation of the product. The aim was to drive growth by targeting the consumer, introduce the new product format and encourage increased frequency of use, particularly in sandwiches. However, as with any established brand, the challenge was to communicate

Photo 5.2

change in a way that attracted new users whilst not alienating existing ones. With this in mind, Unilever's agency DDB London, developed the 'Please Look After this Brand' campaign featuring another British icon, Paddington Bear, across a variety of media including television, radio, cinema, Internet, sales promotion and PR.

In the television advertisement, Paddington decides to try something other than the marmalade sandwiches that he traditionally favours and samples a sandwich that contains 'squeezy' Marmite. Having decided he likes it, he shares a crust with a pigeon and, in a similar vein to the story-lines in the Paddington children's animation, typical slapstick chaos ensues.

Why do you think Unilever chose a children's character like Paddington Bear in this instance? Do you think it was effective? Justify your answer.

Sex and sexual representation

Whilst there is an old adage within the field of marketing that says 'sex sells', in truth this is not always the case. The spectrum of sex and sexual representation within marketing communications is a wide one, ranging in content from the discussion of feminine hygiene products to instances of full frontal nudity. However, whilst the sexual content of marketing communications commonly revolves around visual depictions of attractive individuals, alone or with partners, involved in some form of sexual behaviour, this is not always the case. It can also take the form of explicit sexual references or sexual innuendo in verbal, pictorial or written form.[18]

The attraction of using **sexual appeals** is very simple; they have been demonstrated to be effective in arresting consumer attention and generating high levels of recall.[19] Sexual appeals appear to be particularly effective for younger audiences[20] with theory suggesting that young people for whom sexual experience and sexual expression are relatively new find sexual content informative, novel and salient.[21] However, this is not the case for all consumers. There is some evidence that overt sexuality in marketing communications can give certain consumer groups a negative disposition towards a brand.[22] Women appear more likely to be offended by the sexual content of marketing communications than men[23] and, in particular, the more educated and feminist orientated women consumers appear most critical of those communications that portray women as sex objects.

In addition, there is evidence that the effectiveness of marketing communications that contain sexual material can also be compromised. In situations in which a communication

---

THINK BOX

Models in advertisements

What do you believe the minimum age of models in advertisements that use sexual appeals should be?

Visit the ASA website for the Advertising Codes and compare your response to the current codes. What recommendations, if any, can you make to the regulators regarding the use of models in advertisements that use sexual imagery? Justify your response.

ETHICAL ISSUE TO CONSIDER

Some advertisements targeted at males have historically used female models in seductive poses (e.g. cars and automotive products). In recent times, this approach has been criticized for demeaning women.

Draw on the material in this chapter and in Chapter 3 to discuss the ethical dimensions of using female models in this way.

If the approach was to be parodied and male models used in seductive poses in advertisements targeting women, would there be any ethical issues with this strategy? Justify your response.

contains large amounts or information or complex sets of ideas, the inclusion of a sexual element can actually interfere with consumers' comprehension of the message.[24]

Finally, extreme care must be taken with the content of sexually-based marketing messages when targeting messages at younger consumers. Idealized images of women and their bodies have been shown to influence levels of body dissatisfaction amongst young women,[25] whilst young men exposed to the sexual depiction of women in advertising are more accepting of sexual aggression towards women and sex-role **stereotyping**.[26]

Fear/shock appeals

Persuasive appeals based upon shock and/or fear use the threat of negative consequences to motivate consumers into action.[27] Appeals such as these are most often used within the context of social marketing or public policy with the aim of persuading consumers to make changes that will positively affect their health or wellbeing. A good example of such an appeal was used by the Drug and Alcohol Service for London[28] (Photo 5.3) which sought to raise awareness amongst women of the physical consequences of binge drinking. By increasing levels of involvement and perceived risk, it is hoped that consumers will alter behaviour or reappraise the relative importance of key attributes at the point of decision-making thereby making choices that will yield more positive outcomes.

One of the strongest determinants of the success of fear and shock appeals is the target audience's willingness to interact with them. Protective motivation theory suggests that if shock and **fear appeals** are either too forceful or too subtle, they are likely to be ineffective; the former because consumers will simply 'switch off' and the latter because of a lack of impact.[29] Whilst research has yet to identify a distinct threshold at which fear or shock appears to become effective, four components have been identified that make up consumers' consideration sets and therefore influence the relative efficacy of shock or fear-based communications:[30]

The severity of harm	Consumers weigh up the severity of the harm they are likely suffer relative to the pain or inconvenience of potential preventative action.
The probability of occurrence	Consumers weigh up the likelihood that they will suffer negative consequences if they fail to take the required preventative action. If they believe the likelihood to be small then they are less likely to take action.

If you drink like a man
you might end up looking like one.

Wine doesn't just come with cheese. For women it's also accompanied by hair loss, wrinkles
and obesity, plus the other problems like breast cancer, early menopause and memory loss.
For confidential advice or more information please contact 0208 257 3068.

Photo 5.3

The efficacy of   Consumers weigh up the potential benefits that adoption of preventative
coping response   actions or a 'coping response' are likely to bring. If they believe that it
is going to be effective, they are more likely to react to the communication in a positive way.

Self efficacy   Consumers evaluate their own ability to perform the required preventative action. If they perceive themselves to be unable to take the appropriate action they are unlikely to act in response to the communication.

Expertise/authority

An expertise/authority-based appeal is one in which the product or service is positioned as having a high degree of skill or knowledge in a specific market area.[31] Such appeals can be highly persuasive when used in relation to high involvement products or services where consumers experience a desire to minimize degrees of risk. Organizations and individuals who are perceived to have 'expert' status possess high levels of 'source credibility' with the result that consumers tend to believe that their communications have authority.

Nostalgia

A campaign based upon nostalgia is one that references specific elements of the past that are meaningful and potentially persuasive to the target market. The use of nostalgia is

THINK BOX

Your own consumer behaviour

Very few of us live lives that are devoid of any excess. Some people eat too much sugar or drink too much alcohol. Some gamble to excess whilst others might indulge themselves with an overdose of retail therapy. Reflect upon your own behaviour. Is there anything that you do to excess? What kind of fear appeals could be used to persuade you to moderate your behaviour?

effective on a number of levels. The human tendency to selectively remember the past by suppressing or minimizing painful or unpleasant events means that consumers perceive products associated with past times as more positive than those associated with the present day. Furthermore, the appeal of nostalgia is not limited solely to the old. Nostalgia also holds appeal for younger consumers as the longevity of some brands has the potential to endow them with 'vintage' or 'iconic' status.

The use of nostalgia in marketing communications tends to become more popular during difficult times such as war or economic recession. According to Steve Sharp, Marketing Director at UK retailer Marks and Spencer, 'Nostalgia always becomes more important when times are tough, as traditional values become more important'.[32] Recently, Marks and Spencer and supermarket chain Sainsbury's both used their 100th and 140th anniversary as the basis for their promotional campaigns that highlighted their heritage and values. Similarly detergent brand Fairy Liquid celebrated their 50th anniversary with a limited reintroduction of their white bottles and a montage of vintage Fairy Liquid advertising.

However, the use of 'nostalgia' is not without danger as, if used incorrectly, products and brands can appear old-fashioned or out-dated. Therefore it is essential that the contemporary relevance of the brand in question must also clearly ring out in order for an effective balance in the communication to be achieved.

'Teaser' campaigns

'Teaser' campaigns are those that offer the consumer an incomplete message with the result that they then seek to achieve some form of 'closure'. 'Closure' may be defined as a situation in which individuals seek a form of solid solution to what they perceive to be an ongoing or enduring ambiguity.[33] Gestalt psychology suggests that individuals are driven to 'fill in the gaps' when faced with an incomplete situation[34] which in turn increases their involvement with the message.

THINK BOX

Nostalgia in advertising

Find examples of advertisements that use nostalgia. How effective do you believe these are? Justify your response, drawing on material from this chapter.

Teaser campaigns usually take two forms: an on-going narrative or story that ends with a 'cliff hanger' or an incomplete picture or message that the audience is forced to complete. The narrative approach is particularly flexible as the 'story' can act as a vehicle for a variety of important brand messages. Further, it does not assume prior knowledge of the brand or product and can be used to target messages at consumers new to the brand or product/service sector. In contrast, the aim of the incomplete picture/message option is to increase consumer involvement by getting them to 'fill in the blanks' or to create a 'buzz' of discussion about the communication.

MINI CASE: TEASER CAMPAIGN HIJACKED!

In 2007, Swedish train services company SJ sought to publicize their 95 SEK tickets with the use of a teaser campaign. The underpinning idea was that a large number of brightly coloured posters branded with the number '95' would be posted at key sites around the country. Hopefully, people would question what it was all about and generate a bit of a 'buzz'. A couple of weeks later, SJ would reveal themselves as the source of the message and highlight the good value of their ticket price.

Unfortunately, the 'reveal' was left too late and a short while after the posters went up, owners of a pornography website contacted the major media to claim credit for the campaign. Whilst many reporters didn't fall for the scam, the story of the attempt to hijack SJ's campaign was extensively reported. This was doubly disastrous for SJ, not only did this undermine the impact of their initial campaign, their brand was now in inextricably linked in the minds of consumers with that of pornography.

What lessons might be learned from this incident? Was there anything that SJ might have done to prevent the hijacking?

Words, pictures, sound, smell, touch . . . using all of the senses

The use of words, pictures and, if the medium supports it, sound are also tactics commonly used to enhance the creativity of a marketing communication.[35] High imagery words, strong colours and attractive images and shapes all have the potential to attract and hold the attention of the audience. For print-based communications, the size of a communication relative to those around it can have an impact as can differentiation in terms of shape and colour. This is particularly important in situations such as classified advertisements where the target audience is subject to multiple communications simultaneously.

Sound can also be highly evocative and can convey the mood and message pertaining to a brand in a highly memorable way. Sounds can vary enormously in type and can range from the simple 'jingle' to classical concertos. Jingles have considerable value as they are usually written specifically for a brand. Therefore, if consumers are exposed sufficiently to a jingle, classical conditioning will effect a recollection of the brand in question.

Smell is thought to be one of the most powerful tools when seeking to evoke memory or generate emotion. From a marketing point of view, using scent in the purchase environment is a well-used tactic, particularly by supermarkets. For instance, who has not been tempted by the smell of freshly baked bread from an 'in-store' bakery? However, the use of scent as a creative tactic when communicating through more traditional media can be a more challenging proposition. A particular smell can be conveyed through paper-based communication media by permeating one part of the advertisement with scent. This approach, known colloquially as 'scratch and sniff', has typically been used in relation to products like perfume and fabric conditioner where the majority of the product benefits and brand values reside in the quality of the scent. However, whilst the challenge of using scent in conjunction with the traditional media of television and radio might appear insurmountable, this is not necessarily the case with film. A Hanover-based company called Cinescent, has launched a machine that pumps a barely detectable aroma through a cinema's air conditioning system to accompany on-screen ads. Initial trials in Germany suggest that it is potentially very effective. The trial consisted of two advertisements for Nivea sun lotion; one which was accompanied by the faint smell of the product. According to Cinescent, the aromatic advertisement, boosted consumer recall by 37 per cent and raised advertising impact (gauged over a few weeks) by more than 500 per cent.[36]

Using touch and taste to convey marketing messages can be hugely effective if done appropriately. Not only can it differentiate a piece of communication from others of its type, it can also clearly convey product values and brand values metaphorically or literally. For example, in print media, the use of unconventional qualities and weights of card or the use of textured paper can make a piece of communication stand out from inserts or full page advertisements in more traditional form. Where the value of a product or brand is based around its taste or texture, a more experiential approach such as sampling can provide an excellent opportunity to engage the consumers' senses. However, where it is not possible for consumers to sample the product first hand, brand characteristics can be metaphorically conveyed through touch and taste. For example, if it is the case that a product such as chocolate has a particularly silky texture, a tactile, silky medium might act as a powerful metaphor.

Generating creative ideas

Brainstorming

Whilst some organizations rely purely on the innate talents of their marketing and creative teams to generate creative ideas, there are, in addition, a variety of techniques that can be implemented to good effect. For the main part, these techniques encourage individuals to look at a product/brand/situation from a different or novel perspective and, from that basis, arrive at creative solutions to a defined marketing challenge.

The majority of techniques designed to encourage individuals to think creatively have their roots in a technique called 'brainstorming'. 'Brainstorming' was first developed by Alex F. Osborn in 1939 at a time when he headed up the advertising agency Batten, Barton, Durstine and Osborn.[37] The aim of 'brainstorming' was to facilitate creative thinking by freeing individuals from feelings of inhibition and self-criticism whilst also shielding them from the potential for criticism from others. The aim of a 'brainstorming' exercise was to generate as many different ideas as possible in response to a given brief. Four basic rules characterize any brainstorming activity[38]:

1. *Criticism is ruled out during the course of the brainstorming exercise.* If there should be any cause for criticism, it should be reserved until after the exercise is complete.
2. *'Free-wheeling' should be actively encouraged.* Wild and extreme ideas should be welcomed as they can always be tempered according to circumstances.
3. *Quantity is important.* The more ideas generated, the more likely a good one will be found amongst them.
4. *Seek out combination and improvement.* Having generated a number of ideas, efforts should also be made to see how they might be combined and/or improved upon.

Brainstorming exercises should always be undertaken in response to a brief which contains clear objectives. Without clear objectives, brainstorming activity can be directionless and lack the dynamism needed to generate true creativity. A number of other barriers to effective brainstorming have also been identified[39]:

- Participants can't detach themselves from their day-to-day work and struggle to give the subject at hand their full attention.
- Participants struggle to break away from a group mentality and political correctness.
- Managers are risk averse and shy away from radical creativity.
- The environment in which the activity takes place is not conducive to creative or unconventional thinking.
- The mix of people involved in the brainstorming exercise is unbalanced. If too many people come from one part of the business it will skew the creative process.
- In situations in which the same subject has been continuously revisited it is often the case that responses become clichéd.
- Participants who adopt a negative attitude to either the subject of the exercise or the brainstorming exercise itself will struggle to make a positive or creative contribution.
- Strict limitations on time can result in the limited exploration of the value of individual ideas.

Creative 'pass the parcel'

A good mix of people, ideally from both client and agency should be chosen to make up the 'pass the parcel' team. Using the objectives cited in the brief as a base point, each person writes down an initial response in the centre of a piece of paper. They then pass it to the next person who then 'improves' it. This goes on until everyone has had the chance to 'improve' each idea at least once. The papers are then collected and posted onto a wall in gallery fashion. The ideas are then compared and contrasted by the team in terms of how successfully they address the brief's objectives. The brainstorming rules pertaining to a lack of criticism and the importance of 'free wheeling' also apply to this method as these factors are clear inhibitors of creativity. Suggestions that are clearly too extreme can always be weeded out at the end.

The benefit of this method is that it overcomes the initial feeling of 'creative block' that is often present when first presented with a brief. It is often the case that it is easier to develop and build upon an idea than to generate one in the first place. In addition, the fact that everyone has contributed towards each idea at least once prevents individuals becoming overly protective or defensive over their individual contribution to the ideas generated.

Osbourn's checklist

Whilst this is a method that is cited as being particularly appropriate in situations where marketers are seeking creative inspiration for packaging, brochures, folders and direct mailings,[40] it actually has broad application across a number of communication vehicles.

Starting with a set of raw ideas generated through either a classic 'brainstorm' or 'pass the parcel' style activity, the aim of the 'checklist' is to ensure that each and every idea is thoroughly and systematically interrogated to ensure that its full potential is recognized. For each idea, it is suggested that the following questions should be considered:[41]

- How can the size or proportions be altered?
- How can the shape or function be altered?
- Can the surface be changed?
- How many ways are there to construct it?
- Can it be made more effective?
- How can its performance be improved?
- Can the user do something different with it?
- What materials can be used?
- How can the information be put across better?
- What style could be used?
- What style or personality should it have?
- What about colour?
- What sounds or noises can be used?

Whilst these are the suggested questions, they should by no means be regarded as set in stone. Based upon the communication objectives and the target audience, additional questions can be added to ensure that all relevant alternatives can be considered.

'Zwicky's box'

'Zwicky's box' is one of the most thorough methods of approaching a creative problem. Based on a system of general morphological analysis first proposed by Fritz Zwicky, it is a way of systematically listing and logically addressing every conceivable option associated with the creative objectives using a matrix system or 'box'. All of the elements of the IMC promotional mix are listed down one side of the matrix (i.e. advertising, sales promotion etc.) and under each is listed all of the potential vehicles and their components or elements available. Across the top of the matrix, are listed all of the characteristics that need to be taken into account.

Marketers should then systematically move cell by cell and list all of the creative alternatives in each case. As with the 'checklist' approach, the benefit of this approach is that it ensures that every area is considered and given equal attention. In addition, not only does it help marketers think more creatively about how multiple media can be used individually and in concert to achieve a given objective, it also encourages them to think about issues associated with consistency and **continuity**.

If undertaken correctly, all of these exercises have the potential to generate creative ideas that are the product of both convergent and divergent thinking. On completion of the 'brainstorming' activity, the ideas should then be analysed for practicality and actionability (i.e. can it actually be implemented), affordability (i.e. can the organization afford to implement it) and the degree to which they are likely to effectively address the objectives set out in the brief.

The challenges and pitfalls of creativity

Possibly the greatest challenge associated with the use of creativity in integrated marketing communications stems also from its greatest strength: originality. Central to the concept of creativity is the ability to differentiate one's brand from its competitors in a unique and novel way that sometimes results in marketers pushing the boundaries of truth, taste and decency. To ensure that this does not occur, the Advertising Standards Authority (ASA)

	Consumer benefit	Copy style	Copy length	Audio
Advertising				
Press				
Magazines				
TV				
Radio				
Posters/outdoor				
Sales promotion				
Coupons				
Premiums				
On pack				
In pack				
Added value				
Added volume				

Figure 5.2 An example of Zwicky's 'box' or 'matrix'

has established a set of guidelines and regulations based upon the premise that marketing communications should be legal, decent, honest and truthful.[42] Those that do not comply with the regulations face potential sanctions from both the ASA and the Office of Fair Trading.

A further challenge associated with creativity is maintenance of a balance between the **creative execution** of a piece of marketing communication and the basic functionality required, for example, brand recognition or comprehension of brand values. Research has suggested that there have been many cases in which significant resource has been wasted because of an overemphasis upon the 'creative' at the cost of the functionality of the communication.[43] Problems such as these can be solved through the inclusion of clear objectives within the **creative brief** and close adherence to those objectives throughout the duration of the campaign. This achieved, a clear balance between creativity and functionality can more easily be struck.

Summary

Creativity is one of the most effective tools for marketers when seeking to gain the attention of potential consumers and effectively communicate a message to them about their product or service. It enables marketers to cut through the clutter and noise of consumers' everyday lives and encourages involvement with the marketing message. However, creativity for its own sake is a waste of resources so it is essential that, in formulating creative messages and campaigns, marketers are mindful of its required functionality. Therefore in order to be effective, creative campaigns or messages must satisfy five key criteria; they must be objective driven, distinctive, salient, relevant and non-offensive.

Review questions

1. Define the term 'creativity' using examples to illustrate your answer.
2. What is the value of 'creativity' to brand owners when seeking to generate awareness of their brand amongst their target market?
3. 'Creativity can only be a good thing.' Discuss this statement using examples to illustrate your answer.
4. Discuss the extent to which the use of humour within a marketing communication might interfere with consumers' ability to process the content of the message.
5. A common adage amongst marketers is that 'sex sells'. Using examples, discuss the extent to which sexual appeal or innuendo is used to sell the following product types:

   * cars
   * lipstick
   * holidays.

6. To what extent is it ethical to scare consumers into changing their consumption behaviour?
7. Identify an example of a marketing communication that uses 'authority' or 'expertise' as the basis of its creative approach. Why do you think this approach was chosen for this product/ brand?
8. Identify a brand that you believe to possess 'vintage' or 'iconic' status. How is this communicated by the brand owners?
9. For a brand of your choice, discuss the extent to which sound or imagery has been used to communicate the brand values.
10. Discuss the extent to which the creativity of a campaign is limited by media selection.

Recommended reading

Ang, S.H., Leong, S.M., Lee, Y.H., and Lou, S.L. (2013). Necessary but not sufficient: beyond novelty in advertising creativity. *Journal of Marketing Communications*, 18(1), 1–17.

Ogilvy, D. (2007). *Ogilvy on Advertising*, London: Prion Books Ltd.

Pricken, M. (2008). *Creative Advertising: Ideas and Techniques from the World's Best Campaigns*, London: Thames & Hudson.

CASE STUDY 5.1

Using creativity to drive brand success

Source: Institute of Practitioners in Advertising: IPA Effectiveness Awards 2009. This case has been condensed from *Ella's Kitchen – The First Three Years*. Authors: Agostino Di Falco, Paul Lindley, Nicole McDonnell, Samantha Crossley, Peter Dale, Nick Bampton, Daniel Salem, Bobi Carley, Damon Lafford, Michael Barrett and Alison Lindley. Case material provided by the World Advertising Research Centre (WARC) www.warc.com.

This case study illustrates an unusual partnership/ collaboration designed to address several key challenges facing marketers and communications organizations.

The vision

Ella's Kitchen was founded by Paul Lindley, a father of two young children, who had naturally begun taking an interest in his children's diet. This was a time when the health of the nation had begun to be put under great scrutiny. According to government statistics, approximately 30 per cent of children in the UK are medically overweight and 15 per cent are clinically obese. Much of the blame for this position was being placed on fast food manufacturers and the influence of advertising over kids' eating behaviour. As a father, Paul refused to believe that children (his in particular) didn't want to lead healthy lives and eat healthy foods. In his opinion good food could be made cool in the eyes of children and that involving them in its development would prompt behavioural change. It was around this time that he decided to launch a range of organic fruit and vegetable products aimed at children. He named the brand Ella's Kitchen after his daughter. The next few months were spent determining how he could get the business off the ground and devising a strategy to challenge the establishment.

Market trends

There were three key market trends that drove the Ella's Kitchen product strategy.

The first stemmed from the time-pressured lives of parents these days. They want the best for their kids and work exceptionally hard to achieve a high quality of life but a price being paid was that they sometimes chose convenience foods for their kids to eat and frankly the nutritional quality of some of these foods was not up to scratch. Secondly, parents were already spending more on their children's diet. Having spoken at length with hundreds of parents, Paul was convinced that regardless of price premium they would be willing to spend incrementally on healthy foods for their kids. As an issue, the availability of money was subservient to convenience.

And finally as it turned out, the issue of convenience was also subservient to that of healthy eating. The high profile work of the likes of Jamie Oliver had become a catalyst for forcing parental re-assessment of eating standards to such an extent that it was felt that launching into the market at that time would take advantage of significant attitudinal change.

Kids first

As all parents know, making healthy food available for kids is one thing but getting them to eat it is another. Millions of hours have been spent at the dinner table by frustrated parents trying to force their kids to eat broccoli. Paul knew that in order for Ella's Kitchen to be successful he needed kids to buy into the brand – the taste, the look, the positioning, everything. He spent considerable time trialling fruit and vegetable flavours, textures and combinations and researching them with children of friends and relatives.

A product to sell

Out of this process emerged a set of Smoothie Fruit products in four varieties, packaged in a distinctive re-sealable pouch. The product would initially be sold in multi-packs of five units, ideal for Monday to Friday school lunchbox purchasers. A deal with a manufacturer was agreed. All that was required now was distribution and funds for marketing.

Meanwhile in an office in Camden . . .

Separately and simultaneously to Paul's process, Viacom Brand Solutions (VBS) – the advertising sales house for Nickelodeon – was wrestling with the prospect of losing all HFSS (High Fat Sugar Salt) advertisers from the kids channels at a cost of circa £5 million in advertising revenue. The government was aiming to reduce children's consumption of HFSS products and removing advertising of this nature from children's TV channels was seen as a solution.

VBS knew they were fighting an uphill battle persuading the government not to implement this legislation. They were going to have to think of alternative strategies to recoup this lost revenue. At the heart of the government's strategy there was an assumption – that advertising was bad for kids and TV advertising was the main culprit.

This was a challenge. In the long-term interest of the VBS business it was decided to embark on a campaign that would demonstrate that advertising could be used as a positive force for good. And the category targeted initially was that of kids' health. If it could be demonstrated to the government that they had contributed to changing children's food eating habits positively then not only might VBS generate more advertising revenue through healthier food and drink products but there was a hope that the industry might also compel the government to behave more collaboratively towards the TV industry in the future.

So now **both** Ella's Kitchen and VBS had a cause to fight for.

A meeting of minds

Paul recognized that if he was going to credibly build a brand among children he would have to associate Ella's Kitchen with a partner who already had that relationship. That partner would be Nickelodeon. The meeting of minds took place in May 2005 when Paul met with Nick Bampton, MD of VBS, and was able to outline his vision and current limitations. From a VBS perspective, this was potentially a great opportunity to address the government's issues with TV advertising, show that TV can build brands from scratch and that the medium was not simply the preserve of large multi-national companies with large media budgets. Ella's Kitchen did not have a budget.

Shared risk innovation

Together Ella's Kitchen and VBS constructed an innovative shared risk agreement where VBS would write a letter to Ella's Kitchen guaranteeing £100,000 worth of airtime to the brand in 2006 as long as the brand was able to secure national distribution. In return, Ella's Kitchen would pay VBS 3p per pouch sold. In addition, VBS offered to produce the creative materials for TV and web campaigns. Paul took the letter with him as he pitched the brand to **multiples** and, lo-and-behold, towards the end of 2005, on the basis that there would be nationwide TV support on Nickelodeon, Sainsbury's agreed to carry Ella's Kitchen in 335 stores.

The launch strategy

In 2005, over £100 million* was spent on soft drink advertising, of which £63 million was spent on TV. Ella's Kitchen couldn't compete in terms of scale so a strategy was devised that would focus on a key strategic objective – that is to win kids over and let them act as Ella's ambassadors to their mums. The strategic focus on kids would clearly differentiate Ella's Kitchen versus competitors (Del Monte, Tropicana), who adopted 'gatekeeper' (mums) strategies. To bring this to life some kind of emotional attachment (fun and cool) was needed to go with the rational benefits (healthy and tastes good).

This discovery took place exclusively and intermittently throughout 2006 on Nickelodeon, Nick Replay, Nicktoons, Nick Jr and Nick Jr 2. Nickelodeon is the outstanding kids' network given that kids have the greatest affinity with it, take ownership of it, contribute content ideas to it and watch it in greatest numbers (4 million monthly – BARB).

Creative approach

Given the exclusivity of the deal with Nickelodeon, VBS were able to create work in the same style and tone of voice of the channels. The ads would fit seamlessly in Nickelodeon's programme environment. The emphasis was on fun, play and energy. The series of upbeat executions featured Paul's daughter Ella introducing kids to 'the Red One' (berry based) and 'the Yellow One' (banana based).

Media strategy

The media strategy and plan mirrored the creative approach in that it was based around the idea of congruency. It sought bouncy, energetic, uplifting shows in sync with the brand proposition as opposed to ones which tried to bring energy levels down ahead of bedtime. In addition the spots appeared next to Nickelodeon's own pro-social strand called Nicktrition (a series of 50 short educational films about healthy lifestyles for kids). Short bursts of activity punctuated the year keeping the brand top of mind.

Early results

Aside from an introductory price offer, advertising on Nickelodeon was the sole marketing variable used in 2006. The results were extremely encouraging. Weekly case sales (six multi-packs of five pouches) grew from 300 to 800[†] by the end of May, easily meeting the targets set for the brand by Sainsbury's. After 6 months of trading, the brand had sold over half a million pouches. The biggest endorsement of the brand's performance came from Waitrose who began to stock the product in the summer. With additional distribution secured, by the end of the year the brand surpassed 1,000 case sales per week.

A new arrival

Side by side with the Smoothie launch, Paul began developing a range of baby food products using the same convenient re-sealable pouch technology. Four initial varieties were produced and Waitrose agreed to become Ella's first baby food retailer. VBS produced the

TV copy in the same campaign style and this time the media placement focussed on Nick Jr, the network's pre-school channel. Baby food sales grew rapidly throughout the autumn as the impact of the advertising and mums' word of mouth took effect.

Netting the big one

A successful 2006 was rounded off magnificently by attracting the attention of Tesco. Early in 2007, Ella's Kitchen was to receive nationwide distribution for both Smoothie Fruits and Baby Foods in Tesco Stores.

Year 2 – 2007

The long-term advertising and media strategy had already been established, so 2007 was about ensuring the brand built further distribution and maintained momentum. As well as TV, VBS introduced an online component to the media strategy. Nickjr.co.uk and nick.co.uk were deployed on a continuous basis sending kids to the Ella's Kitchen website to engage with the brand and play games. VBS refreshed the TV and online creative treatments throughout the year and especially to accommodate an on-pack promotional tie-up with Disney. They approached the brand to support the film launch of *Meet the Robinsons* on pack. By the end of 2007 the brand had sold over 6 million units.

Year 3 – 2008

In Year 3, Ella's Kitchen had begun to generate impulse sales in multiples, CTNs and service stations. The brand had also developed a range of Pasta Sauces, again in the same distinctive pouch format, so that kids could literally squirt the sauce on top for themselves. The range came in Italian, Indian and American varieties. Distribution was secured in major outlets without too much trouble, again on the premise that the brand would continue to receive advertising support. A new advertising campaign in the same 'house' style was unveiled to Nickelodeon viewers and browsers for Smoothie Fruits and Pasta Sauces, featuring Ella and younger brother Patrick.

Results

All references made to performance cover the three-year period from February 2006 to January 2009. This period has witnessed Ella's Kitchen grow exponentially – 20 million portions sold in the 36 months since launch. Results focus on a number of key areas:

- customer feedback
- Sainsbury's sales (the only retailer to have stocked the brand from day 1)
- Ella's Kitchen turnover and profit
- VBS airtime investment and return.

Customer feedback

Ella's Kitchen isn't Del Monte or Heinz, so to spend money on tracking studies when the same funds could be used to develop new product variants simply wasn't their style. But that is not to say that the company wasn't aware of what customers thought about them, their products and indeed their advertising strategy. Fascinatingly, the brand is awash with feedback from customers endorsing the strategy. There's absolutely no doubt that an army of advocates has been established. Interestingly, the overwhelming feeling seems to be one of relief and gratitude that a 100 per cent organic fruit and vegetable brand has made healthy eating appealing to kids.

Sainsbury's sales‡

It's important to remember that the measure of advertising effectiveness we have here is extremely 'clean'. The only advertising vehicle used since launch in 2006 has been Nickelodeon. There have been in-store promotions at launch and two on-pack partnerships with film distributors. In all cases, TV advertising supported these events. However, for the vast majority of the last three years, the only tool Ella's Kitchen has used to communicate with its consumers has been Nickelodeon.

The key findings from the Sainsbury's data indicate:

- Since launch there have been 19 waves of advertising across the full range of products. Almost without exception each burst of activity has precipitated a step change in sales (see Figure 5.3). Each year momentum has been built. In Sainsbury's alone unit sales in 2008 increased by 25 per cent for Smoothie Fruits and 147 per cent for Baby Foods versus 2007.
- As Figure 5.4 shows, the rate of sales delivered by the brand has grown steadily through the period analysed.
- To further emphasize this point, Figure 5.5 compares the year-on-year change in rate of sale. It continues to rise to this day.

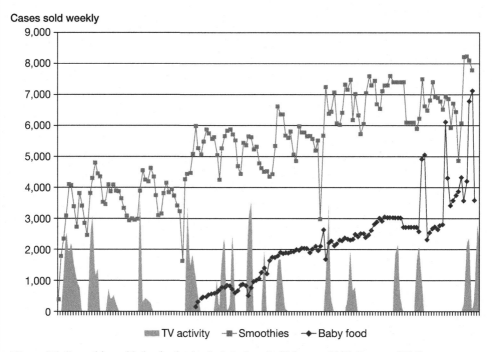

Figure 5.3 Smoothie and baby food sales in Sainsbury's (February 2006–January 2009)

Rate of sale

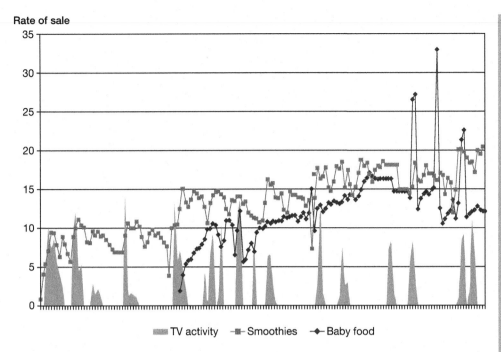

Figure 5.4 Smoothie and baby food rate of sale in Sainsbury's (February 2006–January 2009)

Rate of sale change (%)

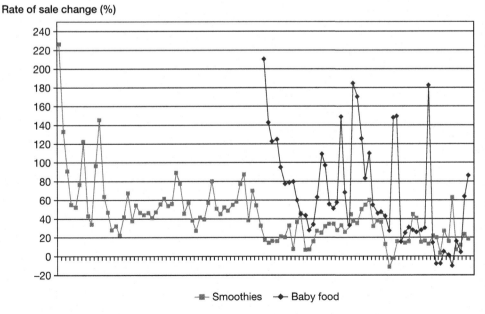

Figure 5.5 Smoothie and baby food rate of sale in Sainsbury's, year on year change
(February 2006–January 2009)

Ella's Kitchen turnover and profit

The table below demonstrates just how quickly the brand managed to build sales:

Table 5.2 Ella's Kitchen turnover (July–June FY)

Year	Turnover	Year on year
2005/6	£0.2M	
2006/7	£1.3M	+550%
2007/8	£3.2M	+192%
2008/9	£8.2M	+115%

The unique partnership with VBS enabled the brand to attain crucial early levels of advertising investment, without having to bear significant capital cost:

Table 5.3 Analysis of advertising value and expenditure with VBS

Year	Market value of advertising (£K)	Price paid through revenue share (£K)
2006	220	50
2007	247	127
2008	298	347

Table 5.4 shows how this approach brought stability to the brand's advertising to sales ratio:

Table 5.4 Advertising to sales ratios

Year	A:S ratios
2006	5.60%
2007	4.70%
2008	6.10%

Finally, Table 5.5 shows that already, Ella's Kitchen is generating high levels of profit. This, despite the fact the company has grown its cost base significantly.

Table 5.5 Key profit statistics

	2005/6	2006/7	2007/8	2008/9*
EBIT (£M)	−0.04	0.1	0.4	0.7
Gross profit (%)	20	23	25	25
Net profit (%)	n/a	8	11	8
Net assets (£M)	0.04	0.03	0.3	0.7
SKUs	2	6	15	22
Staff	1	2	8	12

*projection

Ella's Kitchen took a risk when positioning themselves away from mums and towards kids as influencers of family budgets. In creating a partnership on TV and online with VBS and Nickelodeon they also shied away from the traditional mums' targeted print arena. The evidence overwhelmingly shows that this strategy paid off.

VBS investment and return

There's no doubt that VBS also took a risk when creating this unique deal. However, not only are they now enjoying significant return on their investment (£547,000 revenue between Feb 06 – Jan 09) but a number of other brands in the healthy food sector have been signed up (Kidsnax, Rocks Organic, Good Natured, Babylicious) to advertise on VBS channels.

Another of VBS's initial objectives was to influence governmental attitudes towards advertising, and it is interesting to note that two years after the initiative with Ella's Kitchen commenced, the government has launched a major long-term advertising offensive 'Change for Life' designed to get the general public to eat more healthily and exercise more. This really is a step change in policy and the Ella's Kitchen campaign which was proactively promoted at various governmental and food forums throughout 2006 and 2007 may have played a role in bringing this about.

Summary

There are three key reasons why Ella's Kitchen and Viacom Brand Solutions achievements stand out:

Vision

Both companies showed foresight in identifying how to tackle their respective issues. For different reasons adding value to parents' and children's lives through the consumption of healthy foods was a cause they both sought to champion.

Innovation

One of the underlying themes of this case study is innovation. Wherever one looks there's innovation – the initial product idea, the distinctive packaging, the unique shared risk arrangement, the differentiated targeting of kids, the congruent approach to creative and media placement.

Performance

Ultimately this of course is the acid test. And in this respect, the campaign does not disappoint. The focussed advertising investment with Nickelodeon over three years of just £0.5 million represents less than 0.1 per cent of food and drink category advertising expenditure (Ad Dynamix), and yet the brand generated £13.5 million in revenue. Despite significant increases in distribution and being in its fourth year of trading the brand's rate of sale continues to grow. And crucially a very close bond appears to have been developed between the brand and its customers. For VBS, as well as generating £0.5 million incremental revenue, the Ella's Kitchen initiative has clearly demonstrated the power of TV to positively change behaviour, enabled us to pitch successfully to new food manufacturers, and to lobby the government into behaving more collaboratively.

The last word

We forged a groundbreaking shared risk advertising relationship with Viacom Brand Solutions to achieve such deep and wide awareness among kids. The way we have worked with them has generated much trade comment and praise, together with industry awards. Our advertising is viewed by over 66 per cent of kids in the UK – and seen in an environment that they own and in a language that they understand.

In securing the early support and commitment of VBS and Nickeldoeon since 2006, under the unique risk sharing model, the company secured over £500,000 of advertising airtime on their channels, and shared revenues and sales information as part of a partnership approach. Without doubt this arrangement has driven our marketing strategy. The partnership continues!

Paul Lindley, Founder Ella's Kitchen

Notes

*   Ad Dynamix
†   All sales data is provided by Sainsbury's
‡   Provided by Sainsbury's
\>   Ad Dynamix

CASE STUDY QUESTIONS

1. Critique this case study. What factors do you believe led to the campaign's success?
2. Are there any ethical issues associated with the campaign? If so, how well do you believe they were addressed? What would you recommend be done differently in the future and why?
3. What lessons do you believe government regulators may take from this case study? The case study authors noted the hope of influencing future regulation – how much impact do you believe this case may have had?
4. Critique the ROI data presented – how might their evaluation strategies be improved for the future?
5. What recommendations would you make to VBS regarding future collaborations? What organizations would you specifically recommend they do not enter into collaborative ventures with and why?

CASE STUDY 5.2

Creativity through the use of non-conventional media

Creativity in marketing communication can be exhibited in many forms; from the creation of a whole concept to the selection of individual media. One particular area of growth is the use of non-mainstream art in advertising.

Non-mainstream art can take many forms. The professional use of graffiti is increasingly commonplace as brands seek to communicate their relevance to their target market.

Recently, in the US, McDonalds has used graffiti as part of a strategy to consumers of Latino extraction. Ken Ebo, McDonalds' Regional Marketing Director, was quoted as saying

'We wanted something [that reflects] the lifestyle of the Hispanic consumer'. Whilst on the face of it, this might appear a rather clumsy attempt at negative stereotyping, the use of the 'Mi Encanta' slogan ('I'm loving it') together with a semi-permanent and well-executed depiction of the New York skyline makes this a rather elegant piece of communication. Its distinctive style and durability also suggest that this is a very astute choice of medium.

Rather than using graffiti to create an image on a wall or other medium and obscure the surface, there have also been instances in which the artists have interacted with the medium to enhance the message. An excellent example of this is the award-winning campaign by TBWA/Paris Outdoor in their campaign for K2R stain removers. They used stains and marks found on the ground in public areas and stencilled the outline of a piece of clothing around them with the simple statement 'Try K2R'. Not only was this a clever use of the physical environment, but it was visually striking and clearly communicated the benefits of the K2R brand.

In contrast there has also been growth in what is known as 'reverse graffiti' advertising; where artists use the medium of dirty surfaces and key locations, cleaning it in a way that reveals a logo or a message. UK reverse-graffiti artist Paul Curtis, aka 'Moose' is particularly well known in this field and has done work for HP, Xbox and Big Brother.

However, the use of graffiti as a medium for advertising is not without its pitfalls. Whilst some see graffiti as an art form, others see it simply as vandalism. Indeed, the concept of graffiti itself is an anathema in some societies as Nike, the sports brand, found out to its cost. It was reported that in Singapore, a country with a strong tradition of orderliness, up to 50 people complained that their bus stops had suffered from acts of vandalism. However, it transpired the ads, featuring US basketball star LeBron James, were designed to look like they had been posted over other ads. Obviously their design was just a little too convincing – they really did look like graffiti and it was this that sparked the complaints.

Both Coca-Cola and Pepsi have also suffered from misplaced graffiti. Both companies were questioned by India's Supreme Court about adverts painted onto the rock face of the Himalayas. Not only was concern raised of the ecological damage of the graffiti itself but also the potential damage that might be inflicted by the solvents required to clean it. In their defence, both companies claimed that the graffiti was out of their control because the business in the region was controlled by franchisees.

CASE STUDY QUESTIONS

1. To what extent is graffiti a creative medium for marketing communication?
2. What factors do you think contribute to the relative effectiveness of graffiti as a medium of marketing communication?
3. Discuss the relative benefits and pitfalls of using graffiti as a creative technique.
4. What kind of brands are best suited to the use of graffiti? Are there any that are not?
5. Cultural differences mean that graffiti is more acceptable as a medium of communication in some cultures than in others. What other forms of 'non-mainstream' forms suffer from the same difficulty?

Notes

1   Amabile, T.M. (1988). A model of creativity and innovation in organizations. *Research in Organizational Behaviour*, 10, 123–67, cited in Klebba, J.M., and Tierney, P. (1995). Advertising creativity: a review and empirical investigation of external evaluation, cognitive style and self-perceptions of creativity. *Journal of Current Issues in Research in Advertising*, 17(2), 33–52.

2   Kilgour, M., and Koslow, S. (2009). Why and how do creative thinking techniques work? Trading off originality and appropriateness to make more creative advertising. *Journal of the Academy of Marketing Science*, 37, 298–309.

3   West, D.C., Kover, A.J., and Caruana, A. (2008). Practitioner and customer views of advertising creativity: same concept, different meaning? *Journal of Advertising*, 37(4: Winter), 35–45.

4   Ang, S.H., Lee, Y.H., and Leong, S.M. (2007). The ad creativity cube: conceptualization and initial validation. *Journal of the Academy of Marketing Science*, 35(2), 220–32.

5   Runco, M.A., and Charles, R. (1992). Judgments of originality and appropriateness as predictors of creativity. *Personality and Individual Differences*, 15(5), 537–46.

6   Kilgour, M., and Koslow, S. (2009). Why and how do creative thinking techniques work? Trading off originality and appropriateness to make more creative advertising. *Journal of the Academy of Marketing Science*, 37, 298–309.

7   Smith, R.E., Mackenzie, S.B., Yang, X., Buchholz, L., and Darley, W.K. (2007). Modelling the determinants and effects of creativity in advertising. *Marketing Science*, 26(6), 819–33.

8   Smith, R.E., Chen, J., and Yang, X. (2008). The impact of advertising creativity on the hierarchy of effects. *Journal of Advertising*, 37(4), 48.

9   Till, B.D., and Baack, D.W. (2001). Recall and persuasion: does creative advertising matter? *Journal of Advertising*, 34(3), 47–57.

10 Wright, M. (1985). Schema schema: consumers' intuitive theories about marketers' influence tactics. *Advances in Consumer Research*, 13, 1–3.

11 Petty, R.E., Cacioppo, J.T., and Schumann, D. (1983). Central and peripheral routes to advertising effectiveness: the moderating role of involvement. *Journal of Consumer Research*, September, 135–46.

12 Till, B.D., and Baack, D.W. (2001). Recall and persuasion: does creative advertising matter? *Journal of Advertising*, 34(3), 47–57.

13 Dahlen, M., Rosengren, S., and Torn, F. (2008). Advertising creativity matters. *Journal of Advertising Research*, September, 392–403.

14 Chung, H., and Zhau, X. (2003). Humour effect on memory and attitude: moderating role of product involvement. *International Journal of Advertising*, 22, 117–44.

15 Edell, J.A., and Burke, M.C. (1987). The power of feelings in understanding advertising effects. *Journal of Consumer Research*, 14, December, 421–33.

16 Chung, H., and Zhau, X. (2003). Humour effect on memory and attitude: moderating role of product involvement. *International Journal of Advertising*, 22, 117–44.

17 De Mooij, M. (1998). *Global Marketing and Advertising: Understanding Cultural Paradoxes*, Thousand Oaks, CA: Sage Publications.

18 Gould, S. (1994). Sexuality and ethics in advertising: a research agenda and policy guideline perspective. *Journal of Advertising*, 23(1), 73–80.

19 Lass, P., and Hart, S. (2004). National cultures, values and lifestyles influencing consumers' perception towards sexual imagery in alcohol advertising: an exploratory study in the UK, Germany and Italy. *Journal of Marketing Management*, 20, 607–23.

20 Fetto, J. (2001). Where's the lovin'? *American Demographics*, 23, 10–11.

21 Reichert, T. (2003). The prevalence of sexual imagery in ads targeted to young adults. *Journal of Consumer Affairs*, 37(2), 403–12.

22 Fetto, J. (2001). Where's the lovin'? *American Demographics*, 23, 10–11.

23 La Tour, M.S., and Henthorne, T.L. (1993). Female nudity: attitudes toward the ad and the brand, and the implications for advertising strategy. *The Journal of Consumer Marketing*, 10(3), 317–38.

24 Severn, J., Belch, G.E., and Belch, M.A. (1990). The effects of sexual and non sexual advertising appeals and information level on cognitive processing and communication effectiveness. *Journal of Advertising*, 19(1), 14–22.

25 Harrison, K., and Cantor, J. (1997). The relationship between media consumption and eating disorders. *Journal of Communication*, 47(1), 40–67.

26 MacKay, N.S., and Covell, K. (1997). The impact of women in advertisements on attitudes toward women, *Sex Roles*, 36(6/7) 573–89.

27 Duke, C.R., Pickett, G.M., Carlson, L., and Grove, S.J. (1993). A method of evaluating the ethics of fear appeals. *Journal of Public Policy and Marketing*, 12(1), 120–9.

28 Daily Mail online (2008). The Graphic Image that Warns Binge-drinking Women they Could End Up Looking Like a Man. Online. Available HTTP: <http://dailymail.co.uk/news/article-1023844/The-graphic-image-warns-binge-women-end-looking-like-man.html#ixzz0nWt7Xv2O> (accessed 8 June 2008).

29 Rogers, R.W. (1975). A protection motivation theory of fear appeals and attitude change. *Journal of Psychology*, 93, 93–114.

30 Arthur, D., and Quester, P. (2004). Who's afraid of that ad? Applying segmentation to the protection motivation model. *Psychology and Marketing*, 21(9), 671–96.

31 Braunsberger, K., and Munch, J.M. (1998). Source expertise versus experience effects in hospital advertising, *Journal of Services Marketing*, 12(1), 23–8.

32 Wood, Z. (2009). Milky Bar Kid Rides Out Again as Tough Times Send Shoppers on Nostalgia Trip, *The Guardian*, 12 May. Online. Available HTTP: <http://theguardian.com/media/2009/may/12/nostalgic-advertising-milky-bar-kid-persil-hovis> (accessed 14 April 2014).

33 Van Hiel, A., and Mervielde, I. (2003). The need for closure and the spontaneous use of complex and simple cognitive structures. *The Journal of Social Psychology*, 143(5), 559–68.

34 Solomon, M., Bamossy, G., and Askegaard, S. (2002). *Consumer Behaviour: A European Perspective*, London: Prentice Hall.

35 Percy, L., and Elliot, R. (2005). *Strategic Advertising Management*, Oxford: Oxford University Press.

36 Bloomsberg Businessweek (2010). I Smell an Ad Campaign. Online. Available HTTP: <http://images.businessweek.com/ss/08/07/0731_btw/2.htm> (accessed 23 July 2010).

37 Osborn, A.F. (1957). *Applied Imagination: Principles and Procedures of Creative Thinking*, New York: Scribner.

38 Taylor, D.W., Berry, P.C., and Block, C.H. (1958). Does group participation when using brainstorming facilitate or inhibit creative thinking? *Administration Science Quarterly*, 3(1: June), 23–47.

39 Pricken, M. (2009). *Creative Advertising*, London: Thames and Hudson.

40 Pricken, M. (2009). *Creative Advertising*, London: Thames and Hudson.

41 Pricken, M. (2009). *Creative Advertising*, London: Thames and Hudson.

42 http://asa.org.uk.

43 Kover, A.J., James, W.L., and Sonner, B.S. (1997). To whom do creatives write? An inferential answer. *Journal of Advertising Research*, 37(1), 41–53.

6 The IMC client–agency relationship

LEARNING OUTCOMES

After studying this chapter, you will be able to:

- Accurately describe the industry structure
- Explain and distinguish between the relative roles assumed by client and agency organizations
- Identify the key challenges faced within a client–agency relationship

Introduction

It is often the case that, in the study of the field of integrated marketing communications, an area that is essential for anyone seeking to enter the industry is often ignored; the industry structure and the challenges posed by the client–agency relationship. Understanding the role of the various players within the market is an essential precursor to being able to manage them effectively. To this end, this chapter discusses the structure of the marketing industry, clearly distinguishes between the concepts of 'client' and 'agency' and considers the various roles within the industry. It outlines the briefing and pitching process through which client organizations identify the most appropriate agencies for a given task and then discusses the challenges that arise as a result of the client–agency relationship.

The structure of the marketing industry

The client–agency dynamic

Organizations that function within the marketing industry can be roughly divided into two camps; those that are 'client' and those that are 'agency'. 'Client' organizations, simply defined, are those in possession of a particular product or service with the objective of marketing it to a group of customers or consumers. To achieve this objective, they employ an outside organization or 'agency' with specialist skills to conceive and implement some form of marketing activity on their behalf. By contrast, 'agencies' are the organizations that offer their expertise and service in one or more fields of marketing. On the basis of the client's stated objectives, they offer strategic and creative advice as to how such objectives might be achieved and how much such a programme of activity might cost. If awarded the business, agencies create and execute the campaign and are often involved in the analysis of the results.

Within the context of the client–agency dynamic, the fact that the agency is employed to undertake work on behalf of the client means that the relationship between the two organizations is more complicated than the classic vendor–seller relationship. In effect, the dynamic may be viewed as not so much a transaction but more of a symbiosis or partnership[1] in which the two parties are mutually dependent upon each other. This being the case, it is essential that positive and effective working relationships are established between the participant organizations as clear links have been proven between strong inter-organizational relationships and positive business performance.[2] However, the situation is often complicated when client organizations employ multiple agencies to supply their marketing requirements. Clients are often forced to mediate between agencies vying for restricted budgets whilst agencies find themselves in uncomfortable alliances with their fellow competitors.

The client-side management structure

'Client' organizations can take many forms, from large multi-nationals such as The Coca-Cola Corporation, which market a variety of brands across all continents, to sole traders catering for localized markets. Regardless of their size or scope, all organizations have a requirement to accurately, effectively and efficiently communicate the values and benefits of their products and services to their target market.

Classically, within client organizations, the various roles associated with the integrated marketing communications process are allied with specific layers of management (Figure 6.1). Within smaller organizations, individuals may assume one or more roles, whereas

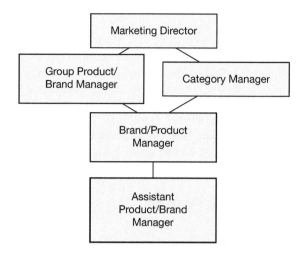

Figure 6.1 The client-side management roles associated with the integrated marketing communications process

within larger multinationals there may be multiple management strings, each associated to a brand or product line, depending upon its size or value. Brand Managers, as guardians of all aspects of their allotted brands, are primarily responsible for the day-to-day direction and management of the integrated marketing communications process. Aided by their Assistant (sometimes called Junior) Brand Managers, they are usually responsible for setting communications objectives, briefing communications agencies, monitoring the process, managing budgets and evaluating campaign results.

Monitoring the performance of Brand Managers is the job of the Product/Brand Group or Category Manager. The Product/Brand Group or Category Manager holds overall responsibility for the broader management and coordination of an organization's portfolio of complementary or competing brands[3] and is primarily focussed upon maximizing **efficiency** of resources and supply chain management issues. Product/Brand Group or Category Managers monitor the relative market position of brands within an organization's portfolio and identify where effort and resources are being duplicated. Also, managers at this level continually monitor changes in the market such as alterations in consumer tastes and preferences, new product and brand developments and competitor marketing communications strategies. They are therefore in a position to work with Brand Managers to coordinate marketing activity across an organization's **brand portfolio** to ensure that opportunities are being maximized whilst threats minimized.

Finally, from a client-side perspective, the Marketing Director holds overall responsibility for the performance of marketing-related activity within an organization. Whilst not directly involved with the integrated marketing communications process on a day-to-day basis, the Marketing Director is responsible for translating the corporate mission statement and objectives into marketing and communication objectives. He or she is then answerable for their successful implementation across the organization's marketing management hierarchy.

Agencies and their management structure

Traditionally, agencies were known as either 'above the line' or 'below the line'; a term derived from the way that, historically, agencies charged for their services. The 'line' in

THINK BOX

Desperately seeking Brand Managers

A recent job advertisement for the role of Brand Manager read as follows:

> Reporting to the Marketing Director, you will lead the development of a strategic marketing plan that maintains our brand's leading position by maximizing customer value and generating opportunities across all UK **distribution channels**. You should have a thorough understanding of the key issues in the market and be able to demonstrate a strong track record of managing integrated communication strategies to target key customer segments. Utilizing all aspects of the marketing mix, you will play a key role in the management and coordination of a portfolio of external agencies and sales teams, based both in the UK and abroad, to ensure global consistency of the brand.

On the basis of the advertisement detailed here, what do you believe to be the personal and professional characteristics required for a candidate for this role? Consider the extent to which you possess these characteristics. What might you do to remedy any areas of potential weakness?

question relates to the one that appears upon an organization's balance sheet and delineates the origin of funds that have contributed to the profit or loss account from those that relate to its distribution. Items that were deemed 'above the line' include posters, television and radio advertising; indeed any media upon which agencies added **commission** for buying the media in addition to the costs of production. Marketing activity such as sales promotion and direct marketing were considered 'below the line' because they were billed on the basis of cost without the addition of commission.

Over the last 20 years, changes in the services offered by agencies and the way that they charge for them has resulted in the original meaning of **above the line** and **below the line** being almost obscured. In some corners of the industry, agencies have broadened the number of services that they offered to include both ATL and BTL and the term **through the line** or TTL emerged to reflect this. Indeed, the growing recognition of the value associated with a more integrated approach to communications programmes has resulted in the emergence of the '**full service**' **agency** that client companies can use: a 'one stop shop' for marketing communications.

For clients, the use of full service agencies has the potential benefit of saving time, effort and money on two counts. Firstly, time and effort can be more efficiently used as there is only one point of contact with whom to meet and liaise over the course of a campaign. In addition, a full service agency has a full marketing communications tool kit at its disposal and therefore has the potential to implement the most effective creative and media strategies to achieve the client's objectives.

However, whilst the full service option has the potential to offer clients a simple and time-efficient communications solution, such agencies are subject to the 'jack of all trades, master of none' phenomenon. Whilst they might be competent in all areas, a lack of specialization means that they struggle to remain at the 'cutting edge' of the field either because of a lack of specific expertise, an unwillingness to invest in untested areas or fears over levels of profitability.

To fill this gap, there is a major role in the market for specialist agencies. Specialist agencies take one of two forms:

1.   Agencies that focus upon a single type of market that is either difficult to access or has unusual characteristics, for example, sports marketing or youth marketing.
2.   Agencies that focus upon the specialist provision of a limited range of marketing tools (for example, Internet marketing, sales promotion or direct marketing).

Agencies that focus upon specific areas in the market offer the benefit of specialist market knowledge, contacts and a raft of market experience that allow them to formulate and execute effective campaigns without having to go through the learning curve that more generalist agencies often have to face. In contrast, agencies that specialize in the use of specific marketing tools have the potential to offer clients specialist knowledge, access to the most up-to-date technology and production-related economies of scale as they buy regularly within a limited range of media.

Whilst it might be tempting for client organizations to seek specialists in each area of marketing communications in an effort to maximize the quality of their communications output, such an approach has three key drawbacks. Firstly, from a management point of view, the time and effort involved in briefing and managing a variety of agencies is likely to be high, therefore eating into the time that the Brand Manager has to perform other aspects of the role such as forecasting, product development and liaison with other departments within the organization. In addition to time, it is likely that management costs will also be higher as each agency will have its own management team (depicted in Figure 6.2) whose time will have to be financed out of the cost of the project. Finally, a number of difficulties arise in assuring that a marketing communications campaign involving a number of different agencies will take a truly integrated form. The onus falls upon the Brand Manager to ensure that all of the agencies involved not only have an identical understanding of the objectives of the campaign together with their role within it, are willing to liase with each other throughout and are willing to put the client's communications objectives ahead of their own profit motivation. We will see later on in this chapter that this is not always the case!

The typical agency structure

Within any agency, there are up to four key departments that work together on specific client accounts, which are depicted in Figure 6.2.

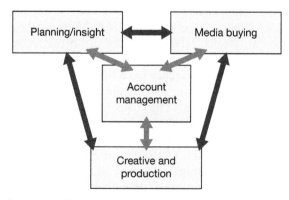

Figure 6.2 Agency departments that work on client accounts

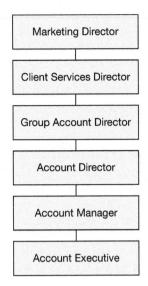

Figure 6.3 A typical agency account management structure

The **account management** team has a hierarchical structure, which is responsible for the logistical and financial management of the account and acts as the primary point of contact between the agency and its clients (Figure 6.3). Generally, within agencies, client accounts are managed on a day-to-day basis by a team of the Account Director, Account Manager and their Account Executive. They are responsible for meeting with clients in order to take a 'brief'; a set of objectives or a desired outcome that requires an integrated marketing communications solution. They then work with the other departments in the agency (Figure 6.2) to formulate a response in the form of a costed and timed proposal that they then present back to the client for consideration.

The account team report to the Group Account Director who has a responsibility for a number of complementary or potentially competing accounts. It is the Group Account Director's role to identify any areas of expertise within the team that might be exploited, to manage the resources across their teams and to spot potential conflicts of interest and avert such difficulties before they arise. The Group Account Director reports to the Client Services Director who, in turn, reports to the Managing Director. The Client Services Director works with the Managing Director to translate the broader business objectives of the organization into workable objectives for the Group Account and Account Directors, and monitor and manage their implementation. Furthermore, it is generally the Client Service Director who takes an overview of all the client-based business to identify systemic strengths and weaknesses and implement strategies to capitalize on the former and rectifying the latter through additional resources and/or training.

Given the client brief, the role of the Planning/Insight Department is to undertake a detailed business analysis and propose a strategy that will most effectively achieve the client's objectives. They are then involved throughout the campaign processes in such areas as the testing of concepts and ideas, the ongoing analysis of responses and the ultimate evaluation of the campaign as a whole.

Unlike the account teams, the management structures associated with Planning Departments are much less traditionally established. Planning Directors are now common in most large agencies and head up departments that comprise individuals with varying titles depending upon the agency in question: 'Consultants', 'Senior Planners', 'Junior Planners' and 'Analysts' are regularly found. Generally however, a team comprised of at least a senior and junior member is attached to each account management team to provide them with ongoing, analytical and strategic support at each stage of the communications campaign process.

Planning/ Insight Departments also work closely with other departments in the agency to ensure that they too can work effectively. For example, it is essential that the Planning Department liaises with the Creative Department to provide them with key aspects of data that they will need to inform their creative processes. This includes profiles of market dynamics, competitor companies and key consumer segments. Of particular interest are target consumers' lifestyle, behavioural, demographic and psychographic data that enable the Creative Department to formulate creative strategies and treatments that will satisfy the client's communication objectives.

Headed up by an overall Creative Director, Creative Departments are generally constructed of a series of creative teams, each attached to a particular client account. The composition of each creative team will depend upon the expertise required within a given sector but will usually include a Copywriter who is responsible for the written or verbal element of the communication and an Art Director or 'Creative' who is responsible for the presentation and non-verbal element. They liaise closely with the Production Team who, depending upon their capacity, resources and expertise, focus upon the production elements, ranging from basic mock-ups to the fully finished communication vehicle.

As with the other departments, the Creative Department does not operate in isolation. Not only do they remain in constant communication with the Account Management team to ensure that their creative treatments reflect the client's objectives but they also work directly with the Media Buying Department to ensure that the format in which they are produced will work across their chosen media.

The role of the Media Buyer is to negotiate for and buy the media that will be used to communicate the marketing message. Taking the Planning/ Insight Department's analysis into account, together with the client's objective and budget, the Media Buyer will identify and purchase the most appropriate mix, taking into account not only what media is to be used but where and how it might be accessed by the target audience. The model cited here assumes that a typical agency has the capacity to buy media in-house. However, increasingly, economies of scale are encouraging agencies to outsource their media buying facility to larger, specialist companies who can buy large amounts of media at more competitive rates.

The agency structure portrayed here is a very generalized one and obviously will differ from organization to organization. In addition, as in the case of client organizations, the number of people doing a single role or the number of roles being fulfilled by a single person can vary. It is largely dependent upon two factors: the size of the agency and the monetary value of the client account. Generally, the greater the value of the account the more resources an agency is willing to employ to manage it. However, whilst the job titles may vary, the types of role and responsibility will remain largely the same. Also, as in the case of media buying, some elements can be contracted out to specialist companies to take advantage of higher levels of expertise and their ability to buy in bulk.

The client–agency process

Within the client–agency process, there are six key points that determine whether an agency will be 'awarded' a client's business or, indeed, whether they choose to take it.

1 The brief

When a client organization identifies a need to implement an integrated marketing communications programme, the first stage is to issue a 'brief'. Ideally, a brief is a clearly structured document that contains all the information a communications agency would need to adequately respond with a strategic integrated communications solution given the timescales involved. At the very least, a brief should include the following:

- Key organizational information: organizational profile, organizational objectives, outline of all brands within the company portfolio, broad marketing objectives.
- Market information: a market overview including market growth figures, key competitors, market share, potential substitutes.
- Brand specific information: the name of the brand/brand extensions involved together with pictures and samples, a history of the brand and the communications strategy to date.
- A detailed profile of the target market(s).
- Clear and measureable objectives for the proposed campaign.
- A budget.
- Clearly stated time-scales: when an agency response is required and when the campaign is proposed to take place.

The brief should be received by an agency's account management team and copies immediately distributed to all those within an organization that are likely to work either on the agency response or, if awarded, on the business itself. This enables anyone on the team to feed questions back to the account management team who, in turn, can raise them with the client for clarification prior to the official response.

MINI CASE: TOO POSH FOR MAINSTREAM EXPERTISE?

In August 2009, it was reported in the UK advertising journal 'Campaign' that Burberry, the high fashion brand, had hired the ad agency Bartle Bogle Hegarty (BBH) to provide strategic support and to revolutionize their digital marketing efforts. Traditionally, fashion houses have shied away from the use of mainstream agencies as they were thought to lack the subtlety and insight required to communicate with consumers of luxury brands. According to Janet Carpenter, General Manager of Atelier, Leo Burnett's agency that specializes in luxury products:

> Mainstream agencies can still be a little too obvious in their general advertising, and obvious campaigns just don't work for high-end brands because luxury consumers don't want to be advertised to.

However, the previous year's recessionary economic climate highlighted the need for fashion houses to rethink their approach. Consumers' attitudes towards luxury brands appear to have altered and, whilst still prepared to pay a premium for the designer names, they are doing so with less frequency and with a greater amount of thought. Further, it was thought that the rather insular nature of the fashion industry and its tendency to rely on in-house creatives had generated two additional problems. The internally focussed nature of the in-house department resulted in some loss of objectivity and a lack of expertise, particularly with regard to potential benefits of digital technology. The concern that digital technology did not have the potential to create the intimacy desired by the design houses was quickly being outweighed by the fear that they were being made to look outdated by their High Street rivals.

For BBH, the challenge is twofold: to develop the brand experience whilst still retaining its integrity and prestige and to develop a digital presence that not only matches the day-to-day experience that its customers have come to expect from brands such as Amazon and eBay, but exceeds it in a way that corresponds with the premium nature of the brands.

Taking the role of the Brand Manager for Burberry, what do you believe to be the greatest challenge when briefing an agency like BBH? What information should be included in the briefing document? What suggestions do you have for overcoming the two key challenges?

---

2 The 'pitch'

Once a response has been formalized by the agency, the next stage is to meet with the client to 'pitch' their ideas. Formal pitches take place when a company is seeking to change from an existing agency or to appoint one for the first time. Alternatively, sometimes an organization has a 'roster' – a list of agencies that they use – and it is the case two or more are asked to compete or 'pitch' for the business. However, in some situations an agency is awarded all of an organization's business within given parameters and is therefore 'retained'. In such cases, a formal pitch is unnecessary and is replaced with a less formal presentation of ideas or concepts.

The number and level of seniority of people attending the pitch from either the client or agency side will depend on the perceived importance or monetary value of the business at stake. As a rule however, at the very least, those who are responsible for the day-to-day management of the business together with at least one senior manager from each side (client and agency) is likely to be present.

Pitches usually take the form of a presentation accompanied by a written proposal document and each pitch can vary in length according to the complexity of the project in question. In instances where the client has asked more than one agency to pitch for business – known as a 'competitive pitch' – clients often include a time limit on each presentation to give greater basis for comparison and also to ensure that all agencies can be given an equal chance within a limited time frame.

The content of a pitch depends upon what is required by the brief. However, features common to many pitches include:

- an introduction to the agency and overview of the agency's credentials;
- an outline of the proposed strategy linked clearly to the client's stated objectives;
- a clear strategy for campaign evaluation;
- a breakdown of the budget/costs involved;
- a detailed set of timings;
- identification of additional benefits associated with either the proposed strategy and/or employment of the agency.

Following the completion of the pitch or pitches, the client team then meets to decide to whom to offer the business. Criteria for such a decision can vary but can include:

- ability to address the campaign objectives
- levels of creativity
- cost effectiveness
- levels of professionalism
- personal affinity for the agency team.

However, if a client organization does not find the pitches satisfactory, they may ask the agency or agencies in question to re-pitch or, indeed, seek alternative agencies to pitch for the business. Conversely if, over the course of a pitch, an agency team decides that it does not want the business, they can simply turn the offer of business down. While this is rare, it does happen and is usually the result of the client making changes to the campaign or budget that renders the business potentially unprofitable.

3 Agreeing agency compensation

In any successful business relationship, both parties must feel they have either benefited or been compensated adequately. Within the client–agency relationship, the client must feel as if he or she is getting good value for money whilst the agency must feel as if it is being adequately compensated for its efforts expended on behalf of the client. Therefore, mutual satisfaction over agency compensation is an essential part of any client–agency business arrangement.

The term **agency compensation** relates to the amount of money paid to the agency by the client for its services. It has been noted that, traditionally, 'above the line' agencies took the majority of their compensation in the form of commission (traditionally 15 per cent[4]) whilst in 'below the line' agencies compensation was based upon the cost of their services. In the 1970s, fee-based systems gained popularity with project charges calculated on the basis of hourly rates, day rates, project fees or even monthly retainers.[5] However, the vagaries associated with these charging structures often raised doubts in clients' minds over the value for money they were receiving.[6] As a result, over the last 20 years there has been a strong movement towards agency accountability and this, in turn, appears to have generated two key trends.[7] In the first instance there has been a significant move away from the use of commission. Where commission is still employed it is often at a significantly lower rate and combined with some other form of remuneration. Secondly, there has been an increase in the use of performance or outcome-based incentives.

From the perspective of the client, such a shift has had the benefit of promoting greater transparency within agencies' system of fees and rewarding those who perform particularly well. However, for agencies, such a system increases the administrative workload as they have to document the time spent on each account according to campaign and provide regular evaluation reports. In addition, such a system does not build in compensation for those small, 'one-off' tasks often asked for by clients but not costed into the wider budget.

4 Managing the process

Efficient management of the campaign process is an essential criterion for a good client–agency relationship. It has already been stated that, once the business has been awarded to the agency, the account management team become responsible for the day-to-day management of the account. To ensure that the process runs smoothly, there are five key tools that need to be employed:

- *An agreed timing plan for the project* – whilst initial timings for a project should have been presented at the pitch, a more detailed timing plan should be prepared by the agency and agreed with the client as quickly as possible. The timing plan should highlight key dates and link them to actions that need to be undertaken by named individuals.
- *Progress reports* – at regular and agreed intervals, the Account Team should produce a progress report that is distributed to every member of the client and agency

team. Using the timing plan as its basis, it should clearly identify the stages of the project and whether it is running ahead or behind schedule. Where delays exist, clear reasons must be given and strategies for making up lost time suggested wherever possible.

- *An effective budget handling system* – both Brand Managers and Account Teams should have an effective system for managing and monitoring their budgets. Where additional costs arise, they must be flagged and written confirmation for approval of an increase in funding must be received from the budget holder. Ideally, the status of the budget should be included at the bottom of each and every Progress Report so that everyone involved in the project is aware of the budget status.
- *Regular meetings* – ideally Brand Managers should meet, face to face, with Account Managers and Account Directors at least once a month to discuss progress and iron out any potential problems.
- *Contact reports* – within 24 hours of every meeting, the agency's Account Manager should produce a 'Contact Report'. The report should detail exactly what was agreed during the course of the meeting, what actions are required, the named individuals responsible for undertaking those actions and the date by which specific points of action require completion. The Contact Report should be distributed immediately to all those attending the meeting and all those who are required to undertake points of action.

Using these simple tools, Brand Managers and Account Teams can ensure that everyone involved with the campaign is aware of its status at all times, knows what they are required to do and when they are required to do it and thus, the likelihood of unpleasant surprises is minimized.

5 Accountability

Agency account teams and client-side management teams are all subject to accountability. From the perspective of an agency, not only is agency compensation increasingly results-based but individual teams are assessed on their ability to retain clients and generate extra business. Brand management teams are also accountable to senior management for the effective use of their budgets and the growth and management of their brands. Therefore, careful documentation is essential for client and agency staff alike. Whilst most of this can be achieved through the Progress Reports that highlight campaign development, at the end of each and every campaign, a thorough evaluation of its relative success is required in terms the initial campaign objectives. In addition, throughout the campaign, careful note should also be taken by both client and agency alike of any additional achievements outside of the specified objectives and included in any final campaign reports.

6 The review

Ideally, a date for a formal review should be set as part of 'due diligence' procedure at the beginning of any new client–agency relationship with the aim of determining whether the objectives of all parties are being achieved over a given period of time, often three years. Within the industry, there is often the perception that a review offers an opportunity for the client whilst posing a threat to the agency. However, this is not quite true as the review offers opportunities and poses threats to both sides.

From the 'client' perspective the aim of the review is to determine whether the creative work and service levels offered by the agency are of an expected quality, whether the strategic, marketing and media objectives are being achieved and whether the relationship offers value for money. On this basis, a review offers the opportunity to re-evaluate all of the original assumptions that were in place when the agency was first appointed. If the relationship is proving unsatisfactory, action can be taken to remedy issues associated with the existing client–agency relationship or, alternatively, a new agency might be sought usually through a 'pitch'.

In contrast, reviews offer the opportunity to agencies to evaluate whether current client requirements in such areas as management hours, objectives and campaign evaluation match those that were originally negotiated in the initial contract. In addition, it gives them the chance to evaluate whether, given the work in progress, the balance of the account team in terms of skills and seniority is appropriate and sufficient to manage the client account effectively. Ultimately, however, agencies should use reviews to ascertain whether an account is profitable. If it is the case that the level of resources needed to manage a client's account is not reflected in the level of agency compensation received (agency fees), then action should be taken to renegotiate the terms of the business relationship or, in extreme cases, it is often the case that the agency resigns and a 'pitch' ensues.

Challenges associated with the management of the client–agency relationship

Whilst it has been noted that the ideal client–agency relationship should be that of a mutually beneficial partnership, sadly this is not always the case. Through the use of agency theory we can identify and understand the underlying causes of friction that often exist between agencies and their clients.[8]

At a basic level, agency theory uses the contract metaphor and relates to any situation in which one party, the client (identified in the theory as 'the principle') contracts another party (identified as 'the agent') to work on their behalf. To this end, agency theory identifies that there are two key areas of potential danger; one that exists at the point at which an agency is appointed and the other once a client–agency relationship has been established.

The first danger is known as the hidden characteristic problem.[9] The 'hidden characteristic problem' recognizes that difficulties can originate when, during the course of a pitch, an agency misleads the client, purposely or otherwise, as to their credentials and the extent to which they have the capability, capacity or even corporate culture to satisfy their side of any contract. Within the context of a competitive pitch, there is the temptation for agencies to overstate their abilities in order to win the business and unless the client has had prior experience of the agency they may take their credentials at face value.

Such a situation has the potential to generate dissatisfaction on the part of the client as, according to expectation disconfirmation theory,[10] the level of satisfaction experienced by the client is determined by the extent to which the agency lives up to the promises that it has made. Whilst it might appear a truism that client organizations are more likely to be satisfied with an agency if it meets or exceeds their expectations, conversely they are likely to be dissatisfied if they feel themselves to be misled. Therefore, in order to ensure maximum levels of client satisfaction, agencies must be realistic in the promises they make to win business.

The second area of danger is known as the hidden action problem and arises as a result of the physical distance between the client and agency together with the resulting necessity for the client to trust the agency to fulfil its promises. Without a watchful client eye, less scrupulous agencies are free to cut corners and fail to resource the account as originally promised at the pitch. In addition, they might choose to recommend strategies that generate high profit margins for the agency in preference to more effective, less profitable ones.

Overcoming the challenges of the client–agency relationship

There are four main ways that such difficulties associated with the client–agency relationship can be overcome.

1. Efforts must be made by all parties to ensure that there is an effective match between the requirements of the client organization and the abilities and culture of the agency. The most profitable relationships are often the most long-term and whilst inadequacies and conflicting priorities can be masked in the short term, over the long term, they will eventually emerge and the relationship will break down. Ultimately, in a situation in which all parties act with honesty and transparency from the outset of a business relationship, the likelihood is that the client–agency partnership is heightened.
2. Contracts between the client and the agency should be clearly structured in terms of expectation and outcome. Should the agency be required to undertake activity outside of the stated contract, the contract should be amended or a new contract agreed.
3. Agency remuneration should be of a level that fairly reflects the amount of resource required to successfully manage the campaign in question. The old adage 'you only get what you pay for' certainly applies and agencies that are offered a fair rate of return are less likely to cut corners. Clients who continually seek to drive down agency rates are likely find that their accounts will be under-resourced and prone to difficulty.
4. Constant two-way communication between client and agency is essential. Having a knowledge of what is happening within a campaign at any given point engenders a sense of confidence in clients and endows agencies with the appearance of professionalism and total competence. It's a 'win-win' situation!

MINI CASE: PEPPERAMI PITCH GOES PUBLIC

In August 2009, it was reported that Unilever, the owner of the spicy sausage snack brand Pepperami, split from its retained ad agency of 15 years, Lowe London. Rather than undertake the conventional pitch processes to appoint a new agency, Unilever launched a worldwide competition using the website www.ideabounty.com; an online community for creatives.

Contestants were issued with a brief which required them to produce creative concepts based upon the 'Animal'; a character previously created by Lowe. The winners will win a 'bounty' of £10,000 and see their ideas translated into a worldwide campaign with the help of London-based production company Smartworks.

If successful, it was suggested that Unilever would pitch out all further briefs for the Pepperami brand in a similar way, rather than appointing retained ad agency.

Why do you think that Unilever chose to adopt this approach? Discuss the benefits and potential pitfalls. Do you think that this is a suitable approach for all brands?

Summary

We have seen over the course of this chapter that, whilst it can be a rewarding partnership, the client–agency relationship can also be fraught with potential danger. Central to a good client–agency relationship is the ability to work together in a symbiotic partnership with a unified sense of purpose. This can only happen when roles are defined, objectives are unified and there is a transparency of reward that fosters a significant level of trust between two commercial organizations. When such a relationship occurs, the benefits to both client and agency have the potential to be great, both in terms of efficiency of effort and financial reward. However, when the relationship breaks down, not only can literally millions of pounds and hours of management time be wasted but brand reputations can also be destroyed. From a management perspective, there can be no greater incentive for getting the client–agency relationship right from the outset.

Review questions

1. Distinguish between the role of 'client' and 'agency'.
2. Outline the typical structure of an 'agency' and explain the role of each of the departments.
3. Discuss the main challenges faced by Brand Managers in managing the client–agency relationship.
4. What do you see as the main challenges to the success of client–agency relationship?
5. Outline a typical account management hierarchy and explain the role of each level of management.
6. What do you perceive the main value of a competitive pitch to be?
7. Define 'agency theory' and distinguish between the challenges posed by the 'hidden characteristic problem' and the 'hidden action problem'.
8. 'Communication is central to a good client–agency' relationship'. Discuss.
9. How might a performance-based method of agency compensation foster better client–agency relationships?
10. Distinguish between the terms 'above the line', 'below the line' and 'through the line' and discuss their relevance as descriptors for modern day communication agencies.

Recommended reading

Hameroff, E.J. (1997). *The Advertising Agency Business*, London: McGraw-Hill.
Pollick, D.G. (2000). *Agency: Inside the World of Advertising*, iUniverse.com.
Roetzer, P. (2012). *The Marketing Agency Blueprint: The Handbook for Building Hybrid PR, SEO, Content, Advertising, and Web Firms*, Hoboken, New Jersey: John Wiley & Sons, Inc.
Simms, M. (2005). *Working with Agencies*, Chichester: John Wiley and Sons.

CASE STUDY 6.1

Saatchi and Saatchi: when bigger isn't always better

The UK advertising agency Saatchi and Saatchi is one of the most iconic names in the marketing industry. Its roots can be traced back to 1969 and the point at which Charles Saatchi and his creative partner, Ross Cramer, left Collett Dickenson Pierce to set up their own agency Cramer Saatchi. Despite the fact that their new enterprize received early acclaim for the Health Education Council's 'The Pregnant Man' and 'What happens when a fly lands on your food' campaigns, the partnership dissolved when Cramer left to become a director of films and commercials.

In 1970, Charles was joined by his brother Maurice who had previously worked in publishing at Haymarket; the producer of Campaign, the advertising industry trade paper. Charles and Maurice then recruited Tim Bell to run the media side of the business and together they launched Saatchi and Saatchi.

At a time in which the advertising industry had developed a reputation for excess, Saatchi and Saatchi occupied a distinctive position with their platform of cost-effective creativity. Charles Saatchi developed a fiery and fearsome reputation and, in his drive for excellence, insisted his staff live up to his own standards of creativity and professionalism. At the same time Maurice set about constructing a business plan with the aim of turning Saatchi and Saatchi into the biggest advertising agency in London.

Maurice's strategy was aggressive. An unwritten industry code of conduct was that agencies refrained from poaching clients away from each other, but this made the acquisition of a portfolio of clients a very slow process. This being the case, Maurice decided to move away from convention and, having identified a priority list of target clients, 'cold called' them, asking for an opportunity to present Saatchi and Saatchi's credentials in the hope of gaining some business.

This unconventional approach was followed by a programme of highly strategic mergers and acquisitions over the next few years. They purposely targeted competing firms with lucrative, established advertising contracts including a highly prized place on the roster of Procter & Gamble, owner of multiple household brands. Not only did this rid them of some of their competitors, but it gave them a ready-made portfolio of 'blue-chip' clients. By 1975, they had vaulted themselves from the position of thirteenth largest advertising agency in the UK market to becoming the fifth and, with it, came a lucrative listing on the London Stock Exchange.

The end of the 1970s saw what many thought to be a golden period in the Saatchi and Saatchi success story. The purchase of agencies Hall Advertising and Roe and Partners positioned them as the premiere advertising agency in the UK market. In addition, they were commissioned to undertake advertising activity for the Conservative Party in the 1979 General Election and the poster campaign entitled 'Labour isn't working' received wide acclaim.

Not complacent with their achievements, the early 1980s saw a move by Saatchi and Saatchi to build upon their success. Whilst they acquired two further UK agencies in Dorland and Crawfords, their sights had shifted to the development of an international platform. A further programme of acquisition was put in place and in 1982 they bought a number of agencies in the US, including the renowned Compton Advertising for £57 million. This was followed in 1986 by the purchase of Ted Bates Worldwide for the then breath-taking sum of $507 million, making Saatchi and Saatchi the world's largest advertising agency.

Yet unfortunately size does not always equate with success. As a result of Saatchi and Saatchi's dramatic growth, a number of problems arose. In the first instance, in advertising, as with any service-based organization, much of what the organization produces, for example, creativity and production management services, are intangible. Therefore clients' decisions are based upon trust, reputation and the relationship between the client and agency teams.

In the US, despite their meteoric success, Saatchi and Saatchi were largely an unknown entity and many of Bates's clients became alarmed at this apparent invasion of the market.

In addition, large payouts to members of the Bates management teams raised questions as to the financial management and stability of the company. As a result, the newly enlarged agency lost a number of lucrative accounts including RJR Nabisco, McDonalds, Michlob and Warner-Lambert.

In addition, cracks began to appear internally. One of the original team, Tim Bell, departed having felt marginalized by the speed of expansion of the Saatchi and Saatchi empire. Martin Sorrell replaced Bell as the brothers' right hand man but soon he too left to set up his own business, WPP. In an attempt to maintain levels of creativity, large salaries were offered to attract new talent but this only served to aggravate existing staff who demanded parity of terms and conditions. Even the Saatchi brothers themselves appeared to have disengaged from the core business of advertising. They shifted their attention to the banking sector and attempted a takeover of the then troubled Midland Bank and later the investment bank Hill Samuel.

This lack of focus, together with the recessionary economic conditions of the late 1980s and early 1990s, had a visible effect upon the business with the result that a number of clients defected to competing agencies. This, together with Sorrell's WPP takeover of the advertising giant Ogilvy and Mather, resulted in Saatchi and Saatchi losing its lead position in the market. For the first time in years, the company registered a reduction in their level of profit and this, together with its precarious financial position, required the sale of some of the company's assets and the implementation of cost-cutting measures.

Over the next few years, the Saatchi brothers became increasingly marginalized within the Saatchi and Saatchi organization. In the mid-1990s, following a boardroom coup, Charles and Maurice offered their resignation from the organization they had founded and, together with a group of close colleagues, they set up a new agency which they called 'M&C Saatchi'.

Despite the fact that the Saatchi brothers' attention had long been diverted from the day-to-day running of the advertising element of the business, the impact of this defection was seismic. A number of Saatchi and Saatchi's clients found themselves unnerved by all that had happened and followed them to the new agency. Also, financially, the upheaval was potentially disastrous. It was rumoured that the client migration resulted in a loss of up to £40 million in potential billings and, together with the £11 million they were forced to pay in severance pay and litigation, the episode was extremely expensive for the Board.

In an attempt to distance itself from its turbulent past, Saatchi and Saatchi Worldwide changed its name to Cordiant. It hived off the Saatchi and Saatchi agency as a smaller, separate, independent entity and in this form it regained some of its creativity and commercial hunger. However, the combination of the iconic name, the rejuvenated commercial spirit and its comparatively diminutive size made it a ripe target for takeover and it did not stay independent for very long. In 2000, it became part of the Publicis Group, a position it has held to this day.

CASE STUDY QUESTIONS

1. Maurice Saatchi strove from the outset to turn Saatchi and Saatchi into a large agency. Discuss the relative benefits and pitfalls of being a large agency.
2. To what extent do you believe that Charles and Maurice Saatchi adopted the right strategy for their organization? What should they have done differently?
3. In this chapter, it has been established that the ideal client–agency relationship should be that of a mutually beneficial partnership. In what way might the 'highs and lows' of

the Saatchi and Saatchi story have affected their ability to maintain a partnership with their clients?

4. The 'Saatchi and Saatchi' brand has often been described as iconic in the world of advertising. Discuss why you think this might be the case.

5. What were the challenges for employees working within the Saatchi and Saatchi organization at the time? Discuss the impact that such turbulence might have had on their work.

Notes

1   Gould, S., Grein, A.F., and Lerman, D.B. (1999). The role of agency–client integrated marketing communications: a complimentary agency theory–interorganizational perspective. *Journal of Current Issues and Research in Advertising*, 21(1: Spring), 1–12.

2   Heide, J.B., and John, G. (1990). Alliances in industrial purchasing: the determinants of joint action in buyer–seller relationships. *Journal of Marketing Research*, 27(February), 24–36.

3   Morgan, N.A., Kaleka, A., and Gooner, R.A. (2007). Focal supplier opportunism in supermarket retailer category management. *The Journal of Operations Management*, 25(2), 512–27.

4   Palmer, M. (2001). A quest for accountability and value – trends in agency compensation. *The Advertiser*, May.

5   Fox, S. (1984). *The Mirror Makers*, New York: William Morrow.

6   Spake, D.F., D'Souza, G., Crutchfield, T.N., and Morgan, R.M. (1999). Advertising agency compensation: an agency theory explanation. *Journal of Advertising*, XXXVIII(3: Fall), 53–72.

7   Beals, D. (2004). Inside information – trends in agency compensation. *The Advertiser*, August.

8   Bergen, M., Dutta, S., and Walker Jr., O.C. (1992). Agency relationships in marketing: a review of the implications and applications of agency and related theories. *Journal of Marketing*, 56(July), 1–24.

9   Spake, D.F., D'Souza, G., Crutchfield, T.N., and Morgan, R.M. (1999). Advertising agency compensation: an agency theory explanation. *Journal of Advertising*, XXXVIII(3: Fall), 53–72.

10   Santos, J., and Boote, J. (2003). A theoretical exploration and model of consumer expectations, post-purchase affective states and affective behaviour. *Journal of Consumer Behaviour*, 3(2), 142–56.

7 IMC and branding

LEARNING OUTCOMES

After studying this chapter, you will be able to:

- Understand the concept of branding
- Appreciate the variety of roles that brands play within the lives of both organizations and consumers
- Understand the process by which consumers conceptualize brands
- Distinguish between the concepts of brand image and brand identity
- Recognize the value of a clear brand 'personality'
- Consider the nature of the different types of consumer–brand relationships and reflect upon their implications for IMC strategy
- Understand the challenges facing marketers when managing IMC strategies across multiple brands
- Appreciate the value that an effective IMC strategy has for marketers seeking to establish a clear brand position

Introduction

The term **brand** is one that has become increasingly common in everyday parlance over recent years. Traditionally, brands were simply a way of distinguishing one product from another but over time it has become clear that the concept is much more complex and can be applied across a wide range of contexts. For example, it is not uncommon for the media often to talk about a team's 'brand' of football or a political party's 'brand' of politics. Brands are everywhere – from tins on the supermarket shelf to 'branded' people (when ex-England football captain David Beckham moved to LA Galaxy, questions were raised about the likely impact upon the 'Beckham brand'). Successful 'branded' organizations, products and services that have developed a currency all of their own fulfil a variety of functions, for consumers and organizations alike. However, from an IMC perspective, attempts to understand the concept of branding raise a number of questions, for example, what exactly does the term 'brand' mean and how is a 'brand' created? Furthermore, once created, how do brands evolve and what are the implications for marketers? In this chapter we address all of these questions and consider the role that integrated marketing communications has to play in both the creation and evolution and management of brands.

THINK BOX

MUFC brand

On 5 April 2009, *The Times* newspaper reported that British football club Manchester United had replaced Real Madrid as the world's top football brand. What do you understand by this statement? In what ways might Manchester United Football Club be considered to be a brand?

Defining 'brands'

Over recent years, a variety of different definitions of a 'brand' have been offered by academics and marketing practitioners alike. The traditional and rather simplistic perspective is that of the brand as a form of trademark; a visual vehicle in the form of a logo with a focus on design and colour that distinguishes itself from its competitors within the marketplace.[1] Such a definition is offered by the American Marketing Association who defines a brand as:

> A name, term, design, symbol or any other feature that identifies one seller's good or service as distinct from those of other sellers[2]

However, the simplicity of this definition does little to give the student of marketing any insight into how a brand differs from a product and offers little explanation as to why a 'brand' might be of greater value than a product for consumers and organizations alike. In contrast, Jones[3] makes such a distinction with his statement that:

> A product is something with a functional purpose. A brand offers something in addition to its functional purpose. All brands are products . . . but not all products are brands.[3]

(p. 9)

Calkins[4] suggests that a logo or a brand on its own does little to add value to a product unless it is linked with a specific set of associations in the mind of the consumer or stakeholder. From an IMC perspective, whilst these associations are generated through personal experience, they can also accumulate through a variety of communications, many of which emanate from sources other than the brand owner. Indeed, according to White and de Chernatony,[5] consumers develop their conceptualizations of brands at every point at which they come into contact with a brand, either directly or indirectly. It is therefore imperative that marketers not only understand the important role of consistent communication strategy in the successful creation and management of brand, but also the potential impact that communications, outside of their control, might have on perceptions of their brands.

Why brands matter: IMC and the function of brands

Brands fulfil communications functions for both organizations and consumers

According to de Chernatony and Dall'Olmo Riley,[6] brands fulfil an important variety of legal, identificational and personal functions for organizations and consumers alike. A clearly branded product effectively implies boundaries between itself and competitor products, allowing consumers to easily distinguish between them. Consumers use brands as a form of heuristic, a mental 'rule of thumb' used by consumers when they might not be in possession of full information about a product or simply do not have the time or inclination to undertake complex cognitive evaluation processes. Brand heuristics can be communicated throughout all aspects of the classic product and service marketing mixes as can be seen in Table 7.1.

Table 7.1 Examples of brand heuristics

Element of the marketing mix	Typical heuristics
Product	Gold packaging – 'premium' Green packaging – 'ecologically sound' Large size – 'good value' Small size – 'premium' Featured product content (e.g. 'with *real* cream') – 'special'
Place	Waitrose – 'high quality product' Lidl – 'low price' Street markets – 'bargains'
Promotion	Functional free gifts/premiums – 'functional product' Premium free gifts/premiums – 'premium product'
Price	High price – 'good quality' Low price – 'lower quality'
Physical evidence	Clean, tidy offices – 'efficient, professional' Dated décor – 'old fashioned'
People	Well trained, helpful staff – 'efficient organization' Unfriendly staff – 'poor product/service'
Processes	Fast, efficient service – 'efficient organization/high quality' Slow service – 'inefficient organization/poor quality'

Brands effectively act as a form of shorthand in the communication of product quality and attributes. They have the potential to add value to the product in the eyes of the consumer in two ways. Firstly by endowing the product with attributes (either real or imaginary) the consumer feels that he or she is buying more than just a basic product. Also, by communicating the values and attributes associated with the brand, it reduces the levels of perceived risk associated with the purchase of any product or service. In both cases, consumers are likely to feel more positively disposed towards brands and are more predisposed towards purchase.

It is therefore essential that, when creating a new brand, it is achieved in a way that communicates those values and attributes distinctively and effectively. To this end, the following factors require special attention when deciding upon the choice of brand name and the characteristics of its graphic representation:

- the product's function
- the product's attributes
- the product's values
- the values of the brand owner
- logos and graphical representations associated with competitor products.

Brands as identity systems

Brands can also be used by consumers to support their self concept or underpin their personal identity systems. **Identity** may be defined as a form of self categorization.[7] According to de Mooij, 'identity' is the idea that one has about one's self, one's characteristic properties, one's own body and the values one considers to be important.[8]

Brands support consumer identity systems by using attributes of the brand to symbolically represent personal attributes or aspects of their **values system**.[9] For example, for many years, the possession of a company car was seen as a **symbol** of status amongst salespeople within organizations; the better the car, the more important the person. In this way, such a consumer is using the attributes of the brand to transmit messages outwardly to other individuals or groups of people. Alternatively, the consumption of a particular

THINK BOX

Brand logos

Look at the logo and consider the brand name itself and the way that it is portrayed. What does that communicate about the product, its attributes and the values associated with both the brand and the brand owner? How is this achieved?

Photo 7.1

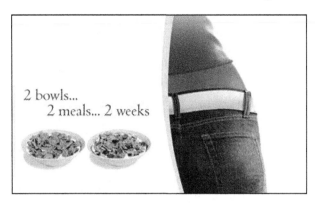

Photo 7.2

brand can be internalized to positively reinforce the consumer's self concept and levels of self esteem.[10]

The **self concept** is defined by Solomon *et al.*[11] as 'the beliefs a person holds about his or her attributes and how he or she evaluates these qualities'. The extent to which these attributes are positively or negatively evaluated is described as **self esteem**. The relative positivity of and individual's self esteem is dependent upon what that consumer perceives to be his or her ideal state or the 'ideal self'. Where a consumer sees that consumption of a brand or selection of brands might support their efforts to achieve that 'ideal', they will make appropriate choices. Take, for example the Kellogg's Special K brand and, particularly, the 'Drop a Jeans Size in Two Weeks' campaign (Photo 7.2). Having recognized the 'ideal' of a slim body in a segment of consumers, Kellogg's positioned the brand as a tool that might be used to lose weight. This proposition was reinforced in their post-New Year campaign that moved the brand from being a supporting 'tool' in consumers' attempts at weight loss, to being the main plank in a specific and branded 'Kellogg's Special K' diet programme.

The **ideal self** is not the only element that comprises the self concept that needs to be taken into consideration when creating an IMC campaign aimed at a specific target market; a number of other 'selves' have also been identified in academic literature (Figure 7.1).[12]

The **actual self**, the way that consumers perceive themselves to actually be (anecdotally described as the 'warts and all self'), acts as the anchoring point from which they locate themselves within their world. In contrast, the 'looking glass self' can be explained as the way that consumers would like others to see them. The '**looking glass self**' is particularly influential in situations in which an individual's consumption choice is on view to others, for example, when buying a dress for a party. In such a case, the consumer will take into account the likely reaction of others when making a brand choice. In contrast, the '**extended self**' reflects the way that consumers use things external to themselves to give themselves an identity. It is often the case that, when asked to describe themselves, they will do so in terms of their family role (i.e. 'mother', 'son', 'daughter' etc.), hobbies (i.e. 'dog owner', 'stamp collector' etc.) or their job (i.e. 'doctor', 'hair stylist', 'bus driver'). The **negative self**, in stark contrast to the other 'selves', comprises those attributes that consumers do not want to be associated with.

Instances of the extended, looking glass and negative selves are regularly exhibited amongst groups of football fans. Football fans can be so fanatical about their affiliation with a single club that they define themselves as a 'Chelsea fan' or an 'Arsenal fan' and in this way, the club becomes part of their 'extended self'. The 'looking glass self' is visible itself when football fans adorn themselves with scarves, team strip and other badges of affiliation to a specific team and the 'negative' self when fans of football disassociate themselves with football hooligans who, they say, go to football games not to watch the match, but simply to fight.

An appreciation of the variety of 'selves' that comprise the self concept is particularly important within the context of IMC for two reasons. Firstly, in understanding consumers' 'actual' and 'ideal' self, marketers can gain an appreciation of the goals that consumers are striving for. They are then in a position to both develop brands that can support consumers in their efforts, and communicate the benefits that their brands can offer consumers seeking to achieve their ideal. Secondly, the variety of 'selves' that underpin the self concept are driven by a system of values and it is recognized that consumers will be drawn to brands whose values coincide with their own and conversely they will actively avoid those that run counter to them. From a communications perspective, it is essential therefore to ensure that the values communicated in any IMC campaign clearly coincide with those of the target audience.

Brands as relationship partners

De Chernatony and Dall'Olmo Riley also recognize the fact that brands have the potential to fulfil relational roles for consumers. Such a perspective goes beyond exchange-based theory and relationship marketing theories normally associated with marketing and proposes that consumers not only obtain functional benefit from brand transactions, but potentially offer psychological and emotional benefits as well. In analysing the variety of relationships that existed between consumers and brands, Fournier developed a typology that identified 15 different types (see Table 7.2).[13]

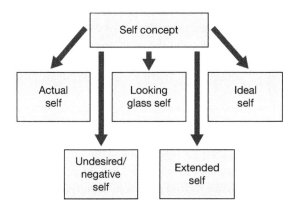

Figure 7.1 An illustration of the variety of 'selves' identified in academic literature

Table 7.2 Fournier's typology of consumer–brand relationships

Relationship type	Definition	Example
Arranged marriages	Non-voluntary union imposed by a third party.	When sharing a flat, the type of washing up liquid is determined by the person who does the shopping.
Casual friendships	Low levels of intimacy; characterized by infrequent and irregular use and low levels of expected reciprocity.	When choosing a snack food, a consumer may choose one brand of crisps one day and a different one the next.
Marriages of convenience	Long-term committed relationship precipitated by environmental factors.	Having moved to a new area, a householder finds that there is only one company that offers a doorstep delivery of milk.
Committed partnership	Long-term relationship. High levels of love and intimacy. Socially supported and committed to stay together despite adverse circumstances.	When a consumer particularly enjoys a brand of premium coffee and is prepared to make sacrifices in the family budget to ensure that he or she can continue to drink it when money becomes short.
Best friendships	Voluntary union based on the principle of reciprocity. Characterized by mutual reward, honesty and intimacy.	Consumers become loyal to a brand of shampoo because it recognizes their shortcomings (i.e. greasy hair/dandruff etc.) and they feel they can rely on it to make their hair look good.
Compartmentalized friendships	Relationships are specialized and situationally confined.	Consumers who only drink eggnog or mulled wine at Christmas.
Kinships	Non-voluntary union with lineage lines.	Teenagers who, on first leaving home, use the same brand of washing powder or toothpaste as their parents did when at home.
Rebounds	Relationship precipitated by the desire to move away from another partner.	People who, on giving up smoking, develop an attachment to a particular brand of sweet.
Childhood friendships	Infrequently engaged relationship based heavily upon nostalgia. Yields comfort and security.	When people buy a brand of jelly out of nostalgia because is was the sort of food they had as a child.
Courtships	An interim relationship state on the road to a more committed partnership.	When someone tries a new brand and likes it but are yet to be totally convinced.
Dependencies	Obsessive, highly emotional. Separation leads to anxiety. Strong feeling that the other is irreplaceable.	Brands that people feel that they cannot live without.
Flings	Time-bounded engagements with high emotional reward but devoid of commitment and reciprocity.	When a consumer breaks up with a boyfriend or girlfriend, he or she indulges in comfort eating with a favoured brand of ice-cream.
Enmities	Negative relationship based upon a desire to avoid or inflict pain on the other.	A consumer boycotts a brand because he or she feels that it has behaved badly or unethically.
Secret affairs	Highly emotive, privately held relationship considered risky if exposed to others.	A member of a diet club who secretly indulges in a love of chocolate.
Enslavements	Non-voluntary relationship that exists because of circumstances that results in a lack of alternative. Involves negative feelings.	Where a consumer is limited to a provider of mobile phone service operator because of a limited signal despite the fact that they feel it is inferior.

An appreciation of the type and characteristics of consumers' relationships with brands is imperative for IMC practitioners when formulating both communication strategy and creative execution. It is important that the timing of the communications, the creative style and the tone of voice should differ according to the relationship type. In order to speak to consumers in a tone and manner they will respond to, the choice of all of these should be tailored appropriately.

Brands as personalities

It has been posited that one of the reasons why consumers have the capacity to develop relationships with brands is their tendency to anthropomorphize inanimate objects.[14] It is common for people to treat pets such as dogs or cats as surrogate children and, from an early age, children endow inanimate objects with life-like attributes in the form of such things as pet rocks. Into adult life, people regularly assign a gender to objects like boats or cars by referring to them as 'he' or 'she' or even give them names.

The creation of **brand personality** is a major challenge for IMC practitioners. Personality can be created via a number of platforms, from the design of the packaging to the choice of media and the content of the creative concepts. Aaker (1997) identified five primary dimensions of brand personality, each associated with specific characteristics. In order to be effectively created, practitioners of marketing should first identify which type of brand personality they wish to convey and then communicate it consistently through all aspects of the integrated campaign. Failure to do so will leave consumers confused as they perceive poorly conceived brands to be lacking in credibility and suffering from a form of 'brand schizophrenia'.

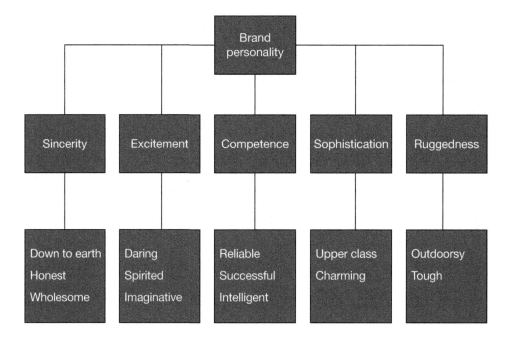

Figure 7.2 Aakers' (1997) Dimensions of Brand Personality[21]

MINI CASE: BUD'S FROGS

One of the easiest ways of endowing a brand with a personality is to associate it with a character or set of characters that the target market will engage and identify with. In the case of Anheuser-Busch, in an attempt to engage with their target audience of the 20-something males, they generated a campaign that contained a series of ads based around a group of frogs. The underpinning idea was to generate a campaign that was ironic and distinctive in a way that would appeal to its target market.

Four ads were made in total. In the first ad, the group of frogs were heard to croak in a seemingly nonsensical way. However, it soon becomes clear that, individually, they are croaking the syllables 'Bud', 'Weis' and 'Er'. Each of the following three ads featured the frogs and used the same quirky sense of humour but involved them in different scenarios. The campaign appeared to be a success on a number of levels. Research suggested that the ads were particularly popular amongst the core 21–27-year-old consumers and the campaign as a whole won a slew of awards; including the prestigious Silver Lion Award at the 1995 Cannes Film Festival.

Yet, not everyone was so pleased with the campaign. Research undertaken by The Centre for Alcohol Advertising suggested children between the ages of 9 and 11 years could more readily identify the 'frogs' than more traditional advertising icons such as 'Tony the Tiger'. Some commentators suggested that in the use of 'critter advertising', Anheuser-Busch were deliberately targeting children, a fact that the company strongly denied.

Discuss the dangers of using characters when creating a brand 'personality'. What might Anheuser-Busch have done to ensure children were not influenced inappropriately by its advertising?

Brands as communities

In addition to one-to-one relationships, brands have the potential to foster relationships at a community level that have many benefits for both consumers and brand owners. A brand community is defined by Muniz and O'Guinn as:

> a specialized, non-geographically bound community, based on a structured set of social relationships among admirers of a brand.[15]

(p. 412)

Traditionally, brand communities were typified by clubs that met at a single geographical point at a given period in time, such as conventions or rallies. However, the development of the Internet has meant that brand communities have increased exponentially in an online format. Brand communities can be created by brand owners or can be generated spontaneously.

A good example of a community developed and managed by a brand owner is that of the Weightwatchers website. In addition to information about Weightwatchers classes, it provides information about Weightwatchers products and services and a forum through which members can share their weight-loss stories. For consumers, membership of these communities offer benefits associated with social contact, support and a feeling of belonging to a wider group as well as informational benefit. However, in most 'managed' communities, there is little scope for voicing complaints or dissent about an organization's activities. Therefore, for marketers, such communities not only provide an excellent way to communicate the variety of products and services associated with a brand, they provide opportunities to lessen risk in the minds of consumers and shorten the learning curves encountered particularly with complex or technical offerings.

Some of the most common hosts for spontaneous online brand communities are social networking sites such as Facebook. For consumers and organizations, spontaneous online brand communities can offer all of the benefits associated with the managed communities. However, the danger for an organization is that they can also act as a forum for complaints and unmanaged communities can generate an unbalanced narrative about the brand without a credible vehicle for response.

Brand stretching: supporting the long-term success of an organization

It has been noted in marketing literature that, for most organizations, effective brand management is an important pillar when seeking to secure their long-term future.[16] Whilst products are considered to have 'product life cycles'[17] that take them inevitably through the stages of introduction, growth, maturity and then into a state of decline, it has been suggested that, for brands, this might not necessarily be the case.[18]

In cases where a brand represents a strong set of values and attributes it can be 'stretched' and developed to apply to other product areas with the result that the life cycle of the brand can be extended indefinitely. According to Elliot and Percy,[19] brand stretching is a process by which brand owners consider all of the elements that comprise a brand and identify how each might be capitalized upon to develop and nurture its position within new and potential markets. The resulting development of products to be marketed under the umbrella of the original brand name are known as brand extensions.

Excellent examples of brand extensions can be found in the confectionary market where there are a number of very well known brands with strong associations and attributes. Take for example the Mars bar whose iconic red logo against the dark background is closely associated with the product attributes of chocolate, caramel, and richness of flavour, energy (to name but a few). In order to capitalize on seasonal markets and the growth of the ready-made milk drink market, Mars 'stretched' the Mars bar brand to create brand extensions in the form of the Mars ice-cream bar, Mars chocolate drink and the Mars egg. In each case, consumers familiar with the Mars brand, will assume that the extensions will possess similar attributes but in a new format.

Riezebos[20] suggests that such developments reflect a change in the way that both consumers and organizations conceptualize brands. There appears a clear move away from a conceptualization of brands as a form of 'product-plus' and towards the idea of the brand as a broader 'concept'. The value of this shift in perspective is potentially immense as it allows brands to modify their product portfolio in line with seasonal fluctuations and changes in consumer preferences, and in addition to Mars there have been many examples of this over the years; Coca-Cola's development of 'Diet Coke' and Lucozade's move into the market for health and fitness products (see Mini Case below) just to name a few.

MINI CASE: RE-ENERGIZING THE LUCOZADE BRAND

The repositioning and relaunch of veteran brand Lucozade was highlighted by the branding consultancy Superbrand as a classic example of good brand management.[1] Lucozade was first formulated in 1927 by a pharmacist in Newcastle as a palatable, easily digestible glucose drink that would help his children recover from illness when they did not feel like eating solid food. Bought by Beechams, in 1938 it was marketed as a way to replace lost energy and support recovery by those suffering ill health. However, over the course of the century, living conditions and general levels of health improved and the market began to fall away. To counter this, the brand was repositioned and relaunched in 1982 as a drink that would supply energy to those living busy, hectic lifestyles.

In 1990, Lucozade Sport, the first mainstream sports drink, was launched in the UK with significant success.[1] GlaxoSmithKline, owners of the brand, have since developed a number of variants such as Lucozade Energy (based upon the original product with the aim of providing energy but not limited to aiding recovery) and Lucozade Sport Hydro Active (a low carbohydrate drink containing electrolytes, vitamins and calcium designed to give better hydration for athletes than water) and new flavours such as orange and lemon. Ultimately, whilst the original product, a drink aimed at the ailing, has long since declined and disappeared, the brand 'Lucozade' still remains vibrant and demonstrates ongoing potential for growth.

1. Why do you think the repositioning of Lucozade was so successful?
2. What attributes of the original product could be transferred to the 'new' product?
3. Lucozade have also launched a range of 'energy tablets'. Can you think of any other product types that might also be appropriate to carry the Lucozade brand?

Contributing to the balance sheet

In the late 1980s, the value of 'intangibles' such as brands became increasingly clear as the gap between companies' book values (the value of tangible assets) and their stockmarket valuations widened. Following the use of brand value by Rank Hovis McDougal (RHM) as a weapon against a hostile takeover by Goodman Fielder Wattie (GFW), there was increasing recognition of the value of brands as intangible assets on balance sheets.

Certainly the value of brands as intangible assets is significant. For Coca-Cola, recognized by Business Week as one of the world's most valuable brands, the value of the Coca-Cola brand accounts for 51 per cent of the stockmarket value of the Coca-Cola Company as a whole. For McDonalds, another major international brand, the figure is as high as 71 per cent.[21]

The implications of brand contributions to the balance sheet are not always obvious yet they should not be ignored by marketers. It is essential that, in the construction of marketing communications objectives, care should be taken that the brand proposition should not be undermined in any way and, indeed, should be actively supported. The temptation of short-term gain at the expense of the long-term value of the brand should be avoided at all cost. To this end, when undertaking a cost/benefit analysis of any IMC strategy, the extent to which the activity supports the creation or maintenance of the brand and its value should be clearly expressed.

Creating and maintaining brand equity

One of the primary ways that brands can contribute to an organization's balance sheet is through the creation of **brand equity**. In both academic and practitioner literature, definitions of the concept are many and varied. According to Aaker,[22] brand equity may be defined as:

the extent to which a brand is valuable to the organization; this value can be manifested in terms of financial, strategic and managerial advantages.

Riezebos[23] proposes that there are four components of brand equity: the size of the market share, stability of the market share, the margin that an organization can realize on a branded article and, finally, the rights of ownership.

In terms of size of market share, Riezebos suggests that equity is derived from two aspects of this component; from the tendency for consumers to attribute higher value to brands if they possess a greater share of the market and from the fact that the higher the market share, the more income the brand is likely to generate. Stable market share has the ability to generate brand equity through its ability to facilitate financial and strategic advantages. Strategically, a stable market share has the potential to dissuade potential new entrants to the market. In contrast, Aaker[24] identified that the reason that financial advantages are gained through a stable market share is because it is a reflection of **brand loyalty** which, in turn, offers the prospect of stable long-term income. The third component, margin, relates to the difference between the cost of producing the branded article and its cost price to the final customer. It is at this point that an effective IMC strategy has the most obvious part to play in the creation of brand equity. Many of the drivers of margin are the result of brand associations created through effective marketing communication. Finally, 'rights of ownership' relate to the potential income that can be derived from the trademarks, patents and other legal vehicles.

Having identified the components of brand equity, the challenge is then to quantify its value. An overview of brand equity literature suggests that there are a variety of ways in which it might be measured and these have been summarized in Figure 7.3.

'Cost approaches' are based upon the cost to the organization of developing the brand. Whilst this is one of the simplest methods to quantify, it does not take into account consumers' subjective perceptions of value and this may be much higher or much lower than the actual costs incurred. By contrast, the 'market approach' not only takes into account the cost of brand creation but also the premium that consumers might place on a brand as well as its capacity to generate income. However, the subjectivity of both the

---

Methods of measuring brand equity

- Cost approaches – age, cost/share of advertising to date
- Market approaches – what the brand would sell for on open market
- Income approaches – the ability to generate income over tax/the premium that a consumer will pay for the brand
- Economic uses methods – the value of the current brand to the current owner
- Brand strength assessment approaches – generally proprietary

Figure 7.3 Methods of measuring brand equity
Source: Riezebos, R. (2003). *Brand Management*, Harlow: Prentice Hall.

measurement of the premium and prediction as to how long that premium is likely to last make any judgements using this method somewhat uncertain. In contrast, the income approach measure focusses solely upon its potential to contribution to the corporate balance sheet. It views a brand as a form of asset and measures the value that it might contribute, not just annually, but over the whole lifecycle of the brand. In contrast to the other approaches, the 'economic uses' method views a brand as an asset whose value might be leveraged in a variety of ways by an organization. For instance, in addition to its ability to generate revenue through sales, a brand can also be used to leverage investment on the basis of its value and can even be 'sold' in the form of franchising. Finally there are a number of proprietary brand strength assessment approaches offered by branding consultancies. The components and their relative weighting of each of these approaches vary and, because they are commercially owned and managed for profit, the theoretical underpinning is not always obvious and subject to commercial confidentiality.

Creating brand identity

Having established the function and value of brands to both consumers and organizations alike, one of the most important long-term objectives for Brand Managers is to establish a clear and distinct **brand identity**. According to Aaker,[25] brand identity differs from brand image in that the latter is passive and looks to the past. In contrast, brand identity should be active and look to the future.

It has already been noted that brands are intangibles that are, in fact, only sets of associations created in the mind of the consumer through every point in which he or she comes into contact with it. To this end, in the creation of brand identity, the starting point for any marketing communications professional must be the existing brand image (i.e. the collection of associations accumulated to date). Then, in order to create a new and coherent brand identity, the next stage must be to identify an 'identity objective' (i.e. the identity that the brand owner seeks to achieve) and map a logical narrative that will allow the consumer to accept the new identity. It must be said that this may take a significant amount of time as consumers do not change their minds about a brand overnight.

In Aaker and Joachimsthaler's model of brand identity depicted in Figure 7.4 we can see the variety of elements that need to be both considered and manipulated in the management of a brand identity project.

From a communications perspective, one of the greatest challenges associated with the creation of brand identity is the generation of an effective brand position. Defined as the unique position that a brand occupies in the mind of the consumer, effective brand positioning will enable consumers to distinguish between the relative value and benefits offered by a brand when compared to alternative options. One of the most common methods for determining a brand's position is through the use of a 'perceptual map'; a graphical representation of a selection of brands against a set of given characteristics using a pair of axis an example of which can be seen in Figure 7.5.

For a perceptual map to be generated, marketers must first ascertain what the most important characteristics of products in a given market might be (in the case of the automotive industry it was level of luxury and function i.e. family or sport). The target market should then be researched to identify the relative position of each brand on the axis. The resulting perceptual maps can then be analysed to identify who the nearest competitor brands are, areas of potential confusion between brands and where gaps in the market might exist. It is then the role of IMC professionals to formulate strategies that will differentiate their brand from the competition.

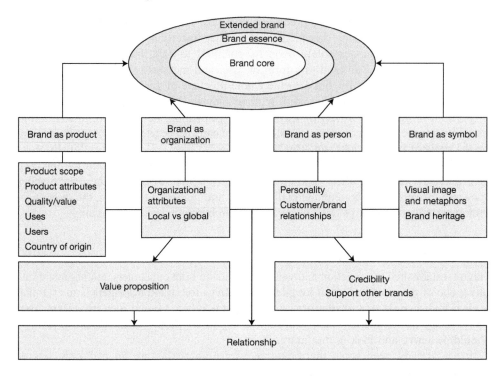

Figure 7.4 Aaker and Joachimsthaler's Model of Brand Identity[26]

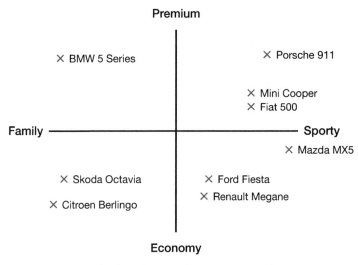

Figure 7.5 A variety of automotive brands mapped onto a perceptual map

Brand portfolios and managing the brand architecture

For most organizations, it is not so much a matter of managing the identity of one brand but managing the identity of multiple brands, or the company's 'brand portfolio' simultaneously. Companies tend to accumulate 'brand portfolios' as a way of spreading risk and avoiding the 'eggs in one basket' syndrome. To this end, if demand falls away for one brand, it is hoped that revenues can be maintained by the remainder of the brands in a company's portfolio.

Another advantage of the possession of a portfolio of brands is that it also allows the company to exploit strategic advantages offered by different sectors within a given market. Take, for example, the recent acquisition of Cadbury's by the American food giant Kraft. Originally Kraft's portfolio consisted of Terry's, most closely associated with the 'All Gold' boxed chocolates range and the Terry's Chocolate Orange, the premium brand Cote d'Or, the distinctively triangular shaped Toblerone, and Milka, which is predominantly sold as a block chocolate. With the addition of Cadbury's they now are in possession of a range of 'countlines' (consumer products that are sold to retailers in packages of multiple items and broken down to be sold singly to consumers) such as Cadbury's Flake or Crunchie and obtained an established position in the premium, organic sector of the confectionary market with the Green and Black's brand.

However, whilst there are undoubted benefits associated with the possession of a portfolio of brands, from a communications perspective, portfolios can also present a significant challenge. Unless each brand occupies a distinct position in the market and is clearly differentiated from other brands in the portfolio, consumers can find themselves confused. This confusion can result in consumers seeking out brands with clearer brand proposition.

One way that consumer confusion can be averted is through the establishment of a clear organizing structure within a portfolio in which each brand has a distinct role and position. This structure is known as 'brand architecture'. Riezebos[27] proposes a model of **brand architecture** composed of four types of brands: **bastion brands**, **flanker brands**, **fighter brands** and **prestige brands**.

According to Riezebos, the 'bastion' brand is the mainstream anchor of the organization's brand portfolio and is the most stable and profitable of the brands in an organization's portfolio. Using the confectionary sector as an example, Dairy Milk might be seen to be one of Kraft's 'bastion' brands. A 'flanker' brand is one which offers a similar quality product to the 'bastion' brand but caters to a slightly different need. Within the context of the Kraft portfolio, this might be seen to be the Whole Nut or Fruit and Nut variants. Kraft's Daim brand might be considered to be one of their 'fighter' brands; one which is used to defend the bastion's position in the market and its strategy often revolves around value-based or cost-reduction options. Finally, the prestige brand is one that offers a premium alternative to the bastion brand. From Kraft's perspective, the Green and Black's or the Cote d'Or brand might fulfil this role very well.

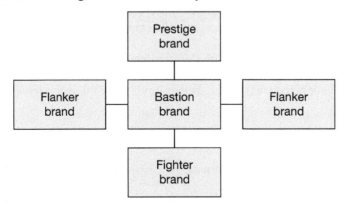

Figure 7.6 Riezebos' (2003) Model of Brand Architecture

Organized in such a way, brands are able to operate along clear and consistent lines and the likelihood of cannibalization of each other's brand share is limited. There is also the added benefit that consumers can move up the structure to the premium brand if they wish to treat themselves or down the structure to the fighter brand if money is tight. Similarly, where consumers seek some variety, the flanker brands offer the opportunity for change. In this way, consumers can move around the portfolio in ways that satisfy their needs at any given moment without significant loss of revenue to the parent company.

Summary

It is apparent that brands assume much more complex roles than simply that of a trademark-style vehicle for differentiation. For consumers, a primary function of a brand is as a communicator of the content and nature of the product they represent. Consumers also employ brands to support their identity and act as partners in consumer–brand relationships. Alternatively, from the perspective of the brand owner, a well managed, well constructed brand can be extended into new product areas which can sustain its business into the future. It can also be a valuable asset which can be used to leverage funding and fend off predatory take-over bids.

Therefore, from an integrated marketing communications perspective, the primary challenge exists to identify the multiple roles that brands play within both the organizational and consumer context. These roles need to be recognized and their ability to support both consumer and corporate needs should be incorporated within the brief for any communication activity. If executed effectively, IMC programmes will allow stakeholders to make brand choices based upon informed judgement. However, if managed poorly, there is potential for confusion and disillusion that is likely to ultimately undermine brand equity and send consumers in search of brands that they can clearly see will satisfy their needs.

Review questions

1. Define what is meant by the term 'brand' and discuss how the concept of a brand differs from that of a 'trademark'.
2. Explain what is meant by the term 'brand heuristic' and give at least three examples of typical brand heuristics used by consumers.
3. Identify three brands that you have recently consumed and reflect how your relationship with those brands relate to the consumer–brand relationships identified in Fournier's typology.
4. Discuss why it is important for IMC professionals to understand the nature of consumer brand relationships such as those identified by Fournier.
5. What are your perceptions of the 'personality' of the following three brands?

   a)   BMW
   b)   McDonalds
   c)   Coca-Cola

   Reflect upon how you obtained these perceptions and what the primary influences were.
6. For a brand of your choice, design a logo in a way that you think clearly communicates its personality. Justify your choices.

7. Discuss why you think that branded products are able to command much higher prices than supermarket 'own-label' branded products.
8. Consider the relative value of each the various methods of assessing brand equity discussed in the chapter and rank them in what would be your preferred order. Justify your decision.
9. For a product sector of your choice, identify what you perceive to be the main criteria for consumer choice and construct a perceptual map of as many brands as you can think of. Where clusters and gaps appear, discuss the implications for marketers and why you believe they have occurred.
10. What role does brand architecture play for marketers who are seeking to establish a clear positioning strategy for their brands?

Recommended reading

Aaker, D. (2010). *Building Brands*, London: Simon & Schuster UK Ltd.
Elliot, R., and Percy, L. (2007). *Strategic Brand Management*, Oxford: Oxford University Press.

CASE STUDY 7.1

Ginsters: brand identity repositioning

Source: Design Business Association: Silver, Design Effectiveness Awards, 2009. Agency: Smith & Milton. Case material provided by the World Advertising Research Centre (WARC) www.warc.com.

This case demonstrates the revitalization of brand image and equity through integrated marketing communications. The complete design overhaul of the Ginsters brand has resulted in significant and tangible benefits to the business. It demonstrates not only the power of re-defining a brand proposition, Real Honest Food, but also how design clarity and consistency can change perceptions and purchasing decisions about a brand.

The case focusses on the strategies used in rejuvenating an established brand that was under threat from all sides: increased competition in the 'impulse/ food-on-the-move market', growing threat of own label, the inexorable trend towards healthier eating and limited distribution (multiples).

Ultimately this is a success story about a rejuvenated Ginsters brand that:

- Gained record total market share 10.1 per cent.
- Enjoyed +24 per cent growth, year on year.
- Sterling share grew 600 per cent faster than the market, in the all important multiples sector.
- Successfully entered new product sectors (multi-packs).
- Attracted over 1 million new households to the brand.
- Distribution gains in all the major multiples. The brand is now regarded as the new benchmark against which other savoury brands are judged.
- The programme significantly raised internal and external perceptions of Ginsters, as a brand they have confidence in, as the quote from a supermarket product buyer shows.

Looks excellent on shelf & brand strategy fits with my category goals

Debbie Allwright, Tesco buyer

Project overview

Outline of project

The overall objective was to build on the strong brand recognition in the 'impulse/food-on-the-move' market and increase appeal amongst housewives in the main meal sector. Increasing visibility in multiples and warding off growing competition from local producers and own-label products was key.

Central to meeting this objective was defining Ginsters brand essence 'Real Honest Food' – and bringing this to life in the form of a revitalized design strategy.

This would include establishing a clear personality for all brand communications that would align packaging, advertising and all other brand communications. The development of a new brand identity programme would also set the standard for a clear and memorable tone of voice, establishing a design discipline for all elements of the brand design identity. The aim was to give Ginsters a strong, motivating and impactful brand presence in whichever category it appeared.

> The biggest rebranding of the company involving the design of the company's packaging, point of sale, website, uniforms, sales fleet and fridges.
>
> Larry File, Ginsters Communications Manager

Description

From a family-run, egg-packing business in Callington, Cornwall, the Ginsters name has grown steadily since the 1960s, when it converted into a small bakery and started making authentic Cornish pasties. Their Original Cornish Pasty is still based on that original recipe. Back then, it was just 30 people working at the Ginsters bakery. Today, over 700 people produce over three million pastries a week using, as always, fresh ingredients from local suppliers. Following 10 years of continuous growth, Ginsters needed to broaden its appeal in the face of growing competition and healthier eating trends. The decision to invest in a major programme of brand development was therefore taken.

Overview of the market

The market for pies and pasties had shown steady, if unspectacular, growth over the previous three years. In 2008 the market was estimated to be worth £901 million, 1 per cent up on the previous year.

Outline of design issues

Key challenges

The products are familiar to many consumers but have an image of being rather old-fashioned and unhealthy with a high calorie content.

The market was under pressure from not only a growing interest in healthier eating and home cooking but also from an increasingly competitive snacking market. Additionally, the category was primarily driven by men, who were the core consumers.

Other challenges

To create a presence and greater stand-out in the multiples and create a synergy across both the savoury range and the new product areas, such as sandwiches. To engage the housewife shopper and evoke a greater impression as a main meal, (for the men in her household), whilst not diminishing its real credentials and appeal to men. The campaign also needed to add meaning to the 'Real Honest Food' proposition to engage these housewives. 'Locally sourced' was a key brand equity and would be highlighted to establish a more compelling food/meal message.

The business also has plans to develop the brand into a number of new markets over the coming years. As such, there was a requirement for a strong, memorable and enduring presentation of the brand, uniting its Real Honest Food proposition.

Design strategy approach

Design strategy

A rigorous brand review to coordinate the total brand expression from packaging, advertising, promotions and internal delivery.

The problem

Successive packaging redesigns and advertising campaigns had created schizophrenic brand messages confusing and alienating consumers.

Photo 7.3

The insight

The statement at the brand's heart – 'Real Honest Food' – demands a clear provenance and a singular, unfussy approach.

The solution

Re-establish the brand's idiosyncratic Cornish values and strip away the veneer of decoration and muddled messaging.

The approach

- Conduct a forensic **audit** of the brand's history and brand truths.
- Establish, refine and reinstate the key brand visual and verbal equities.
- Rediscover what being Cornish means.
- Rejuvenate the brand communications, creating templates for all media, and develop a comprehensive and easy to use brand identity guidelines.
- Redesign packaging across 35 lines and new product development.

Project launch date

September 2008

Results

1 Design discipline

A refreshed, organized and distinctive presentation of the Ginsters brand. This was achieved by exploiting Ginsters original Cornish heritage and keeping to a simple, truthful message: 'Real Honest Food'.

2 Increase in market value

Ginsters achieved growth of £15m year on year, which accounted for an incredible 42 per cent of the total market growth over the same period.

3 Increase in market share

Since the re-brand, data shows that Ginsters have now achieved 10.1 per cent market share (a record). This equates to 24 per cent increase, year on year.

4 Growth in all sectors

Ginsters achieved 24 per cent growth in the multiples but good overall growth in all sectors.

5 Brand consideration

Ginsters continue to lead the sector in consideration, with 37 per cent (source: TNS).

6 Increased market penetration

Year ending December 2008, Ginsters achieved an extra 1 million households purchasing Ginsters (source: TNS).

Testimonials

Smith & Milton's single-minded creative approach helped us to achieve real clarity in the market for what Ginsters stands for. As an immediate result, multipack sales have increased by 34 per cent in 2007 to 62 per cent in 2008.

Andy Valentine, Head of Brand Marketing, Ginsters

Thought I'd drop you a note about your recent brand face lift. As a student of the Ginsters "look" for almost 12 years, I think this is the best brand revamp I've seen – the range looks absolutely fantastic on shelf. It achieves the impact on block as well as individual pack, a neat trick. I think it has moved the brand forward brilliantly.

Gary Johnson, Managing Director, The Sandwich
Centre, Milton Keynes

Other influencing factors

Increased staff attitudes

Ginsters conducted an internal employee survey following the re-brand run by IPOS-MORI. The survey results were the highest in four years. On the measure of 'I have confidence in the way the company is managed', Ginsters scored 63 per cent compared with the industry norm of 57 per cent.

Production costs and improved materials

New materials used for the redesigned packaging resulted in a 5 per cent cost saving in overall production and compared to previous materials used, the new material is far easier to recycle.

CASE STUDY QUESTIONS

1. Critique the case study. Drawing on the material in this and preceding chapters, what do you believe are the major factors that led to the campaign's success?
2. It is noted in the case study that there were some concerns regarding the 'unhealthiness'/ high calorie content of the product. Given ongoing concerns regarding healthy eating, lifestyles and about rising obesity levels and some of the issues raised in Chapter 3, discuss the long-term implications for the brand. What action do you recommend they take?
3. How would you recommend Ginsters responds to any criticisms of the high calorie content of their product? Justify your response.
4. Develop and justify recommendations for measuring and tracking Ginsters brand equity and brand image over time.
5. Visit your local supermarket and evaluate the category in which Ginsters products are placed. How would you recommend competitors counter Ginsters activity and what contingency plans would you recommend that Ginsters develop to counter any likely competitive activity?

CASE STUDY 7.2

Repositioning the brand and refreshing the cider market

In the UK, the market for alcoholic drinks has always been rather fickle and prone to fads. Whether it is Mexican beer with a slice of lime stuck in the neck of the bottle, alcopops or 'ice' beer or cider, certain brands or categories of drinks appear to grab the imagination of the drinking public and sales take off radically. Sadly, for many brands, sales also tail off equally as fast. Magners, the cider brand owned by Irish company C&C, is one such example.

In 2002, Magners faced challenging market conditions when seeking to enter the UK market. Already in place were strong, well known mainstream brands such as Strongbow, the market leader, Gaymers Olde English, Woodpecker and Dry Blackthorn. These brands had long histories in the market and had established distribution networks through both the 'on' and the 'off' trade. A further problem for cider was that, as a category, it had a poor reputation. It was perceived as the drink of teenagers, yokels or 'down and outs' to the extent that 82 per cent of drinkers said that they never considered drinking cider.

However, on analysing the UK market, C&C and their agency, the Media Planning Group, recognized an important gap in the cider market: the authentic, premium cider. On analysing wider market trends, it became clear that there was a growing consumer preference for natural, authentic, premium products. Premium ciders such as K, Red Rock and Diamond White had previously enjoyed popularity in the 1990s, but their 'premium' label was largely based upon their alcoholic strength of up to 8.4 per cent alcohol by volume. Unfortunately for the cider makers, their sales soon started to tumble as imitators entered the market in larger bottles and with much lower price points. Further damage was inflicted on the sector by the increasing popularity of the alcopops (sweet alcoholic drinks) and ready-mixed drinks brands such as the Bacardi Breezer that emerged towards the end of the decade. At the same time, the mainstream cider brands descended into cycles of competition that focussed on price reductions and value promotions and did little to emphasize the heritage or value of their brands.

In response, in 2003, C&C undertook a region-by-region launch of the Magners brand in the UK. Packaged in a pint-sized bottle, the Magners brand was positioned as a premium product whose communication strategy was based upon attributes that simply screamed 'quality' and 'authenticity' at its target market. A totally natural product, made from the juice of 17 different varieties of apple grown on C&C's own orchard in Clonmel, its provenance was clear. Its heritage and authenticity as a product was reinforced by the traditional processes and the location of production at the same cider press that had been used for 70 years. Quality was clearly conveyed through the claim that every drop of Magners cider, once pressed, was allowed to mature in order to create a 'unique' taste. To emphasize the originality of the brand, a unique serving ritual was also developed; to serve the cider in a pint glass full of ice. The price too was premium and, despite the small margin it offered to publicans, whilst consumers asked for it, they were happy to stock it. However, probably the most distinctive aspect of the brand was its position as an 'Irish' cider. In the UK, cider is a drink that is most often associated with the West Country and the 'Irishness' was one attribute that competitor brands might find hard to replicate.

Magners was rolled out on a region-by-region basis and, supported heavily by advertising, aided by a hot summer and football's World Cup, by 2006 they had achieved significant success. Magners had captured 30 per cent of total cider sales and was the number one selling packaged long alcoholic drink in the UK. In effect, Magners had not just repositioned itself in the UK market, it had created a whole new drinks category. Reflecting this success C&C's share price quadrupled from 3 euros to 12 euros and, to meet projected consumer demand, two million apple trees were planted on 5,000 acres of land.

However, all success has its imitators and such was the case with Magners. Having re-established the credibility of cider, other makers lost no time in jumping onto the bandwagon in order to profit from this new drinks category. Scottish and Newcastle, makers of Strongbow resurrected its Bulmers Original Cider brand to defend its position in the market. Meanwhile publicans and buyers in both the 'on' and 'off' trade started to look to these new brands as potential alternatives that might satisfy consumer demand for premium, authentic cider but also yield a better margin. By 2009, the *Sunday Times* reported that whilst the category continued to grow by 11 per cent in the first half of the year, Magners sales were only up by 2 per cent. With its competitors making up ground, the big question for C&C is how to re-establish its dominance of the market; through the vehicle of Magners brand, or through the establishment of a completely new brand.

CASE STUDY QUESTIONS

1. Discuss what functions the Magners brand might fulfil for the following stakeholder groups:

   - consumers
   - publicans
   - supermarket buyers
   - the brand owners, C&C.

2. Describe the kind of personality that C&C and its agency have developed for the Magners brand? How have they achieved this?
3. To what extent do you think that 'authenticity' is an important attribute for a cider brand?
4. Why do you think that the drinks industry suffers from 'fads'? What are the implications for brand owners and what are the implications for valuing brand equity?
5. What ethical issues are involved in marketing communications for alcoholic beverages? How should advertisers such as Magners take these into account?

Visit the ASA website and select the 'Adjudications' section – where decisions regarding complaints about or challenges to marketing communications campaigns are reported. Review recent decisions for alcoholic beverages. What lessons can be learned from these adjudications?

Notes

1 de Chernatony, L., (2009). Towards the holy grail of defining 'brand'. *Marketing Theory*, 9, 101–5.
2 American Marketing Association (2010). www.marketingpower.com (accessed 2 February 2010).
3 Jones, J.P. (1986). *What's in a Name? Advertising and the Concept of Brands*, Massachusetts: D.C. Heath and Company.
4 Calkins, T. (ed.) (2005). *Kellogg On Branding*, Chichester: John Wiley & Sons.
5 White, J., and de Chernatony, L. (2002). 'New Labour: A Study of the Creation, Development and Demise of a Political Brand'. In: Bruce I. Newman and Dejan Vercic (eds) *Communication of Politics: Cross-Cultural Theory Building in the Practice of Public Relations and Political Marketing*, Haworth: The Haworth Press.
6 de Chernatony, L., and Dall'Olmo Riley, F. (1998). Defining a 'brand'. beyond the literature with experts interpretations, *Journal of Marketing Management*, 14, 417–43.
7 Stets, J.E., and Burke, P.J. (2000). Identity theory and social identity theory. *Social Psychology Quarterly*, 63(3), 224–37.
8 de Mooij, M. (2004). *Consumer Behaviour and Culture: Consequences for Global Marketing and Advertising*, London: Sage Publications.
9 Belk, R. (1988). Possessions and the extended self. *Journal of Consumer Research*, 15, 139–69.
10 Solomon, M., Bamossy, G., and Askegaard, S. (2005). *Consumer Behaviour: A European Perspective*, London: Prentice Hall.

11 Solomon, M., Bamossy, G., and Askegaard, S. (2005). *Consumer Behaviour: A European Perspective*, London: Prentice Hall.
12 Lloyd, J. (2006). A Dynamic Model of Consumer Conceptualization of Political Brands, Unpublished PhD Thesis.
13 Fournier, S. (1998). Consumers and their brands: developing relationship theory in consumer research. *Journal of Consumer Research*, 24, 343–64.
14 Fournier, S. (1998). Consumers and their brands: developing relationship theory in consumer research. *Journal of Consumer Research*, 24, 343–64.
15 Muniz Jr., A.M., and O'Guinn, T.C. (2001). Brand community. *Journal of Consumer Research*, 27, 412–32.
16 Doyle, P. (1989). Building successful brands: the strategic objectives. *Journal of Marketing Management*, 5, 77–95.
17 Brassington, F., and Pettitt, S. (2005). *Principles of Marketing*, London: Pitman Publishing.
18 Doyle, P. (1989). Building successful brands: the strategic objectives. *Journal of Marketing Management*, 5, 77–95.
19 Elliot, R., and Percy, L. (2007). *Strategic Brand Management*, Oxford: Oxford University Press.
20 Riezebos, R. (2003). *Brand Management*, Harlow: Prentice Hall.
21 Lindeman, J. (2004). 'Brand Valuation'. In Rita Clifton and John Simmons (eds) *Brands and Branding*, New York: Bloomberg Press.
22 Aaker, D.A. (1991). *Managing Brand Equity: Capitalizing on the Value of a Brand Name*, New York: The Free Press/Maxwell Macmillan International.
23 Riezebos, R. (2003). *Brand Management*, Harlow: Prentice Hall.
24 Aaker, D.A. (1991). *Managing Brand Equity: Capitalizing on the Value of a Brand Name*, New York: The Free Press/Maxwell Macmillan International.
25 Aaker, D.A. (1984). 'Building Brand Equity'. Cited in M. Dahlén, F. Lange, and T. Smith (2010). *Marketing Communications: A Brand Narrative Approach*, Chichester: Wiley, 219.
26 Aaker, D.A., and Joachimsthaler, E. (2000). *Brand Leadership*, New York, NY: The Free Press.
27 Riezebos, R. (2003). *Brand Management*, Harlow: Prentice Hall.

8 Traditional media

LEARNING OUTCOMES

After studying this chapter, you will be able to:

- Discuss the evolution of traditional mass media

- Discuss the strengths and weaknesses of major media

- Discuss the challenges to the efficiency and effectiveness of mass media from fragmentation and the evolution of new media forms

- Review qualitative factors that should also be considered in planning media

Introduction

In the UK, the media landscape has altered hugely over the last 40 years. The development and introduction of digital and satellite technology has resulted not only in an increase in the number and type of media on offer, but has also increased the variety of ways in which they might be consumed.

This change is most clearly illustrated by the change in output of UK television and radio. In the late 1960s, UK consumers had the choice of three television stations, four or five BBC radio stations and a small number of pirate radio operators from which to obtain their political brand information. These stations were often restricted in terms of both their content and the number of hours they broadcast per day.

Today, one digital television provider alone, Sky, offers consumers in excess of 100 channels of television and radio and, in many cases, broadcast content is available 24 hours a day. With regard to radio, in addition to the national stations offered by the BBC radio, Virgin, Classic FM and TalkSport, there are currently 17 regional stations, 40 BBC local radio stations and 280 commercial independent local radio (ILR) stations.

Media choices

Different media forms such as television, radio or newspapers have different strengths and weaknesses. Seldom can one medium accomplish all the objectives that might be sought in planning a campaign. Using a combination of media can extend reach or the number of weeks during which the target group(s) have the opportunity to be exposed to the messages.

Consider a mid-winter campaign to encourage overseas holidays to warmer and sunnier climates. Television may be used to provide reach and to portray the obvious emotional connection of white sandy beaches, blue skies and waving palm trees. Television is expensive and maintaining a campaign throughout the winter period may not be affordable. Images from the television commercial may be used in magazines or as posters in travel agents to recall the television commercial (imagery transfer). The music from the television soundtrack may be used in radio advertising. Television commercials are usually of short, often 30 seconds, duration, with approximately 75 words possible in the time.

Other media will therefore be used to provide the details of prices, packages available and conditions of travel that would not be possible to communicate in the television advertisement. For example, magazines may feature a visual from the television commercial and give summary details of the travel agency outlets, or provide website details. Newspapers may provide specific details of local travel agency branches, including street address, telephone numbers and website details, and may also provide more information regarding specific prices and packages than is possible in other media.

THINK BOX

Multi-media campaigns

Multi-media campaigns may be effective, but the cost is beyond many small advertisers. What combinations of media might be viable for a regional advertiser with ten branches in the region? How might this advertiser gain synergies in marketing communications activity?

Cinema might complement media such as television by repeating the television advertisement – or a longer version of it.[1] Radio, using the soundtrack of the television commercial, may be used for 'imagery transfer', to recall the television advertisement and extend activity between or beyond more expensive television flights. Radio or newspapers may also be concentrated only in selected areas that are deemed to be the most important markets.

Obvious factors to consider in deciding on which media to include and how much of the available budget to allocate to each one are:

- The overall marketing objectives for the product or service and the way all elements of the marketing mix may work together. It would be futile to plan for a media schedule centred on television advertising that enabled an up-market image to be portrayed if there are plans to heavily discount the product or to undertake major price discount-based sales promotion activity. The planned creative approach intended may also influence the type of media that may be considered, such as whether a detailed product demonstration is recommended, or whether the creative approach will be based on the portrayal of emotional or rational appeals.
- A thorough understanding of the primary target group for the advertising (and any relevant secondary target groups that should be considered). The more that is known about them, especially their media usage habits, the more precisely targeted the advertising activity can be.
- A detailed analysis of past competitive activity in order to predict likely future activity and to decide whether to match their activity in terms of media options or to find channels with lower levels of competitive activity which may reduce the risk on potential effectiveness being adversely impacted by the 'clutter' of other messages.[2]
- The resources available. There is no point in planning a substantial multi-media programme with heavy weights (in terms of TARPS) of advertising if there is insufficient funding available to sustain the programme.

THINK BOX

Fragmentation of audiences

Consumers have an ever-growing range of news and entertainment options available to them and the number of people using one medium at any given time is considerably smaller than in the past when there were far fewer options available.

What are the implications of continued 'fragmentation' of audiences across multiple media options?

Discuss the challenge of fragmentation for marketers with very precise target groups versus those whose targets are much broader.

MINI CASE: GOVERNMENT COMMUNICATION

Large scale mass media campaigns are frequently used to communicate government policies or to raise awareness of a range of policy, health and safety issues. Consider the following quote.

> Only 6 per cent of the population trust and act on all government advice regarding diet. 37 per cent said they did not trust any government advice and 20 per cent said they completely ignored it.[3]

(p. 18)

1. How successful do you believe campaigns aimed at raising awareness of government policies are?
2. Select a recent government-sponsored communications campaign and critique it in terms of the message being sent and the likely response of the target group(s).
3. How would you recommend this be amended for the future? Justify your answer.
4. What do you recommend that government agencies do to improve their credibility and trust and how do you recommend they do this?
5. For what other organizations is the issue of low credibility and trust likely to be an issue and how do you recommend they address the problem?
6. Taking the specific issue of low levels of trust in government advice regarding diet noted above, governments around the world have invested large amounts of resources in trying to address problems with rising obesity rates and in trying to improve the quality of diets (such as through encouraging the consumption of five helpings of fruit and vegetables per day). What are the implications of low levels of trust in government sources regarding diet?
7. How would you go about investigating what sources of information different segments would trust regarding diet and other health-related issues and how people would like to obtain this information?
8. How would you go about investigating how the issue of low levels of trust in policy communication should be addressed?

We now provide a brief overview of the strengths and weaknesses of each of the main traditional media in turn:

Media strengths and weaknesses

Television

Television has credibility, both with consumers and retailers, and reaches substantial audiences. The combination of audio and video allows portrayal of excitement and emotion (tearful reunions, etc.). It also enables product demonstration, however both advertising time and commercial production costs are expensive and thus often beyond the budgets of small firms and many not-for-profit organizations.

While much of the television advertising you may have seen will have been scheduled on a national basis, regional advertising allows for different weights of advertising to be placed in specific areas. Additionally, **cooperative advertising** enables retailers' details to be placed on a manufacturer's television advertising, thus highlighting specific regional/ local availability and enabling individual retailers some access to a medium that they might not otherwise be able to afford.

Television can provide high **reach**, although lower than in the past due to the proliferation of channels and the fragmentation of the available viewing audience. Additionally, whereas in the early days of television, viewers might have sat through entire advertising breaks, the advent of remote controls meant that viewers were able to mute the sound or change channels during breaks, leading to concerns about the effectiveness of advertising.

The sheer volume of advertising has lead to concerns regarding clutter and its potential impact on advertising effectiveness.[4,5] This has also lead to attempts to find new ways of using the medium to avoid clutter and stand out from conventional advertising formats. One of the major recent developments has been the growth in product placements[6] which are discussed in more detail in Chapter 10.

Production costs may be substantial, often placing the effective use of the medium beyond many advertisers. Conversely, excessive **frequency** of exposure can lead to irritation ('wearout'),[7] with lengthy debates over the last 30 years about how much is 'enough'.[8]

There are also a number of ongoing debates regarding the exact impact television advertising has on behaviour[9] and how to measure effectiveness[10]; these debates will no doubt continue in the future. One of the most high profile debates links exposure to advertising for foods deemed of low nutrition value and obesity.[11,12] This remains a hotly contested subject, with claims of direct and indirect effects being disputed[13]

MINI CASE: CELEBRITY SPOKESPEOPLE

Sainsbury's have used the celebrity chef Jamie Oliver as their **spokesperson** for several years. While popular, he is also somewhat controversial due to his blunt views on people's dietary habits and the quality of some mass-produced foods.

1. Discuss the pros and cons of using a high profile spokesperson such as Jamie Oliver as the central spokesperson for an organization such as Sainsbury's.
2. Assume you are one of Sainsbury's competitions – what options are there for countering the impact of Jamie Oliver's continual involvement with Sainsbury's? Which option do you recommend and why?
3. How would you determine if and when Jamie Oliver might become over exposed or less influential as a spokesperson?

For any campaign, planners need to determine how different media are used individually and in combination by target segments in order to gain a clearer understanding of the impact persuasive communication of all kinds is likely to have on different segments of the population.[14]

THINK BOX

Refer back to Chapters 3 and 5. Is it ethical to use shocking imagery for campaigns such as this? When would this type of tactic not be appropriate?

Radio

Radio offers more regional, **demographic** and **psychographic** selectivity than television and offers immediacy of messages. Deadlines are shorter than for television and production costs considerably cheaper. It is an extremely flexible medium, providing options in terms of areas, time zones etc.

Often it performs a valuable role in reinforcing key communication points on television, extending a campaign's duration or providing continuity between television advertising **flights**; it can stand alone as an effective medium.

Radio is often not a 'high participation' medium, requiring no conscious effort to use it and, at times it can often be seen as a passive 'background' medium. Another criticism of radio is that it cannot demonstrate products and cannot convey emotion. We discussed imagery transfer earlier – advertising that has been specifically developed or modified for radio can, with creative copywriting, communicate emotion, drama and excitement.

Many of the concerns discussed in relation to television regarding clutter, frequency of exposure and how to measure effectiveness also apply to radio.

THINK BOX

Radio campaigns

Assume you have recommended a radio campaign to a client whose target is adolescents and young adults. The recommendation has been rejected on the basis that radio is just musical wallpaper and no one remembers anything they have heard. How would you respond to this?

Newspapers

Newspapers provide high reach and wide geographic selectivity, with shorter deadlines and lower costs than television. While some supporters claim it to be the last true mass medium, readership profiles indicate readership to be strongest in older age groups.[15] Some control over the environment in which an advertisement appears is possible, such as news, sports or business pages, although this may at times work to the advertiser's detriment if the specific content of an editorial piece detracts from the advertiser's message (such as airline crash editorial adjacent to travel advertising).

To some extent, they offer a degree of catalogue value in that readers can refer back to an advertisement and study it several times, something that is not possible with television or radio, however few readers would stockpile newspapers – today's paper is likely to be discarded today. Newspapers lack the high colour reproduction qualities of magazines (other than via pre-printed inserts) but can communicate a large amount of detail that is not possible via short radio or television advertisements.

Magazines

Magazines can be broad, mass appeal media or extremely specific, targeted at a very clearly defined target. They generally offer good quality reproduction through the use of glossy pages, and longer life than electronic media – readers may keep a magazine for days, weeks or longer, referring back to issues and/or specific advertisements that have captured

THINK BOX

Magazine advertisements

Browse through a selection of glossy women's magazines, especially those with a focus on fashion. You will notice that there will be several competing brands, such as cosmetics or perfume, placed close together.

How can an individual brand stand out from the clutter of competing brands? What are the implications of not placing advertising in these magazines?

their interest. In addition, as well as the primary readership (generally the purchaser of the publication), magazines can often have a substantial secondary (pass-on) readership.

Cinema

This tends to be more popular with younger rather than older age groups, with impact provided by the large screen, offering entertainment and involvement to a level beyond that achievable with television; quality advertisements are seem as mini-movies.[16] Its effectiveness is less well researched than other media and it is rarely used as the sole or primary medium for a campaign. Advertising is generally placed during the dates that specific movies are likely to attract audiences matching the advertiser's target groups. Reach is relatively limited due to the small numbers of seats in each theatre and repeat exposure to the same advertisements can lead to irritation for frequent movie goers, potentially diminishing the impact of the advertisement.

Outdoor/out-of-home/hoardings

Outdoor is claimed to be the earliest form of advertising, dating back thousands of years.[17] Outdoor advertising used to refer only to large static hoardings or billboards, such as those placed at the side of roads. As such it has suffered from a 'cheap' image of peeling paper posters, blank or defaced sites.

It now encompasses dynamic three-dimensional, often electronic, signs, including advertising on buses and bus shelters and other forms of transit-related signage such as on taxis or trucks, sports ground advertising, shopping mall displays, inflatable signs etc. As technology changes, new, and at times radically different forms of signage are appearing.

What all these forms of advertising have in common is that they are seen by consumers outside their homes, often close to the point at which an actual purchase is likely to take place. Their value, apart from the novelty associated with new advertising forms as they appear, is largely in providing a reminder function – featuring the key message from an advertising campaign that may appear in a number of other media.

Drawbacks include the lack of selectivity of those exposed to the message and relatively short exposure times. In addition, there are concerns regarding 'pollution' of the environment by intrusive signs and the potential for some signs to be a traffic hazard if they distract drivers. Given the diversity of outdoor advertising forms, finding a common and credible means of assessing the impact of the medium is recognized within the industry as a significant challenge.[18]

THINK BOX

Humour and fear in advertising

Refer back to the discussion of humour and fear/shock tactics. Discuss how humour and shocking imagery can be conveyed via all the different types of media discussed in this chapter. What are the advantages and disadvantages of each medium in communicating these messages?

Simultaneous media use

An additional aspect of media use that has also been largely ignored in much of the academic literature is the issue of **simultaneous media use**, in which consumers may be using several media forms such as the Internet and either television or radio at the same time.[19] The following provides an indication of the extent of simultaneous media usage in the USA:

> 32.7 per cent of males and 36.4 per cent of females watch television while they are online, with the two media becoming either foreground or background depending on the task and interest.[20]

There is no data available on simultaneous media use in other markets, and the way in which messages across these media may interact and reinforce each other is totally un-researched.

MINI CASE: IMAGERY TRANSFER AND SIMULTANEOUS MEDIA USE

Assume you are developing a recommendation for a campaign involving the use of television, radio and the Internet. Given the discussion earlier in the chapter regarding imagery transfer and the fact that simultaneous media use is a reality, although poorly understood:

1. How would you measure the impact of simultaneous media use for your campaign?
2. What research do you recommend be undertaken to improve knowledge of this phenomenon?

In addition to the factors discussed here, other, more subtle factors need to be considered, including the impact of media context on communication effectiveness.

Media context

Imagine the way an advertisement for an airline would be perceived within a television programme or a magazine feature on romantic overseas holidays versus within a programme or feature on the dangers of travel, including accidents, risk of illness, robbery or violence. An advertisement for cake mixes is likely to be perceived very differently within an environment centered on the benefits of cooking versus an environment which shows graphic images of reconstructive surgery as a result of accidents.

Where there is low involvement in a product category, advertisements embedded in a context that is similar ('congruent'), attitudes towards the advertisement have been found to be more positive than when they appear in an environment that sharply contrasts with the tone of the advertisement.[21,22] Positive contexts appear to lead to more positive attitudes to advertisements placed within them, although different effects may occur for familiar versus unfamiliar brands.[23]

There may be some very pragmatic reasons for avoiding placing advertisements within a movie or television programme containing high levels of violence as there is evidence that communication effectiveness may be compromised; advertisements shown in this type of environment achieve less favourable reported attitudes both towards the specific advertisement and the advertised brand than when the same commercial is used in an environment that does not contain violence.[24]

The rational **hierarchy of effects models** reviewed earlier reflect a very positivist view of 'what advertising does' to apparently passive receivers[25] rather than reflecting the reality that people may construct their own realities and meanings from the combinations of communications to which they choose to pay attention.

As noted in Chapter 2, social contexts may influence the effects of advertisements such as in group interactions involving the interpretation of advertising or its use in discussions regarding creative executions; lack of familiarity with specific advertisements may result in exclusion from group interactions.[26] The impact of these types of interactions on brand purchase is not clear.

MINI CASE: GRAPPLING WITH VIOLENCE

Assume your company has been invited to sponsor a television series of murder mysteries which is expected to be very popular with the age groups that are your key target groups. Some of the programmes will contain graphic scenes of violence and there has been some negative advance publicity regarding 'gratuitous violence'.

1. What are the pros and cons of this potential involvement for your brand image?
2. What research would you need to help make your decision?
3. If you did sponsor the series, but adverse publicity grew and your company was criticized for its involvement in what is seen as 'normalizing violence', what action might you take? Justify your answers.
4. Would there be any difference in your response to Question 3 if the series was based on police solving the murders and thus being seen to keep society safer?

Summary

What is becoming increasingly clear is that marketers must adopt a very different mindset to that of the past and consider what people do with the range of marketing communications they use[19] – which may or may not include conventional advertising. In today's volatile and rapidly changing marketplace, 'the communication challenge is to consider all contact points with customers and thus every channel of communication is a medium'[27] p. 51. This becomes particularly important when considering new, primarily electronic media forms in which people may co-create the context of the media, as evident with social media sites. The implications of the Internet and new media for effective communication strategies are the focus of the next two chapters.

No one medium or combination of media is going to be appropriate for all advertisers. You should be able to draw up an extensive list of the strengths and weaknesses of all media likely to be under consideration for a specific campaign, with different items taking on more or less importance according to the nature of the product or service for which the advertising programme is being developed. Each selected medium should complement other media selected so that the cumulative effect is greater than their individual contribution.[28,29]

THINK BOX

Choice of media and target audiences

Think about the following:

Returning to our earlier example of exotic holidays in warmer climates: How might the choice of media alter if the primary target audience was families with young children, young singles, or older but unconfident holiday makers?

Now repeat this exercise for a company promoting domestic travel.

Review questions

1. How important do you believe traditional media are in the current environment relative to newer communication options?
2. How might you determine the impact of simultaneous media usage among adolescents?
3. You are considering purchasing advertising time in a newly released movie showing in cinemas. The movie has received severe criticism for gratuitous violence. Does this affect your decision as to whether to buy advertising or not? Would your decision change once the movie is released for screening on television?
4. You are considering purchasing television advertising in a US-originated programme which rates well against your primary target group but which is known to contain product placements for a competing brand. How does this affect your decision?
5. How might creative factors affect media choices? Give examples to illustrate your answer.
6. Draw up a table of the strengths and weaknesses of:

    *   television
    *   radio
    *   newspapers
    *   magazines
    *   cinema
    *   outdoor advertising (posters, hoardings etc.)
    *   the Internet.

    Now critically discuss how the importance of any factors you listed might change for:

- fast moving consumer goods
- durable goods such as washing machines
- cars
- overseas holidays
- charity fundraising
- social marketing for energy conservation and for sun protection.

Recommended reading

Ambler, T. (2000). Persuasion, pride and prejudice: how ads work. *International Journal of Advertising*, 19(3), 299–315.

Baron, R. and Sissors, J. (2010). *Advertising Media Planning*, 7th edition, New York: McGraw Hill.

Heath, R., and Feldwick, P. (2008). Fifty years using the wrong model of advertising. *International Journal of Market Research*, 50(1), 29–59.

Pilotta, J.J., and Schultz, D.E. (2005). Simultaneous media experience and synesthesia. *Journal of Advertising Research*, 45(1), 19–26.

Pilotta, J.J., Schultz, D.E., Drenik, G., and Rist, P. (2005). Simultaneous media usage: a critical consumer orientation to media planning. *Journal of Consumer Behavior*, 45(1), 19–26.

CASE STUDY 8.1

Ancestry.co.uk

Source: Institute of Practitioners in Advertising: IPA Effectiveness Awards 2009. Authors: Mark Buttress and Paul Cooper, Brilliant Media. Contributing authors: Rachel Empson, Steve Leonard, Lisa Haynes, Louise McKee and Ben Bisco, Brilliant Media. Case material provided by the World Advertising Research Centre (WARC) www.warc.com.

This case study illustrates how a very specific niche market can be effectively reached. As you read it, consider topics such as targeting and the use of the Internet as a communications medium.

Background

Ancestry.co.uk was launched in 2001 and is the UK's leading family history site. The popularity of family history has grown exponentially over the last two years, partially due to programmes such as the BBC's *Who Do You Think You Are?* Ancestry has over 820 million searchable names, and this has made it much easier and quicker to research family history as people can search for their family members in online collections such as Censuses, phone books, newspapers, parish records and birth, marriage and death indexes to get very detailed information about their ancestors in minutes.

Ancestry.co.uk is part of a global network of Ancestry sites that includes Ancestry.com in the US, Ancestry.ca in Canada, Ancestry.com.au in Australia, Ancestry.de in Germany, Ancestry.it in Italy, Ancestry.fr in France, Ancestry.se in Sweden and Jiapu.com in China.

There are a number of players within the online genealogy market, with Ancestry and Genes United taking the lion's share of web visitors.

The revenue model varies across sites, with Ancestry.co.uk being very much a premium product, charging an annual subscription of £83.40. Genes United do not charge the end user a fee, but instead operate an advertisement-based revenue model. Many smaller players operate a combination of the two.

With Ancestry's simple annual subscription model there is a clear correlation between site visitors and revenue.

Target audience

Generally genealogy has greater appeal among an older audience with a slight female bias. The target audience for Ancestry.co.uk has been defined as AB Women, aged 55–64 with broadband access and heavy Internet use. The characteristics of this audience include a low consumption of media, which is mainly consumed for information purposes rather than entertainment, and a thirst for knowledge.

TGI Touchpoints reveals that this audience

- Use magazines for the following:

  o   education/information, index 127
  o   research, index 124
  o   practical advice, index 118
  o   treat/reward myself, index 106
  o   keep up to date, index 103
  o   relax/escapism, index 101.

- Are strong users of the Internet both at home and at work:

  o   at home, index 150
  o   at work, index 145.

- Internet usage at the weekend is high with 3–4 hours a day indexing highest at 186, followed by 2–3 hours a day at 178.
- The top five types of websites visited in the last month are:

  o   gardening
  o   business
  o   home improvements
  o   personal finance
  o   electrical equipment.

Context

With annual subscription being the sole source of revenue for ancestry.co.uk, each customer's potential value was capped. Therefore the key task was to build volume of annual subscriptions by driving maximum traffic to site, and optimizing visitor-to-trial and trial-to-subscription conversions. Considerable work had been done in the previous year to optimize subscription conversions, the task in 2008 therefore was to focus on driving additional volume of site traffic and to keeping cost-per-visits to a minimum.

While **offline** marketing (primarily in press) had a part to play in generating interest in family history research and building brand awareness, the bulk of site traffic was attributed to online search, with online display activity accounting for a large portion of spend, yet no direct link to site visits or subscriptions. Questions were therefore raised over the continued use of online display advertising.

However with the most cost-efficient acquisition channel being in limited supply (search volumes were low due to the niche nature of the product) it was important to understand the true value of online display advertising, and go beyond the traditional methods of evaluating online display campaign effectiveness. The current norm was to use click-and-view-based conversions using the last event metric. However in reality this gave a distorted picture (only 7.45 per cent of conversions were click-based and it was known that display affects other media such as search), so the team wanted to build a more realistic performance model.

This case study therefore focusses solely on the Engagement Mapping project, the learnings it delivered and the influence on future campaign planning and marketing effectiveness.

Approach

The approach was to look at a high volume of display ads delivered and to map these onto individual response patterns, to try to map the entire online customer journey prior to subscription examining the relationships between the many different influencing factors.

Data requirements

The team needed a robust data set to be able to achieve their objectives and to validate the findings over a wide period, therefore we decided to use the period Jan to Jul 2008. Atlas, the primary data source, gave us a full 6 months of data. Atlas provided us with data covering 20 per cent of the UK population for this period. This included all impressions served, clicks and conversions of people that interacted with any display or search ads for ancestry within this time period.

Variables for the impression data included date and time, unique ID (this related to the cookie tag), advertiser and creative delivered. Over 132 million display impressions were included in the model and more than 500,000 clicks.

Key steps

The primary steps towards achieving the overall objective were to understand key metrics of the display campaign.

1 Optimum ad frequency

Throughout the campaign period – the total number of impressions served per individual are detailed in the chart below as a percentage of the total. The average number of impressions delivered per individual was 7.32, with 71 per cent receiving no more than 5 ads.

Individuals that converted the number of impressions delivered prior to sign-up was on average 9.78, but 70 per cent saw fewer than 10 ads prior to conversion.

Those converting were seeing more ads than non-converting individuals. Therefore we knew that we needed to increase the frequency of the inventory by 2 in order to communicate the key points of the brand, message and product to the consumer.

2 Optimum time period

We needed to determine the time period between first or last impression and sign-up. These were separated between search and display on the attribution model. The more immediate impact was noticed on search, where 28 per cent of individuals saw their first ad and converted via search within a week, for display this was 20 per cent.

Table 8.1 Period between first ad and sign-up by media

Period	Search	% search	Display	% display	Total	% total
Same day	2,156	10.04	939	3.77	3,095	6.67
1 day	939	4.37	800	3.21	1,739	3.75
2–3 days	1,173	5.46	1,288	5.17	2,461	5.31
4–7 days	1,672	7.79	2,132	8.56	3,804	8.2
2 weeks	1,885	8.78	2,547	10.22	4,432	9.55
3 weeks	1,303	6.07	2,082	8.36	3,385	7.3
4 weeks	1,115	5.19	1,701	6.83	2,816	6.07

The difference is even more pronounced in the first day where the differential between search and display is 10.04 per cent and 3.77 per cent respectively (Table 8.1).

This data illustrates what we already suspected – display activity builds awareness and communicates the message yet does not tend to be an activation medium. Search tends to be an activation channel but the data illustrates that in this case it is not as conclusive as the actual keyword journey is much more complex and a longer conversion process than we normally see in other industries.

This data led us to the conclusion that display ads were having an effect on search conversion.

When viewed from the last impression perspective then the conversion period contracts – and the differential between search and display is no longer apparent.

Between last ad and sign-up is 42 per cent for both search and display (Table 8.2).

This illustrates that display is acting as directional and activation when looked at from a last action model (in addition to driving brand, awareness and engagement) and is essentially playing two crucial roles. With the low cost of online display inventory in comparison to other media this is how we really took advantage of these findings by increasing both volume and frequency.

Table 8.2 Period between last ad and sign-up by media

Period	Search	% search	Display	% display
Same day	2,955	13.76	2,827	11.32
1 day	1,672	7.79	1,966	7.87
2–3 days	1,957	9.11	2,588	10.36
4–7 days	2,419	11.26	3,302	13.22
2 weeks	2,398	11.17	3,395	13.6

3 Attribution and touchpoint analysis

The next step was to review whether there are any flaws within the last event metric when evaluating supplier and creative effectiveness. This was done by examining sign-ups against first ad delivered, last ad and seen between these **touchpoints**. The differential between first and last is expressed as a percentage of the total sign-ups of those seeing a display ad within the campaign period.

Bespoke sites show little variance, Advertising UK is the highest at –5.8 per cent, with Adviva and Adconian showing a positive differential.

This illustrated that if we give equal prominence to the first ad as well as the last ad (i.e. brand, engagement and activation) then it completely changes our view of the efficiency of the media placements. We used this to then re-plan the media taking into account the weight and cost we pay for activity to balance out against our objectives.

For creative, the efficiency ratio between first and last ads viewed show a positive increase for larger formats but a negative one for smaller ones. These findings are as you would imagine (the half banner and super skyscraper did not have enough volume to be statistically valid) larger sizes tended to be more effective when giving the initial ad seen equal prominence to the last ad seen from a conversion perspective.

4 Display within the customer journey

From the above learnings the team was accurately able to place media within the customer journey cycle.

These have been split into five key periods:

- 49–40 days: first touchpoint – network display
- 39–23 days: second touchpoint – targeted sites
- 22–13 days: closer to conversion, Ad.com seen within this period
- 12–6 days: visited site – PPC searches
- 5 days: brand searches.

Again this clearly illustrates the role display plays as the introducer and search as the activation channel (in addition to more targeted display activity from a content targeting perspective).

5 Display impact upon search

The next step was to evaluate the impact of display ads on search conversion rates. This was crucial to truly understanding the role and effect of display media. If search plays a large part in the activation of a user how much of that activation is as a direct result of the display activity? For the campaign period, search converts were separated between those that had viewed an ad and those that had not. From these two groups we looked at the overall conversion rate from click to signup:

- not seen an impression click to sign up = 1.8 per cent
- seen an impression click to sign up = 4.6 per cent
- this represents an uplift of 260 per cent.

When looking at brand searches alone:

- not seen an impression click to sign up = 3.1 per cent
- seen an impression click to sign up = 10.9 per cent
- this represents an uplift of 350 per cent.

For generic searches:

- not seen an impression click to sign up = 1.4 per cent
- seen an impression click to sign up = 3.4 per cent
- this represents an uplift of 240 per cent.

This clearly shows that display activity was directly driving over 50 per cent of all brand search conversions and a large proportion of generic keyword search conversions.

To this affect the team was able to start to report these conversions attributing the right uplift back to the display campaign to give a true customer acquisition cost for the channel/ activity.

6 Conversion exposure

This analysis gives an overall picture where online sign-ups were derived from. 74 per cent were either from display, search or a combination. This illustrates that in order to run the most effective campaign to drive new acquisition you need to use the two channels in unison with clearly defined ways as outlined in this document.

7 Display impact upon sales

From the search uplift results the team was able to build a formula and apply to search generated sign-ups in 2008 (Table 8.3):

> display impact = search sign-ups − (search clicks × conversion rate (not seeing impression))

Table 8.3 Potential sign-ups impacted by display activity (2008)

Clicks	All sign-ups	Search	Display
3,157,442	78,165	44,204	33,961

Summary

The engagement analysis has shown that:

- The optimum frequency of ads (9.78) shown to elicit a conversion. Capping the amount of ads shown has increased cost effectiveness.
- 47 per cent of sign-ups fall within 4 weeks of the first impression exposure. The immediacy is more apparent for search sign-ups (10.04 per cent on same day).
- Taking into account first exposure as well as the last illustrates different results between networks and sites.
- Larger creatives have an influence at earlier exposures (+1 per cent) and smaller ones are used later in the conversion journey (-0.25 per cent).
- Significant uplift in search conversion from customers viewing ads (260 per cent). Greater uplift in brand keywords (350 per cent) than generic overall (240 per cent).
- The learnings from this project have had a considerable impact on the media schedule for this year, and subscriptions for Quarter 1 2009 has shown an increase of over 50 per cent based on the same period last year. This cannot be attributed entirely to changes in the media schedule as 2009 saw the introduction of access to the 1911 Census. There is no historical evidence of the impact of a new survey being added to the Ancestry.co.uk site since its inception.

CASE STUDY QUESTIONS

1. Critique this case, drawing on material covered in all chapters, but particularly discussions regarding ROI.
2. How would you recommend Ancestry.co.uk monitor ongoing web visitor activity in the future?
3. How would you recommend they measure user satisfaction with the site structure and content?
4. How would you determine what other sources of information are used by people researching their family histories and how valuable Ancestry.co.uk's material is seen in relation to those other sources?

5.   Discuss the implications of your potential findings for the future development of the Ancestry.co.uk services.

CASE STUDY 8.2

Watch your own heart attack (British Heart Foundation)

Source: Case study taken from Institute of Practitioners in Advertising Effectiveness Awards. This case has been condensed from *Watch Your Own Heart Attack*. Author: Nick Hirst, Grey London. Case material provided by the World Advertising Research Centre (WARC) www.warc.com. This case won a bronze medal in the 2009 Effectiveness Awards.

This case illustrates how traditional media can be used in an unusual and unexpected way in order to maximize the impact of the marketing communication message.

Overview

94,000 people die of a heart attack every year in the UK. For those trying to reduce that number, a key area of focus is patient delay, measured through 'pain to call time'. The key factor in terms of survival and quality of life is the total time from onset of myocardial infarction (heart attack) to reperfusion (thrombolysis (drugs)) or angioplasty (balloon in artery) of which pain to call time is a part. As the NHS has improved the call to reperfusion times and services in recent years, much of the delay is now down to the time taken by the patient or carer calling the NHS (ideally the ambulance service).

Patient delay is important because speed of treatment directly impacts on both survival and quality of life after a heart attack. From the minute symptoms start, heart muscle starts to die, irrevocably, hampering the heart's ability to function. So patient delay also reduces quality of life, including ability to work and exercise. This is a given in the British medical community; but a US study quantified its importance:

*   Survival rates are improved by up to 50 per cent if drugs are administered within 1 hour of symptom onset.
*   Delaying treatment by 30 minutes can reduce average life expectancy by 1 year.
*   For every 15 minutes that the start of treatment for heart attack is delayed, the odds of death increase 1.6 times.

Waiting to call 999 can kill. Waiting to call 999 can leave you disabled. 90 per cent of people know that. And yet for some reason, people don't call immediately. This campaign by the British Heart Foundation tries to change this.

Deadly ignorance

The key reason is ignorance. A study conducted in Glasgow found that three quarters of people delay more than an hour. And in all cases where delay was more than one hour the main reasons for the delay were thinking that symptoms would go away or that they were not serious. Everyone *thinks* they know a heart attack when they see one. Sudden chest pain. Collapse. Death. This is the 'Hollywood heart attack'.

In reality, every heart attack is different. And yet awareness of the range of symptoms varies widely, ranging from nausea to pain in the jaw.

There are an estimated 2.4m people at risk of heart attack in the UK right now – men and women, middle-aged to elderly. Just over one in 20 of these people will have a heart attack in any 12-month period. Even with individual medical screening, it's extremely difficult to tell who they are, or where they are.

This large audience, very difficult to communicate to on an individual basis, makes marketing communications a vital part of efforts to reduce patient delay.

The British Heart Foundation has been running its 'Doubt Kills' campaign since 2006. It aimed to reduce pain-to-call time by raising awareness of chest pain as a symptom, using the device of an invisible belt around a man's chest. But by 2008 awareness of symptoms other than chest pain was still 'extremely low'.

This called for a new campaign. The overall objective remained the same: to save lives and improve the quality of life amongst those experiencing heart attacks by reducing the pain to call time.

But now the *range of symptoms* was a key part of the communications objectives:

- Increase awareness, knowledge and understanding of the range of heart attack symptoms.
- Highlight the relevance of heart attacks (and hence this knowledge) to the target audience.
- Motivate people to take action to learn more about heart attack symptoms from the British Heart Foundation.

Five factors made the problem difficult to solve:

1. Complexity

The campaign needed to communicate a range of eight symptoms, and tell people they needed to call immediately if they were experiencing any of them. This meant the audience had to understand and remember a complicated message.

2. Broad target audience

Because there is no way to predict who will have a heart attack, the campaign needed to communicate to the broadest possible audience. 45+, C1C2D men are most at risk, and represented the best chance to communicate to the right people cost-effectively.

3. Denial and resistance among the audience

Time and time again, research has demonstrated that those likely to suffer a heart attack simply don't see themselves as 'at risk'. This means they're unlikely to listen as a matter of course to messages, and unlikely to call 999 unless they're certain they're having an attack.

4. Limited budget

Despite a complex message and a tough target audience, the campaign had a budget of only £1.35m. So many of the obvious media options for delivering a complex, hard-hitting message to large numbers of people were unavailable.

5. No clear recipe for success

Research has shown that there is 'little evidence that media/ public education interventions reduced delay'. And even taking into account non-communications interventions, there are few clear 'rules' for success: 'Studies that were effective in reducing delay appeared similar to those that were ineffective.'

The communications approach

The strategy that solved these problems was based on two insights from qualitative research:

> People who have had a heart attack before are more likely to know when they're having one and take immediate action.

And

> It's often the partner of a victim that prompts or makes the 999 call.

Furthermore, the first four problems outlined above gave the agency several channel and creative imperatives:

- **Complexity** of message meant that the communications had to be richly detailed.
- The **broad target audience** meant that the team had to use a traditional broadcast medium.
- **Denial and resistance** meant two things: first, that creative had to be visceral and compelling (rather than simply informative); second, that the team would have to ensure communications were seen in a shared environment so that partners could take action where sufferers would not.
- Given the above, TV was rapidly emerging as the optimum channel; however, the **limited budget** meant that there were not sufficient resources to be able to use it in the traditional way (repeating commercials that were long enough to carry a complex message).

The solution

The idea was to give the audience a 'dry-run' heart attack, together. Communications would simulate, rather than inform, to ensure the resistance audience would internalize our message.

The simulation itself was a two-minute film, aired on ITV, advertised through announcement media, to ensure large numbers of the right people watched together. It was subsequently made available online so people could recommend it or watch it again.

As such the campaign had three distinct phases: **invitation**, **event**, and **repeat**.

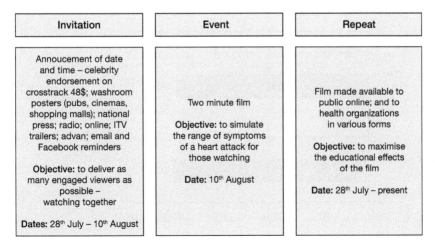

Figure 8.1 Communications model

Invitation

The invitation phase invited people to watch 'the most important two minutes of TV you'll ever see'. Posters were simple announcements; in film and radio, celebrities like David Cameron and Chris Tarrant lent a sense of scale. People could also request reminders.

Event

In the film itself, Stephen Berkoff 'inflicts' the symptoms of a heart attack upon the viewer. TV allowed us to demonstrate a number of symptoms, in dramatic and involving fashion, to millions of people watching together.

Repeat

The repeat phase allowed people to watch the film again, and share it with others. The film was made available at www.2minutes.org and on **YouTube**. It was also offered to healthcare organizations.

Success

Did people watch the film? And more importantly, did they remember it?

Minute-by-minute BARB data indicates that 6.07m people (or about 13 per cent of the adult population) watched the film. Tracking data indicates 17 per cent recall among all adults.

This suggests that everyone who saw it remembered it – including an estimated 3.2m of our 45+ C1C2D target audience.

Furthermore, the invitation phase played a part in delivering that audience. Tracking data shows that 38 per cent of viewers in the target audience had planned to watch the ad.

In addition, 10,000 requested email or text reminders from 2minutes.org.uk. And to date, the film has been watched 370,000 times on 2minutes.org.uk and 75,000 times on YouTube. This suggests that all three phases of the communications model worked as intended.

Four out of five of those who saw the film understood there's more to heart attacks than just chest pains (Figure 8.2).

Awareness of the *five* key symptoms featured in the film increased significantly (Figure 8.3).

92 per cent of viewers in the target audience understood that it was 'Vital that you call 999 straight away when experiencing even mild symptoms.'

Furthermore, awareness and understanding was sustained over time, as demonstrated by a second survey three months later.

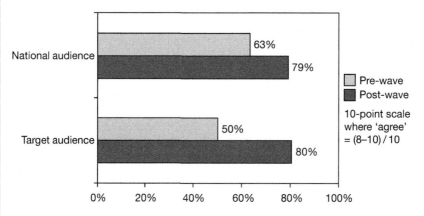

Figure 8.2 Agreement that 'Every heart attack is different, there is a variety of symptoms'

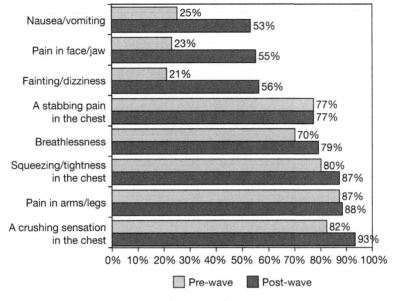

Figure 8.3 Pre- and post-wave awareness of heart attack symptoms

Relevance

Personal concern about heart attack among the target audience increased almost fourfold, from 17 per cent to 58 per cent (Figure 8.4).

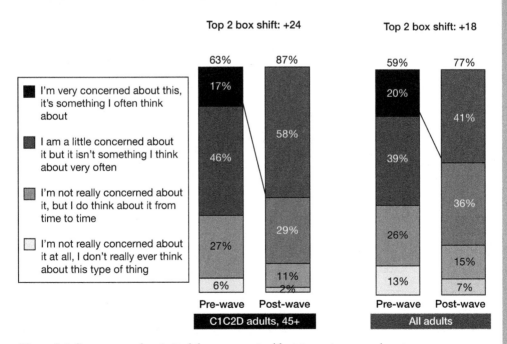

Figure 8.4 Concern over heart attack by agreement with statements, pre- and post-wave

There was also a significant increase in the importance of knowing about heart attack symptoms – vital given that it's often someone else who calls 999 (Figure 8.5).

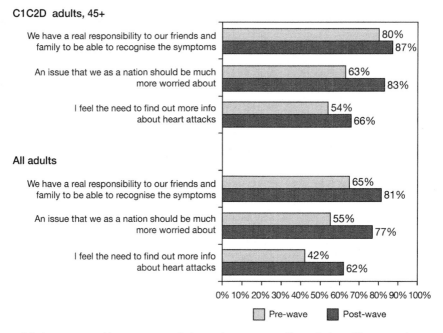

Figure 8.5 Agreement with statements relating to importance of knowledge of heart attack symptoms

Motivate people to take action

Nearly half discussed the TV ad; 32 per cent of target audience viewers reported looking for more information on the Internet (Figure 8.6).

		Talk about TV ad	Talk about symptoms	Look on Internet for more info	Watch again on BHF website myself	Watch again with friends/ family	Find out more GP	Find out more NHS Direct
C1C2D adults, 45+	Done	52%	44%	32%	24%	21%	13%	7%
All adults	Done	51%	46%	44%	35%	27%	16%	6%

Figure 8.6 Further action taken following film

Google search data for August show a significant and unprecedented uplift in search traffic for 'heart attack' (Figure 8.7), and 28 per cent of the target watched the film again with friends and family (suggesting an even wider audience than those who initially tuned in).

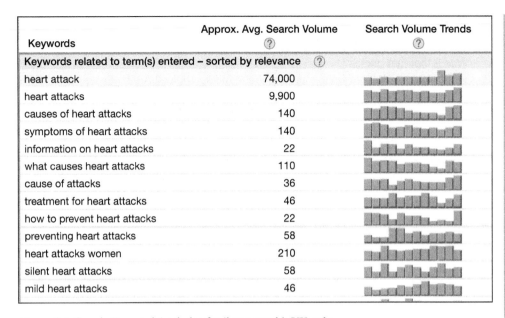

Figure 8.7 Google Keyword Analytics for 'heart attack', UK only

Results: patient delay

The film clearly achieved its communications objectives. But did this strategy reduce patient delay, and achieve the primary objective, which was:

> To save lives and improve the quality of life amongst those experiencing heart attacks by reducing the pain to call time.

MINAP data for Q3 2008 shows that pain-to-call time fell to 53 minutes, its **lowest level since 2005** during the campaign, and was **two and a half minutes** lower for the second half of 2008 than for the average of previous years.

Furthermore, those slowest to call delayed even less. This is important because these sufferers are often the ones experiencing the 'less acute' (though no less dangerous) symptoms of which awareness was lowest.

Table 8.4 Average time taken to call emergency services from onset of symptoms

	Average for all cases	Average for slowest quartile
Average national pain-to-call time, 2006–Q2 2008	57 minutes	129.5 minutes
Average pain-to-call time since campaign (H2 2008)	54.5 minutes	125 minutes
Drop in pain-to-call time after campaign	2.5 minutes	4.5 minutes

Two-and-a-half minutes doesn't sound much, but every minute saved is vital.

CASE STUDY QUESTIONS

1. Discuss why the agency chose to run the campaign using traditional broadcast media. Was it the right choice?
2. What message factors were important in the media choice? Are there alternative ways of delivering a complex message?
3. How was the media usage different from a 'normal' campaign you would usually see?
4. Why was it useful to have a 'three phase' approach – rather than repeating the message more frequently? Would such an approach be good for all types of adverts? Why or why not?
5. Do you think the combination of new media in the repeat phase and traditional media worked well? Discuss other ways of using new and traditional media together.
6. For what other marketing communications campaigns is this type of approach likely to be effective? Justify your response.

CASE STUDY 8.3

DWP/COI – giving it to you straight

This case has been condensed from Nairn, A. and Kenny, J. (2008). 'DWP/COI – Giving it to you straight', Case Study Institute of Practitioners in Advertising Effectiveness Awards. Case material provided by the World Advertising Research Centre (WARC) www.warc.com.

This case study illustrates how traditional media were used to inform the public of a key change to the way state benefits and pensions would be paid. It is unusual in that it did not seek to 'sell' anything, to canvass support or encourage behaviour change. It set out to inform people that their behaviour had to change and what they needed to do.

Overview

From 2003, the government began to move towards electronic transfer as a normal method of paying social security benefits and state pensions, a move that would impact on 13 million people whom research showed to be 'overwhelmingly negative' about the change, with practical concerns such as managing bank accounts and the loss of social contact if they no longer collected their entitlements in person. Post Office staff actively lobbied against the plans, with concerns regarding possible branch closures. Media coverage was also negative, but the changes were pursued as they offered significant savings, estimated at £450 million annually in processing costs and fraud reduction.

A consumer-facing brand was developed using the 'Direct payment – giving it to you straight' premise that summed up the essence of the campaign.

For the first stage of communication, a straightforward, yet high-standout approach was taken, using a TV campaign featuring familiar faces chosen for their credibility with the target population (the actors Annette Crosbie and Chris Walker) talking matter-of-factly about the changes, and reassuring people that they'd be receiving 'a letter and leaflet with information about what to do next'.

All other channels (from print and radio to DM) then used ordinary people to explain the implications of the change for specific customer groups (e.g. Income Support, Incapacity

DWP Department for Work and Pensions

There's a new arrangement for Income Support.

Your money gets paid straight into your account.

direct payment giving it to you straight

Direct Payment is the way all benefits will be paid, because order books and giros are being phased out. But to make changing easy:

• You'll receive a letter and a leaflet telling you all about Direct Payment and what to do next if you need to change.

• You'll still receive the same amount of money as you do now.

• If you don't have a suitable account, the leaflet explains your options.

• Using cash machines, you can get your money out any time you like, anywhere in the country.

• And you can still use the Post Office™ to get your money.

In the meantime, for more information please call us on **0800 107 2000** (textphone 0800 107 4000 if you have hearing difficulties) or visit www.dwp.gov.uk/directpayment. All lines open 8am to 9pm weekdays, 9am to 5pm weekends.

Photo 8.1

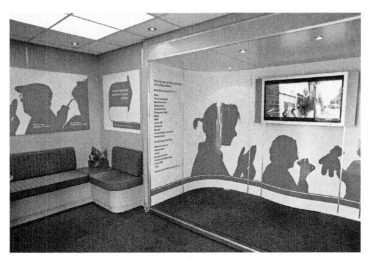

Photo 8.2a

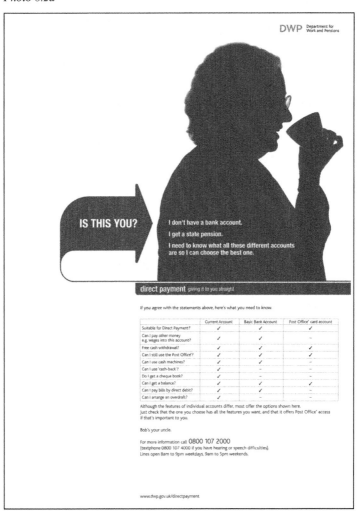

Photo 8.2b-1

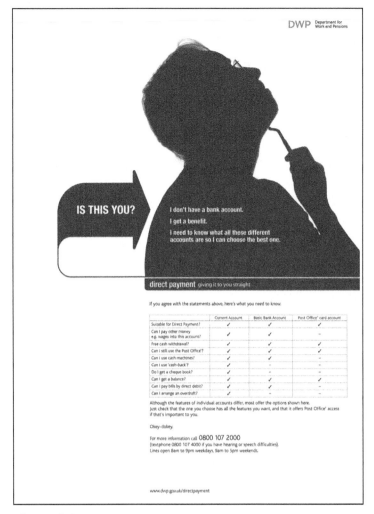

Photo 8.2b-2

Benefit, Disability Living Allowance recipients). Naturally, the Direct Payment brand device ran across all activity, ensuring an extremely coherent campaign feel (Photo 8.1).

A second phase provided details of what the changes entailed, offered reassurance and addressed misconceptions; space prevents us from reproducing samples of the material used. The advertisements are attributed with providing the main source of awareness and information.

The key target (for 85 per cent of claimants to opt for Direct Payment by the end of 2005) was met one year early – against all predictions. It has since continued to grow, to virtually universal levels (Figure 8.8).

The shift was far smoother than anticipated, with 95 per cent of users declaring themselves happy with the new system and 86 per cent describing it as an improvement. Ofcom now cites Direct Payment as an example of best practice when delivering large switchover campaigns to vulnerable audiences. Likewise, the National Audit Office, in a review of 24 successful change programmes from around the world, cites Direct Payment as a rare example of a project which has 'delivered real and lasting benefits to citizens'.

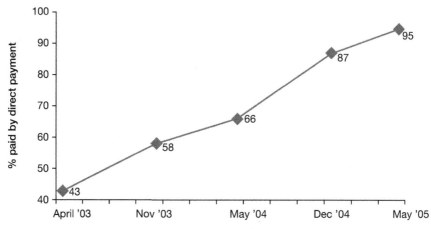

Figure 8.8 PSA target was met 1 year early

CASE STUDY QUESTIONS

1. Why do you believe the campaign was so successful?
2. Critique the combination of media used – what role did each perform?
3. What do you believe was the rationale for selecting the two actors as spokes-people?
4. Central and local government frequently communicate with the public regarding decisions that are to be made on their behalf. This type of communication therefore does not seek to persuade, but to inform people of choices, canvass views or clarify actions that may need to be taken if specific alternatives are selected. Find examples of this type of information provision and critique the approach taken.
5. What challenges do information and opinion-seeking campaigns face compared to those for more conventional advertising?
6. How well do you believe these types of campaigns use different media types? What improvements can you suggest for future activity?

CASE STUDY 8.4

Novartis: tissue overload

Case study taken from Institute of Practitioners in Advertising Effectiveness Awards. This case won a bronze medal in the 2010 Euro Effies Awards. Case material provided by the World Advertising Research Centre (WARC) www.warc.com.

Not all products are, in themselves, exciting – but they are often necessary. This case study outlines the creative and media strategy used for a nasal spray. It shows how even a mundane product can be positioned as a 'hero' by offering a solution to a problem with both health and social dimensions – a nasal cold.

The challenge for Otrivin was how to launch a true innovation in a category that is so dormant that people have stopped paying attention because they don't expect there's anything new going on. This is a story of a forgotten category: there has been no innovation offered in the past 10 years for nasal congestion based on the common cold. All nasal sprays do and communicate the same: they unblock your nose so you can breathe better. Many people think that all the nasal sprays are the same; they unblock your nose and that is it.

Novartis Consumer Health exceeded its objectives in launching Otrivin Complete in Europe, during the severe economic crisis. The overall rise in market share has been 50 per cent over target and each market has exceeded target, while showing a very healthy growth rate.

Objectives

- Increase value share for the total Otrivin brand by 2 points (by successfully launching new Otrivin Complete while minimalizing cannibalization on the Otrivin base SKU).
- Differentiate Otrivin Complete from all the other brands.

Target audience

Men and women who suffer from a nasal cold that hassles them in the everyday course of their busy lives – no matter if it's full-time and overtime at work, or juggling a family and a job and an active personal life. The truth is, there's too much to do and they never quite get around to taking good care of themselves. A blocked and runny nose from a cold becomes a persistent annoyance that keeps getting in the way of them being able to stay focussed and fresh for the day.

Creative strategy

Otrivin's opportunity was to reveal how, in fact, nasal cold sufferers are putting up with an incomplete solution by pointing out the negative attention that people receive from others because of their ongoing reliance on using tissues. This is especially aggravating when people are out in public and trying to be at their best. It shows that they're not completely in control of how they wish to present themselves.

Media strategy

In order to create high levels of awareness for the new product and the need to illustrate the effect of Otrivin Complete, TV had a leading role supported by print. As the target audience is so busy, in store and outdoor had an important role as well. On top, PR was used to drive additional interest and publicity.

Budget
€ 5–10 million

Markets
Belgium, the Netherlands, Norway, Poland, Sweden

Evidence of results

- Total Otrivin brand value share has seen an overall rise in market share of 50 per cent over target and each market has exceeded the target, while they have shown a very

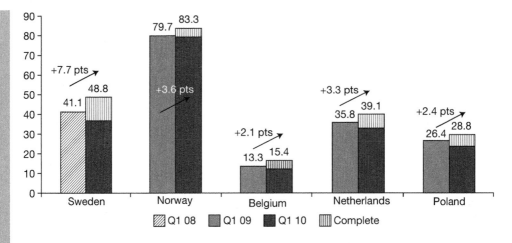

Figure 8.9 Value market share for total Otrivin brand per market

healthy growth rate. The growth has been mainly incremental and there was only a limited cannibalization effect for the existing business.

- Consumers believe that Otrivin Complete is different from all the other nasal sprays. The campaign created tremendous interest, and was appreciated with the audience. With a correct message identification of 'Tissue Overload' scoring 24 per cent higher than the benchmark.

CASE STUDY QUESTIONS

1. The lead medium was television, supported by print. Discuss why radio was not considered as a medium.
2. The identification of busy lifestyles among the target group saw the inclusion of in-store and outdoor activity. Explain the roles these two media channels played relative to television and print.
3. How would you ensure that all selected media supported each other?
4. How would you determine which combination of media were seen by the target prior to their purchase and what their relative influence was?
5. What role do you believe PR played in the campaign and how would you measure its effects?

CASE STUDY 8.5

Road safety strategies

This case has been condensed from Lyle, D., Bailie, J.A., McCartney, D., Lyle, R. and Martin, D. Department of the Environment (NI)/Road Safety Authority (ROI) – The longer-term effects of seatbelt advertising 2001–2007. Case study: Institute of Practitioners in Advertising Effectiveness Awards. Case material provided by the World Advertising Research Centre (WARC) www.warc.com.

Road safety is a difficult area, with campaigns over time having used a range of strategies from fear-based appeals, educational approaches and even humour (for an example of this, see the Australian 'Pinkie' campaign which stated that speeding was due to the drivers' sexual inadequacies!) to address a range of issues such as alcohol impaired driving, speeding and seatbelt use.

The campaign discussed here set out to reduce the number of road deaths and serious injuries in both Northern Ireland and the Republic of Ireland through changing attitudes towards wearing of seatbelts and, ultimately, seatbelt use.

The primary target was the 15–34 year age group as they are over-represented among road traffic casualties both in Ireland and many other countries. Research identified attitudes and perceptions regarding seatbelt use as factors that would motivate people to wear

Photo 8.3a

Photo 8.3b

Photo 8.3c

Photo 8.3d

Photo 8.3e

Photo 8.3f

Photos 8.3a–f Initial hard hitting creative 'Damage'

Photo 8.4a

Photo 8.4b

Photo 8.4c

Photo 8.4d

Photo 8.4a–d 'Get it On' creative strategy 2006

seatbelts, particularly the prospect of killing a family member or friend or of being seriously disabled.

The **creative strategy** therefore focussed on realistic dramatization of the potential consequences of not wearing seatbelts, stressing personal relevance and risk with all activity branded, 'No Seatbelt – No Excuse' to summarize the moral consequences of not wearing a seatbelt – and disprove the perception that a seatbelt is a personal freedom or personal choice.

From 2001, shocking imagery was used to encode long-term memory and to dramatize the selfishness of not wearing a seatbelt by showing how brain damage and death are the outcomes, as shown in the storyboard from a 'Damage' focussed advertisement.

A separate advertisement 'Selfish' was developed to target parents, with the aim of emotionally engaging them by dramatizing the immoral selfishness of not ensuring that their children are correctly restrained in the car. This continued to build on the 'selfish' proposition to win the moral argument regarding child restraints in the light of the new legislation. The advertising had to persuade parents that 'the most selfish thing I can do to my children is to allow them to travel unrestrained'.

To address social norms and the acceptability of wearing seatbelts, 'Get it On' was launched to reinforce the fact amongst younger drivers and passengers that wearing your seatbelt is the cool thing to do as shown in the creative samples.

During the six years pre-launch of the seatbelts campaigns, 1,775 people were killed or seriously injured while not wearing a seatbelt. In the six years post-launch, the number of deaths and serious injuries fell to 953.

The public's perception of the most influential factors in saving lives on the roads was used to calculate the proportion of the €401.3 million (£378.4 million) economic saving (NI and ROI combined) which can be attributed to each of the influential factors. The road reduction payback of the TV ads as a "very influential" factor in saving lives is estimated at £66.29 million, with other factors such as police enforcement, news coverage and road engineering among other factors also influencing the results.

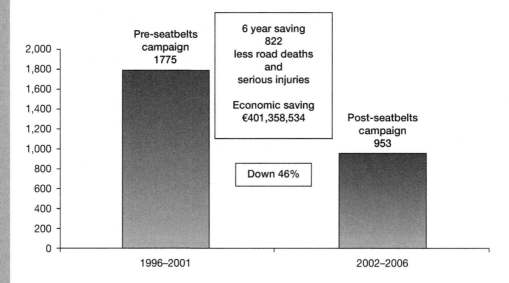

Figure 8.10 ROI road deaths and serious injuries without seatbelts pre- and post-damage/selfish/get it on – compared Republic of Ireland

CASE STUDY QUESTIONS

1. Discuss the use of traditional media as the foundation for the campaign.
2. How can the momentum be maintained and the message kept fresh?
3. How would you test when each message was becoming stale (wearing out)?

Notes

1 Ewing, M.T., du Plessis, E., and Foster, C. (2001). Cinema advertising re-considered. *Journal of Advertising Research*, 41(1), 78–85.
2 Ha, L., and Litman, B.R. (1997). Does advertising clutter have diminishing and negative returns? *Journal of Advertising*, 26(1), 31–42.
3 National Social Marketing Centre (2006). *It's Our Health! Realizing the Potential of Effective Social Marketing*, London: National Social Marketing Centre.
4 Pieters, R., Warlop, L., and Wedel, M. (2002). Breaking through the clutter: benefits of advertisement originality and familiarity for brand attention and memory. *Management Science*, 48(6), 765–81.
5 Rotfeld, H.J. (2006). Understanding advertising clutter and the real solution to declining audience attention to mass media commercial messages. *Journal of Consumer Marketing*, 23(4/5), 180–1.
6 Balasubramanian, S.K., Karrh, J.A., and Parwardhan, H. (2006). Audience response to product placement. An integrative framework and future research agenda. *Journal of Advertising*, 35(3), 115–41.
7 Kirmani, A. (1997). Advertising repetition as a signal of quality: if it's advertised so much, something must be wrong. *Journal of Advertising*, 26(3), 77–86.
8 Krugman, H.E. (1984). Why three exposures may be enough. *Journal of Advertising Research*, 24(4), 15–18.
9 Ambler, T. (2000). Persuasion, pride and prejudice: how ads work. *International Journal of Advertising*, 19(3), 299–315.
10 Baker, W.E., and Lutz, R.J. (2000). An empirical test of an updated relevance-accessibility model of advertising effectiveness. *Journal of Advertising*, 29(1), 1–14.
11 Bandyopadhyay, S., Kindra, G., and Sharp, L. (2001). Is television advertising good for children? Areas of concern and policy implications. *International Journal of Advertising*, 20(1), 89–116.
12 Garde, A. (2008). Food advertising and obesity prevention: what role for the European Union? *Journal of Consumer Policy*, 31(1), 25–44.
13 Livingstone, S. (2005). Assessing the research base for the policy debate over the effects of food advertising to children. *International Journal of Advertising*, 24(3), 273–96.
14 Hallward, J. (2008). 'Make measurable what is not so': consumer mix modeling for the evolving media world, *Journal of Advertising Research*, 48(3), 339–51.
15 Case, A. (2001). The last mass medium? *Brandweek*, 42(18), 12–14.
16 Philllips, J. and Noble, S.M. (2007). Simply captivating. *Journal of Advertising*, 36(1), 81–94.
17 Shimp, T.E. (2003). *Advertising, Promotion and Supplemental Aspects of IMC*, 6th edition, Independence, KY: Thompson South-Western.
18 Anonymous (2005). Outdoor audience measurement. *Campaign*, 25 February, p. 10.
19 Pilotta, J.J., and Schultz, D. (2005). Simultaneous media experience and synesthesia. *Journal of Advertising Research*, 45(1), 19–26.
20 Pilotta, J.J., Schultz, D.E., Drenik, G., and Rist, P. (2005). Simultaneous media usage: a critical consumer orientation to media planning. *Journal of Consumer Behavior*, 45(1), 19–26.
21 De Pelsmacker, P., Geuens, M., and Anckaert, P. (2002). Media context and advertising effectivness: the role of context appreciation and context/ ad similarity. *Journal of Advertising*, 31(2), 49–61.
22 De Pelsmacker, P., Geuens, M., and Anckaert, P. (2002). Media context and advertising effectivness: the role of context appreciation and context/ ad similarity. *Journal of Advertising*, 31(2), 49–61.

23 Janssens, W., and De Pelsmacker, P. (2005). Advertising for new and existing brands: the impact of media context and type of advertisement. *Journal of Marketing Communications*, 11(2), 113–28.

24 Prasad, V.K., and Smith, L.J. (1994). Television commercials in violent programming: an experimental evaluation of their effects on children. *Journal of the Academy of Marketing Science*, 22(4), 340–51.

25 Heath, R., and Feldwick, P. (2008). Fifty years using the wrong model of advertising. *International Journal of Market Research*, 50(1), 29–59.

26 Ritson, M., and Elliott, R. (1999). The social uses of advertising: an ethnographic study of adolescent advertising audiences. *Journal of Consumer Research*, 26(3), 260–77.

27 Jenkinson, A. (2006). Planning and evaluating communications in an integrated organization. *Journal of Targeting, Measurement & Analysis for Marketing*, 15(1), 47–64.

28 Naik, P.A., and Raman, K. (2003). Understanding the impact of synergy in multimedia communications. *Journal of Marketing Research (JMR)*, 40(4), 375–88.

29 Kliatchko, J. (2005). Towards a new definition of integrated marketing communications (IMC). *International Journal of Advertising*, 24(1), 7–34.

9 Electronic, new and social media

LEARNING OUTCOMES

After studying this chapter, you will be able to:

- Provide an overview of the role of electronic media in the marketing communication process

- Discuss the development of electronic media from traditional Internet forms through to new and emerging media, including the emergence of social networks

- Discuss the implications of using social networks for marketing and the challenges this provides

- Provide an overview of the ways in which effectiveness and return on investment may be measured

- Debate the ethical aspects of engaging in social media optimization

Introduction

The Internet emerged in the 1990s as a major mainstream communication tool. Originally limited to text-only-based communication (mostly using email), the Internet has emerged as a major tool for social communication while also evolving from the rather static environment in the early days to today's rich-media environment delivered over the Internet. Equally, during this time the Internet has changed from having a very narrow, mostly technical and academic audience to a widespread audience in most of the developed world.

While the technical foundations of the Internet have changed, so has the use of the Internet as a marketing (communications) tool. While in the early days there were only very limited creative opportunities, these barriers had been mostly overcome by the late 1990s, when the creative possibilities started to make the Internet, and especially the world wide web, almost equivalent to traditional, offline, static advertising tools, and enabled organizations to use the Internet in very much the same way as they would use printed information.

During the late 1990s, the Internet also emerged as both a communications tool as well as a distribution channel. One of the pioneers who capitalized on the expansion of the Internet and used the medium as a distribution tool was Amazon.com, which launched in 1995 and quickly expanded beyond the US into Europe and Asia. Yet while some companies have been extraordinarily successful in capitalizing on the emerging media many more companies have failed. Especially during the 'dot-com-bubble', which lasted roughly between 1995–2001[1] the Internet was hailed as the most fundamental business change in centuries – and many investors tried to jump on the bandwagon with little or no understanding of what operating in an increasingly interactive technology-driven environment entailed.

One of the problems encountered was that many organizations, especially traditional brick-and-mortar companies and smaller Internet start-ups treated the Internet as just the same as their real-world presence, which resulted in many websites being a carbon copy of their paper-based marketing tools, or at least treated in a similar fashion. This static approach to an interactive environment was evidently not what consumers wanted, and soon the approaches had to change to encompass more interactivity.

However, it would be too simple to say that only the static treatment of the traditional Internet lead to difficulties. Some companies tried to embrace the possibilities of the Internet before most of their customers were ready. The high-profile dot-com demise of Boo.com is a good example of this. The company launched in 1998 to much fanfare in the UK and promised to reshape the fashion retail business. However, the website was complicated to use, made excessive use of features, such as **Flash** and **JavaScript**, which were too advanced for most of its client base, and eventually folded in 2000.

Other companies found it hard to attract customers to go online and to present a compelling argument why customers should use their online-based services. Pets.com for example struggled to entice pet-owners to shop for products online despite its often high profile advertising campaigns featuring a talking sock-puppet, which in addition to appearing in the company's adverts appeared on a variety of television shows and in the New York Macy's Thanksgiving Parade. Yet, the company failed to attract sufficient orders and folded only two years after it launched. However, the case of Pets.com is interesting in more than one way, as it illustrates how difficult it is firstly to entice people to get to know a brand and visit or use a particular website and secondly then capitalizing on the brand name and/or turn the website visitors into actual customers who are prepared to spend money on a particular website.[2]

Finally, another reason why some companies found it hard to deliver on the Internet, was the often costly infrastructure required to make an attractive offer. In terms of opportunity cost, the time lag between order and delivery is a major concern for most Internet-based companies. Often this opportunity cost is reflected in substantially lower prices than on the high street, for example for fashion and electronic items, books and so forth. However, for many items even a one day delay may be too much, and thus companies offering those items required a substantial infrastructure to deliver those items. For example the online supermarket Webvan.com and the anything-delivery service Kozmo.com ultimately could not operate a profitable business combining online-ordering and real-life fulfilment.

THINK BOX

Online retailers

- Which websites do you use regularly to buy from?
- Why do you buy from them?
- How does your buying behaviour differ from going to a real ('bricks and mortar') shop?
- What items do you exclusively buy in a real shop?
- When do you check items on websites before going to a real shop to make a purchase? How many of the sites you visit are for brands versus retailers?
- What are the implications of your combined website visits/traditional outlet purchase for marketers and for retailers?

While many lessons can be learned from the failures of the early days of the Internet, probably the most important lesson that can be learned is that ultimately it is technological advancement and customer-orientation that drives growth online, and that just as in the real world, wherever the customer-orientation is lost, no matter how innovative, useful or well-advertised a brand or website is, it is unlikely to succeed.

THINK BOX

Website evaluation

Take any website that you are familiar with and evaluate it in terms of the eight Cs presented on p. 204.

- How well does it rank?
- Which Cs are the most important ones, and why?
- How does this differ from website to website?
- Now repeat this process for a website you have not found useful. How could the website be amended to offer better value for site visitors?

What are the implications of your evaluations for both useful and non-useful websites?

Table 9.1 Eight Cs

C	Meaning
Content	Relevant, interesting and up-to-date content, which engages the user. This content can be either centrally-generated (for example a news website) or user-generated (for example Facebook and other web 2.0 sites).
Context	The provision of relevant and useful context to the content and or searches provided. For example, the provision of links to restaurant reviews on a website for hotels.
Community	Building of a community of users, for example by providing a space where users can interact (e.g. forum) – which is especially important in case of non-user-generated content.
Customization	The ability to adopt a site to the specific needs of the user. For example, adding regional news headlines on the front page of a national website like the BBC.
Communication	Providing a real two-way communication environment, e.g. the user can interact with the website (owner) or other users.
Confidence	Enticing confidence in the seriousness and reliability of the website, the information provided and the safety and security of any data divulged by the users of such a site (e.g. credit card data).
Connection	Enabling the necessary technical infrastructure to successfully connect to the website and use the offers at reasonable speed.
Commerce	The possibility to spend on the website, for example in the form of 'value-added' memberships or in the form of buying products and services.

The other, increasingly important factor is interactivity and ultimately customer-empowerment. Although the later parts of this chapter will deal more specifically with customer-participation and interaction (e.g. **web 2.0**), it is nevertheless important to note that treating the Internet as just an extension of printed material has been highlighted as one of the major reasons why online retailers fail to be successful. Rather, various combinations of 'Cs' are suggested as success factors. For example, a three Cs framework of Communication, Context and Community,[3] others talk about Content, Connection and Commerce. Yet others talk about Content, Connection and Confidence,[4] or extend the three Cs to eight Cs: Content, Context, Community, Customization, Communication, Confidence, Connection, and Commerce.[5] (See Table 9.1.) Most importantly, however, is that with all the frameworks suggested, the commercialization (or Commerce) is just one of several Cs which make up a successful online environment.

Online advertising

Apart from general websites, one of the traditionally most important forms of marketing communications activity on the Internet is online advertising – either for products or services available offline, for other websites, or a combination of the two, i.e. for other websites which contain information about services or products available offline.

The most obvious difference from traditional, paper-based advertising is of course the added interactivity of online advertising, or even a **rich-media** type advertising, combining static images, video and sound. Online ads can interact with the consumer, for example by letting the consumer play games in order to claim a prize, or they can interact with the context in which they are displayed. For example, in 2007 Apple targeted readers of Microsoft-based PC reviews with an online ad which proclaimed 'Give Up on Vista' (full replay here: www.youtube.com/watch?v=ZRAUlK8_2VE), in which the well-known characters of 'PC' and 'Mac' debate if it is time to 'give up' on the Microsoft Vista operating system and switch to a Mac.

However, while the ability to interact with either content or user is a major advancement over all traditional media, it is also a potential source for user annoyance,[6] for example in the case of visiting a website, which then loads advertising that contains sound, which the user may find disturbing. In fact, some authors suggest that online advertising as a whole causes more annoyance than traditional advertising and may itself damage a brand.[7] Given that annoyance with advertising can potentially lead to advertising avoidance and even negative brand images, most 'annoying' forms of advertising are increasingly less likely to be used – at least when visiting serious websites. For example, **pop-up ads** and **superstitials** or **interstitials**, which prevented the users from directly clicking through to the wanted content, are less frequently used today – not least, because almost all modern browsers will block these types of advertising by default, thus making this type of advertising unviable.

However, while there is evidence that untargeted and 'annoying' advertising may alienate users, well targeted and relevant advertising may also enhance user experience.[8]

In fact, the Internet offers the most viable and effective targeting possibilities. For example, advertising can be targeted to reach only users in specific areas (by using IP selection and IP location), it can be context relevant (for example new PC buyers reading reviews), it can be dynamic (for example adapting to keyword searches) and it can be specific to dynamic content on remote websites (for example Google's AdSense, which delivers advertising specific to the website context for each user).

MINI CASE: GOOGLE ADSENSE

Google AdSense is an online advertising service, which delivers small adverts to websites based on the content of their webpages, i.e. a website that deals with nutrition would have adverts that relate to food and a website that sells cars would display adverts about buying and selling cars.

Most of the adverts are in the form of links to other websites (like in the example above), though occasionally they can also include additional information, images and even video.

In addition to the website content, the adverts can also be targeted depending on who views the adverts, for example where the viewers are from or what computer operating system or browser they are using.

The links are displayed based on a bidding process, in which the advertiser promises to pay a set amount for each person who clicks a link (i.e. not simply for displaying the link).

- What do you think are the positive points of this type of targeted adverts?
- What do you think are the potential negative points?
- Do you think you can successfully use this type of advertising to build a brand?

---

eCommerce/mCommerce

Electronic commerce (eCommerce), or using the Internet to purchase goods and services over the Internet has steadily increased in recent years, so much so, that eCommerce grew by 14 per cent in December 2012, compared to 2011 and accounted for 12 per cent of all retail sales in the UK in 2012, the highest percentage in Europe.[9]

With the widespread **adoption** of the Internet, individuals buying goods online, trading in stocks or shares or transferring funds has become an almost everyday occurrence for many consumers. Equally, on a B2B level, ordering goods and services online or arranging for payments online has simplified many tasks.

In addition to 'normal' goods, such as books and CDs, and services for delivery at a later date, eCommerce also enables the delivery of instant access digital content, for example when using the iTunes movie store to purchase and rent digital movies, which can instantaneously be downloaded and played on an iTV player, can be stored and consumed later once or in the case of a movie purchase, can be permanently stored on a digital device for multiple playback etc.

However, a major drawback of eCommerce is the computer dependency of the actual transaction, i.e. a transaction can generally only take place where the consumer has access to a computer and Internet connection. While this enables the consumer to shop from home, compare prices and eventually purchase goods or services, it leaves consumers who are out and about without any means of purchasing goods or services unless they purchase these in the traditional 'bricks-and-mortar' way.

mCommerce, or Mobile Commerce, tries to close the gap between 'bricks-and-mortar' commerce and eCommerce, by bringing commercial application to mobile devices. For example, mobile phones can be used to purchase tickets for trains and buses in Germany, thus avoiding the need to queue for a ticket or to have enough change to pay a bus driver. Similarly, mCommerce is being used for parking fees in Germany, and Austria, where a user can call a specific number upon arrival, and again upon departure and the parking fee is then collected from his mobile phone provider.

SMS/MMS/WAP/i-mode and mobile Internet

With the more widespread adoption of mobile phones, marketing communications and commercial solutions have become more important as an extension of mCommerce. Although limited to very basic text communication, similar to the early days of email, **SMS (short message service)** communication can be a timely, easy and convenient channel to reach a large amount of potential customers almost simultaneously no matter where they might be at any particular time (provided they have mobile phone coverage). This technology can be used for example to update customers with breaking news or special or time limited offers.

Improving on the text-only version, **multi-media messaging services (MMS)** can enhance the message by adding **layout** options (e.g. text size, font options etc.), and the messages can include pictures and sounds. However, although most modern mobile phones support MMS, some older models may not support the technology – thus resulting in the message getting lost or not being delivered to the consumer. Also, generally the costs for sending MMS messages is significantly higher, even in bulk, than SMS messages thus this form of communication is used significantly less often. However, similarly to email, it is conceivable that as old phones are phased out and the cost of MMS messages is declining, it may in future become a defacto standard for short messaging on mobile devices.

Another service often talked about is **WAP** services, or **wireless application protocol**-based services, which at the most basic level offer a simplified version of Internet services similar to basic websites 'on the go'. The main difference to SMS and MMS services is that with WAP services the user is usually required to actively navigate to the appropriate

WAP site in order to access the service, which in turn requires that the user knows about the site and address. There is, however, an advanced version of push WAP available, which 'pushes' content to compatible phones. However, although WAP was much hyped, it seems to have been overtaken by more advanced and competing technologies, such as **i-mode**[10] or more recently, with near-complete **HTML** rendering at high speeds on mobile devices such as the iPhone and Blackberry devices. This latest technology enables users to access most normal websites 'on the go', thus removing the additional cost and effort involved in developing specific websites for a still relatively small audience. Largely, it can therefore be argued, that **mobile Internet** is similar to 'desk-bound' Internet, although the usage and types of websites visited may be different. For instance, someone on the move may be more interested in fast and easily accessible information, for example travel updates, rather than browse through a number of websites to find a certain product or similar.

MINI CASE: IPHONE MOBILE APPS

After the introduction of the iPhone, mobile Internet usage rose dramatically. But, the iPhone also enabled retailers to have their own, dedicated applications. Amazon, eBay and NatWest among others have developed applications that enable them to bring their services to iPhone users. Getting users to download an mCommerce application to their iPhone is hoped to enhance brand loyalty and customer retention.

* What do you think makes a good mCommerce iPhone application?
* How would you use an mCommerce application like the one from Amazon?
* What additional functions (if any) would you want an application to have over the traditional website?

NFC, Bluetooth and location-based services

While SMS, MMS and WAP/i-mode and mobile Internet services have made it possible for information to be delivered to or requested by consumers almost everywhere, and therefore closed an important gap in terms of communication coverage, it nevertheless left another important gap: communicating with potential consumers in a particular location only, for example by allowing consumers passing a certain shop to be informed of a special offer when they are passing nearby.

There are currently three ways to identify users in a particular area: Near Field Communication, Bluetooth and cell-radius/node-based systems.

At the closest level, **near field communication** (**NFC**), a chip-based system can be used to identify users in a range of around 0.2 metres. This technology can be used to identify users at very short range, and thus is primarily used in travel cards (such as the London Oyster card or the Paris Navigo card) and in 'wave and pay systems', such as the OnePulse card introduced by Barclays Bank in the UK, which combines a traditional credit/ debit card, a 'wave and pay' system for transactions under £10 and an Oyster travel card. Although there are currently only limited applications of targeted marketing communications using NFC technology, systems that display user-specific communication are available. For example, if a user who likes to eat out exits an underground ticket gate, it would theoretically be possible to display to him or her information about a nearby restaurant.

Bluetooth reaches potential customers in an extended radius of around 10 metres, however, it depends on the customer having Bluetooth enabled on his or her device and usually agreeing to receiving some form of communication. Typical examples of this are generally ring tones, small movies or java-games, which can be downloaded from Bluetooth-enabled 'posters'. The main advantage of Bluetooth is that it can transfer fairly large amounts of data at virtually no cost to the end-user, as it does not rely on any given network, but the sending 'base station' connects directly to the handset. However, as there are compatibility issues between different phones, and a low uptake by most consumers, Bluetooth is only fairly infrequently used, and if so generally seems to target a fairly young and tech-savvy segment of the market (e.g. consumers who are likely to play games on their phone, have different ring tones etc.) and tends to rely on the novelty factor. In addition, many consumers have security fears and privacy concerns and this may well hinder uptake and usefulness of Bluetooth-based communication services in the future.

Finally, most providers have in recent years enabled 'cell-based' systems, which determine where a particular phone or mobile device is at present. This can either be achieved by triangulation, where the signal from different mobile phone cells is used to determine the position, or by simply determining in which cell the phone is currently operating. Additionally, modern phones also have a built in A-GPRS chip that uses GPRS signals to locate a phone. Similarly, on modern phones or mobile devices which operate with Wi-Fi-based Internet connections, such as the iPhone or the Nokia N95 users can be located by identifying Wi-Fi node is registered in, and then location specific services and information can be displayed. For example, Apple teamed up with Starbucks to enable users to purchase the music currently playing in the Starbucks store they are in for their iPhone or iPod Touch from the iTunes music store.

MINI CASE: STARBUCKS AND IPHONE

Since the introduction of the iPhone, Apple and Starbucks have worked closely together. Starbucks has released two applications specifically for iPhone users: the myStarbucks application allows users to locate the nearest Starbucks stores using the phone's built in GPS system to where the phone is at the moment, and it allows customers to check opening times, food menus and even invite friend via SMS for a coffee.

The second application lets you check your Starbucks Card balance, top up and even pay using your iPhone rather than your card.

In addition, Starbucks also integrated with the iTunes Music Store, which is available on all iPhones and iPod Touch. If you open your iTunes Music Store application, then it will display the most recently played songs in the Starbucks you are in, and you can then purchase these directly from the Music Store online.

- Do you think the brands of Apple and Starbucks fit?
- Can you think of other uses of **location-based** services, for example for other stores?
- Why do you think people would use location services?

Viral marketing/blogs/social media and social networks: web 2.0

While the previous communication channels largely rely on organizations to both generate and communicate messages to potential individual users, the Internet has empowered individuals to also generate content and/or distribute content among their network of friends or acquaintances. At the very basic level, this may simply be the passing along of commercial messages – for example in the form of an email signature, such as the signatures appended to many free email services, such as Yahoo or hotmail. This practice is known as **viral marketing**, as the messages are spread in a virus-like form among **social networks**. Of course, viral marketing is not limited to signatures, but may also include hybrid media, which will be discussed in the following chapter in more detail, such as video clips, advergames or branded presentations being emailed or shared among social networks.

However, with generation of content becoming increasingly easy and with less technical skills needed to publish on the Internet, the Internet has also enabled users to generate and promote and distribute increasing amounts of content, and at an advanced level, interact with each other based on the published content. At the most basic level this could be in the form of online diaries, or **blogs** on a given topic. And with free services such as blogger and WordPress etc., it has become fairly easy even for non-tech-savvy Internet users to generate and share content with anyone on the Internet.

However, while traditional blogs tended to be fairly extensive – and thus require often a fairly high level of commitment by the blog owner, more simple blogging tools have become available in the last few years. **Microblogging** usually limits updates to around 160 characters and are often also not computer based, but, for example services like Jaiku and Twitter enable the generating and sharing from microblog entries via a web interface, instant messaging services and SMS.

Services like blogs, or microblogs, are a viable communication tool that enable companies and organizations to share insights and go 'behind-the-scenes' as well as updates and news items with customers or service users. For example, presidential candidates in the US have used Twitter to communicate with potential voters (for example twitter.com/BarackObama).

On the other hand, online communities or social networking sites, such as Facebook, **MySpace** or Orkut have become increasingly popular. While these sites rely largely on users contributing content, these websites do offer services for commercial communications. For example Facebook groups and pages offers the possibility to recruit 'user-groups' and 'fans' of a product, service or person. For example politicians can recruit 'fans' such as Hillary Clinton on Facebook (www.facebook.com/hillaryclinton) or 'friends' on MySpace (http://myspace.com/hillaryclinton), or commercial organizations can develop applications which appear on users profiles, for example the 'send Starbucks' application on Facebook, which enables users to send Starbucks products to each other.

THINK BOX

Product reviews

- Do you ever share your feelings about particular products, brands or services on social networking sites? Why/why not?
- Do you read the opinions and/or feelings of others about products, brands or services? If so, what influence do you think this has on your own behaviour?
- Do you think applications like 'send Starbucks' have an impact on you? If so, what?
- Why would you become a fan of a product or service? And what would you want in exchange or expect to happen once you are a fan?

One of the main issues facing social networking sites, or in fact any site that relies heavily on user-generated content is the concern about copyright and defamation and privacy issues. For example, in 2007 MTV-owner Viacom tried to sue YouTube for $1bn in damages over Viacom shows being made available on the YouTube website by YouTube contributors.[11]

Defamation issues are also potentially problematic, as user-generated content is hard to police and check for accuracy. In a high profile case, a British television producer won £17,000 in damages after a former school-friend set up a bogus profile page suggesting the producer was gay.[12] However, libel and defamation cases are often problematic, and may create more publicity than the original defamatory statement. And even without defamatory statements, social networking sites can be used to damage brand image.

For example, Facebook has various groups opposing global brands such as Starbucks, McDonalds etc., yet, it could be argued that this is nothing but an extension of such groups existing 'in real life', and thus may have no more impact onto consumer decision making than non-web-based groups. One of the fundamental problems with either side of the argument is that the evaluation and measuring of how much 'buzz' and eventual influence on decision making is created by both real-life and **virtual word of mouth** and viral campaigns remains hard to quantify.

MINI CASE: IMAX AND AZIZ ANSARI

With Twitter, Facebook and other social networking sites around, it is often easy to spread good and bad experiences very fast among a massive number of friends or followers. In 2009, the American TV presenter Aziz Ansari went to watch Star Trek: The IMAX Experience at his local cinema in Burbank, paying $5 more for the IMAX effect.

However, Anziz was very disappointed that the screen in the cinema was not nearly as large as a traditional IMAX screen (and in fact only slightly larger than a conventional screen), though the cinema was charging extra money. He immediately sent out an update via Twitter and his blog to warn other cinema goers.

IMAX responded a few days later, stating that the smaller IMAX screens were still worth the extra money, though within the blog-sphere the sentiment and comments about the IMAX defence remained negative, with comments like 'LOL at Richard Gelfond, weak argument dude. People aren't going back to Imax because of these lies.' (User Haha at www.mainstreet.com/node/12157/comment.) Indeed, IMAX sentiment nosedived almost immediately.

How do you think the blogging and Tweeting impacted sales of IMAX tickets?

How would you respond if you were acting for IMAX?

Measuring effectiveness and return on investment

As mentioned in the previous section, there are considerable problems trying to measure the effect and effectiveness of communication taking place on the Internet, especially in the social media space, although this also heavily depends on the measurements and target objectives as well as the message types.

On the one side, measuring effectiveness of online advertising, e.g. banners on websites, is fairly straightforward, and measures such as click-through rates and unique visitors generated by any particular campaign are easily measured. In fact, they are probably easier to measure, thanks to cookie technology and IP-number tracking than for any other marketing communication campaign.

Thus, if the objective of a particular banner advertising campaign is to generate sales of an online shop, then this is easy to measure, as the visitor can be tracked through from seeing the ad, to visiting the website, entering the online shop and purchasing and even possibly re-purchasing goods or services. Yet, if the ultimate target is not generating online sales, but rather generating brand image or enhancing brand reputation – or even just increasing sales in an offline environment, the measurement becomes complicated. While it is easy to generate statistics about how many visitors a particular website had, the reasons for visiting the website and the links used are not always clear, and it is therefore complicated to show how a visit is related to any particular mentioning of a brand or website, for example, a brand may be discussed in a **podcast**, which then results in users searching for the brand or the brand's website in a search engine, and then visiting the site. However, although the site statistics will be able to show that the visitor is coming as a result of a search engine search, and even the search terms used, it won't be able to tell why the visitor has performed the search in the first place. As search engine traffic is often a major source of traffic to a website, this ultimately means that the major referral source for visitor traffic is potentially unknown.

Similarly, discussions in the blogsphere are highly problematic to quantify in a sensible way to measure effectiveness. While there are enormous amounts of statistics available on each individual blog, for example by using blogstatistic sites such as xinureturns.com, which measures ranking in various search engines, social book marking popularity, back links and syndication of content, or by measuring how often a specific term is used or tagged, by using websites such as technorati or Nielsen's blogpulse, the effect of this communication remains problematic to quantify, as it is lacking the final link to any measureable outcomes, such as sales outcomes.

This lack of the final connection between 'buzz' and sales often generates significant problems when trying to argue for funding for online, and especially social media, projects. This lack of a direct measure is not dissimilar to the difficulties discussed for public relations campaigns. However, while there are no really reliable models for measuring word of mouth both online and offline effectiveness, anecdotal evidence suggests that such a link is indeed present.

Ethical issues

While there are many possibilities for using technology to target, segment, and to deliver relevant and timely communication to these consumers, such as keyword-sensitive advertising campaigns, there are equally very serious concerns about the ethical aspects of using such technology.

Most of the concerns focus around the privacy issues involved in using technology to deliver personalized communication, especially the extensive data collection, storage and mining and then profiling of individual consumers. For example, the company Double Click continues to collect information about users and the adverts they have seen and on which sites these adverts have been viewed in order to generate consumer profiles. Historically, the company had tried to compile a database of consumer profiles, including names and purchase history of individual web users, which was only abandoned after the company was taken to court in 2002 in a case that was ultimately settled outside of court.[13] Such behaviour has generated a large amount of mistrust in the privacy of online data, above and beyond the safety concerns that many users already have when giving out personal details on the Internet.

At the moment, **cookies**, and therefore tracking of Internet traffic trough cookies, is not regulated at all, and continues to be a concern for some, though most countries and companies have adopted an 'opt-in' approach to other forms of online and mobile personal data, such as email addresses and location specific information i.e. the consumer has to actively activate such services, or at least consent to, in order to receive them. Of course such concerns are also extremely serious, if for example, mobile devices are potentially being tracked, and data about their location stored and used for commercial purposes – and if this data is potentially combined with purchasing data.

THINK BOX

Consumer data

- What data are you happy to share with companies? What data do you not want to share?
- Why do you think companies would be interested to harvest personal data?
- What steps do you take to protect your personal data?

Finally, another criticism of using social media for commercial purposes comes if user generated content is hijacked to promote buzz, especially if it is not directly clear that such content is generated for commercial purpose. For example, it is conceivable to discuss products or services 'incognito' for marketing purposes on consumer review websites, thus trying deceptively to increase positive word of mouth.

Although word of mouth agencies (especially when operating in the real world) require their 'agents' to disclose that they are generating word of mouth (see for example Buzzagent.com), many users do still remain somewhat sceptical of such tactics.

Summary

This chapter introduced the role that emerging, new and social media can play in marketing communication, especially the changing nature of communication through electronic media.

ETHICAL ISSUE TO CONSIDER

- What are the ethical implications for activity such as the Starbucks promotion or the computertan.com case in Chapter 3 which invited site users to 'hoax a friend'?
- How do you view social networks being used by marketers without other site users being aware of their identities and persuasive intent?
- Given that this type of activity is beyond the control of regulators, what action do you believe should be taken to expose this type of activity and who should taken the action you recommend?

While in the early days of the Internet, much of the content was simply a reproduction of previous marketing material, with the emergence of new and social media this has changed dramatically. Much of the communication using these media can be used in a much more targeted fashion, for example by displaying search term relevant advertising and location-based, specific information. The more traditional forms of online advertising also have a great advantage in that they are easily measurable (e.g. by click-through rates), and often a consumer can be tracked right through from seeing an online ad to making a purchase.

With the rise of the mobile Internet, many of the online services have become easy to use on the go, and enable consumers for example to compare prices and product reviews online while in a store before making a purchase decision.

One of the main challenges however has been the loss of message control, especially with the rise of social networks like Facebook and Twitter, where messages can be multiplied potentially thousands of times within seconds. Yet, similarly to public relations activity, it is hard to determine how much influence buzz in cyberspace really has on achieving sales or other communication outcomes.

Review questions

1. Critically discuss the current and potential role of the Internet in:

   a. fast moving consumer goods promotion
   b. consumer durables (for example, refrigerators, washing machines etc.)
   c. medications, including both non-prescription and prescription medicines.

2. Assume you are a marketing executive for an insurance company. You have received several complaints about annoying Internet pop-up ads for your company's products. How would you assess what action might need to be taken?
3. Discuss the **ethics** of viral marketing using electronic media and of the use of cookies to track Internet use.
4. Discuss how you would assess how social networking sites might be used for:

   a. a range of cosmetics aimed at mature women
   b. social marketing activity aimed at reducing excessive alcohol consumption among young people.

5. How could return on investment be measured for each of the activities in question 1 and question 4?
6. Assume you are a marketing executive for one of the global brands noted as being subject to negative Facebook comments. How would you monitor this activity and what action might you take to minimize its effects?
7. 'The Internet is the potential saviour of small business in a very competitive world'. Discuss this statement in light of recent developments of electronic, new and social media.
8. For a brand of your choice, explore the value of using social networks to communicate brand values. Are there any brands that would not be suited to this medium? Explain your reasons.
9. Although there are no definite figures available, there is an estimated 60 million blogs worldwide and that number is growing daily. In such a crowded media market, discuss the products, services and brands most suited to coverage by this medium and explore the value of blogs to both the brand, the blogger and the consumer.

10. New media is usually associated with younger target groups. Consider how the value of each of the following media might be communicated to older consumers (65 years and over):

- social networking sites
- blogs
- SMS.

What challenges do marketers face in trying to engage older consumers with new media?

Recommended reading

Blood, R. (2002). *We've Got Blog: How Weblogs Are Changing Our Culture*, New York: Perseus Books.

Kamal, S., and Chu, S.-C. (2013). Materialism, attitudes, and social media usage and their impact on purchase intention of luxury fashion goods among American and Arab young generations. *Journal of Interactive Advertising*, (13)1, 27–40.

Lister, M., Dovey, J., Giddings, S., Grant, I., and Kelly, K. (2007). *New Media: A Critical Introduction*, 2nd edition, Abingdon: Routledge.

Nahai, N. (2012). *Webs of Influence: The Psychology of Online Persuasion*, London: Pearson.

Scoble, R. (2006). *Naked Conversations: How Blogs Have Changed the Way that Businesses Talk with Customers*, New Jersey: John Wiley & Sons.

Yang, J. (2006). *The Rough Guide to the Blogging*, London: Rough Guides.

CASE STUDY 9.1

Marmite

Source: Institute of Practitioners in Advertising: Bronze, IPA Effectiveness Awards 2008. Authors: Kirsty Saddler, Sarah Carter, Les Binet and Alex Vass. Case material provided by the World Advertising Research Centre (WARC) www.warc.com.

Marmite is a much loved (or hated!) British institution, a sticky, dark brown savoury spread made from yeast extract. Traditionally, Marmite was consumed on toast, though with a change in breakfast habits, less and less Marmite was being purchased, with the younger generations being especially reluctant to eat Marmite, as they are the most likely to skip breakfast. As Marmite is high in salt, it was no longer allowed to market directly to children, which used to be the source of much of their growth previously, when Marmite was sold as a vitamin-rich spread for mothers and children.

In 2005, Marmite introduced a newer, squeezy packaging to replace the traditional glass tub, and the recipe was changed slightly to make it more squeezable and less sticky. It was also sold at a 35 per cent premium to the traditional Marmite.

Despite the added convenience, much of the response to the change was less than positive, with many bloggers and comments being very negative, and the main challenge for Marmite was to turn the negative buzz into an advantage.

Marmite responded with a mix of new and old media responses, combining PR, cinema, television and online advertising and social network activity.

In a first response, the company used traditional advertising creating awareness for the more convenient Marmite. The advertising focussed on a man with a broken arm, who could not get Marmite out of the glass tub. This was then followed by an award winning 'Marmart'

Photo 9.1a

Photo 9.1b

Photo 9.1c

Photo 9.1a–c 'Marmart' posters

poster campaign, showing designs 'squeezed' in Marmite, highlighting the fun aspect of the new squeezy Marmite.

The poster campaign was backed up by a website encouraging people to submit their own designs. In a second wave, Marmite ads also featured another British cultural icon, Paddington Bear.

Marmite also actively recruited people to become fans of its product on Facebook, and used YouTube to show off the Paddington Bear-themed advertising campaigns.

On their Facebook page, fans of Marmite could exchange recipes, images and stories about using Marmite, and the page was used to show videos of Marmite in use. The Facebook page in particular was a success, with more than 230,000 fans by 2009.

The launch of Squeezy was a big success, with sales increasing by 8 per cent from 2005 to 2007. During the 'Marmart' campaign, more than 60,000 people logged onto the 'Marmart' website, and 290 images were uploaded.

CASE STUDY QUESTIONS

Drawing on the material in the chapter, discuss the following questions:

1. Now that Squeezy Marmite has been established in the market, how can you maintain the buzz about the product? Create a campaign that helps to maintain the excitement about Marmite, combining traditional and new media forms. Explain why you are using which media and what it brings to the communication mix.
2. How can you evaluate the impact new media buzz has? How can you evaluate traditional media (newspapers, television etc.) impact on overall sales figures?

CASE STUDY 9.2

BT – bringing it all together in digital

This case has been condensed from Cudhilly, M., and Preston I. (2009) 'BT – Bringing it All Together in Digital', Case Study Institute of Practitioners in Advertising Effectiveness Awards. Case material provided by the World Advertising Research Centre (WARC) www. warc.com. Campaign developed by LBi.

This second case illustrates several points from the chapter, including the need to recognize that customer knowledge is sometimes not as great as marketers assume.

The business of being BT

There is no brand more recognized in the world of telecommunications than BT. As the world's oldest company in its field, the business carries both significant heritage coupled with the challenges of running an operation which supports the backbone of the UK's communications network. The current business situation for BT is one under scrutiny in the marketplace. With declining share prices, job cuts and well reported losses from the Global Services division, what often goes unnoticed is the positive performance of individual parts of the company. BT.com is such an example, where as BT's second largest sales channel, it has a critical impact upon the company's performance.

BT.com represents everything the brand stands for and offers its customers a wide range of communications and entertainment services, from the traditional BT territory of calls and phone lines, through broadband and most recently TV. It acts as BT's most direct interface for customers, servicing over 2 million customers every month delivering information to help them learn about or buy something new. It needs to be constantly and rapidly fine-tuned to meet the ever changing needs of customers if it is to continue to perform at an optimal level. Like any large organization, there are stringent processes surrounding the release of any form of communication to the world at large. Probably more than any other area of the business, BT.com needs to manage the tension of rigorous communication policies with the very real need of remaining relevant and in touch with consumer's needs.

The challenges for BT.com

Do more with less

For BT.com, 2008–2009 was a financial year of flat and in some cases declining traffic on the site. As the global recession began to bite in the second quarter, marketing budgets were frozen. It was definitely a case of needing to do more with less. The key levers to pull on an ecommerce channel are obviously traffic (input) or conversion (output). In a cost-saving period when you cannot buy more traffic, it's obviously important to convert more existing customers. This was the major challenge faced in mid-2008 by BT.com.

Confusing customer experience

The overall design language had stayed the same for over four years. During this time, presentation of the brand and design language had become dated. Equally, the customer experience was disjointed and confusing. In particular, the sales channel experience was disparate – it had a different look and feel depending on where you were, and wasn't realizing

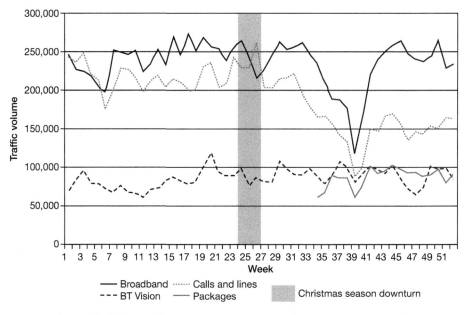

Figure 9.1 Flat and declining traffic on BT.com

its sales potential – the average sales conversion rate was only 1.72 per cent for the last six weeks of the second quarter.

Creating the successful approach

LBi took inspiration from user-centred design and agile software development processes as well as assembling a highly diversified cross-functional team (business consultants, planners, experience architects, technologies, researchers, SEO experts to name but a few) to help deliver this solution, an approach labelled 'Nimble'.

The communication and iteration principles existed, thus enabling rapid turnaround of new designs, continual integration with build and launching these to market immediately. The process works in four-week cycles, or iterations, with strategy, user research, experience architecture, design, interface development, testing working as a single, self-organizing team. BT were required to nominate a 'product owner'; someone who would, on a daily basis, make all the critical decisions on behalf of all business stakeholders as part of this creative unit.

With the 'Nimble' process, all the traditional documented processes were eschewed in favour of drawing key insights directly from customers, through workshops, one-to-one interviews and task-oriented online exercises. The team acted on the findings of these sessions, along with business and market information, to create designs and pages for release. The principle of releasing early and realizing immediate results, whilst measuring the performance of any changes and repeating the process to enable continual improvement was central to activity.

It was an approach that required huge commitment and belief from BT. The only formal checkpoint for the wider business is a weekly status meeting, which serves to review the decisions that have been taken and look ahead to the coming deliverables. It presented risks compared to the traditional processes inside BT, but they recognized the potential of working in this way was enormous if it could deliver its promise.

Another consideration was the fact that the inconsistency across the site would actually increase for a period while all the packages were launched. Due to the iterative release programme, new designs would be launched as they were ready, not as a full site. However, having seen the BBC go through a similar exercise with their new wider site, there was confidence that provided the remaining product sections could be swiftly updated, it would be successful.

The first test for the new process

In August 2008, BT set the first challenge in this new way of working. The brief was simple: Sales, sales and more sales!

LBi were tasked with re-designing what BT terms the Pre-Sales journey; the pages visitors to BT.com browse before they click a button to buy a product and enter an order. The main goals were to increase sales, in particular sales conversion on the site.

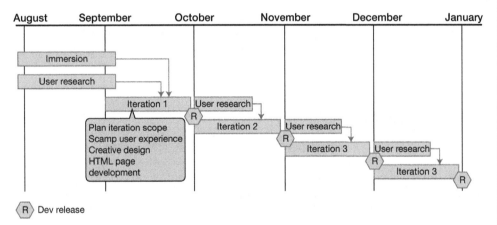

Figure 9.2 'Nimble' process

Key insights

The four week immersion phase examined three strategic pillars:

- the business – through stakeholder interviews and data analysis;
- the market – through competitor benchmarking and user experience evaluation;
- the user – one-to-one user sessions on the current BT site.

Clearly, all these steps are important to forming our creative approach. Both the business and market were sending a clear message that by bundling up BT products to create packages, a consumer-friendly converged service proposition would be created. By doing this, all the information showed that market demands would be met and additional revenue delivered. However, the most crucial piece of the puzzle to understanding how to deliver a creative solution were the comments from BT's existing and prospective customers. They simply didn't understand BT's product offerings. They were very functional, not benefits led, and moreover BT Vision was a total mystery to people!

The conclusion was clear: you couldn't hope to sell packages of products that people didn't understand! So simply packaging up what BT had wouldn't work. The research identified there were particular comprehension issues with the BT Vision proposition.

Essentially, it was not clear that BT Vision would act as a replacement for normal television – this needed to be simplified. Our customer insight showed the need to unlock the proposition for Vision to help customers understand the converged proposition for all BT's products. And not only is it a key business objective, it's also a market imperative for BT to sell bundles. If consumers couldn't understand Vision, we couldn't fulfil this goal.

Add the lack of understanding around propositions with a fragmented user-experience, the conclusion was to recommend a complete re-design delivering the appropriate brand expression for all significant services and effectively meet overall communication goals to deliver increased sales. So we began with Vision.

Building believable brands

The old world was about brands controlling messages they designed and delivered to audiences they defined. Digital channels have changed that situation completely and forever. The new world is about consumer empowerment.

This tends to expose gaps between a company's brand promise and the service and experience the brand delivers online. BT believed in LBi's insight that brands that don't respect this and don't react to it by communicating honestly, transparently and intelligently in digital channels will be exposed. The task therefore was to provide active demonstration to consumers of BT's brand proposition: 'Bringing it all together'.

The creative strategy

LBi's approach to the creative strategy began with adopting the unwavering imperative to support the BT's brand proposition of 'Bringing it all together'. After investigation it was felt the there were three main components required for the brand proposition to feel believable in the digital space.

Firstly, customers needed to be aware that BT's portfolio of products and services has been designed so that they are complementary with one another, rather than a set of mutually exclusive offerings, which was how they had previously been presented. This was achieved by ensuring each product and service was described in a manner that made sense as part of the whole brand proposition, whilst also actively up-selling the benefits of the next tier of products. Secondly, it was vitally important that the site had a look, feel and tone-of-voice that was consistent throughout the entire customer journey, and which also presented BT as a credible, contemporary communications brand that was providing access to a desirable digital lifestyle. Lastly, the site needed to support a broader level of familiar brand expression, something that had not previously been one of BT's strongest points. By working closely with BT's other key agencies, we've ensured that BT.com works as part of a multi-channel strategy, most notably by integrating the BT Family from their iconic TV ads.

As noted previously, customer knowledge is sometimes not as great as marketers assume. Demystifying the proposition for Vision was the first crucial step. The team took the insights gained from user research to formulate a simple, clear and comprehensible proposition for the service. BT Vision goes against people's accepted model for television consumption. Instead of pre-defined channels, the service is entirely on-demand, meaning people can choose whatever shows or movies they want to watch at any time. The site's existing content had incorrectly assumed people understood what 'on-demand' meant; the fact was they didn't. The consumer needed to be educated about this concept, making them comfortable with this new paradigm for TV, then enticing them by the convenience and flexibility this would bring to their lives.

The next step was to completely overhaul the site's look and feel. Following the principles outlined in the creative strategy, the team developed an entirely new design language and expression for the brand online. Due to the constraints of the content management tools, they needed to ensure that all changes would avoid any changes to back-office systems or underlying templates and thus simultaneously avoid being sucked into the complexities of a full BT release programme. It is testament to the skills of the interface developers and BT.com content team that they were able to exact a completely new design and experience without changing a single line of back-end code. Instead, everything was done in the presentation layer, so consumers would see the new site but as far as the back-end was concerned, nothing structurally had changed. The back-end is still in 2005, 'believing' the site not to have changed, while the consumer is up-to-date again. In terms of effectiveness, this saved costs and time as back-end re-development was not required. And delivered something that had not been achieved in over four years; a radically new design.

By re-writing the presentation code, the pages were automatically transformed from their previous width of 800 pixels to the larger 1024 pixel format, a move which reflects the larger screen sizes customers now have access to. The designers further gained additional space by removing the existing left hand navigation and re-presented it as a horizontal strip in the body of the page. Lastly, all existing graphical assets (such as buttons and brand imagery) were replaced with new versions that reflect the evolution of BT's brand identity. Prior to launch, the Vision pages were again tested with users. The response demonstrated a much clearer understanding of the proposition and all participants confirmed they were more likely to consider purchasing Vision as a result of the changes made.

Results of the BT vision re-launch

The new designs were launched Week 30 and it immediately had an impact.

For the first time since 2007, Vision sales met their online sales targets, without new promotions or additional traffic driving activities to deliver new customers. And in the first six weeks of the re-launch, BT Vision conversion increased from 0.44 per cent to 0.74 per cent. Since then, the site has achieved a consistently higher conversion rate.

Turning attention to other areas of the site – packaging things up

Knowing the complexity of content in the calls and lines and broadband sections of the site, the team decided to test the effectiveness of introducing packages of products, but without changing the individual product sections. As the product sections would still be in old templates, we had to create a sufficiently compelling experience inside the Packages section in its own right to convert sales. Research showed that consumers also expected when buying more than one product from the same provider there is generally a 'deal' to be had. It was decided that this would be the perfect opportunity to test the effectiveness of introducing 'The BT Family' into the online space. By doing this, the team hoped to aid recall and offer customers a sense of familiarity with the ATL campaigns, even though these wouldn't relate to this new combination of products.

Results of launching packages

The launch of the Packages area on BT.com marketed dual- and triple-play bundles of services under unique names with simple explanations. The average value of a sale of multiple products on BT.com moved from £250 first year revenue to £353, an increase of 41 per cent after the launch of Packages on BT.com in November.

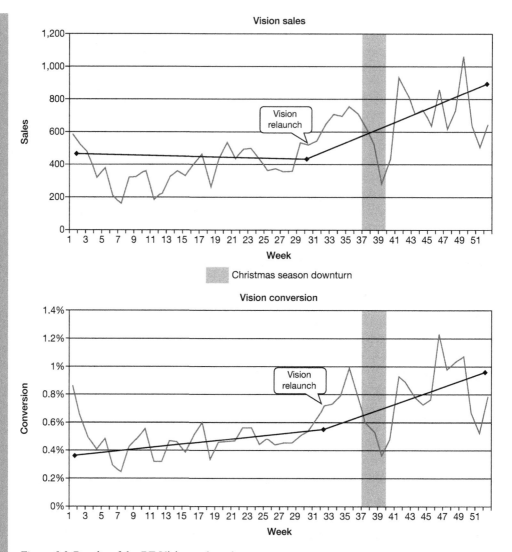

Figure 9.3 Results of the BT Vision re-launch

Turning attention to broadband

The online proposition for broadband has historically been a better offer than the proposition sold in call centres, but in the shrinking marketplace the proposition was levelled in the second and third quarters of the financial year to ensure that the high acquisition volume remained in the main telesales channel. With flat traffic overlaid by a less rich online offer, there was a need to increase conversion, as well as more simply explain the BT Total Broadband proposition. With the two areas now in-market, the lessons learnt and continued customer feedback from user sessions were used to deliver a consistent presentation for the broadband section.

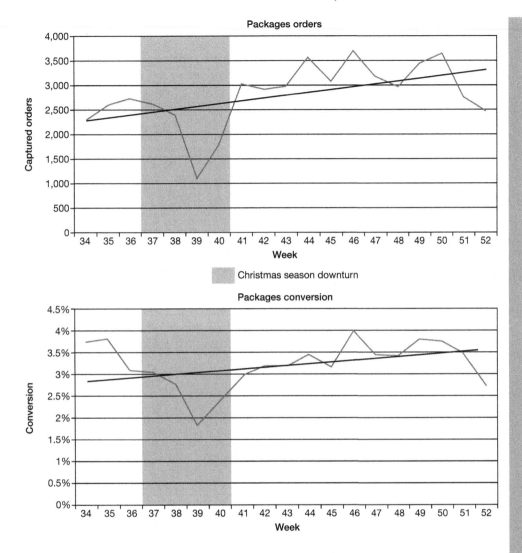

Figure 9.4 Packages orders

Results for broadband

Broadband conversion rate increased after the site re-launch by a third, from 1.92 per cent to 2.54 per cent.

And finally where BT started out

To deliver the last main product area, attention returned to BT's heartland. Calls and lines traditionally was not a product sold online on BT.com, the start of 2008–09 launched the voice proposition online completely, and then work was put into optimizing the user experience. Calls and lines was the last part of the site to be redesigned, and was released just prior to Christmas (the week before!). The redesigned site on BT.com was re-positioned and re-architected to focus on user needs over product features. It segments those

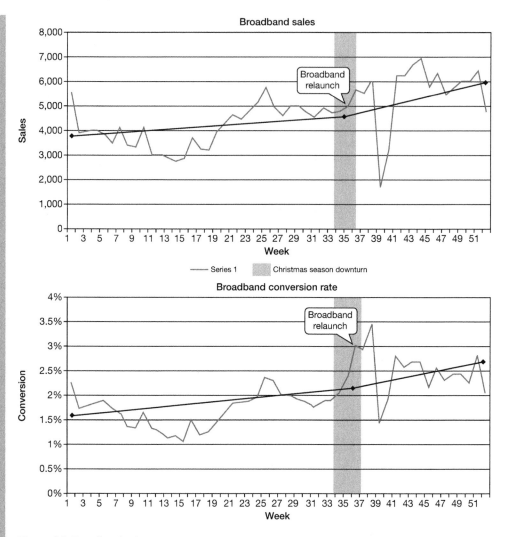

Figure 9.5 Broadband sales

customers who are installing a new line in a new build for example, those moving home, or existing customers who want to enjoy savings as part of an inclusive calling plan.

Results for broadband

By segmenting the customers in this way the process of looking at acquiring or upselling customers was much simpler. Conversion rates ran at an average of 2.14 per cent up until the end of Q3 (Christmas time) – after this Q4 conversion rate was an unprecedented 4.89 per cent.

Conclusion

Bringing it all together in the digital space is both a science and an art in the creation of an effective business transforming website. This case study demonstrates that creating the

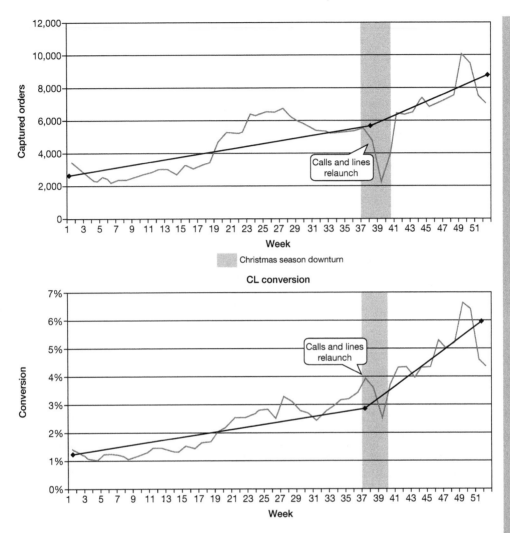

Figure 9.6 Results: conversion rates

right processes for client–agency engagement is an important ingredient to allow truly effective business digital creative work to be created. This paper demonstrates that the world of marketing 2.0 is not just about clients and agencies learning about how to do one-off campaigns but rather it is about learning to embrace and harness the immense iterative potential of the medium. The case shows how BT and LBi have embraced continual optimization to achieve real business results. And we show how, by bringing to life BT's brand promise online, we help create a believable brand.

CASE STUDY QUESTIONS

1. Critique this case drawing on material from this chapter and the preceding chapters (including client–agency relationships) – what specific challenges are highlighted in it? How well do you believe these challenges were addressed? Justify your responses.

2. Visit BT.com and assess the site against the material presented in the case study. How well do you believe the site meets the information needs of potential customers? How should site visitor satisfaction with information provided be tracked? Justify your response.

3. Compare the BT.com site with the sites of their major competitors. How would you expect competitors to respond to BT's redesign activity and what actions would you recommend BT take to combat them?

4. The case highlighted assumptions that had been made regarding consumers' understanding of relatively new terms such as 'on demand'. How would you recommend researching consumers' understanding of new media and its related terminology and the impact that less than complete knowledge may have on adopting new technology? What are the implications for marketing communications?

5. What segments might exist and how would you recommend communications be directed at each segment regarding the benefits of new media, overcoming consumer concerns regarding potential complexity and relative advantage over more traditional media?

Notes

1   Cooper, M.J., Khorana, A., Osobov, I., Patel, A., and Rau, P.R. (2005). Managerial actions in response to a market downturn: valuation effects of name changes in the dot.com decline. *Journal of Corporate Finance*, 11(1–2), 319–35.

2   Lanxon, N. (2008). The greatest defunct websites and dotcom disasters, C-Net UK. Online. Available HTTP: <http://crave.cnet.co.uk/gadgets/0,39029552,49296926–8,00.htm> (accessed 26 November 2009).

3   Shah, D.V., McLeod, J.M., and Yoon, S.-H. (2001). Communication, context, and community: an exploration of print, broadcast, and internet influences. *Communication Research*, 28(4), 464–506.

4   Cunliffe, D. (2006). Opening address at Government Technology World New Zealand Conference, Duxton Hotel, Wellington. Online. Available HTTP: <http://beehive.govt.nz/speech/government+technology+world+new+zealand> (accessed 1 July 2008).

5   Lee, Y.E., and Benbasat, I. (2003). Interface design for mobile commerce. *Communications of the ACM*, 46(12: December), 48–52.

6   McCoy, S., Everard, A., Polak, P., and Galletta, D.F. (2007). The effects of online advertising. *Communications of the ACM*, 50(3: March), 84–8.

7   Rettie, R., Robinson, H., and Jenner, B. (2001). Does Internet Advertising Alienate Users? Academy of Marketing, Conference, July 2001, Cardiff Business School, UK.

8   Robinson, H., Wysocka, A., and Hand, C. (2007). Internet advertising effectiveness. *International Journal of Advertising*, 26(4), 527–41.

9   Centre for Retail Research (2012). *Online Retailing: Britain and Europe 2012*. Online. Available HTTP: <http://retailresearch.org/onlineretailing.php> (accessed 22 March 2013).

10 Teo, T.S.H., and Pok, S.H. (2003). Adoption of WAP-enabled mobile phones among Internet users. *Omega*, 31(6: December), 483–98.

11 VerSteeg, R. (2009). Viacom v. YouTube: preliminary observations. *NC Journal of Law and Technology*, 9, 43.

12 Sturcke, J. (2008). £17,000 damages for victim of fake Facebook profile, *The Guardian* (24 July).

13 Rendleman, J. (2002). DoubleClick Settles Lawsuit, But Still Can Track Web Surfers, *Informationweek*. Online. Available HTTP: <http://informationweek.com/news/security/privacy/showArticle.jhtml?articleID=6502942> (accessed 7 July 2008).

10 Emerging, hybrid media and experiential marketing

LEARNING OUTCOMES

After studying this chapter, you will be able to:

- Describe hybrid media forms and discuss their current and potential future significance as marketing communication tools
- Discuss the concerns raised regarding hybrid media as forms of stealth advertising
- Discuss the ethical issues regarding hybrid media forms
- Critically evaluate product placements as marketing communications tools
- Critically evaluate advergames, particularly those targeted at children
- Discuss ways by which return on investment from hybrid media may be assessed

Introduction

Up until the mid-1990s, marketing communications debate centred on traditional media and the growth of online (Internet) advertising. As more experience was gained with different types of Internet activity,[1] after considerable disappointment that the initial promise of electronic media as a replacement for conventional advertising had not been fulfilled[2] and a lot of hype over the forecast death of advertising[3] was shown to be considerably overstated, ways of blending available media forms (called hybridization of media) began to be explored.

Hybrid media is the strategic use of traditional and new media and marketing communications tools to communicate the message in a more effective way. The field continues to evolve rapidly, with product placements and games containing embedded advertising being a prominent example. Other forms of media-decentred advertising and marketing communications include the merging of social media and real-life experiences, and the merging of live reality and computer-based information in the form of 'augmented' reality.

THINK BOX

Hybrid media

- What are the advantages of merging media, i.e. the development of hybrid media for consumers?
- Are the increasing number of converging media channels an advantage or disadvantage for marketers? Can you identify the challenges and opportunities?
- How do you think a marketing professional should react to the new media landscape?
- What ethical issues should be considered?

Drivers of hybrid media development

Technology has been the driver of many forms of hybrid media, especially in relation to interactive games. For example, by the middle of the 1990s new media forms centred on playing video games became increasingly common. Although video games were originally developed in the early 1950s,[4] it was not until the 1980s that they became a common feature in many households. Early game consoles were seldom connected to other devices, and games came preloaded on disks or special memory sticks. This made social gaming problematic and thus the game experience less interactive, as all the people playing a videogame had to be in the same room and play at the same time.

From a games developer's perspective the non-connectedness meant that games could not be updated, changed or new levels etc. added once a customer had bought a game. At the same time increasingly connected devices, e.g. personal computers, could also be used to play video games and soon began to rival the dedicated gaming consoles as a major gaming platform during the 1990s.[5]

At the same time cell phones emerged as a convenient portable way to play games,[6] enabling consumers to take games with them and play on the move. However, the often limited data networks meant that, similarly to the games consoles of the 1990s, many cell phones were unable to be used for social gaming.

By the early 2000s, gaming had emerged as a major pastime, and was increasingly available on a number of platforms: personal computer games, mobile phone-based games, console-based and Internet-based online gaming. Since the middle of the 2000s, many of these platforms have started converging, allowing games to be played online and offline as well as social gaming, i.e. playing with other players either known or unknown in the wider community.[7]

By 2002, around 37 per cent of the American adult population had played games online,[8] and with the emergence of social online gaming, both Internet and console-based, this proportion is expected to rise dramatically. With the number of games available rising dramatically, and more and more people gaming routinely often for extended periods of time, the gaming platform became a viable alternative to and competition of the more established media forms (such as television). By 2012, around 25 per cent of Europeans had played games at least once a week.[9]

In 2006, at least for young males, online gaming had overtaken watching television as a major form of spending their leisure time.[10] Many of these games contain products and/or persuasive messages for products and services, but in a form in which the actual persuasive content may not be readily discernable.[11,12]

ETHICAL ISSUE TO CONSIDER

- What ethical issues might arise in relation to children and hybrid media such as games?
- What responsibility do marketers of these games or any organization considering joint promotions with specific games have?
- What research should be carried out to determine the impact of hybrid media forms and by whom?

Concerns regarding hybrid media

As with many new innovations, there has been considerable concern regarding the impact of hybrid media, especially claims that it is merely advertising by stealth[13] as it may affect users of the media without their conscious knowledge. This links to earlier concerns regarding claimed (and subsequently discredited) influence of **subliminal advertising** over the late 1950s to mid-1970s.[14]

More recent research indicates that the effects appear to be small and indirect, impacting on attitudes towards brands, not on the cognitive (thought) but rather the **affective** (feeling) component of attitudes.[15] Part of the challenge of research into the impact of sub-liminal messages has been determining the perceptual threshold for a stimulus. Not only does this threshold, or 'limen' (hence the term subliminal), vary substantially between individuals; it also varies within each individual across time.[16]

However, stimuli that are not directly attended to are not necessarily subliminal and it is suggested that subtle message forms such as product placements may directly influence brand preference and, ultimately, brand choice through a form of low involvement processing of messages which is not as yet fully understood.[17,18] This is of particular concern in relation to children as there is ample research illustrating that their cognitive abilities are not as developed as adults.[19,20] Specific areas of concern relate to product placements and joint promotions such as those involving the release of movies or television programmes popular with young age groups.[21]

Product placement/joint promotions

Product placement involves the use of a recognizable branded product in traditional mass media such as movies or television programmes and in newer electronic media such as videogames. This placement may be paid for directly, be provided as part of an exchange of goods or services, or be a part of a joint promotional package.[22] Placement can take many forms in traditional media, from passive (the product is shown as part of the setting, but is not actually used), through to active (the product is used by an actor with or without verbal acknowledgement as part of the script). Placement therefore provides an indirect form of celebrity endorsement for the product featured.[23] The practice of product placement in entertainment media is growing and with this growth has come growing uneasiness about its impact and whether the practice should be subject to greater control than it is currently.[24]

While much of the debate relates to the growth of product placements in new electronic media, the concept of product placement in commercial media is not new. It has its origins in the early years of the twentieth century. Early radio serials (in the 1920s) were actually scripted by the sponsoring advertiser's advertising agency. Long running programmes thus routinely included the advertiser's name in the programme title, contained advertisements for the advertiser's products and product mentions by the programme's characters as part of the script.[25] Since the 1950s, product placement also occurred in movies, helping to offset the often substantial production costs.[26] By 2005, product placement in the US was estimated to generate around US $3.4 billion.[27] In films alone, the amount spent on product placement is expected to rise from US $722 million in 2005 to more than US $1.8 billion in 2010.[28] And, although individual deals are seldom disclosed, individual amounts reported can vary from US $25 million paid by companies to feature their products in the movie *Minority Report* to over US $200 million paid for by Volkswagen to NBC Universal for product placement in film and television programmes produced by the company.[29]

In the UK, the paid-for product placement was estimated in 2011 at 0.1 per cent of total advertising revenue (£7 million or $10.5 million), estimated to rise to 0.9 per cent (£38m or $57.8 million) in 2015.[30]

Product placements extend well beyond traditional media forms such as movies and television shows to include placements within videogames available for purchase and games hosted on Internet sites.[31,32] McDonalds are reported as having offered to pay rap artists to include specific mentions of their products in songs, with payment based on the number of times each song was played.[33] In electronic media such as video or computer games, the product is often an integral part of the game itself, such as accurately depicted cars in a motor racing game.[34]

However, not all product placements are paid for. There are in fact three types of product placements, of which two do not involve direct payment: gratis placements, barter-style agreements and paid for product placements. For gratis placements, products are used free of charge and often not even with the consent of the brand owner. Normally this may be the case where the brand image enhances the credibility of the show or the character it is associated with. Barter-style agreements are probably the largest source of product placements,[35] representing around 64 per cent of all product placements.

In the case of barter-style agreements no money is exchanged, but the company may provide assistance in terms of providing products for the set, expertise or free advertising and linked promotions for a film, television show or video game. This can add up to a substantial saving for the film producers in terms of production cost: For example, BMW supplied 32 Mini Cooper cars for the filming of *The Italian Job*.[36]

Because of the increasing popularity of product placement many more placements are now paid for. While during the 1970s, only around 18 per cent of placements were paid for, this number had grown to around 29 per cent in 2004.[37]

The main rationale for product placements is the increased viewer involvement in the content, particularly in an environment where consumers frequently easily ignore traditional advertising in an increasingly cluttered environment.[38] However, the tactic is often criticized as inherently deceptive, as directly or indirectly paid for promotion is normally not separated from content.[39] Conversely, product placement advocates argue the use of brands, especially by movie characters, help to define the characters on screen and add realism to the environment on screen.[40] While much of the focus is on consumer-oriented products, evidence of increased recall, attitudes and purchase intentions are evident in relation to the placement of business-to-business products.[41]

While there is largely anecdotal evidence that product placement is an effective way to promote products and services in movies and on television, attributed largely to the increased viewer involvement, it seems hardly surprising, that repetitive exposure to placed products in video games that may be played several times with maximum involvement would be even more effective.[42] What is totally unknown is whether the same potential for wearout exists for product placements as for traditional media.

The impact of product placements remains under-researched, but subject to considerable debate regarding potential effects. In relation to children specifically, one study reports that, while up to half of children do recognize the commercial intent of programme placements, 72 per cent reported 'seeing a favourite character using a certain brand makes them want to use that brand at least some of the time'[43] p. 14. This may indicate a link between involvement in, and loyalty to, the programme and loyalty to the products the programme characters explicitly or implicitly endorse.[44]

Additional concerns relate to promotional tie-ins with movies that may or may not involve direct product placements. A long-standing link between Disney and McDonalds, estimated to have been worth US $100 million (£54 million) a year in royalties ended in 2006.[45] However, McDonalds then signed a two-year deal with DreamWorks Animation, beginning with *Shrek III* in mid-2007.[46]

THINK BOX

Product placement

Several popular television programmes involve the stars using a particular brand of product (e.g. cars). In police dramas, 'good guys' drive only the sponsor's brand of car – 'bad guys' cannot drive this brand.

Consider the implications of this for the brands not part of the product promotion – are there likely to be any negative impacts on their brands? If so, what might these be and how would you recommend dealing with the problem?

Under the current rules, there is technically nothing to prevent a product placement being arranged that specifically featured unpleasant characters using a competitor's brand. While this has not actually occurred (yet), what should marketers do to protect their brands from being used in this way?

ETHICAL ISSUE TO CONSIDER

Should there be restrictions on the types of tie-ins permitted for movies and television programmes? Justify your response.

As product placements become more common, is it likely that their impact may lessen? What do you recommend marketers do?

It has been suggested[47] that viewers of programmes or movies that contain product placements should be informed in advance that the product placements exist. What impact do you believe that this might have on viewer's perceptions of the programme or movie and the products it contains?

THINK BOX

'Cartoon character' endorsement

While we have noted concerns regarding product placements, there have also been several moves to use the popularity of cartoon characters to promote health food options. Nickelodeon has linked with fruit and vegetable marketers to enable cartoon characters such as *Dora the Explorer* and *SpongeBob SquarePants* to be used to promote 'branded' fruit and vegetable products; US sales of the specific products is reported to have increased by 30 per cent. Tesco, the giant UK-based grocery chain, obtained the rights to use several Disney characters including Winnie the Pooh on branded fruit products.[48]

Discuss the use of popular television characters, including cartoon characters, to promote healthy eating and healthy lifestyles. Given that young children are unlikely to be able to understand the way in which their favourite characters are being used, are there any concerns with this type of activity? How should such arrangements be monitored to determine their effects and who should be responsible for this?

MINI CASE: PRODUCT PLACEMENTS IN THE PUBLIC INTEREST

According to the US magazine *The Advocate*, the AIDS Healthcare Foundation in California is planning on petitioning for a law to require condoms being used in adult movies.[49] The arguments that the AHF uses are that workers in the adult industry should be protected, which is of course a very valid point. Another point though is absent from the statement, and that is the question whether or not what is happening in adult movies may influence perceptions of 'normality', and 'what is expected', which is part of ongoing research project grounded in the Theory of Reasoned Action/Theory of Planned Behaviour (see Figure 10.1).

In other words, what we are interested in is, if people do form their views of what is expected and 'normal' from media consumption, even if this is not (usually) a major plot line (as using a condom or not using a condom would be) – and how that then in turn does (or does not) influence their intentions and potential behaviours, especially behaviours that are often very private and for which there are only limited other experiences apart from media and own experiences.

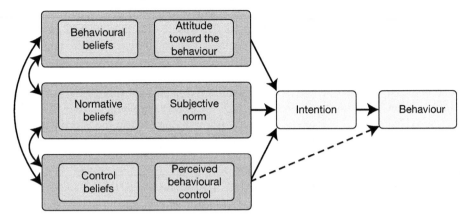

Figure 10.1 The Theory of Reasoned Action*

This is, of course, ultimately leading us to ask if and how this can be used for social marketing purposes. In other words, while the original AHF petition may be mostly about workers in the adult industry, it may be, that if such a ban comes into force, and if the TRA/TPB model guides us in the right way, such a ban on condomless sex on screen may have also a prevention effect in the much wider public that consumes adult movies.

- Is using condoms on screen a viable solution?
- Would you use condoms because you have seen them being used on screen? Because of other reasons?
- Why would you use some products because they are endorsed by stars? Why not others? And are there limits?

Product placement in video games ('advergames')

Products and games can be linked in one of two ways: either by placing the product into the game environment, similar to traditional product placement in movies, or by developing themed video games, for example games which feature a well known brand character as a main character of the game.

The sector of advertising or product placement sponsored games (or 'advergames' for short), has rapidly evolved in the last few years, with computer games based on movies or TV series claimed to generate double the revenue of the film industry.[50] The advergame sector itself is a reflection of the increasingly 'blurred boundary between entertainment and persuasion'[51] in marketing communications.

Product placements within games are claimed to be 'more effective than placements on television or in films because, in a game's immersive environment, players can interact with the products they see'[52] p. 24, but there is little empirical evidence to support such assertions. Several caveats are offered regarding effectiveness being, unsurprisingly, dependent on how well the product fits with the environment in which it is featured.[53]

Advergames provide virtual interaction with a product or a brand name. Similar to traditional product placement, the aim is to create an emotional connection between the game, the gamer and the brand featured.[54] However, when compared to conventional advertising, the potential interactivity and elective involvement of advergames makes these forms of advertising more attractive and potentially more effective.[55] Child gamers may play games up to 100 times,[56] and adults can spend up to 30 hours playing one game.[57]

Also, research on advertising recall rates show impressive results, with one research claiming rates of 30 per cent of in-game adverts are recalled immediately after the game, and an impressive 18 per cent after five months.[58] This more positive view is supported by other studies, showing higher recall rates.[59,60] Concerns are evident regarding advergames provided by food marketers, with sites primarily promoting foods deemed high in sugar and fat[61,62,63] (and which are now, as noted in previous chapters, subject to increased regulation of advertising in traditional mass media such as television).

Video games allow for more flexible levels of product placement than do movies or television programmes. Products and advertising can be placed in the background of the games, such as pitch-side advertising in football games. Alternatively, they can be an integral part of the game itself, for example in car racing games, in which the cars are shown fully branded and extremely detailed.[64] In a way, customers can therefore virtually test drive a placed car, and potentially build an emotional association to the brand of the car.

Experiential marketing

Experiential marketing combines both customer experience with a brand and a wider emotional experience. Often direct contact is made between the marketer and the customer, with the intention of involving the customer in the brand and providing a positive brand experience, leading to an emotional connection for the customer associating the brand with this positive emotion, which in turn leads to purchase intention and/or increased brand loyalty.

Traditionally this approach often relied on a live experience combining retail and other forms of events – thus going beyond the mere selling/ purchasing experience. Increasingly, this often means combining social networking techniques with real live events in an attempt to create a positive customer experience, which can be experienced and shared amongst consumers. For example, the mobile phone company T-mobile used flash mob-like events for marketing purposes.

This was based on the social networking phenomena of flash mobbing, where people invited each other, often randomly, using Twitter, Facebook or SMS to be in a specific place at a specified time, and to then perform a designated activity together (for example dancing in a public place). However, not all experiential marketing events have to combine real live with virtual events. Some events can be entirely virtual, for example by using networked multi-player games events – where participants are only partaking virtually, for example by playing interconnected games.

THINK BOX

Experiential marketing

- Discuss if and how experiential marketing can create added value.
- Would this work for all types of products? Why or why not?
- What are the advantages of combining social networking and real-life events?
- What are the advantages and disadvantages of entirely virtual events?

Augmented reality marketing

Augmented reality combines live, direct views of the real world with computer generated elements that 'augment' – or enhance – the reality, for example by providing additional information in real time. Alternatively, reality can be 'mediated' – or changed in real-time. At the most simple, this can take the form of textual information displayed inside a live view of the environment. In these cases, sponsored information is 'added' into the picture, for example by showing the location of a nearby bar. However, augmented or mediated reality can be more technically and graphically advanced, inserting not only information, but also logos, pictures and even interactive figures into a live image.

In marketing it is used for example when during a live sport broadcast large adverts are displayed 'as if' they were painted on the pitch, when in reality there is no such advert. Equally, mediated reality can be used to target different advertising segments: target market specific adverts can be 'inserted' on pitches during sports broadcasts, thus enabling the change of adverts seen on screen depending on where the event is being watched.

Effectiveness/pre-testing/measuring return on investment

There are numerous, mostly anecdotal reports of product placement success yet there is no real way of empirically measuring its effects.[65] Examples of claimed successful product placement included Tom Cruise's use of Rayban sunglasses in two separate movies which is reported to have positively impacted on the product's sales.[66]

A major commercial success was claimed for the placement of Hershey Foods' Reese's Pieces confectionary in the 1982 movie *E.T. The Extra-Terrestrial* with sales of the confectionary increasing 65 per cent following the movie's release.[67] However, a more critical report suggests that much of the sales increase may be because of a linked sales promotion,[68] rather than the movie itself. In fact, most research on product placement seems to suggest it's direct effect is rather weak, however, the effect in traditional media is multidimensional, and therefore difficult to measure.[69]

Conversely, when considering product placements in non-traditional media, the research seems to support a more positive view, with brand recall rates after five months as high as 18 per cent.[70] Practitioners largely rely on brand recall as a measure of effectiveness, either unprompted or prompted and viewers' brand recognition within a movie.[71] However, in either case, the reliance of the measurement of product placement effectiveness on mere brand recall or recognition is often criticized as being only a crude measure, and argue that both explicit measures such as product recall and implicit measures should be used.[72]

Ethical issues

There are a number of specific ethical issues regarding product placements in particular which we have noted throughout this chapter. One of the major concerns is the potentially deceptive nature of the placement, especially as the source and nature of the communication can no longer be identified,[73] i.e. it is not clear if the actor, producer, writer, or in fact the brand owner are the originator of a brand related message. This in turn makes effective regulation complex if not impossible. This is of particular concern in areas where product types are controversial, for example in the case of tobacco or alcohol use.

Of particular concern is the finding that portrayal of movie stars smoking increases the likelihood of teenagers smoking.[74] Similar concerns are evident in relation to possible links with exposure to persuasive communication regarding food deemed to be of low nutrition value and obesity,[75] particularly when the tactics used would not be acceptable in conventional media.[76]

In the wider hybrid media area, children's limited ability to understand the nature of persuasion knowledge and thus defences against persuasive communication is held by lobby groups to be justification for limiting the type and amount of exposure to subtle forms of persuasive communication that children may not recognize as such.[77] There is, however, little specific research in this area and it remains a very difficult – and hotly contested topic.[78]

It could be argued that an extreme form of product placement is represented by programmes such as the US *Sunset Tan*, set in a tanning salon. Regular use of sunbeds is known to increase the risk of skin cancer.[79] This programme regularly features celebrities such as Britney Spears praising tanning.[80] While it does not currently screen in the UK, it is available online.

Thus, there are potential legislative and ethical issues that need to be debated in relation to all forms of hybrid media, particularly in terms of growing concerns regarding the impact of persuasive communication on vulnerable groups such as children. There are continual pressures for reviews of current regulations in individual countries and across wider markets such as the EU[81] and these will no doubt continue in the future.

Summary

The hybridization of media has been enabled by the rapid developments in technology. In the second part of the 1990s, moving-image culture went through a fundamental transformation. Previously separate media – live-action cinematography, graphics, still photography, animation, 3D computer animation and typography – started to be combined in a number of ways.

These changes have been also affected by the development of the Internet and the opportunities it brings with it. The hybrid media has been noticed and used by marketing communications practitioners to engage consumers in brand-related activities, for example, through the use of advergames or online gaming. In addition to hybrid media, other forms of engaging consumers with the brand, such as experiential marketing or product placements have emerged. The technological developments present marketers with new and interesting opportunities for communicating with consumers.

Review questions

1. Discuss the growth of hybrid media forms as a means to achieve cut through and avoid the increasing clutter of conventional advertising.
2. What impact is the increase in product placements likely to have on their effectiveness?
3. Discuss the ethics of hybrid media forms where the receiver of communications may not be aware of the persuasive intent.
4. Discuss the potential impact of the portrayal of alcohol consumption, excessive speeding or food of low nutritional value in hybrid media on subsequent behaviour.
5. Visit the websites of five major UK/EU food marketers whose products have particular appeal to children and who include interactive games on their websites. Critique this activity and recommend action to address any concerns.
6. Should regulations be tightened with regard to exposure of children to product placements, advergames and other forms of subtle commercial messages within television programmes?

7. Discuss the arguments for and against placing warnings in television programmes, movies or advergames signalling that product placements are included in the content.

Recommended reading

Colliander, J., and Erlandsson, S. (2013). The blog and the bountiful: exploring the effects of disguised product placement on blogs that are revealed by a third party. *Journal of Marketing Communications*, DOI: 10.1080/13527266.2012.730543, 1–15.

Hudson, S., Hudson, D., and Peloza, J. (2008). Meet the parents: a parents' perspective on product placement in children's films. *Journal of Business Ethics*, 80(2), 289–304.

Kretchmer, S.B. (2004). 'Advertainment: The Evolution of Product Placement as a Mass Media Marketing Strategy'. In: M. Galician (ed.), *Handbook of Product Placement in the Mass Media: New Strategies in Marketing Theory, Practice, Trends and Ethics*, Binghamton, NY: Haworth Press, pp. 37–54.

Redondo, I., and Holbrook, M.B. (2008). Illustrating a systematic approach to selecting motion pictures for product placements and tie-ins. *International Journal of Advertising*, 27(5), 691–714.

CASE STUDY 10.1

Bebo's *Kate Modern*: using online product placement to monetize social networking websites

This case has been adapted from: Bebo's 'Kate Modern': using online product placement to monetize social networking websites. Source and author: Meg Carter: www.megcarter.com. Case material provided by the World Advertising Research Centre (WARC) www.warc.com.

Social networking websites were initially viewed by advertisers mainly as places to seed TV commercials or create profile web pages for brands. But as leading online networks such as Bebo and MySpace embraced original content production, the potential to offer another marketing technique came into focus – namely, product placement.

Global paid product placement across all media is forecast by PQ Media, the specialist researchers, to be worth $7.55bn in 2010 – an almost 20 per cent compound annual growth rate between 2005 and 2010. It may prove a way to turn to commercial advantage the huge audiences on networking websites, which have not developed as conventional mass advertising platforms since they emerged in the mid-2000s.

Kate Modern: investing in original content

Bebo, which has 40 million members worldwide including 11.2 million in the UK and 3.4m in the US (at January 2008), was early into product placement, commissioning the online-only video series, *Kate Modern*, in 2007.

The *Kate Modern* format was created for Bebo by the producers of Lonelygirl 15 – a series of video clips which became a cult phenomenon on YouTube, as an interactive teen drama series.

This included online profile pages for characters and actors through which additional plot developments were introduced to the Bebo community. Users were also invited to castings as well as to shape story developments.

Series one of *Kate Modern* comprised 155 video-based four-minute episodes. It ran between July and December 2007 and accumulated more than 35 million online video viewings – an average 1.5 million a week: good news for the six brand partners which each paid up to £250,000 ($475,000 at Jan 08 rates) to be associated with the show.

Profiting from 'brand integration'

Bebo called its strategy 'brand integration' rather than product placement. A participating brand owner received a combination of media exposure through Internet banner advertising on the site or profile pages and integration of its product into the *Kate Modern* plot.

Following *Kate Modern*, Bebo decided to roll out this commercial model across other original content commissions including *Sofia's Diary*, another teen soap, and global online reality TV travel show, *Gap Year*. At the time of writing, both were due to launch in early March, 2008.

Mark Charkin, vice president of Bebo sales, said:

> We set out to add value to the Bebo experience by giving Bebo users access to original entertainment content they could interact with. We did not intend this to be a loss leader, however. It had to be economically viable from day one.

Bebo committed to spend up to £6,000 per four-minute episode. Setting the price it would charge brands to be associated with *Kate Modern*, however, was less clear cut.

Charkin said:

> We estimated the number of views per episode that would make it a success as 100,000. Then we set a price for brand association based on the predicted degree of exposure brands would have in *Kate Modern*. As it happened, the average number of views achieved per episode was twice that, with some even getting more than a million.

Rates charged to advertisers were charged by calculating the value of conventional Internet media placement – banner ads, profile pages and so on – and the degree to which their brand or product was integrated into the storyline of the online video drama. Background pack shots commanded a lower price than full product integration into the storyline.

'We were looking both for category sponsors willing to associate themselves for the duration of the series and also brands wanting integration for shorter periods to promote more time sensitive products,' Charkin added. Bebo signed up Atlantic Records, Buena Vista International, Microsoft, Orange, Paramount and Procter & Gamble.

Buena Vista used the association to promote the release of three movies: *Hallam Foe*, *Ratatouille* and *Enchanted*. For *Hallam Foe*, the film's star, Jamie Bell, appeared in *Kate Modern* bumping into one of the drama's characters in a bar.

Procter & Gamble used *Kate Modern* to promote Pantene, Gillette and Tampax. For Pantene, it was written into the script that one character worked at the brand's PR company. Over a number of episodes she was seen developing creative briefs to promote the haircare range and filmed at a shoot for a new Pantene ad. Microsoft used its association to demonstrate a number of MSN products including its mapping service.

Impact and evaluation

Estimating the value and impact of each brand association was challenging for both sides. To evaluate its pricing strategy, Bebo used a combination of traditional media modelling used for movie product placement plus brand exposure measurement and analysis of the relevance of a brand's involvement to the drama's plot. Most of the brand owners undertook their own brand tracking studies and focus groups to gauge brand awareness generated by the association as well as changes in viewers' purchasing intent.

This set-up was typical of many product placement deals – even those involving more tried and tested media, according to John Blakemore, former advertising director of Glaxo-SmithKline and co-founder of Ash Blakemore Product Placement, a specialist consultancy. Blakemore said:

> Evaluation remains a grey zone. Even with TV – at first glance and by comparison an easier medium to monitor – measurement is down to working out how many people saw you for how long at what time then analysing this against the equivalent exposure you would have got in a conventional TV spot.

Such techniques can help with pricing. Evaluating effectiveness and value for money remains a highly subjective process, Blakemore added.

In the run-up to the launch of *Sophia's Diary*, Bebo planned further research on the impact of its brand integration approach on Bebo users. This involved profiling more closely the demographics of who was watching and when. The company also considered commissioning its own tracking and brand evaluation study.

While remaining tight-lipped about the financials of the first series of *Kate Modern*, Mr Charkin said: 'All I can say is we made a profit and came out ahead.'

The future for online product placement

In January 2008 Bebo launched a second series of *Kate Modern* with advertisers including Cadbury-Schweppes and Toyota. The results were closely watched, and not just by Bebo insiders.

At that time, YouTube – better known for distributing user-generated clips or extracts from broadcast TV uploaded to its website – also considered more original content investment. MySpace, which sold its first original web drama Quarterlife to NBC, the US broadcaster, also confirmed plans to expand advertiser-funded programming and product placement.

At the time of writing, many commentators argue that online product placement has the potential to generate far deeper levels of engagement between consumer and brand than television or movie-based product placement.

In January 2008 Hitwise and Experian Integrated Marketing published research entitled, 'The Impact of Social Networking in the UK', which argued for the online advertising potential of social networking websites.

The authors claimed sites such as Bebo, YouTube and MySpace, would be the primary online arena for future targeted marketing and advertising campaigns and the dominant channel for viral marketing.

David Fletcher, head of MediaLab at mediaedge:cia, the media buying group, told warc.com: 'Online social networks allow unprecedented interactivity and engagement – even when compared to more traditional Internet portals'.

> The deeper someone interacts with a piece of online content, the deeper their engagement both with that content and the environment in which they consume it. That has clear benefits both for the social network and its advertising partners.

CASE STUDY QUESTIONS

1. Which tools and media channels were used in the case?
2. How effective do you think such an integrated approach is? List advantages and disadvantages.

3. Discuss the ethical aspects of mixing paid for banner advertising and product placement in a social media environment. What concerns could be raised?
4. How would you evaluate a campaign such as this? Think of ways to calculate a Return On Investment (ROI).

Notes

* Adapted from Ajzen, I., and Fishbein, M. (1980). *Understanding Attitudes and Predicting Social Behaviour*, Englewood Cliffs, NJ: Prentice-Hall.

1   Anonymous. (2003). Cashing in on the SMS phenomenon. *Computer Weekly*, 37.
2   Elvin, J. (2001). www.Bust.com (cover story). *Insight on the News*, 17(12), 10.
3   Rust, R.T., and Oliver, R.W. (1994). The death of advertising. *Journal of Advertising*, 23(4), 71–7.
4   Mau, G., Silberer, G.N., and Constien, C. (2008). Communicating brands playfully. *International Journal of Advertising*, 27(5), 827–51.
5   Anonymous. (1997). At home with computers. *Crain's Small Business Southeast Michigan Edition*, 5(2), 18.
6   Anonymous. (2003). Cashing in on the SMS phenomenon. *Computer Weekly*, 37.
7   Goldsborough, R. (2006). That's advertainment. *Information Today*, 23(3), 33–4.
8   Williams, D. (2006). 'A Brief Social History of Game Play'. In Peter Vorderer and Jennings Bryant (eds) *Playing Video Games: Motives, Responses, and Consequences*, Abingdon: Routledge.
9   Ipsos Media CT. (2012). Videogames in Europe: Consumer Study. Online. Available HTTP: <www.isfe.eu/sites/isfe.eu/files/attachments/euro_summary_-_isfe_consumer_study.pdf> (accessed 28 March 2013).
10 Kim, R. (2006). Video games no longer child's play. *San Francisco Chronicle*, 12 June, cited in Vedrashko, I. (2006). *Advertising in Computer Games*, GamesBrandsPlay.com. Online. Available HTTP: <www.gamesbrandsplay.com/files/vedrashko_advertising_in_games.pdf> (accessed 27 March 2009).
11 Balasubramanian, S.K. (1994). Beyond advertising and publicity: hybrid messages and public policy issues. *Journal of Advertising*, 23(4), 29–46.
12 Banerjee, S. (2004). Playing games. *Billboard*, 116(20), 3–4.
13 Mutel, G. (2004). Product placement reaches maturity in the US. *Campaign (UK)*, 49, 17.
14 Rogers, M., and Seiler, C.A. (1994). The answer is no: a national survey of advertising industry practitioners and the clients about whether they use subliminal advertising. *Journal of Advertising Research*, 34(2), 36–45.
15 Aylesworth, A.B., Goodstein, R.C., and Kalra, A. (1999). Effect of archetypal embeds on feelings: an indirect route to affecting attitudes. *Journal of Advertising*, 28(3), 73–81.
16 Moore, T. (1982). Subliminal advertising: what you see is what you get. *Journal of Marketing*, 46(2), 38–47.
17 Heath, R. (2000). Low involvement processing – a new model of brands and advertising. *International Journal of Advertising*, 19(3), 287–98.
18 Moore, E.S. (2004). Children and the changing world of advertising. *Journal of Business Ethics*, 52(2), 161–7.
19 Moses, L.J., and Baldwin, D.A. (2005). What can the study of cognitive development reveal about children's ability to appreciate and cope with advertising? *Journal of Public Policy & Marketing*, 24(2), 186–201.
20 Mallalieu, L., Palan, K.M., and Laczniak, R.N. (2005). Understanding children's knowledge and beliefs about advertising: a global issue that spans generations. *Journal of Current Issues and Research in Advertising*, 27(1), 53–63.
21 Moore, E.S. (2004). Children and the changing world of advertising. *Journal of Business Ethics*, 52(2), 161–7.
22 Karrh, J.A. (1998). Brand placement: a review. *Journal of Current Issues and Research in Advertising*, 209(2), 31–49.

23 Law, S., and Braun, K.A. (2000). 'I'll have what she's having': gauging the impact of product placements on viewers. *Psychology & Marketing*, 17(12), 1059–75.

24 Auty, S., and Lewis, C. (2004). Exploring children's choice: the reminder effect of product placement. *Psychology & Marketing*, 21(9), 697–713.

25 Kretchmer, S.B. (2004). 'Advertainment: The Evolution of Product Placement as a Mass Media Marketing Strategy'. In M. Galician (ed.), *Handbook of Product Placement in the Mass Media: New Strategies in Marketing Theory, Practice, Trends and Ethics*. Binghamton, NY: Haworth Press, 37–54.

26 DeLorme, D.E., and Reid, L.N. (1999). Moviegoers' experiences and interpretations of brands in films revisited. *Journal of Advertising*, 28(2), 71–95.

27 Russell, C.A., and Belch, M. (2005). A managerial investigation into the product placement industry. *Journal of Advertising Research*, 45(1), 73–92.

28 Wiles, M.A., and Danielova, A. (2009). The worth of product placement in successful films: an event study analysis, *Journal of Marketing*, 73(July), 44–63.

29 Wiles, M.A., and Danielova, A. (2009). The worth of product placement in successful films: an event study analysis, *Journal of Marketing*, 73(July), 44–63.

30 NMG Product Placement (2012). Latest Research Study by NMG Product Placement values UK 'Paid for' Product Placement Market Size at £9.7m to £29.1m. Online. Available HTTP: <www.newmediagroup.co.uk/?p=904> (accessed 23 March 2013).

31 Jones, M. (2006). Official sites. Movies, games and the blurry lines of genre. *Metro Magazine*, 148(22 March), 160–3.

32 Nelson, M.R., Yaros, R.A., and Keum, H. (2006). Examining the influence of telepresence on spectator and player processing of real and fictitious brands in a computer game. *Journal of Advertising*, 35(4), 87–99.

33 Hackley, C., and Tiwsakul, R. (2006). Entertainment marketing and experiential consumption. *Journal of Marketing Communication*, 12(1), 63–75.

34 Moltenbrey, K. (2004). Adver-driving. *Computer Graphics World*, 27(6), 30–1.

35 PQ Media (2005). *Product Placement Spending in Media*, Executive Report, Education and Public Policy Research Unit, Arizona State University.

36 Lehua, J.-M., and Bressoudb, E. (2007): Effectiveness of brand placement: new insights about viewers, *Journal of Business Research*, 61(10), 1083–90.

37 PQ Media (2005). *Product Placement Spending in Media*, Executive Report, Education & Public Policy Research Unit, Arizona State University.

38 Karrh, J.A. (1998). Brand placement: a review. *Journal of Current Issues and Research in Advertising*, 209(2), 31–49.

39 Banerjee, S. (2004). Playing games. *Billboard*, 116(20), 3–4.

40 Balasubramanian, S.K., Karrh, J.A., and Parwardhan, H. (2006). Audience response to product placement. An integrative framework and future research agenda. *Journal of Advertising*, 35(3), 115–41.

41 Lord, K.R., and Gupta, P.B. (2009). Response of buying-centre participants to product placements. *Journal of Business & Industrial Mareting*, 25(3), 188–95.

42 Gunn, E. (2001). Product placement prize. *Advertising Age*, 72(7), 10.

43 Kennedy, D.G. (2004). Coming of age in consumerdom. *American Demographics*, 26(3), 14.

44 Karrh, J.A., McKee, K.B., and Pardun, C.J. (2003). Practitioners' evolving views on product placement. *Journal of Advertising Research*, 138–49.

45 BBC News. (2006). *McDonalds and Disney End Tie-up*. Online. Available HTTP: <http://news.bbc.co.uk/1/hi/business/4752885.stm>.

46 LA Times. (2006). *Studios Feast in Fast-Food Tie-ins*. Online. Available HTTP: <www.calendarlive.com/movies/la-et-goldstein21nov21,0,6882446.story?coll=cl-nav-movies>.

47 Watson, R. (2006). EU legislators lock horns over product placement. *Times Online*, 1.

48 Food Navigator. (2006, 24 July). *Nickelodeon Characters Prepare to Entice Kids to Veg*. Online. Available HTTP: <www.foodnavigator-usa.com/news/ng.asp?n=69355-nickelodeon-fruits-and-vegetables-cartoon-celebrities> (accessed 11 January 2007).

49 The Advocate (2009). California May Require Condoms in Porn. Online. Available HTTP: <www.advocate.com/News/Daily_News/2009/12/17/California_May_Require_Condoms_in_Porn/> (accessed 17 December 2009).

50   Lindstrom, M. (2005). Get a jump-start on playing the new brand game. *Media Asia*, 28 January, 21.

51   Shrum, L.J. (ed.) (2004). *The Psychology of Entertainment Media: Blurring the Lines Between Entertainment and Persuasion*, Mahwah, NJ: Lawrence Erlbaum.

52   Edery, D. (2006). Reverse product placement in virtual worlds. *Harvard Business Review*, 84(12), 24.

53   Peckham, M. (2007). Brand-aid. In-game 'advertainment' is poised to change the way you play. *Games for Windows*, 1(2), 46–8.

54   Arnold, C. (2004). Just press play. *Marketing News*, 38(9), 1–15.

55   Deal, D. (2005). The Ability of Online Brand Games to Build Brand Equity: An Exploratory Analysis. Paper in Proceedings of 2005 DIGRA conference. Online. Available HTTP: <www. gamesconference.org/digra2005/viewabstract.php?id=46>.

56   Gunn, E. (2001). Product placement prize. *Advertising Age*, 72(7), 10.

57   Nelson, M.R., Keum. H., and Yaros, R.A. (2004). Advertainment or advercreep? Game players' attitudes towards advertising and product placement in computer games. *Journal of Interactive Advertising*, 4(3), 1–30.

58   Grigorovici, D.M., and Constantin, C.D. (2004). Experiencing interactive advertising beyond rich media. Impacts of ad type and presence on brand effectiveness in 3d gaming immersive virtual environments. *Journal of Interactive Advertising*, 5(1), 1–26.

59   Schneider, L.P., and Cornwell, T.B. (2005). Cashing in on crashes via brand placement in computer games. *International Journal of Advertising*, 24(3), 321–43.

60   Molesworth, M. (2006). Real brands in imaginary worlds: investigating players' experiences of brand placement in digital games. *Journal of Consumer Behaviour*, 5(4), 355–66.

61   Culp, J., Bell, R.A., and Cassady, D. (2009). Characteristics of food industry websties and 'advergames' targeting children. *Journal of Nutrition Education and Behaviour*, 42(3), 197–201.

62   Dahl, S., Eagle, L., and Baez, C. (2008). Analyzing advergames: active diversions or actual deception. An exploratory study of online advergame content. *Young Consumers*, 10(1), 17–34.

63   Lee, M., Choi, Y., Quilliam, E.T., and Cole, R.T. (2009). Playing with food: content analysis of food advergames. *Journal of Consumer Affairs*, 43(1), 129–54.

64   Moltenbrey, K. (2004). Adver-driving. *Computer Graphic World*, 27(6), 30–1.

65   Atkinson, C., and Fine, J. (2004). Nielsen plumbs product placement. *Advertising Age*, 75(37), 47.

66   Karrh, J.A. (1998). Brand placement: a review. *Journal of Current Issues and Research in Advertising*, 209(2), 31–49.

67   Gupta, P.B., and Gould, S.J. (1997). Consumers' perceptions of the ethics and acceptability of product placements in movies: product category and individual differences. *Journal of Current Issues and Research in Advertising*, 19(1), 37–50.

68   Pechmann, C., and Shih, C.-F. (1999). Smoking scenes in movies and antismoking advertisements before movies: effects on youth. *Journal of Marketing*, 63(3), 1–13.

69   McCarty, J.A. (2003). 'Product Placement: Practice and Inquiry'. In L.J. Shrum (ed.) *The Psychology of Entertainment Media: Blurring the Lines between Entertainment and Persuasion*, London: Psychology Press.

70   Nelson, M.R., Keum. H., and Yaros, R.A. (2004). Advertainment or advercreep? Game players' attitudes towards advertising and product placement in computer games. *Journal of Interactive Advertising*, 4(3), 1–30.

71   Karrh, J.A., McKee, K.B., and Pardun, C.J. (2003). Practitioners' evolving views on product placement effectiveness. *Journal of Advertising Research*, 43(2), 138–49.

72   Law, S., and Braun, K.A. (2000). I'll have what she's having: gauging the impact of product placement on viewers. *Psychology & Marketing*, 17(12), 1059–75.

73   Hackley, C., Tiwsakul, R.A., and Preuss, L. (2008). An ethical evaluation of product placement: a deceptive practice? *Business Ethics: A European Review*, 17(2), 109–20.

74   Distefan, J.M., Pierce, J.P., and Gilpin, E.A. (2004). Do favourite movie stars influence adolescent smoking initiation? *American Journal of Public Health*, 94(7), 1239–44.

75 Lee, M., Choi, Y., Quilliam, E.T., and Cole, R.T. (2009). Playing with food: content analysis of food advergames. *Journal of Consumer Affairs*, 43(1), 129–54.

76 Dahl, S., Eagle, L., and Baez, C. (2008). Analyzing advergames: active diversions or actual deception. An exploratory study of online advergame content. *Young Consumers*, 10(1), 17–34.

77 Bray, H. (2004). 'Advergames' Spark Concerns of Kids Being Targeted, *Boston Globe*, 30 July. Online. Available HTTP: <www.boston.com/>.

78 Livingstone, S. (2005). Assessing the research base for the policy debate over the effects of food advertising to children. *International Journal of Advertising*, 24(3), 273–96.

79 Murray, C.D., and Turner, E. (2004). Health, risk and sunbed use: a qualitative study. *Health, Risk & Society*, 6(1), 67–80.

80 Poorsattar, S.P., and Hornung, R.L. (2008). Television turning more teens toward tanning. *Journal of the American Academy of Dermatology*, 58(1), 171–2.

81 Hatfield, S. (2000). EU turning into battleground over more curbs on marketing. *Advertising Age*, 71(39), 60–1.

11 Integrated campaign development
Advertising

LEARNING OUTCOMES

After studying this chapter, you will be able to:

- Understand the concept of advertising and explore its role within the wider communications mix
- Appreciate the process of advertising and understand the strengths and weaknesses of a range of models of how advertising has been assumed to work
- Understand the factors that affect the effectiveness of advertising
- Appreciate the components of an effective advertising brief
- Understand how to evaluate the effectiveness of an advertising campaign
- Understand the legal and ethical limitations associated with advertising

Introduction

The basic concept of advertising has been around almost as long as the concept of commerce itself. Wherever a buyer–seller relationship had the potential to exist, so did the potential for advertising. The earliest evidence of advertising has been found as far back as 3000 BC in the form of a Babylonian clay tablet that lists information relating to the services offered by an ointment dealer, a scribe and a shoemaker.[1] Furthermore, there is also significant evidence that tradesmen of the early civilizations of Greece, Egypt, Rome and Mesopotamia used signs to communicate the existence of their wares to potential customers.[2]

Over the course of time, whilst the complexity of brands, the media and even the markets themselves have developed exponentially, many of the basic principles of advertising have remained the same; simply to communicate a specific message to a target audience. The aim of this chapter is to explore the nature of advertising, how it works and the factors that affect its relative effectiveness. It will look at the variety of media available to those seeking to reach their target markets and the various methods of advertising open to them. Finally it will examine two types of barriers faced by advertisers; psychological ones that are self imposed by the target audience and regulatory barriers either imposed by an industry code of practice or by wider government legislation.

What is advertising?

Interestingly, when perusing texts and articles that relate to the topic of 'advertising', it is a striking fact that very few authors offer a definition of the term. Texts regularly proffer explanations of what advertising does or what media it encapsulates, but to find a formal definition of the term 'advertising' is rare. Dictionary definitions of 'advertising' focus upon the process of making people aware of positive features of a product or service or 'selling' it yet its scope is much wider than that. The word 'advertising' is derived from the Latin term 'ad vertere' which means 'to turn the mind toward'. To this end, advertising may be defined as any form of communication that serves to achieve one or more of the following: to inform, to advise, to persuade, to remind and to provide information to aid the process of informed decision making on the part of the consumer or customer.

How does the process of advertising work?

Hierarchy of effects models

At its most basic level, the underlying premise of all advertising communication is the transmission of a message from one party (an information source) to another (the destination) via one or more media. The background to this process has been covered in Chapter 2 in the discussion of communication theory. However, within the context of advertising, the focus shifts from the logistics associated with the movement of communication to processes determining impact and outcome.

Over the last century, advertising theorists have generated a number of models to explain how advertising works. The earliest models emerged from the literature on personal selling, and focussed upon a 'hierarchy of effects' in which advertisers lead consumers through a sequence of steps until they reach a decision.

Figure 11.1 depicts one of the earliest models and most widely cited is that of AIDA (Awareness, Interest, Action, Desire).[3] In its earliest incarnation in 1898, St. Elmo Lewis[4] theorized that in order to maximize their success, salespeople had to attract the attention

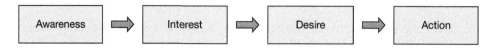

Figure 11.1 The AIDA model

of consumers, maintain their interest and then generate a level of desire. The final stage, that of prompting the consumer to action, was added shortly after and the model became known as AIDA.

The success of the **AIDA model** prompted the development of a number of other 'hierarchy of effects' models[5] depicted in Table 11.1. All of these models assume the same initial goal of drawing consumers' attention to the brand in question. Consumers are then lead through a sequence in which their interest is engaged with the result that they become so well disposed toward the product or service in question that they take positive action at the point of decision-making or 'action'.

In 1961, Colley's publication entitled *Defining Advertising Goals for Measured Advertising Results*,[6] added a further dimension to the hierarchy of effects field. Whilst he too proposed a hierarchical model that moved consumers from a state of **awareness**, through **comprehension**, then conviction and finally to 'action', there was an additional focus upon marketers' ability to measure the effectiveness of their advertising campaigns. Like many of the models that preceded it, 'DAGMAR' as it became known, proposed

Table 11.1 Early hierarchy of effects models[3]

Year	Author(s)	Form/description of model
1910	Printers Ink	AICA (attract **Attention**, develop **Interest**, produce **Conviction**, induce **Action**)
1911	Arthur Fredrick Sheldon in *The Art of Selling*	AIDAS (favourable **Attention, Interest, Desire, Action,** permanent **Satisfaction**)
1911	International Correspondence School	PAICSH (**Preparation** for approach, **Approach, Interest, Closing, Sale, Holding** the customer)
1915	Samuel R. Hall, *Writing an Advertisement*	AICCA (**Attention, Interest, Confidence, Conviction, Action**)
1920	West Coast Life Insurance Company	ADICA (attracting **Attention**, creating **Desire**, removing **Inhibitions**, inspiring **Confidence**, impelling to **Action**)
1921	Harry D. Kitson, *The Mind of the Buyer*	AIDCA (**Attention, Interest, Desire, Confidence, Action**)
1922	Alexander F. Osborn, *A Short Course in Advertising*	AIJA (**Attention, Interest, Judgement, Action**)
1923	Daniel Starch	SRBRA (**Seen, Remembered, Believed, Read, Acted** upon)
1938	Edward K. Strong	AD(W)C(S)PS (**Attention, Desire (Want), Conviction (Solution), Purchase, Satisfaction**)
1940	Clyde Bedell, *How to Write Advertising that Sells*	AIDCA (**Attention, Interest, Desire, Conviction, Action**)

that consumers should be moved through a series of stages; from a point of ignorance of a brand, to awareness of its existence, through to comprehension of its attributes, conviction of its superiority and then finally to a state of action in which they make a purchase. Evaluation of the success of the campaign was then measured in terms of the extent to which a specific campaign moved consumers up the ladder from one level in the hierarchy of effects to another'.[7]

THINK BOX

Hierarchy of effects

For a branded product that you have bought recently, try to remember when you first became aware of it. Based upon your own experience, construct your own 'hierarchy of effects' from the point of awareness to the point of purchase. Compare your construct with those listed on p. 246. How similar are they and how can you account for the differences?

ETHICAL ISSUE TO CONSIDER

Refer back to material in earlier chapters, particularly Chapter 3. What ethical issues may arise from the 'Desire' component of the AIDA model?

Consider a range of possible target groups, especially children. Does the creation of 'desire' for products or services lead to pestering of parents to buy the advertised products for them?

If so, what, if anything, should marketers and regulators do?

Challenges to the hierarchy of effects models

To this day, 'hierarchy of effects' models retain a degree of popularity and are widely cited in academic and practitioner literature. Their logical structure makes them simple to teach and easy for students of marketing and advertising to remember. Yet, despite this, they are not without criticism.

One of the strongest challenges to the concept of hierarchical models is that of a potential lack of relevance to the 'real world'. Whilst from a theoretical perspective they might be psychologically sound, critics accuse them of not adequately reflecting the markets they seek to portray on a number of counts.[8] Firstly, critics question the assumption that there is a direct causal link between advertising and sales.[9] For example, take an advertisement for a new brand of breakfast cereal. Critics of the hierarchical model concept suggest that, just because a consumer sees it and is persuaded of its positive benefits, he or she is not necessarily driven to purchase a box at the next available opportunity.

Further, concerns are raised over the extent to which such models have the capability to either reflect or explain the dynamics of market share. Logically, the causal link proposed by standard hierarchical model structures suggest that a brand's share of total market sales should be a direct reflection of its relative share of advertising. If the link truly existed, new brands whose launch activity includes high levels of advertising should automatically see high levels of sales. Yet as even the most intensely advertised new brand launches can see high levels of brand failure, this blatantly is not the case. Conversely, if an established brand ceases to advertise, the causal link suggests that its sales would immediately start to fall but evidence suggests that such falls only occur after a time lag if at all. Finally, in an instance where all the brands in a given market advertise, it would be expected that total demand for the product group would increase but it has been shown to only generate a marginal effect.

Yet despite this criticism, there does appear to be some evidence that advertising does stimulate sales in the short term.[10] Persuasive advertising is at its most effective the day after the consumer has received the advertising message and is therefore capable of generating immediate lifts in sales. However, questions associated with its sustainability and ability to affect long-term shifts in behaviour or attitude must be raised as the impact of the communication has been seen to lessen significantly with each passing day.

One potential explanation for this uplift is Ehrenberg's proposition that the hierarchical sequence that consumers travel through is that of 'awareness, trial, reinforcement'.[11] He suggests that there is evidence that consumers take greatest notice of advertisements for brands for which they have a prior history of purchasing. To this end, having been made aware of the product, consumers may then try the product when they next experience a need for it or something similar. According to Ehrenberg, the final sequence in the advertising process is therefore to reinforce the correctness of the choice of that brand in the minds of consumers and thereby increase the likelihood of repeat purchase.

THINK BOX

Low involvement products

There are a large number of products such as toilet cleaners, floor and window cleaners that are unexciting. These products are not high profile – they are not on display within homes and they are not likely to be the topic of conversation for many people.

Many of these products are packaged in similar containers, there is minimal difference in pricing across products and product differences are likely to be minimal (e.g. smell or colour rather than superior product performance).

Purchasers expect the products to perform the functions they are intended to perform, but are unlikely to show high levels of interest in the products and often unlikely to show high levels of brand loyalty, often buying one of a range of brands on the basis of price discounts.

How can you make your brand one of the range that may be considered, if not preferred, in the category?

Advertising is a major tool in creating a personality for brands in these categories, often using humour to show how the product can help perform mundane chores quickly and effectively.

Locate advertising for three brands in one of these 'low involvement' categories – how do they compare? What do they have in common and how does each brand differentiate itself from its competitors? What lessons can be learned from your findings?

The role of advertising

In light of all of these criticisms, if advertising is not a pure and direct generator of sales, the question arises as to what exactly *does* it do?

Whilst no true consensus exists, there appears to be broad agreement that advertising's primary role is to establish the place of a brand in the market by raising awareness of its existence and imparting information about its attributes and benefits to potential consumers.[12] In effect, the role of advertising is to place a brand into a pool of alternative products or brands that a consumer would consider purchasing to satisfy a given need and this pool is known as the **consideration** or **evoked set**.[13]

In order to achieve this, the advertiser must ensure that a brand's attributes are communicated in a way that makes them salient to consumers' needs and to do so in a way that will distinguish it from all of the other brands in its product group. In order to do this effectively, the precise nature of need experienced by a particular target group must be clearly identified. Then, an advertising message should be communicated in a way that configures (or reconfigures) the brand's attributes in the minds of those consumers so that the brand stands out as the obvious solution to that need.[14] If undertaken successfully, the next time the consumer experiences the need, the brand and its ability to satisfy it will spring immediately to mind and its chance of selection will be enhanced.

Once the brand has been selected the role of advertising is to positively reinforce the correctness of the choice in the minds of consumers. Effective positive reinforcement is important in that, when they next seek to satisfy a similar need, the brand is at the top of their shopping list.

What makes advertising effective?

Having established the *role* of advertising, the next question arises as to what constitutes *effective* advertising. The most obvious answer must be that the most effective advertising is that which secures the place of a brand in a target consumer's consideration or 'evoked' set. In order for this to be achieved, three things must have happened:

1. The advertising message must have been clearly transmitted through a medium or media that reached the target consumer.
2. The consumer must have registered and processed the message to a greater or lesser degree.
3. The consumer must have developed or retained a positive disposition toward the brand.

Therefore, when looking at what makes advertising effective, each of these elements requires individual consideration.

Transmission of the advertising message through the media

In order to receive an advertising message effectively, an appropriate medium or set of media should be chosen to convey it and the message itself should take an accessible form. To this end, the following points should be observed:

1. *There should be a clearly defined target audience.* If advertisers are unsure of who they are trying to communicate to, they will struggle to formulate an effective message or select an appropriate set of media to reach them. At its most basic level, the target

audience should be defined in terms of their demographic profile, their geographical location, their underlying values and attitudes towards the product area and competitor brands and any patterns of purchasing behaviour.

2. *The target audience should have access to the advertising media.* If the target audience cannot access a particular medium, then they will not receive the message. For example, the use of banner advertising on websites would be inappropriate if the target audience for the advertising message displayed a low level of computer ownership.

3. *The advertising message should be in a form that the target audience can understand and process.* When identifying the target audience for a specific message, it is also important to understand any potential limitations that might prevent them from being able to process or respond to an advertising communication. Levels of literacy and numeracy should be considered in the construction of any communication together with any physical limitations that the target population might experience. For example, if a target population included a number of hearing-impaired consumers, then visual media should be used in preference to purely audio-based platforms. Similarly, a highly complex, technical explanation of a product might be inappropriate for an audience with a very low level of education.

When considering the various types of advertising media, most academic and practitioner texts tend to focus upon the traditional media listed in Figure 11.2.

One potential reason for such a focus is that, traditionally, advertisers have been able to purchase a quantifiable aspect of these media on the basis of number (i.e. number of poster sites, number of advertising slots or 'hits' on a website), time (i.e. 10, 15 or 30 second advertising slots on television or radio) or space (i.e. size of the poster, size of the advertisement in the magazine or newspaper). In addition, these media share an additional characteristic in that the content and form of the message may be determined by the advertiser. In this way, these media may be defined as 'controlled' media.

However, over recent years it has been recognized that controlled advertising channels are not the only information sources used by consumers in the construction of their

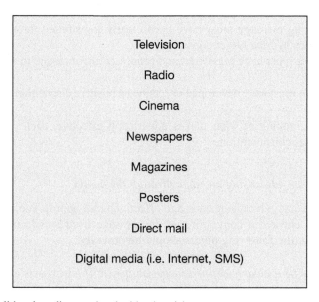

Television

Radio

Cinema

Newspapers

Magazines

Posters

Direct mail

Digital media (i.e. Internet, SMS)

Figure 11.2 Traditional media associated with advertising

consideration or 'evoked' sets. Consumers collate information from a variety of sources and form conceptualizations of brands at every point at which they come into contact with them.[15] This has particular implications for what can be recognized as an advertising medium. In effect, everything that can impact upon the way that consumers conceptualize brands should be considered – from a brand's packaging to the celebrity who wears a particular brand in public.

ETHICAL ISSUE TO CONSIDER

Regulations relating to advertising of foods deemed to be of low nutrition value (i.e. high in fat, salt and sugar) now prohibit advertising for these products being placed in programmes predominantly watched by children. It does not, however, prevent them being placed in programmes which may primarily appeal to older age groups, but which are viewed by substantial numbers of children.

This may result in the anomaly of more actual numbers of children being exposed to these advertisements than are protected through the current regulations from seeing them in child-focussed programmes.

Should anything be done to rectify this situation? If so, what do you recommend?

Now consider the possible impact of flyers and leaflets delivered to homes. These may promote the types of foods banned from appearing in children's television programmes. It is, of course, impossible to prevent children from reading this type of material. Little is known about what effect, if any, this material has on dietary patterns. What do you recommend should be done to research this area?

MINI CASE: THE HIGHS AND LOWS OF FASHION

Burberry, the international fashion label most renowned for its distinctive beige check, is a classic example of a situation in which a brand's values can be hijacked and transformed by the consumer markets.

At the turn of the millennium Burberry successfully re-launched its range and quickly became the darling of A-list celebrities. However, fashion labels have little control over the people associated with them and media pictures of controversy-ridden soap actress Daniella Westbrooke and her daughter, bedecked head to toe, in Burberry were met with ridicule.

The situation worsened for Burberry when the brand was adopted by label conscious '**chavs**' and counterfeiters took no time to jump on the bandwagon. Fake 'Burberry' appeared on unscrupulous stalls in markets across the country as the famous beige check became the uniform of football hooligans throughout the UK.

- To what extent might a celebrity be considered a medium of communication?
- How would you recommend measuring their effects and effectiveness in communicating different types of messages?
- What are the benefits and pitfalls for brands if they become associated with a particular celebrity?

- Think of other situations where celebrities may be role models and thus influence behaviour. Consider, for example, the influence of celebrities (for example, Katie Price) endorsing the use of sun beds when medical evidence suggests that their use can increase the risk of skin cancer.
- Consider also celebrities whose private behaviours include excess alcohol consumption, reckless driving and/or drug use. What influence do you believe they have on people's behaviours and what are the implications for marketers considering their suitability for brand promotional activity?
- Then consider the influence of celebrities who provide positive role models or endorsement of recommended behaviours such as health screening checks.
- What advice can you give marketers and regulators?

ETHICAL ISSUE TO CONSIDER

In the celebrity role model situation outlined above, what are the ethical issues from the perspectives of:

- the celebrities themselves
- the media who carry images of the celebrities and who repeat their comments and/or report their behaviour
- regulators.

In addition, in the eyes of increasingly savvy consumers, some sources of brand information possess greater credibility than others. Such consumers are suspicious of advertising communications and there is evidence that there is a growing tendency for them to reject advertising that they consider is overtly selling a brand.[16] To this end, brand communication through non-controlled sources such as **word of mouth** and consumer advocacy are gaining in credibility at the expense of the traditional controlled media.

Taking both controlled and uncontrolled media into account, a prime consideration of all advertisers seeking to construct an effective integrated advertising campaign must be to understand the strength and value of the individual media within a specific product area. The most effective combination of media must then be selected to ensure that the target audience has access to the advertising message and then, finally, it is essential that there is coordination across the media to ensure that a clear and consistent message is sent.

Registering and processing of the advertising message by the target consumer

It has already been noted in the previous section that one of the basic requirements for effective advertising is that the target audience should be able to access the message and that they should be physically and mentally capable of processing it. Further, the increasingly brief nature of television and radio advertising[17] generates the further qualification that advertising should be constructed in such a way that the key components of the message can be conveyed briefly concisely – often in a matter of just seconds.

Krugman was one of the first people to identify consumer **involvement** as one of the factors to affect the degree to which a consumer registers and processes an advertising message.[18] The concept of involvement within the communication process is described in detail in Chapter 2, but within the context of advertising, involvement takes two main forms; involvement with the product class and involvement with the message. Where a consumer experiences high levels of involvement with a product class, there is evidence that he or she will be more attentive to brand related communications and will process them more actively than would be the case for a low involvement product area.[19] For example, a woman who has just had a baby is more likely to take notice of an advertisement for a brand of nappies and will process its content more actively than a woman without children.

However, for the majority of product areas, consumers experience very low level involvement[20] and therefore in order to engage with consumers, advertisers must seek to generate involvement through the creative treatment of the advertising message itself. This may be achieved through the use of a number of creative tactics that challenge existing perceptions of a product area and/or the brand in question and a number of these are summarized in Figure11.3.[21]

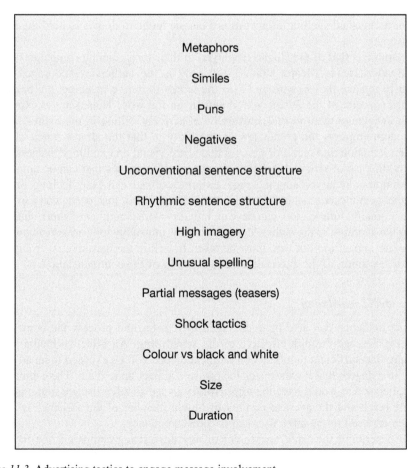

Figure 11.3 Advertising tactics to engage message involvement

A basic principle underlying all of these tactics is the use of advertising to create a challenge to convention or received wisdom. This may take the form of a metaphor or simile that subtly endows the brand with distinctive attributes and with it challenges the target audience to think of it in a different way.

Sexual metaphors are often used and a good example of this is the Herbal Essences television campaign in which the product benefits are linked to the female orgasm.

Alternatively, the use of high imagery, bright colours, and strong contrasts can also be an effective way of emphasizing key components of the advertising message as they catch the audience's attention and leave a clear visual imprint in the memory. Historically, these have often been paired with shock tactics as such an approach has been proved to successfully increase involvement.[22] The campaign by the World Health Organization, 'Bob, I've got cancer' is an example in which an anti-smoking campaign uses an image that displays clear echoes of image of the iconic Marlboro cowboy but juxtaposes it with an inferred statement that one of the riders has cancer. These two elements work closely together to infer to the reader a causal link between smoking and cancer.

The construction of words and phrases or the use of puns within an advertising message can also be used to increase involvement. In line with gestalt principles or 'laws'[23] that suggest that receivers of a stimulus such as an advertising message will seek continuity and symmetry by filling in the missing pieces of a message or by drawing meaning from past experience. The use of unusual letters, the replacement of a symbol in the place of a letter or an unusual spelling of a word is a classic tactic to draw and hold the attention of a consumer.

An example is that of the slogan employed in their long-running campaign for Heinz Baked Beans: 'Beanz Meanz Heinz'. Not only is the audience encouraged to sub-consciously replace the 'z' with an 's' in the words to derive meaning, the baked bean tin images (instead of the letters 'e', 'i' and 'n' in the word Heinz) are employed as a devise to encourage them to seek closure by effectively 'filling in the blanks'. Further, the campaign employs the gestalt law of similarity in that the almost poetic structures encourage retention and recall of phrases that share visual and auditory likenesses.

Finally, the use of size and duration are also creative tactics that can be employed to draw attention to an advertising message. Extremes of size can exact feelings of wonder in an audience but care must be taken that the message is not lost, particularly in the case of the very small! Duration too, can have an impact – with a number of short, sharp bursts grabbing the attention of the audience. Alternatively, unusually long advertising messages can generate impact too but care must be taken to ensure the narrative is strong enough to hold the attention of the audience for the duration of the communication.

Effective media scheduling

The target audience can also be encouraged to register and process the content of an advertising message through effective media **scheduling**. An effective media schedule will ensure that sufficient numbers of a target audience will be exposed to an advertising message to a degree that it maximizes the positive impact upon them. The estimated size of the audience that would have the **opportunity to see** an advertising communication is called the reach and the average number of time a member of the audience is likely to have been exposed to the advertisement is called frequency.

When describing the 'size' or weight of any advertising campaign, the term gross rating points is employed which is calculated by multiplying 'reach' by 'frequency' as is depicted in Figure 11.4.

GROSS RATING POINTS (GRP) = REACH × FREQUENCY

Figure 11.4 Calculating the size of an advertising campaign

Whilst there is no definitive measure for the perfect campaign, for many years, there was widespread acceptance of Krugman's proposition that at least three exposures were necessary as, at exposure 1, it introduces the audience to the advertising message, at exposure 2, they have the opportunity to process its content and, at exposure 3, they recognize it.[24] This process is described as **wearin**; a form of habituation in which any hostility to a new or unfamiliar message is overcome.[25] However, from this point onwards, a process of **wearout** may occur in that the additional value obtained from each further exposure decreases as a process of disengagement begins.[26] This process is thought to be prompted by the onset of tedium; a situation in which the audience experiences boredom, a decreased opportunity to learn and a negative reaction against the repeated message.[27]

There are several tactics that can be used to prevent wearout. Different versions of advertisements may be rotated to keep the message fresh, or an advertisement may be withdrawn for a period of time before being reintroduced. There are a number of different variables that impact on whether and at what point wearout becomes a factor. These range from the type of product or service being advertised to the style of advertisement, similarity to other advertisements in the same category and the weight of advertising in any specific period of time. Most large companies maintain **tracking research** programmes (see Chapter 16 for a more detailed discussion) that monitor the performance of marketing communication elements and which should detect wearout before it becomes a major barrier to communications.

An additional factor to consider is that the work of Krugman and others was conducted when considerably fewer media channels were available and thus fewer channels had much larger individual audiences than they do today. Additionally, the research was conducted before the popularity of newer electronic media, hybrid media forms or the growth of simultaneous media use and areas such as effective frequency of exposure is now one of many topics that require considerably more research.

It is now accepted that there is no 'golden rule' regarding advertising weight and frequency. Decisions will be made on the basis of a combination of past advertising performance, experience, judgement, marketing and competitor analysis, predictive modelling (where available) and, of course, the budget available.

The importance of 'ad liking'

Whilst the use of an engaging creative treatment may well increase potential levels of involvement and a maximization of gross rating points will ensure that the target audience will actually be exposed to the message, the ultimate test as to advertising's effectiveness is whether it has a positive impact upon purchase intent[28] To this end, 'ad liking', defined as the degree to which the audience likes a particular advertising message, has been shown to be a precursor to advertising recall. In turn, it appears to act as a multiplier of the effectiveness of a campaign and has a significant impact upon purchase intent.

Advertising campaigns that appear to generate high levels of 'ad liking' tend to be those that rate highly on the dimensions of entertainment, personal relevance and empathy (i.e. a situation that the viewer might aspire to). By contrast, those that result in low levels of liking tend to be overly repetitive, confused or even alienate their audience either in terms of the message or mode of delivery.[29]

MINI CASE: RAISING EYEBROWS AT CADBURYS

In 2009, Cadbury's 'Eyebrows' campaign became an Internet sensation. The advertisement is set at a photographic studio where a young boy and girl are about to sit for a portrait. When the photographer is distracted by telephone call, the boy touches his watch which sets off a dance music track. With a deadpan expression on their faces, the children's eyebrows appear to dance and, at one point, the little girl accompanies the music with noises made with a balloon. Watched over four million times online it has prompted 54 video responses on YouTube and inspired parodies by stars such as Lily Allen, on Channel 4's Sunday Night Project.

Whilst this campaign was very popular, to what extent do you think it actually generated sales of chocolate bars? Justify your answer.

The role of the creative brief in effective advertising

In order for an organization to execute an effective advertising campaign, a creative brief must be generated to ensure that all parties involved in the process are working toward the same objectives.

A creative brief in its simplest form is a document that is used by agencies to define the objectives of a project and outline key deliverables. There are no hard and fast rules as to who should draw up the document and what it should contain. However, it is often the case that it is the product of joint meetings and total agreement between a client and its chosen agency.

In the construction of the brief, it is essential that time is taken to ensure that it is clear, concise and contains information of a suitable quality and quantity that will allow the agency to generate an effective response. There is a term that is often used in advertising – Garbage In, Garbage Out – in reference to the fact that an inferior brief is likely to produce inferior results. In addition, care should be taken on the part of the client to avoid ultra-prescriptiveness. Ideally, a balance should be struck between being specific without being restrictive in that it should function as both an aid to judgement and also a source of inspiration.[30]

Therefore, in order to ensure that a brief contains information of both a suitable quality and quantity, every document should contain a checklist of elements that require inclusion before it is considered complete. The following items should be included:

1. *An overview of the company and its market.* This should include a broad statement of the corporate objectives, market figures, other brands in its portfolio.
2. *Background information on the brand in question.* This should include market figures (i.e. sales, market share), a history of the brand and its communications/promotions strategy to date, a list of brand extensions and an outline of the broad brand vision and long-term objectives. The brief should describe the brand's values and personality

as they are currently portrayed/ perceived and the benefits that the consumer should gain from using the brand.

3. *Clear objectives for the campaign.* These should be both specific and measurable.
4. *A detailed description of the segments of the market to be targeted.* Ideally, where there are multiple target segments, some indication of priority should also be included.
5. *Clear campaign objectives.* These should be both specific and measureable. Requirements should be plainly stated as to any required changes in levels of awareness, attitude or behaviour and related to specific target segments.
6. *Additional requirements or limitations should be noted.* This might take the form of legal limitations or business agreements that prevent the client from communicating with specific target groups.
7. *A budget.*
8. *A time scale.*
9. *Criteria for the evaluation of the success of the campaign.* These should relate directly to the objectives of the activity.

Once the brief is complete, the agency and client should both approve the content so that, in effect, it can be 'signed off' and the agency can progress the campaign with speed and efficiency.

ETHICAL ISSUE TO CONSIDER

If the brief or the marketing communication agency's response to it raises ethical issues regarding targeting, strategy or tactics, how should this be resolved?

What are the possible consequences of their not being addressed before a campaign is run?

Evaluation of an advertising campaign

Evaluation of an advertising campaign is essential for client and agency organizations alike. For both parties, it generates information about the dynamics of the market and where multiple media are employed, it facilitates the evaluation of individual components.

Techniques for the analysis of return on investment are covered extensively in Chapter 16. However, for the purpose of this chapter it is worth noting that, ideally, evaluation should take place in a continuous fashion over the entire course of an advertising campaign. Continuous evaluation allows marketers to identify any areas of particular strength and, conversely, where areas of weakness emerge, allow remedial action to be taken as soon as possible. Evaluation takes three stages; **pre-testing**, tracking and **post-testing**. Pre-testing is a piece of research that focusses upon the objectives stated in the creative brief and establishes the base point from which the effect of any advertising activity will be measured. This established, an ongoing tracking procedure should be implemented to ensure the campaign is on track and to identify any areas that might require attention. Finally, post-testing measures the impact of the campaign after it has finished and compares the results with that of the pre-test research to measure the extent to which the objectives have been achieved.

Legal limitations, industry guidelines and ethical issues

As noted in earlier chapters, in the UK and in many other countries, the practice of advertising is regulated by a combination of legal requirements and industry Codes of Practice. The industry code of practice is administered by the Advertising Standards Authority (ASA) but is managed by two Committees of Advertising Practice (CAP) – one that focusses on broadcast media and one that focusses on non-broadcast media.[31] Across both committees the basic principles are the same; that advertising should be legal, decent, honest and truthful. The industry code is self-regulatory, i.e. developed by industry members with public consultation, rather than having the full power of legislation. In cases where advertisers do not comply with orders to amend or withdraw advertisements, they can be referred to the Office of Fair Trading where there is potential for prosecution under the Control of Misleading Advertising Regulations 1988.

There are a number of other legal restrictions that govern both the content and the delivery of an advertising message.[32] In the first instance, whilst advertisers are allowed to highlight the benefits of their product or service, the Sale of Goods Act 1979 states that they must not exaggerate in a way that misrepresents them. Communications that are deemed overly aggressive or misleading are banned by The Consumer Protection from Unfair Trading Regulations Act 2008. 'Business-to-business' communications are similarly governed by The Business Protection from Unfair Marketing Regulations 2008. The variety of laws that relate to fairness, decency and copyright are multiple and any organization that is ignorant of them and disparages another organization may find themselves liable for damages.

THINK BOX

Product claims in advertising

For most marketers, there is a fine line between stating the benefits of their brand and exaggerating them. Review a selection of marketing communications (television advertisements, press ads, radio commercials etc.) and reflect upon the way that they convey the benefits of their product without overstating them.

Are there any that you believe go beyond a reasonable level of claims of product or service benefits? How and why do you think this is the case?

ETHICAL ISSUE TO CONSIDER

Visit the adjudications section of the ASA website and review recent adjudications that have resulted in marketing communications campaigns being ordered to be withdrawn.

Given that the Codes of Practice have existed for many years, why are these advertisers continuing to breach the codes?

What action do you recommend be taken?

Summary

Over the course of this chapter we have examined the concept of advertising and the factors that affect its effectiveness. Like any medium of communication, successful advertising requires effective delivery, clarity of expression and needs to give the recipient a reason to engage with it. In order to do so, the client and agency need to work in tandem to generate a clear set of objectives that the campaign should seek to achieve. Only then, armed with a detailed insight into the target audience and a thorough understanding of the strengths and uses of the advertising tools at his or her disposal, should an advertising campaign be formulated, implemented and evaluated.

Review questions

1. Consider an advertisement that you have seen recently. Discuss the extent to which you believe it was 'effective'.
2. For a product you have purchased recently, list all of the other products that you might have purchased to satisfy that need (i.e. your 'consideration' or 'evoked' set). Discuss the extent to which the brands' advertising influenced your choice.
3. Discuss the extent to which you believe 'hierarchy of effects models' reflect the 'real world'. Use examples to illustrate your discussion.
4. Mark Twain was reputed to have once commented that 'Many a small thing has been made large by advertising'. Explain what you think he meant and, using examples, discuss the extent to which you believe this to be true.
5. For a product or service of your choice, create a poster that employs one or more of the creative tactics outlined in this chapter. Explain how your choice might increase potential message involvement amongst its target market.
6. Visit the Advertising Standards Authority website (www.asa.org.uk) and look at the 'Adjudications' page. Select a recent adjudication and discuss whether you agree with it. What other approaches might the advertiser have taken to avoid complaint?
7. For a brand of your choice, identify what you believe to be its target market(s). Discuss what advertising techniques the brand owner might use to communicate specifically with specific target groups.
8. You are a brand owner for a market leading brand of chocolate. For a brand of your choice, write a creative brief for a Christmas campaign.
9. For a brand of toothpaste, discuss the ways in which advertising can raise levels of consumer involvement.
10. Make a list of your 'top 10' advertisements and discuss the following:
    a. What makes these advertisements stand out as special?
    b. To what extent are they subject to 'ad liking'?
    c. Did you purchase any of these brands on the basis of their advertisements? If not, why not?

Recommended reading

Altstiel, T.B., and Grow, J.M. (2013). *Advertising Creative: Strategy, Copy, and Design*, 2nd edition, London: Sage Publications Ltd.

Geuens, M., De Pelsmacker, P., and Faseur, T. (2011). Emotional advertising: revisiting the role of product category. *Journal of Business Research*, 64(4): 418–26.

The Advertising Codes – www.asa.org.uk/asa/.

CASE STUDY 11.1

Taxi insurance

Source: Institute of Practitioners in Advertizing: Silver, Best Small Budget, IPA Effectiveness Awards 2009. The case has been condensed from 'Swinton Taxi Division – Swinton Mystery Tipper Campaign'. Authors: Adrian Rowe, Helen Lawson (Red C). Contributing authors: Katharine Allen, Amy Estcourt (Red C); David Savage, Rhian Thomas (Swinton Group). Case material provided by the World Advertising Research Centre (WARC) www.warc.com.

This case study illustrates what can be achieved with a well planned, targeted and executed small budget campaign. It also illustrates the effective use of often overlooked traditional forms of advertising.

Context and market background

The insurance sector is a complex and increasingly challenging marketplace. For most of us, insurance has always been a distress purchase – something we grudgingly concede we need to have, and resent the increasing premiums. Three key innovations in the last decade have had a significant impact on the broader market. The launch of Direct Line's online insurance offer, in 1999, following the formula of its breakthrough approach to offering insurance by telephone a decade earlier, forced every insurer and broker to reassess their approach – here was a company that made buying insurance simple and fuss-free, cutting out the middleman and talking everyday language. This sparked an extended period of discounting in the sector that still has ramifications today.

The rapid growth of Internet penetration in the UK, and its growing acceptance by consumers as a search tool for products and services, has altered the media landscape for insurers significantly since 2006. Yellow Pages, traditionally the bedrock of lead generation for every insurer and broker, has rapidly been replaced by search engines for all insurance markets. Most recently, the development of insurance comparison sites, initiated by insurer the Admiral Group with the launch of Confused.com and quickly imitated by Moneysupermarket, Tesco Compare and others, has changed the insurer business model beyond recognition.

Taxi insurance

Every taxi driver has to have a licence to operate, granted and regulated by the local authority, and proof of valid comprehensive insurance is a mandatory requirement for obtaining and annually renewing the licence. There are approximately 250,000 licensed taxi drivers in England and Wales, 70,000 of whom drive purpose-built taxis and the remainder operating private hire vehicles. Most are self-employed, and the average insurance premium is £1,100. For a full time driver, who can earn £25–45k outside London, this is a significant, unavoidable operating expense.

In the last five years, the taxi insurance market has seen a rapid increase in competition, to the point where in 2008, the period of this case study, more than 30 insurers and brokers were regularly advertising in the specialist press. Most are small companies specializing in a few niche markets – many prompted by the impact of the heavy price discounting and transactional online marketing in mainstream insurance products.

Despite the powerful impact of the Internet on most insurance markets discussed earlier, penetration of online channels is low, and most taxi insurance leads still come in via more traditional channels. This is less surprising when you pause to consider the typical working day for a cabbie, with long hours spent in the cab and on the road – with no access to the Internet.

One aspect of this case study that is noteworthy, therefore, is the extensive use of promotional methods that might be considered 'old-fashioned', harking back to the days of the major national newspaper and radio sales promotion campaigns, where readers might be rewarded by a passing promotional girl while promenading at a seaside resort with a copy of the *Sun* under their arm. The Swinton Mystery Tipper campaign presented a unique opportunity to directly 'touch' the target audience, face to face, in large cities and small towns alike. In doing so, it leveraged what remains the most powerful marketing channel in this 'Age of Reference' – word of mouth – in this case, on the cab ranks.

Objectives of the campaign

The business objective set by Swinton's marketing team was to increase the volume of policies sold by 10 per cent in the 2008 calendar year. In practice, this was quite a challenging target, as after a period of rapid growth up to 2002, Swinton's taxi division had plateaued as a result of increasing competition in the market. By 2007, there were over 30 specialist insurers and brokers marketing to taxi drivers, resulting in a fragmented market and downward pressure on premiums. In the context of Swinton's overall business, the Taxi Division is a small but profitable niche market, one of several specialist units that the company has bought or acquired over the last decade.

A key marketing objective was to uncover a campaign strategy that could differentiate Swinton's taxi proposition from the burgeoning number of competitors it faced, many marketing the same policies from a limited number of specialist insurance providers. Swinton had successfully used prize draw promotions during 2007 in other specialist units (caravan and motorhome, modified cars) to create a differentiated profile in a fragmented insurer landscape. The marketing brief included a £20k prize draw pot to be used in this context. It is important to recognize that, unlike some insurance markets, there are no significant seasonal peaks in renewals, so the campaign developed needed to be able to sustain momentum over the whole 12 month period.

The solution

The campaign that emerged to address the brief sought to exploit the key characteristic of the marketplace at which it was aimed – that on a frequent basis our target audience congregated . . . on town centre cab ranks, at train stations and airports . . . in private hire cab offices. The aim was to develop some kind of visible symbol or 'badge' that would represent participation in our promotion and act both as a talking point and a reason to call. In such a fragmented and competitive market, core traditional channels such as Yellow Pages and the sector press (*Private Hire & Taxi Monthly* and *Taxi Talk*), were crowded environments. If such a badge could be found, a conversation point could be created amongst cabbies and free brand promotion gained – Swinton could 'punch above its weight'. Taxi drivers are hard-working, hard-done-by, no nonsense characters. Getting their business can be tough, but once you've got it they can multiply it by talking on the ranks.

Enter The Swinton Mystery Tipper, a sassy cartoon character inspired by Dick Tracy with just a dash of Jessica Rabbit. The Mystery Tipper has a £1,000 tip to give away every month to cabbies throughout the UK but only when she spots her sticker in their window. To get that sticker, cabbies had to get a quote.

Photo 11.1

Taxi drivers had previously been involved in research, and it was known that tips and tipping were a source of much conversation in between fares. A campaign featuring a mysterious character that offered 'the tip of a lifetime' was clearly going to resonate with this target audience. Buying insurance of any kind is a dour business and busy taxi drivers have less time than most to arrange theirs. If they're not behind the wheel of their cab, they're not earning money and because you're more likely to find a cab driver at work, the campaign went to them with a physical presence on the streets. Given this target audience is so time-poor, it was crucial to minimize objections and win them over quickly. So a fun, original campaign was created that was simple to enter and offered a handsome reward for very little effort.

Although a wide range of communication materials were developed for the campaign, the key element was the sticker. Using a 110mm by 110mm area, it provided visual shorthand for the entire campaign that taxi drivers would not object to invading their workplace – the cab. Chicago-based illustrators Kunoichi, who provide illustration for Marvel and DC Comics, were commissioned to bring the Mystery Tipper to life. The imagery, with strong 1940s film

Photo 11.2

noir undertones, created a powerful unifying identity for every element of the campaign, from direct mail to sector press advertising and PR and exhibition stands.

Lapsed customers received a direct mail pack encouraging them to come back to Swinton Taxi Division and to make contact to get their sticker and their chance to win £1,000. Current customers also received tailored mailpacks with stickers to give them a chance to win too, and exploit the 'cab rank visibility' to aid retention.

To get the Swinton Mystery Tipper sticker, new customers had to call for a quote. The campaign used trade press, DM, flyers and local radio to get the word out about a mysterious woman tipping cabbies a grand in different UK cities throughout 2008. Advertorials in 'detective speak' ran in the trade press before and after every tip, showing a photo of the winner and announcing the next location. No skill required, just a sticker. And to get a sticker, you had to get a quote. Easy, effective and successful, the Mystery Tipper's appeal was its simplicity.

As Tony Mite, Director and Chief Editor of *Taxi Today*, noted: 'The concept is a brilliant bit of marketing. It gives the drivers something back and it can be at a local level, making it personal. When drivers see that it's coming to their area they love it'.

The activity

Taxi drivers read newspapers, listen to the radio and browse the sector publications like *Taxi Talk* and *Private Hire & Taxi Monthly* – so adverts and editorials were placed there every month. Editorial is typically serious and newsy so the image of the Mystery Tipper with a fist full of cash really stands out. Over the course of 2008, as the promotion gathered steam, an increasing amount of free press coverage was gained in the sector press and on their websites. As Liza Lipson, the National Advertising and Exhibition Coordinator for *Private Hire & Taxi Monthly* observed: 'It is more important than ever to build brand awareness and encourage loyalty in this very competitive market. While taxi drivers may have initially doubted that anyone would win, the regular stories and pictures in PHTM prove the point and can only inspire them to get involved'.

Not every local authority would allow the Tipper into their town, so tip destinations were chosen by the client to include a mix of large and small cities in areas where they performed well.

The first tip in Liverpool in March caused some anxiety, as at this early stage in a year-long campaign, only existing and lapsed customers would have much prior knowledge of the promotion. Thankfully, the leafleting of local offices in advance and PR through the sector press had created awareness, and several taxis sporting the sticker were spotted. Compare the first tip in Liverpool with the last tip of 2008, in Norwich, and the sense of expectation and excitement on the ranks was palpable. The cabbies knew the Mystery Tipper was coming and even the driver from Norwich airport quizzed the team to try to elicit information. The strategy had worked. In Leeds, Sheffield, Derby, Chester, Bristol, Newcastle, Norwich, Liverpool, Cambridge, Blackpool and Manchester, taxi drivers called to get their stickers in their thousands. Announcing the date of the city she would visit next through flyers, trade press and on Facebook made sure a sense of excitement greeted every tip.

Despite the relative antipathy of taxi drivers towards online channels, a small investment was allocated from the limited budget to utilize the most cost-effective aspects of the web. A single page microsite ensured that the more web-savvy of the target audience could register their details (including that data capture jewel, their renewal date) at www.mystery tipper.co.uk. On the site a shadowy figure of the tipper ambles across the page to Sam Spade style music to add a little extra mystery.

The single biggest gathering of taxi drivers occurs in May every year at the Coventry *Private Hire & Taxi Monthly* exhibition. Swinton was a lead sponsor at the exhibition, and the powerful visual identity of the Mystery Tipper delivered record numbers of visitors to the stand, data capture forms and quotes on the day. Four £1,000 tips were awarded to drivers of 'stickered' cabs located in the adjacent car parks.

Results and payback

Twelve consecutive record months of results – in a mature market, for a long-established division – is an exceptional result. The success of this year-long campaign, driving up business by almost 30 per cent, proved that it captured the imagination of no-nonsense cabbies. A powerful concept, executed with acute attention to detail across every touchpoint from exhibitions to Facebook, it has created an uplift in enquiries, quotes and policies that will benefit the business for several years. The campaign was so successful that it was an easy decision for the Swinton marketing team to extend the 2008 Mystery Tipper campaign into 2009, and makes the campaign even more cost-effective, as the origination costs of the campaign material are amortized over a longer period (some materials have been 'refreshed').

Photo 11.3

What's more, the very nature of the campaign, with its 'guerrilla marketing' aspects, means that the growing success we observed during 2008, with each tip enjoying greater success and anticipation than the last, has continued into 2009. Although outside the measurement scope for this paper, as we write this in April 2009 the previous month's results (March 2009) are the biggest in the company's history, with almost 8,000 calls to the business unit.

Campaign performance is measured at Swinton through three key metrics – calls, quotes and policies. Calls and quotes have an additional long-term value to the company, even if

Swinton doesn't successfully convert first time around, in that vital information on renewal date and (for quotes) vehicle details is captured. 'Quotes not taken up' (QNTU) is the most cost-effective recruitment method (after referrals) of all channels, so the call uplift created by the campaign has a long-term value to the business.

Calls to the Taxi Division increased by 26.4 per cent year on year to 55,678 from 44,056 in 2007. Quotes increased by 23.8 per cent to 22,455. Quote to policy conversion rates held up well – there was some nervousness initially that the campaign would result in more 'frivolous' quotes – at 16.0 per cent versus 16.47 per cent in 2007. The net result was a 20.3 per cent uplift in policies year on year, producing £637,000 of incremental premium business at an average premium of £1,040. Average retention rates for Swinton in this sector are 70 per cent, which means that the incremental business generated in 2008 will yield an estimated extra premium income of around £2m over the lifetime of the incremental business written. Add to this the extra 11,500 calls that will provide a rich source of renewal-dated data for future campaigns. There is also the cost amortization of rolling out the campaign through 2009, and perhaps beyond, and the cumulative effect we have observed throughout 2008 and early 2009.

The total 2008 marketing budget for the Taxi Division, including administration, outbound call centre costs, all marketing materials and prize funds, was £463k. This is the most rigorous, but perhaps the fairest, measure against which to judge the campaign, as we observed a campaign impact on every single channel, even those that did not directly exploit the Mystery Tipper campaign elements, such as Yellow Pages.

When considering payback, therefore, the 'worst case' ROI is to directly attribute the £2m of lifetime premium income against these costs, giving a Return on Marketing Investment (ROMI) of 431 per cent, or £4.31 of premium per £ invested in marketing. In practice, the cumulative growing impact of the promotion, the exploitation of the additional renewal data, and the cost amortization of the campaign over 2009 and beyond will all contribute to an even better final reckoning.

Summary

The enormous success of the 2008 campaign gave the client a compelling reason to extend the campaign for a second year. In the market context of increased competition in a fragmented market, Swinton Taxi Division has seen a sharp and sustainable rise in new business that would never have happened without a campaign that so ferociously injected new life into this distress purchase market. It was a simple idea, with its roots in traditional marketing and promotional techniques, but it became a winning campaign by being virtually impossible to miss. By putting in the hours, pounding the streets all over the UK and keeping up the momentum in every city visited its success continued to grow and outperform expectations.

By taking the campaign directly to the streets, the Mystery Tipper sticker created conversations on the ranks as cabbies speculated about where she would appear next. They encouraged each other to get their sticker, which helped Swinton Taxi Division collect valuable data. This data was a crucial part of this campaign's success and renewal dates in particular, are the jewel in the data capture crown across the insurance sector.

The campaign has been recognized with several awards. More importantly, the Swinton Mystery Tipper completely smashed the 10 per cent target in the initial brief and has given the client a database of prospects and renewal dates that will benefit the business over a several year time frame.

CASE STUDY QUESTIONS

1. Critique the campaign. What are the key factors you believe led to its success?
2. How would you expect competitors to react to the campaign and what should Swinton plan to do to counter any competitive activity?
3. How can Swinton keep the momentum of the campaign going and keep the central message fresh and interesting for the target group (consider wearout factors discussed earlier in the chapter)?
4. In the case study, the aversion of this particular target group to Internet-based information delivery is noted. What are the implications of this? How would you evaluate whether other electronic media such as mobile phones might be an effective channel of communication with this group?
5. Assume Swinton are considering using a similar strategy to target other insurance sectors. How would you go about testing whether the concept would work as well, need to be amended or would be unlikely to be effective?

CASE STUDY 11.2

Key 103 – radio station

This case has been condensed from 'Key 103 – The Sound of Maney' Case Study Institute of Practitioners in Advertising Effectiveness Awards. Principal authors: Ian Mitchell, Marcus Leigh. Contributing authors: Caroline Hart, Thomas Hill (BJL). Case material provided by the World Advertising Research Centre (WARC) www.warc.com.

This case study demonstrates how advertising can be effective as part of an integrated marketing communications campaign.

Introduction

This case study demonstrates how a new approach to radio station promotion was able to change the fortunes of Key 103, a local Manchester radio brand whose market share and historical pre-eminence had come under sustained pressure from competitors and changing media consumption patterns since the turn of the millennium. The success of this initiative lay in its ability to link the familiar 'phone-in' promotional mechanic to the brand's core music offering in a way that gave both an instant and sustained rise in listener figures. Indeed, it was so successful that it increased total listening hours by over 20 per cent, thereby increasing the station's capacity to meet advertiser demand, and hence grow profitability.

It achieved this through an idea whose execution, in both creative and media terms, was so simple and effective it made the brand famous across its transmission area and encouraged consumers to participate in the initiative and the execution. It also generated unprecedented engagement from all quarters of the radio station, a 'multiplier' effect that ensured the promotion exceeded all expectations.

Background

Since the late 1990s, commercial radio has been under increased pressure from the strong performance of BBC Radio brands. More recently, new technology has enabled people to listen to what they want, when and where they want to, and this has impacted on the levels of recorded radio listening. Despite there being a 30 per cent growth in the number of UK (terrestrial) radio stations since 2000, the total hours spent listening to radio has hardly changed.

Granted, listening to the radio via Internet or other digital platforms has grown to some 16m adults annually. But the biggest winner here is also is the BBC. Little wonder, then, that commercial radio's share of listening has fallen from over 50 per cent in the late 1990s to less than 42 per cent in March 2008, with local commercial stations accounting for just 31 per cent. Like many original commercial stations, Key 103 not only had to contend with these factors, but also a series of competitive station launches/re-launches that inevitably impacted on its performance.

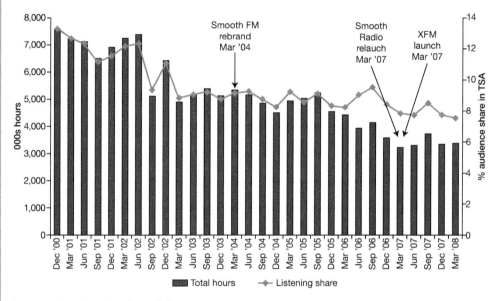

Figure 11.5 The scale of our challenge

The last six quarters up to March 2008 constituted the lowest listenership figures recorded by Key 103. Its last on-air promotion (a competition format) had run in September 2007, and had failed to stimulate a growth in listenership when measured in Quarter 4 2007. It was against these long-term trends (and the more recent promotional activity) that Key 103 embarked on developing a campaign for Quarter 2 2008. The objective was simple – *maximize total listener hours to increase station airtime capacity, which would meet over-demand from advertisers and thus grow profitability.*

If it is broke, do fix it

A review of four years of activity showed us that traditional on-air promotions were the staple diet of stations trying to grow their audience figures for RAJAR (radio audience measurement) sweeps. However, of the 19 promotion-led campaigns we reviewed between 2005 and 2007, only seven saw an increase in listener figures during the sweep they were trying to affect. And of these, only three maintained or grew the audience further in the subsequent survey. Clearly, the traditional promotion was not working terribly hard. Interestingly, further research

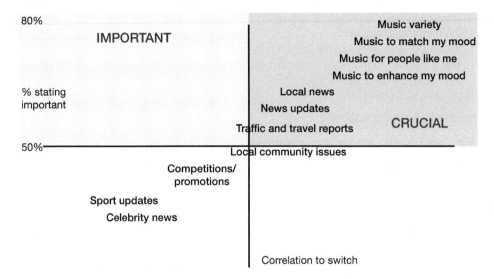

Figure 11.6 What makes people switch radio stations?

also revealed that the music a station plays is a hugely important factor in attracting and retaining an audience.

The intention was to devise a strategy that used music played to drive switching *as well as* a phone-in to generate excitement. Might we be able to breathe new life into a format that was perceived to be tired and failing? What was needed was an idea that went beyond the promotional mechanic of the phone-in – one that also successfully promoted Key 103's core offering. The currency of music had to be central to the promotion, which itself was just the framework through which involvement was stimulated.

The station and the agency set about developing an idea that could bring a fresh, memorable and compelling identity and execution to a promotion. It had to be relevant and engaging, and, just as importantly, it had to be easily understood on and off air to drive take-up and give us interaction outside our core media. Furthermore, it needed to become 'famous' in a way that would attract an audience beyond our usual listeners as well as more listening time from existing listeners.

Research with the station's listener panel identified that almost 80 per cent were more motivated by multiple lower-value prizes than by one big one. The clear-cut results enabled the development of the mechanics of the phone-in competition:

- it would run every weekday for 10 weeks, with a £1,000 prize each day;
- the chance to win would be spread across different programmes throughout the day, with on-air promos and Internet prompts providing clues as to which programme would feature in that day's competition;
- entrants would be randomly selected from listeners who correctly identified artist and song.

This was a known format with the attraction of lots of chances to win. However, the differentiator was to present it in a way that also:

- enabled communication of the breadth and depth of the station's music output;
- clearly positioned the brand to lapsed and non-listeners;
- was entirely ownable by the brand;

- would be clearly understood and was therefore more likely to be successful in attracting interest and interaction;
- would generate word of mouth publicity;
- was simple enough in its execution to be easily elaborated upon by Key 103's DJs and marketing/promotional teams.

The execution – creative

Called 'The Sound of Money', the campaign inextricably linked the station's musical offering with its promotional activity by visually combining 'street' words for cash with the names of Key 103 playlist artists.

So, Kaiser Chiefs became Cashier Chiefs; Snow Patrol became Dough Patrol; Kanye West became Kanye Wedge; and so on. The connection between promotion and core station currency was made quickly, clearly and with humour. Both were being communicated with equal emphasis. The idea therefore enabled selling of both the music and the prize. It successfully delivered our message in an easily understood and immediate way, and contributed a music positioning statement for the station to boot.

As a result of on-air trails, online activity and presenter encouragement, people took the idea and played with it outside the phone-in competition. As they did so, Key103 became a part of the conversation and interaction amongst our audience.

The execution – media

Increasingly, many brands develop channel strategies that are multi-layered and integrated. And while the creative concept lent itself to this perfectly, the budget of £130,000 did not.

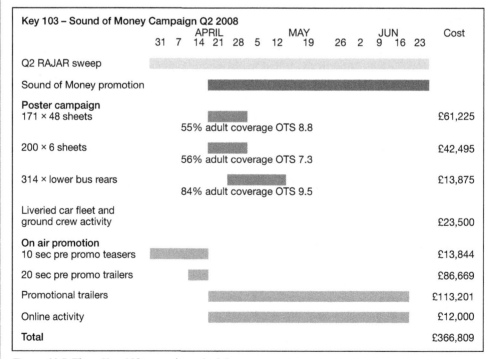

Figure 11.7 Three Key 103 campaign schedule

High impact was needed quickly in a medium that allowed the station to dominate the local urban landscape, and allowed the use of multiple creative executions. It also had to be visible for long enough to embed the idea in the public's mind, so that the 10-week promotion maintained momentum. Outdoor provided this.

On-air teasers, trailers and presenter-mentions were crucial on the run-up to the start of the campaign. The whole concept leant itself to presenters playing the name game on air, thus knitting it more deeply into the station's fabric.

Deepening the connection

On-air promotion started two weeks prior to the competition, with pre-promo teasers and trailers as well as presenter clues. Throughout the campaign, station promos across the day kept the competition top of mind for listeners. Online, a range of features in and around the Key 103 site were used.

- For the duration of the promotion the home page featured the promotion, and seeded clues were placed throughout the site pointing to when the £1,000 song would be played.
- Visitors could find the letters throughout the site and having rearranged them to identify an artist, they'd be told when to listen for the song that day.
- Listeners were directed by programme presenters to go online and create their own posters. The winning entrants for each week were then shortlisted, with the winner having their poster made up and displayed throughout Manchester. Many did (147 actually) though some did better than others.
- Station presenters used their Facebook pages to interact with listeners, and promote the competition. The station's online community were emailed and encouraged to spread the word, as well as giving them insider knowledge of when to listen. Station presenters 'Toolan & Chelsea' even took it upon themselves to make their own videos. They created a Sound of Music spoof, posted it on YouTube, and promoted it on air (4,344 views).

This was just one of the initiatives taken by Key 103 presenters and the station promo teams. The simplicity of the creative execution, lent itself perfectly to the wide range of merchandise, including station vehicle livery. Beyond this, teams took to the streets with abandon, generating free publicity with their own bizarre yet relevant outfits, and even running in the Manchester 10k with placards.

The results were chart topping!

A strong and immediate and consistent response was seen from the folk of Manchester. Daily call volumes consistently exceeded over 2,200, which exceeded anything achieved before for phone-in competitions.

Website traffic rose for the first weeks of the promotion with people going to the site to find out more about the competition and how to play. A peak towards the end was seen as the online promos switched to a 'last chances to win message' for both the phone-in and 'make your own poster' online competitions. Over 10,200 people interacted with the 'puzzle' and 'make your own poster' pages.

The impact on RAJAR figures

While Key 103 had in the past responded well to the challenges it had faced, often recovering some of its lost listeners, the last three years has seen a steady deterioration in listenership

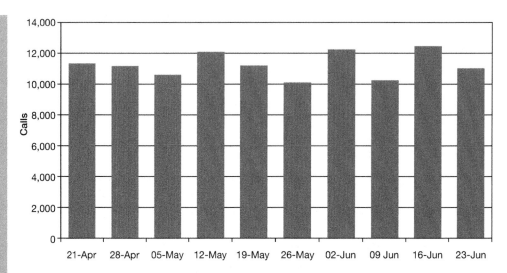

Figure 11.8 Weekly competition phone-in volumes

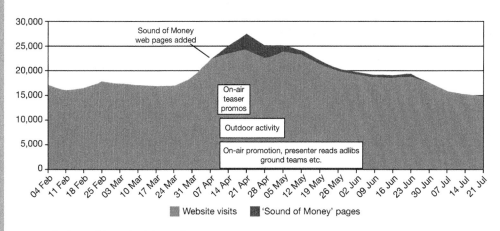

Figure 11.9 Weekly web visitor volumes

Table 11.2 Quarter 2 08 RAJAR results

Key 103 – Total hours performance (all individuals 15+)

	Quarter 2 '08	Quarter 1 '08	Quarter 2 '07
Total hours (000s)	4068	3383	3307
% change Q2 08		+20.2%	+23.0%

Key 103 – Reach (all individuals 15+)

	Quarter 2 '08	Quarter 1 '08	Quarter 2 '07
Total hours (000s)	525	490	502
% change Q2 08		+7.12%	+4.6%

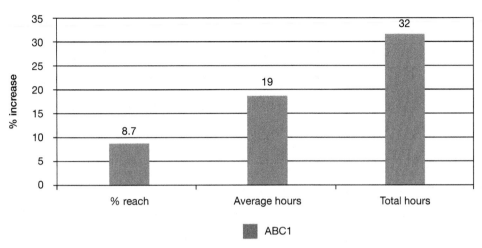

Figure 11.10 Building our audience against key demographics

figures. A measure of the success of the activity would be the June 2008 RAJAR figures. Total listening hours rose by 20 per cent equating to a gain in hours of 685,000 vs the previous quarter and 23 per cent up on Q2 07.

This equated to an increase in station reach of 7 per cent quarter on quarter, and almost 3 per cent, year on year. These were the biggest gains seen since 2002. Like many media brands, Key 103's revenue potential is improved if it can increase its ABC1 profile. Figure 11.10 illustrates that the activity succeeded in increasing delivery against this important demographic segment.

The strategy of spreading the money songs throughout the weekday segments paid dividends, whereby the increase in hours was even across daypart, thus maintaining the daypart profile for the station.

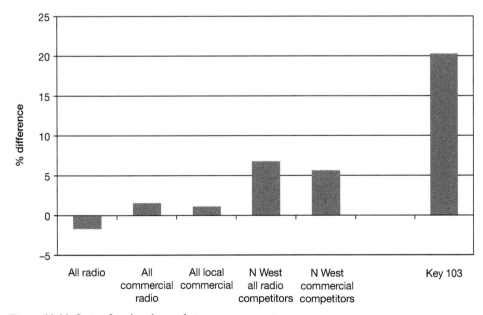

Figure 11.11 Outperforming the market quarter on quarter

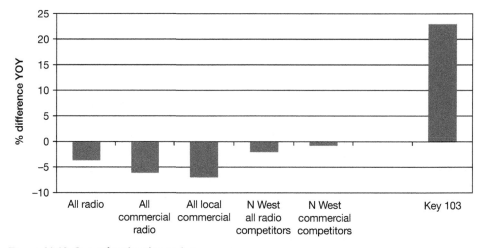

Figure 11.12 Outperforming the market year on year

The size of Key 103's success in gaining audience can be seen when it is compared to overall performances at a national and regional level.

Proving the communications campaign had an impact on results

To find out both listeners (via our online listener online panel) and non-listeners (on the streets of Manchester were researched using an in-house research team) half way through the campaign. The ad campaign delivered strong levels of awareness for the promotion and this awareness was strongly attributed to Key 103.

The research also confirmed that the campaign was driving engagement with the promotion and potentially increased station listener levels.

The promotion's popularity is demonstrated by the fact that 45 per cent of those surveyed participated more than five times. The final piece in the jigsaw is to compare Key 103's performance against its sister station Forth One, where the promotion also ran. Unlike Key

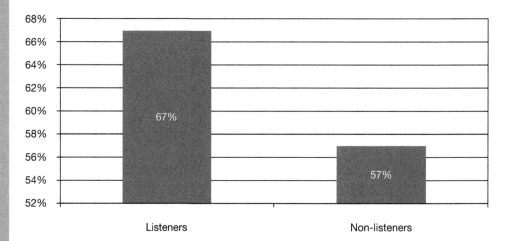

Figure 11.13 Clear evidence of strong awareness

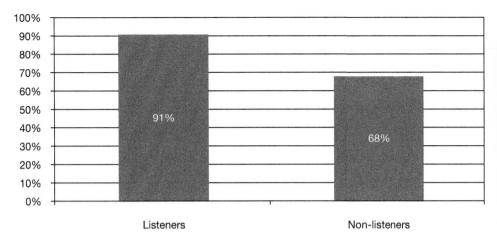

Figure 11.14 Strong evidence of correct attribution

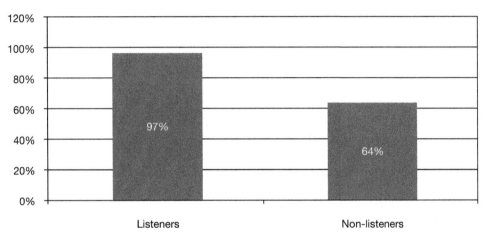

Figure 11.15 Evidence the campaign was driving engagement with the station

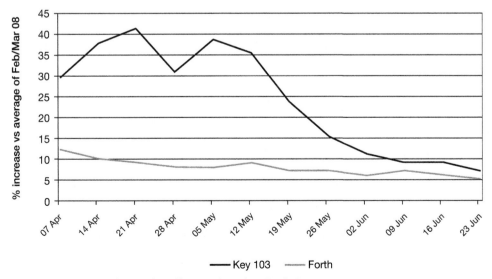

Figure 11.16 Comparison web traffic growth against Forth One

103, Forth One did not support the promotion with advertising. Their support was confined to the same level of on-air promotion with promo-spots and presenter reads, with the station's vehicle fleet also being re-branded and their Ground Teams being similarly active. This said, Forth faced a less competitive marketplace, with both the Real Radio and XFM formats (both present in Manchester) seeing declines between June 2007 and March 2008. A comparison in the increase of web traffic across the two stations shows the impact of a poster campaign in and around Manchester.

Comparing total hours performance, there is a significant difference in performance of the two stations after the promotion, demonstrating the impact of the communications activity undertaken by Key 103.

Table 11.3 Total hours performance – Key 103 vs Forth One

Total hours	Jun 07	Mar 08	Jun 08	Y on Y % change	Q on Q % change
Key 103	3307	3383	4068	+23%	+20%
Forth One	2558	2885	2660	+4%	−8%

The campaign's contribution to increased RAJAR figures

This case study has demonstrated evidence that the campaign drove people to engage with the station and the competition. By exploring several scenarios that could have contributed to the increase in listenership the impact can be judged on likely outcomes predicted had the campaign not been successful.

Table 11.4 A range of scenarios to establish the contribution of the campaign

Scenario	Scenario hours (000s)	Additional hours from the campaign (000s)	% of additional hours attributable to the campaign
If Key 103 performed in line with the average hours of the last 6 quarters	3,419	649	95%
If Key 103 performed in line with Q2 listening trend	3,362	706	103%
If Key 103 performed in line with quarter on quarter change in North West commercial radio	3,375	493	72%
If Key 103 performed in line with quarter on quarter change in North West commercial radio listening	3,281	787	115%
Average	3,409	659	96%

These scenarios suggest that at least 72 per cent (and an average of 96 per cent) of the increase in audience can be attributed to the campaign. Without the campaign, total listenership hours are likely to have remained static or indeed declined.

The success continues

Since the publication of the June RAJAR figures, Key 103 has continued to grow its audience and share. This ongoing success is in part due to the success of the 'Sound of Money' campaign in engaging the people of Manchester, and successfully communicating the artist line-up and music offering that Key 103 provides. The ongoing success and consolidation of audience figures has also in part been achieved by Key 103, and its sister AM station Magic, regaining (after many years) the exclusive rights to broadcast live commentary of all United's and City's home and away and domestic and European matches. Thus laying another brick in the wall of reclaiming its position as Manchester's radio station.

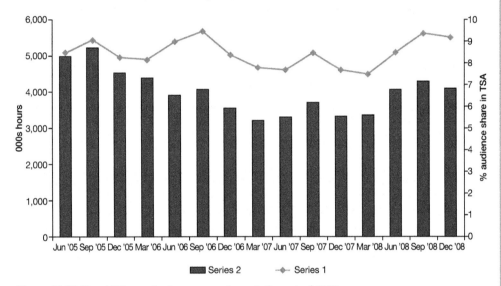

Figure 11.17 Key 103's continuing success through the rest of 2008

What it wasn't

Whilst on a quarter-on-quarter basis some of Key103's growth could be down to an overall growth in the radio listenership in the area, this cannot explain the scale of the improved figures. The increases seen by Key 103 quarter on quarter cannot be explained by seasonal trends in listenership.

Key 103 did not change its presenter line-up over the periods under examination. By contrast, XFM did introduce a new daytime presenter line-up in June 2007 and took over live commentary of Manchester United matches for the 07/08 season. Both these initiatives made Key 103's marketplace even more competitive.

Key 103's Quarter 2 2007 is likely to have been affected by the double whammy of the launch and re-launch of XFM and Smooth; but in the intervening period since then the station had made limited progress in recapturing listeners. While this may have given a lower base for comparison year on year, there were no events or changes in the first quarter of 2008 that would indicate an artificially low base for the quarter on quarter comparison.

Calculating return on investment

The 'Sound of Money' benefited from almost £214K free media coverage, including on-air promotional spots and presenter mentions. Key 103 budgets were based on every extra 1,000 total listening hours (for an all individual audience) added to the station's figures, being able to generate £2,500 additional advertising revenue over the following two trading quarters. This enables a value to be put on the contribution of the 'Sound of Money' campaign. Calculations are based upon Key 103's individual audience, and have been calculated for the six months for which the station used Q2 RAJAR figures as a trading currency.

Taking the average of the extra hours attributable to the campaign we have calculated the revenue attributable as 659K extra hours × £2,500.

Costs

Actual costs (paid for media and production. Includes vehicle livery, extra ground team activity, online activity) = £170,595
Complete costs (paid for media and production + station airtime costs) = £384,390

Revenue attributed to the campaign

Based on average of 659K extra listener hours = £1,647,500.

Based on complete costs, the campaign is projected to have generated almost £1m of extra ad revenue, from a total investment of £384,390, equating to an ROI of £4.28.

New learning

This is not the first case study based on the promotion of a radio station (there have been others focussed on station launches or re-launches). The case reveals some new and important lessons for a radio industry that according to NMR, has spent more than £73m on advertising over the last five years (much of which was used to advertise listenership-hiking promotions and competitions).

From the research and the promotional team's experience of supporting Key 103, it seems clear that when using the familiar promotion mechanic to attract new long-term listeners, and encourage existing listeners to spend more time with the brand, there is real and tangible benefit to be gained by putting the brand's core offering at the very heart of that promotion. Beyond this, there are significant gains to be made if the communication of such a promotion is simple and engaging enough to generate a desire for interaction, involvement and participation not only from the public, but from the station's personnel, too.

CASE STUDY QUESTIONS

1. Review this case study. What do you believe are the factors that led to its success? Justify your response.
2. Discuss the issue of short-term promotional activity coinciding with audience measurement periods. Are the audiences measured an accurate reflection of listening patterns? What advice would you give to marketers considering purchasing radio advertising?
3. Could the promotional format be repeated with the expectation of achieving the same effect on audience levels? Justify your response.
4. How would you expect other radio stations to respond to this campaign, both in the short and longer term?
5. What advice would you give to Forth One, Key 103's sister radio station, regarding future promotional activity?

Notes

1 Russell, T.J., and Lane, W.R. (1993). *Kleppner's Advertising Procedure*, New Jersey: Prentice Hall Inc.

2 Tellis, G.J., and Ambler, T. (eds) (2007). *The Sage Handbook of Advertising*, London: Sage Publications Ltd.

3 Barry, T.E. (1987). The development of the heirarchy of effects: a historical perspective. *Current Issues & Research in Advertising*, 10(2), 251.

4 Strong, E.K. Jr. (1925). *The Psychology of Selling and Advertising*, New York: McGraw-Hill.

5 Barry, T.E. (1987). The development of the heirarchy of effects: a historical perspective. *Current Issues & Research in Advertising*, 10(2), 251.

6 Colley, R.H. (1961). *Defining Advertising Goals for Measured Advertising Results*, New York: Association of National Advertisers.

7 King, S. (1967). Can research evaluate the creative content of advertising? *Admap*, June.

8 Ehrenberg, A.S.C. (1998). 'Repetitive Advertising and the Consumer'. In J.P. Jones (ed.) *How Advertising Works: The Role of Research*, London: Sage.

9 Ehrenberg, A.S.C. (1998). 'Repetitive Advertising and the Consumer'. In J.P. Jones (ed.) *How Advertising Works: The Role of Research*, London: Sage.

10 Jones, J.P. (1998). *How Advertising Works: The Role of Research*, London: Sage.

11 Ehrenberg, A.S.C. (1998). 'Repetitive Advertising and the Consumer'. In J.P. Jones (ed.) *How Advertising Works: The Role of Research*, London: Sage.

12 Joyce, T. (1998). 'The Advertising Process'. In J.P. Jones (ed.) *How Advertising Works: The Role of Research*, London: Sage.

13 Howard, J.A. and Sheth, J. (1969). *The Theory of Buyer Behaviour*, New York: Wiley.

14 Krugman, H.E. (1965). The impact of television advertising: learning without involvement. *Public Opinion Quarterly*, 29(3: Fall), 349–56.

15 White, J., and de Chernatony, L. (2002). 'New Labour: A Study of the Creation, Development and Demise of a Political Brand'. In B.I. Newman and D. Vercic (eds) *Communication of Politics: Cross-Cultural Theory Building in the Practice of Public Relations and Political Marketing*, Haworth: The Haworth Press.

16 Powell, C. (2002). Targeting the media-savvy consumer. *Marketing Magazine*, 107(45: 10 October).

17 Joyce, T. (1998). 'The Advertising Process'. In J.P. Jones (ed.) *How Advertising Works: The Role of Research*, London: Sage.

18 Krugman, H.E. (1965). The impact of television advertising: learning without involvement. *Public Opinion Quarterly*, 29(3: Fall), 349–56.

19 Laczniak, R.N., Kempf, D.S., and Muehling, D.D. (1999). Advertising message involvement: the role of enduring and situational factors. *Journal of Current Issues and Research in Advertising*, 21(1: Spring), 51–61.

20 Ehrenberg, A.S.C. (1998). 'Repetitive Advertising and the Consumer'. In J.P. Jones (ed.) *How Advertising Works: The Role of Research*, London: Sage.

21 Percy, L., and Elliott, R. (2005). *Strategic Advertising Management*, 2nd edition, Oxford: Oxford University Press.

22 Dahl, D.W., Frankenberger, C.D., and Manchanda, R.V. (2003). Does it pay to shock? Reactions to shocking and non-shocking advertisements to university students. *The Journal of Advertising Research* (September), 268–80.

23 Sternberg, R.J. (2002). *Cognitive Psychology*, 3rd edition, Belmont, CA: Wadsworth.

24 Krugman (1965). Cited in Du Plessis, E. (2005). *The Advertised Mind*, London: Kogan Page.

25 Campbell, M.C., and Keller, K.L. (2003). Brand familiarity and advertising repetition. *Journal of Consumer Research*, 30(Sept), 292–304.

26 Du Plessis, E. (2005). *The Advertised Mind*, London: Kogan Page.

27 Anand, P., and Sternthal, B. (1990). Ease of message processing as a moderator of repetition effects in advertising. *Journal of Market Research*, 27(August), 345–53; Blair, M., Henderson, R., and Michael, J. (1998). Advertising wearin and wearout: ten years later – more empirical

evidence and successful practice. *Journal of Advertising Research*, (September–October), 7–18; Calder, B.J., and Sternthal, B. (1980). Television commercial wearout: an information processing view. *Journal of Marketing Research*, 17(May), 173–86.

28 Du Plessis, E. (2005). *The Advertised Mind*, London: Kogan Page.

29 Du Plessis, E. (1994). Understanding and using likability. *The Journal of Advertising Research*, 34(5), RC3–RC10.

30 Storey, R., and Smit, E. (2007). 'The Creative Brief and its Strategic Role in the Campaign Development Process'. In G.J. Telis and T. Ambler (eds), *The Sage Handbook of Advertising*, London: Sage Publications Ltd.

31 www.cap.org.uk.

32 www.businesslink.gov.uk.

12 Integrated campaign development

Sales promotion

LEARNING OUTCOMES

After studying this chapter, you will be able to:

• Define the main types of sales promotions and discuss their role within the marketing mix

• Discuss the strategic and tactical roles sales promotions may play

• Critically evaluate the advantages and disadvantages of sales promotion activity both in the short and long term and from a manufacturer and retailer perspective

• Discuss the impact of competitor reaction to sales promotional activity

• Discuss the issues relating to contentious sales activity such as that directed at children

Introduction

Sales promotions are incentives used to stimulate sales of a specific product or service by changing prices or adding perceived value in the short term. For example, price-based sales promotion may involve a 25 per cent reduction in the normal selling price, or offers of 'buy one, get a second one for half price'. An added value sales promotion may involve buying a product at the normal price but receiving accessories or **complementary products** free. For example, getting a specified number of photographs printed may entitle the purchaser to a free photo album. A food manufacturer may offer free recipe books in return for evidence of a specified number of product purchases.

The objective of a sales promotion may be to stimulate sales of existing products, combat competitive activity or support the introduction of a new product range. Sales promotions may therefore be aimed at any or all of the following: the end purchaser, the retailer (trade promotion), a company's own sales force to generate enthusiasm and commitment for the product range.

Factors driving increased sales promotional activity

Sales promotions have increased in frequency and importance for several reasons. Firstly, functional differences between brands have become less signficant and thus competing brands may be seen as easily substitutable for each other.[1] Secondly, the increased fragmentation of traditional media and the ease with which advertisements can be avoided[2] means that reaching and motivating potential purchases via traditional advertising has become more difficult – and expensive.[3] Additionally, measuring the return on investment from traditional advertising is difficult, whereas the short-term nature of sales promotion activity means that the impact on sales can be more easily measured.

Thirdly, the growing power of retailers, particularly large retail chains such as Tesco means that, for fast moving consumer goods at least, most purchasing decisions take place within a retail store.

In the UK, as in many other countries, a small number of major organizations control the bulk of grocery retailing. The market share of the major supermarket chains as at February 2013, the latest period for which data is available, were:

Tesco:	29.7 per cent
Sainsbury's:	17 per cent
Asda:	17.7 per cent (part of the American Wal-Mart organization)
Morrisons:	11.8 per cent
Waitrose:	4.8 per cent (part of the John Lewis retail chain, with an upmarket emphasis)[4]

THINK BOX

Retailers

What impact will the growing power of major retail chains such as Tesco have on small independent outlets? How should the latter position themselves in the market?

THINK BOX

Sales promotions

Assume you have a quantity of old model stock that has remained unsold, and a new model due to be released in three months time.

1. What types of sales promotions would you recommend to help sell the old stock?
2. What implications are there both for the overall brand and the new model if the stock does not sell?
3. What role might your sales force play in stimulating sales of the old stock?

Examining the power of Tesco alone, this organization not only has some 1/3 of grocery sales (after the horse meat scandal at the end of 2012, Tesco's market share dropped below 30 per cent for the first time in eight years[5]), it accounts for 11.5 per cent of all UK retailing; one pound in eight spent in retail stores is spent at Tesco. It is involved in banking, insurance as well as operating a number of petrol stations; 20 per cent of their sales comes from non-food items. While the chain originated in the UK and this remains their core market, Tesco is a major global force, with a total of 6,234 stores worldwide (2,318 in the UK). Countries in which they are active include China, Thailand, Malaysia, South Korea, Japan, Taiwan, Ireland, Poland, Turkey, Slovenia, Hungary, the USA (Fresh & Easy brand) new stores open at the rate of some 200 per year.

In terms of sales and profitability, Tesco sales for the 2011–12 year were £72 billion, with profits of £3.8 billion.[6] Retail giants such as these use sales promotional activity as an integral part of their marketing communication activity, with individual Brand Managers often having little control over the nature (usually price-based) or timing of in-store promotions. These retail giants operate their own product ranges or house brands (e.g. Tesco's Finest) that compete with manufacturers' own brands for shelf space and market share.

Types of sales promotion

Generally, sales promotion activity can be broken into three main categories:

Financial incentives such as price discounts, either direct or via coupons or savings cards (buy five cups of coffee and get the sixth free) or free offers such as 25 per cent extra volume at no extra cost.

Sweepstakes/contests which usually involve proof of a product purchase and the completion of a simple skill/knowledge task such as correctly completing a current advertising slogan.

THINK BOX

Examples of sales promotions

Find examples of each of the different types of sales promotional activity listed above. Critique them in terms of creativity and potential effectiveness. Justify your criticism.

THINK BOX

Self-liquidating premiums

Find examples of self-liquidating premiums. Critique them on the same basis as the other types of sales promotional activity in the previous Think Box.

What impact do you believe they have on actual product/service purchase, brand image or brand equity? Justify your response.

Samples/premiums (value added) which involve offering free product such as small sample packs, or obtaining an additional benefit such as the photo album example given in the opening section of this chapter, or a free sun hat with the purchase of sunglasses, free pens when buying stationery or free glasses/drink recipes with bottles of alcohol. The latter is particularly common at key gift giving times such as Christmas.

Self-liquidating premiums are usually used to influence repeat purchases and involve obtaining a free product in return for proof of purchase and a small financial charge to cover the cost of the premium and postage etc. The premium products involved are generally not available through normal retail outlets, and seek to add an element of scarcity and status to the product.

The selection of the type of sales promotion will be dependent on the specific objectives set for the product range overall and for the specific promotional activity and is influenced by the strength/desirability of the existing brand relative to competition (no one will want to invest in a premium offer if the product does not have strong brand equity) and the category in which the brand is situated. Knowledge gained through past experience on the likely sales response of different sales promotion activity and different forms of communicating to the target group will guide this selection.[7,8] For example, free offers communicated via text messages to mobile phones have shown mixed effects depending on the perceived relevance and appeal of the offers.[9]

There are a number of legislative and regulatory provisions relating to sales promotional activity, particularly those involving sweepstakes, contests or any form of promotional activity directed at children. You should always check these provisions before designing a sales promotion as breaching the requirements may result in a sales promotion being forcibly withdrawn, resulting in damage to a brand's equity through adverse publicity – and also possibly resulting in legal action against the brand owner.

THINK BOX

Text messages

How effective do you believe sales promotional text messages are? Under what circumstances are they likely to be accepted or rejected by their target?

Strategic and tactical considerations

While the objective of any single sales promotion is generally a specific sales volume in a finite time period, the sales promotion may be part of a long-term strategic plan or a short-term tactical response to competitive activity or market conditions.

Long-term strategies may include using sales promotions to support the introduction of a new product, both to retailers and consumer purchasers. Given the large number of new product introductions each year, a sales promotion about which retailers are positive can aid in obtaining desirable shelf locations or other in-store displays such as end-of-aisle positions during the launch period.

In addition, sales promotions may be used during the launch period to encourage trial of the product by potential consumers, possibly by in-store tastings if appropriate, or small sample packs, price discounts etc. If initial trials are favourable, the product may become a preferred item, or at least be added to the range of brands seen as acceptable by consumers. For strong brands, the ongoing objective may be to encourage repeat purchase and overall increased usage.[10]

Sales promotions cannot compensate for weaknesses in other parts of the marketing mix, such as a lack of advertising budget or inadequacies in the sales force or distribution system.[11] Sales promotions also cannot compensate if other products provide superior performance or are deemed more acceptable to potential purchasers.

As noted in earlier chapters, the boundaries between sales promotion and other activity may be blurred; advertising and increased display space may support a sales promotion

---

THINK BOX

Examples of sales promotions

Assume you are the marketing manager for a confectionary company. You are considering running a sales promotion linked to the launch of a movie that is predicted to be popular with children. You are aware that previous movie tie-in promotions have received considerable criticism for promoting unhealthy foods to children.

1. Find examples of sales promotions of this type and critique them. On what basis do you believe the decision would have been made to run the sales promotion?
2. What would have been the key benefits to the organizations participating in the promotion?
3. What potential negatives might there have been?
4. How would you expect the short-term and long-term impact of the sales promotion to have been evaluated?
5. Analyse the pros and cons of this type of activity in general.
6. What type of sales promotions involving children might be considered for different types of products or services and why? What types should not be considered and why?
7. Repeat question 6 for older age groups.
8. What ethical issues might arise as the result of sales promotional activity and on what basis should they be resolved?
9. How would you deal with adverse media coverage of any sales promotional activity?

and it may therefore be difficult to separate out the relative impact of each component. A 'classic' example of this is Hershey Foods' Reese's Pieces confectionary, which was featured in the 1982 movie *E.T. The Extra-Terrestrial* and, although US sales increased 65 per cent,[12] it is difficult to separate the effects of the product placement from the associated sales promotional activity as US$ 1 million was spent by Hershey's promoting the movie.[13]

Advantages and disadvantages of sales promotions

There has been considerable debate about the short-term versus long-term impacts of sales promotions. There is evidence of both short- and long-term positive benefits for some products that can be attributed to the impact of sales promotional activity; short term effects appear stronger.[14] The type of sales promotion activity is a factor; we have noted that the overall aim of sales promotions is to increase trial and brand selection relative to competitors and, hopefully, result in more frequent purchasing.

However, there is no guarantee that price reductions alone will result in purchase if the perceived brand equity is weaker than that for competing brands.[15] Frequent use of price-based sales promotions may in fact damage the equity of a brand.[16] Further, while sales promotions have become more common, there is some evidence that they are delivering diminishing returns.[17]

There are concerns that purchasers will become accustomed to regular promotions and alter their buying habits to anticipate appealing promotions, resulting in high purchasing levels during the promotional periods but lower than normal subsequent purchases outside the promotional period as purchases use up the stockpiled product bought during the promotion.[18] Thus, over time, price sensitivity may increase – it is suggested that consumers are 50 per cent more price sensitive than they were 25 years ago,[19] but whether or how this varies across product types and categories is not clear.

There is also evidence that, unsurprisingly, price sensitivity increases during economic downturns and decreases during more prosperous periods and may be reflected in the growth of retailer own brands which are usually priced lower than manufacturer brands.[20] Thus a retailer may be able to leverage off a manufacturer brand's promotional activity to the advantage of the retailer's own brand through strategies such as provide preferential shelf placement to house brands in order to attract price-sensitive shoppers.[21,22] Once again, it appears that brand equity is a significant factor as brands with high brand equity tend

---

THINK BOX

Impact of sales promotions on brand equity

How would you evaluate the impact of sales promotions on brand equity across a range of fast moving consumer goods, consumer durables and services?

How would this knowledge impact on decisions regarding the type of sales promotions that might be appropriate for different brands within each category?

How might sales promotional activity alter during periods of economic prosperity versus economic recession? What impact might any changes in strategy have on brand image and brand equity?

to achieve stronger and longer lasting benefits from sales promotions than brands with weak equity.[23]

Manufacturer and retailer perspectives

With the strength of retailers in sectors such as fast moving consumer goods noted previously, manufacturers may have little control over the type or timing of sales promotion activity, potentially resulting in sub-optimal marketing mix decisions due to retailers having, understandably, more short-term perspectives on individual brands than manufacturers.[24] In addition, retailers may not view categories of products in the same way as manufacturers may wish to do, resulting in the way that products are featured in store, such as location and the products that are placed adjacent to them may not be as manufacturers might wish.[25]

The true cost of undertaking sales promotions is often underestimated. Once direct costs are combined with reduced margins (from lower prices), some 50 per cent of sales promotions are not actually profitable for retailers.[26,27] However, a retailer may recognize this and be prepared to accept a loss on an individual promotion if it generates additional store traffic and therefore potentially increased sales of other products, or it counters competitive activity.

Remember that, through checkout scanner data, retailers have considerably more detailed data regarding the purchase response to a range of individual, category and store-wide promotional activity than manufacturers do and are able to leverage off this to their advantage. This data forms the foundation of retailer **loyalty schemes**, which enable incentives such as price discount coupons to be tailored to match individual purchaser history and apparent brand preferences.[28]

Trade responses to temporary price reductions initiated by a manufacturer that are intended to reduce retail pricing may not necessarily be followed through as the manufacturer intends, with retailers potentially opting to not pass the discount on, or to only pass some of it, thus improving the retailer's own margins.[29]

THINK BOX

Price-based sales promotion

Assume that one of your sales force suggests a major price-based sales promotion involving giving away small packs of one of your popular products with every purchase of a product that has seen static sales in the last six months.

1. What factors should you take into account in evaluating whether or not to proceed with this type of promotion?
2. What are the major potential risks? What are the potential major benefits?
3. How would you expect your retailers to react to the promotion?

Competitor response

Sales promotion activity does not occur in a vacuum and many sales promotions that have achieved initial success in increasing sales volume in the short term find that this benefit is eroded or cancelled completely by competitive activity. For example, a promotion to

THINK BOX

Coordinating sales promotions

Assume you are a major fast food organization who is reliant on independent franchise holders to operate the individual food outlets under your brand name.

The majority of customers are probably not aware that you do not actually own or operate the outlets.

What particular challenges does this type of structure present in co-coordinating sales promotions activity and how can you, as the overall brand owner, minimize problems at the retail level?

In the event of problems occurring, what action should you take to protect your brand image?

increase sales of Coca-Cola may be followed by a similar promotion for Pepsi, involving both brands in additional costs but neither brand being able to achieve any significant long-term sales volume.

The decision as to whether to react to a competitor's sales promotion and, if so, in what way will depend on the strength of the brand, the resources it has available and potentially to retailer demands for action. It may be that a competitor may choose to react not by a counter sales promotion but by increasing advertising, providing additional support to retailers, or to not react at all, relying on competitor impacts to be short-term only.[30]

A retailer may change the prices of other brands in the category, possibly asking these brands to contribute to the costs of any price reductions to enable the retailer to maintain their own margins[31] or manipulate both price and position of their own house brands to protect a particularly profitable manufacturer brand.[32]

Ethical issues in sales promotional activity

We have discussed ethical issues in the preceding chapters, but sales promotions are often seen as somewhat more 'suspect' than other forms of marketing communication. There are many examples in the Advertising Standards Authority adjudications of sales promotion activity being declared misleading due to a lack of information being provided about actual prizes, or the conditions under which prizes will be awarded. For example, 'free' holidays may only include airfares and accommodation, not taxes, food and other transport costs, or they may only be available at specific times that make them inaccessible to some people who are required to take leave at specific times of the year.

Think of the various sales promotions you have seen and the impression you got of the promotion and of the company behind it.

Summary

Sales promotions, as an instrument that is primarily used to increase sales in the short run, have become increasingly important as a result of communication clutter, fierce competitiveness amongst retailers, less brand loyalty and short-term orientation of many companies. Sales promotions in consumer markets can take different forms: financial

THINK BOX

Sales promotions and legal regulations

Visit the ASA website www.asa.org.uk and find three examples of sales promotions that have been judged to be in breach of the codes relating to marketing communication.

What can we learn from these adjudications? What are the short- and long-term implications for the companies involved?

THINK BOX

Sales promotion effectiveness

Assume you are the marketing manager for a large FMCG company with multiple beverage brands. Your largest competitor has run sales promotions for cold drinks each year in spring and autumn in an attempt to stimulate sales before and after the main peak summer period. You have never run sales promotions during these periods, and have tended to run promotions only in conjunction with major retailers (reluctantly) and to support high profile charity fund raising events during which you give a percentage of your profits to the charities.

Your own sales tracking data indicates that the overall sales volume in the category does not increase during these sales promotions – but your competitor is gaining short term sales increases at your expense. Once the sales promotions are over, your relative share of sales returns to the pre sales promotion ratios.

1. Analyse what is occurring and outline the various courses of action open to your company.
2. What implications are there for your sales force and for key retailers in each option?
3. Which option do you recommend and why?
4. What competitive reaction would you expect as a result of your implementing the recommended option – and how do you recommend responding to the competitors?

incentives, sweepstakes/contests, and samples/premiums. Using sales promotions may help achieve a number of objectives: increasing market share, increasing sales, attracting news consumers, encouraging brand switching, or rewarding loyal consumers. The use of sales promotions tools depends on the specific objectives the company wants to achieve. When employing this marketing communications tool, businesses need to consider both its advantages (increasing trial, loyalty and profitability) and disadvantages (deal-proneness, brand-switching, the negative effect on brand image).

Review questions

1. Discuss the types of consumer-focussed sales promotions that might be appropriate to support the launch of:

   - a new range of swimwear from a relatively unknown brand
   - a new range of soups from a well known brand with high market share
   - a new integrated television and video recorder for a brand with a small market share.

   Justify your recommendations.

2. Discuss the types of trade-based sales promotions.

3. Discuss the possible impact of a retailer wanting to feature a manufacturer's brand in a series of price discounted promotional activity spread throughout a year. How would you evaluate the potential impact on the brand's equity? Discuss this from the perspective of fast moving consumer goods and consumer durable products.

4. If you were the direct competitor to the brand in question 5, how would you react to this activity?

5. Discuss the advantages and disadvantages of turning the retailer's proposed promotional programme into a value added type of promotion.

6. How would you determine what types of sales promotions would be most likely to motivate a manufacturer's own sales staff and the retailer's sales staff?

7. Return to question 1 and outline recommended ways of measuring return on investment for the sales promotional activity.

Recommended reading

Bolanda, W.A., Connelly, P.M., and Erickson., L.-M. (2013). Children's response to sales promotions and their impact on purchase behavior. *Journal of Consumer Psychology*, 22(2), 272–9.

Irwin, R.L., Sutton, W., and McCarthy, L. (2008). *Sports Promotion and Sales Management*, 2nd edition, Champaign, IL: Human Kinetics Publishers.

Tellis, G.J., and Ambler, T. (eds) (2007). *The Sage Handbook of Advertising*, London: Sage Publications Ltd.

CASE STUDY 12.1

Thomas Cook

Source: Institute of Practitioners in Advertising: IPA Effectiveness Awards 2008. Authors: Charlie Makin, Clay Gill and Lorraine Green. This case has been adapted from Makin, C., Gill, C. and Green, L. 'Thomas Cook – The "Peaks" campaign: making Thomas Cook's world revolve around its customers'. Case material provided by the World Advertising Research Centre (WARC) www.warc.com.

This case study illustrates how a multi-media campaign was used to support a specific promotional programme that was reliant on sales support through the marketer's retail outlets.

Overview

The package holiday became a mass phenomenon in the 1970s, and was a clear indication of the emergence of the consumer society. A generation of families, who had previously never travelled outside the UK, were able to enjoy cheap, simple, safe, foreign travel.

Supply of holidays was relatively limited and travel companies were able to manage demand because customers were concerned that they might not get the holiday or resort they wanted. The tour operators, in effect, had a monopoly on mass market foreign travel; few people would have considered the prospect of making their own travel arrangements. To stimulate demand, the major travel agents advertised immediately after Christmas and consumers (literally) queued to book.

However, digital access has revolutionized consumers' relationship with travel companies and foreign travel is a core part of any people's lifestyle. Digital has empowered people to book travel directly at reduced prices. If you believe the press, it's destroyed the package holiday but the reality is that demand for the packaged travel market is still healthy. CAA ATOL statistics show that packaged holiday passenger numbers have remained roughly static at 30 million per year in 2006, but the share of total travel bookings has fallen from 90 per cent of leisure trips 10 years ago to less than 50 per cent now.

The four major travel agents at the time of the launch of this campaign (Thomas Cook, Thomson, First Choice, Mytravel) were extremely complex, multi channel businesses. They were vertically integrated, in that they owned the whole supply chain. In comparison, the new digital entrants, such as Expedia, are effectively retailers; they don't create products (although they will 'dynamically package' other operator's inventory for customers). It's an industry experiencing great change both structurally and in terms of changing consumer behaviour, ultimately the consumer has greater choice and leverage.

The historical communication model no longer works. The consumer has changed, they take more holidays, to more destinations and they are used to interacting directly with operators and airlines. Effective advertising needs to be more honest and demonstrate that the travel agents act in the consumers' interest, and is constantly price competitive. Modern communications needs to both stimulate consumers and provide an incentive for them to interact with a particular retailer. Consumers expect to use any convenient channel (retail, phone, digital or TV) they choose. Therefore any effective campaign needs to be totally integrated and channel neutral (customers will interact frequently during the booking process).

To make it even more challenging the January to March ('peaks') period is vital to the business. Although booking patterns are flatter across the year, 28 per cent of all summer holidays are still sold over this period. Any company that performs well in 'peaks' is in a far stronger position to manage the inventory for the rest of the year, discount less and hit performance targets.

The campaign

The chosen strategy aimed to put the consumer at the heart of communication activity has evolved over two 'seasons'. The first season (2007) focussed on a more honest and consumer centric approach but was effectively a test. The second season (2008) was a full blown iteration of a consumer centric campaign.

Objectives for 2007

2007 was a turning point for Thomas Cook in the UK. It was in the final stages of achieving a stock market listing and the market was about to consolidate (TUI and First Choice merged in September 2007 and Thomas Cook and Mytravel in June 2007). It needed to be relevant for its customers and stakeholders, but budgets were tight and had to deliver demonstrable business performance.

The objectives for peaks 2007 were complex:

1. To achieve 12 per cent year on year passenger growth: market growth was likely to be minimal at 2 or 3 per cent, therefore we had to win share in a highly competitive market with a budget less than £1 million (possibly 1 per cent of all travel advertising).
2. Drive multi channel flow and drive sales to in house channels: sales had to be directed through Thomas Cook retail outlets.
3. To leverage the brand and deliver a campaign in which tactical and price messages are delivered confidently within a brand leader style: we had to stimulate demand, but not purely through a price promotion.
4. To achieve differentiation within a commoditized and cluttered market.
5. To communicate consistently across all channels and customer touchpoints.

Thomas Cook have an array of consumer channels from online, its own TV channel – Thomas Cook TV – to shop windows and 11,000 staff. We needed to harness every consumer touchpoint, and create an integrated campaign at every point where the consumer could come into contact with the brand.

Insight into the consumer and their relationship with travel agents

High street retail travel agents enjoy little retail loyalty. Logically this is understandable, travel is not a frequent purchase, there are a lot of easily available sources of information on travel and consumers are looking for choice. The decision making process often starts with the choice of destination and the operator and agent can be secondary. As consumers have more choice, more opportunity and take more holidays, consumers booking two consecutive holidays through the same agent is as low as 25 per cent (although industry figures are difficult to verify).

The solution and decision making process

Our own research shows that holiday choice is complex and consumers assimilate information from a wide range of sources, reducing a long list of opportunities down to a specific short list. We also know it's not a linear process, that consumers often change their decisions during the process and are looking for stimulation and ideas.

Consumers go through a number of stages choosing holidays and may consider a number of options at the same time and may move back up the cycle.

An audience analyst confirmed that a plethora of channels are important and 'new' media does not necessarily outperform 'old' media. It's a melange of sources from direct marketing to word of mouth, national press still being influential. This doesn't dismiss the role of digital, but diminishes its role as a lead medium. Our experience in travel also led us to believe that television advertising would have the most profound effect in generating an instant call to action.

It would allow Thomas Cook to:

*   deliver both a price and brand message
*   access the audience at the point of consideration and action
*   motivate staff – 'when we advertise on TV, I know its going to drive people through the door' – area manager, Glasgow.

Additionally, it has a strong multi channel effect, TV activity drives uplift on key online search terms. Television was chosen to be a key part of the campaign.

However, a conventional four-week 400 rating TV campaign was unaffordable; the available budget was minimal in any conventional sense. A key insight was that many advertisers use television as a slow burn medium to build effect over a long period by constantly repeating the same message. Thomas Cook used television as a point of sale medium; a mechanism to drive people directly either to the store, phone or website, by dominating key days and changing the message on a weekly basis.

The campaign

In terms of store traffic and transactions, Saturday is by far the most important day for making bookings. The recommendation was to run two days of intensive activity from midday on Friday to mid-afternoon Saturday for four weeks and be dormant for the rest of the campaign. The message would change every week and focus on a different holiday destination, which would be promoted in store, online and in national press.

Messaging

In all retail markets, consumers react to a mix of brand promises, product and price. In the holiday market, consumers react positively to suggestions about holiday locations, but price competitiveness is critical in the holiday market. Dreamy holiday imagery or spurious superiority claims are cynically regarded and no longer drive traffic.

Thomas Cook wants to be seen as being on the consumers' side, in an honest and relevant way. Although mass market travel can be problematic, the company wanted its customers and stakeholders to believe it was open, listened and was prepared to address issues that mattered to them. This was encompassed in an advertising line that focussed on the globe shaped logo: 'our world revolves around you'.

The peaks retail strategy has traditionally been based around week long, destination specific promotions. These are usually promoted solely in store. Our recommendation was to move into a more intrusive medium. In total, four key trading weekends received TV and press advertising support. These were specifically chosen to be slightly away from destinations normally chosen by consumers, so we avoided obvious choices like Spain and the US:

- 12–13 January: Turkey
- 19–20 January: Cuba/Dominican Republic
- 26–27 January: Greece/Cyprus
- 2–3 February: Egypt.

Four separate low cost commercials were developed. They were only 20 seconds long, and managed to communicate a price promise, a specific offer to a destination and a unifying brand device.

Each of the four executions was destination-specific and relevant extant footage was edited and enhanced for the purpose. Whilst we delivered a hard hitting price promotion, we were able to also communicate 'softer' travel imagery and Thomas Cook brand credentials.

The activity

The campaign was effective because of complete 'visual' integration of every possible touch point with the consumer:

- a pricewatch promise in Thomas Cook stores
- TV advertising

- national press with a free reader offer
- national press supplement (*Mail on Sunday*)
- regional press to support specific airports and routes
- DM to existing travel customers
- online banner advertising
- PR.

A key element was to launch the campaign to staff at the staff conference in Malta in December 2006, where 2,500 representatives from every branch, call centre and other channels saw the campaign. The message that Thomas Cook was returning to television was electric and the presentation was given a standing ovation!

Campaign schedule

Although the total peaks 2007 media cost was £650,000, we believe that the visual integration of all consumer touch points delivered a total communication value in excess of £2,250,000. Although, as predicted, we achieved only 12 per cent share of total communication, we achieved 50 per cent of communication share on the key Thursday to Saturday midday window.

The results

Whilst our campaign centred on the combined effect of advertising price leaders with a retail focus, advertising is shown to be the material driver, increasing performance from 6 per cent without advertising to 65 per cent with it.

Simon Carter, Executive Director of
Marketing, Thomas Cook

Performance against objectives

The core objective was to achieve 12 per cent year on year passenger growth, Thomas Cook passenger numbers grew by 13 per cent. We achieved this by performing 8 points ahead of the market, thereby taking share as we predicted.

Passenger numbers

All of the destinations experienced sales growth directly driven by advertising. However, locations that only had in-store price promotion, without advertising support, performed much less effectively.

Payback

The campaign achieved a year on year uplift of 13 per cent. Most importantly, the campaign brought sales forward from the more heavily discounted summer lates period, which is traditionally a less profitable period.

Revenue uplift

Before the campaign period, revenue was down 1 per cent. What is particularly significant is that the campaign had a longer shelf life than just the weekend, with positive campaign effects evident mid-week too. The campaign helped to drive people in store mid-week, as well as on Saturdays.

Retail reaction

The trade press gave the campaign the thumbs up with the highly influential travel trade gazette writing on 18th January '. . . sorry, Peter (Long, CEO of TUI), but I think Manny (Fontenla-Novoa, CEO of Thomas Cook) has won the first round of the year for a campaign with a message that has greater impact & its commercial potential . . .' '. . . Thomas Cook's campaign is marketing genius . . .'.

CASE STUDY QUESTIONS

1. How would you expect competitors to respond to this type of activity?
2. How should activity such as this be revised in recessions/tight economic times when the media tends to carry frequent editorial exhorting people to holiday at home instead of travelling overseas?
3. How would you recommend Thomas Cook respond to criticisms of the travel industry to CO_2 emissions/global warming and environmental damage?
4. What coordination and control would have been required to ensure that all retail outlets supported the programme?

Notes

1 De Pelsmacker, P., Geuens, M., and Van den Bergh, J. (2001). *Marketing Communications*, Harlow, England: Pearson Education.
2 Rojas-Mendez, J.I., and Davies, G. (2005). Avoiding television advertising: some explanations from time allocation theory. *Journal of Advertising Research*, 45(1), 34–48.
3 Eagle, L.C., and Kitchen, P.J. (2000). IMC, brand communications and corporate cultures: client/advertising agency coordination and cohesion. *European Journal of Marketing*, 34(5/6), 667–704.
4 www.grocerynews.org (2013). UK Supermarkets (market share). Online. Available HTTP: <http://grocerynews.org/2012–06–16–08–27–26/supermarkets-market-share/grocery-stores> (accessed 24 March 2013).
5 Neville, S. (2013). Tesco is Still UK's Top Retail Brand Despite Horsemeat Scandal, Says Report. Online. Available HTTP: <http://guardian.co.uk/business/2013/mar/19/tesco-retail-brand-horsemeat-scandal> (accessed 24 March 2013).
6 Tesco. (2012). Tesco at a Glance. Online. Available HTTP: <http://tescoplc.com/files/pdf/factsheets/at_a_glance.pdf> (accessed 24 March 2013).
7 Freo, M. (2005). The impact of sales promotions on store performance: a structural vector autoregressive approach. *Statistical Methods & Applications*, 14(2), 271–81.
8 Pauwels, K. (2007). How retailer and competitor decisions drive the long-term effectiveness of manufacturer promotions for fast moving consumer goods. *Journal of Retailing*, 83(3), 297–308.
9 Wang, A. (2007). How consumers percieve free offers: implications for mobile marketing. *International Journal of Mobile Marketing*, 2(2), 35–41.
10 Ailawadi, K., and Neslin, S.A. (1998). The effect of promotion on consumption: buying more and consuming it faster. *Journal of Marketing Research*, 25, 390–8.
11 Shimp, T.E. (2003). *Advertising, Promotion and Supplemental Aspects of IMC*, 6th edition, Independence, KY: Thompson South-Western.
12 Gupta, P.B., and Gould, S.J. (1997). Consumers' perceptions of the ethics and acceptability of product placements in movies: product category and individual differences. *Journal of Current Issues and Research in Advertising*, 19(1), 37–50.
13 Pechmann, C., and Shih, C.-F. (1999). Smoking scenes in movies and antismoking advertisements before movies: effects on youth. *Journal of Marketing*, 63(3), 1–13.

14   Baidya, M.H., and Basu, P. (2008). Effectiveness of marketing expenditures: a brand level case study. *Journal of Targeting, Measuring and Analysis for Marketing*, 16(3), 181–8.

15   Alvarez, B.A., and Casielles, R. V. (2005). Consumer evaluations of sales promotion: the effect on brand choice. *European Journal of Marketing*, 39(1/2), 54–70.

16   Aaker, D.A. (1997). Should you take your brand to where the action is? *Harvard Business Review*, 75(5), 135–43.

17   Ziliani, C. (2006). Target promotions: how to measure and improve promotional effectiveness through individual customer information. *Journal of Targeting, Measurement & Analysis for Marketing*, 14(3), 249–59.

18   Mela, C.F., Jedidi, K., and Bowman, D. (1998). The long-term impact of promotions on consumer stockpiling behavior. *Journal of Marketing Research (JMR)*, 35(2), 250–62.

19   Lodish, L.M., and Mela, C.F. (2007). If brands are built over years, why are they managed over quarters? *Harvard Business Review*, 85(7/8), 104–12.

20   Lamey, L., Deleersnyder, B., Dekimpe, M.G., and Steenkamp, J.-B.E.M. (2007). How business cycles contribute to private-label success: evidence from the United States and Europe. *Journal of Marketing*, 71(1), 1–15.

21   Corstjens, M., and Lal, R. (2000). Building store loyalty through store brands. *Journal of Marketing Research (JMR)*, 37(3), 281–91.

22   Oubina, J., Rubio, N., and Yague, M.J. (2006). Strategic management of store brands: an analysis from the manufacturer's perspective. *International Journal of Retail & Distribution Management*, 34(10), 742–60.

23   Slotegraaf, R.J., and Pauwels, K. (2008). The impact of brand equity and innovation on the long-term effectiveness of promotions. *Journal of Marketing Research (JMR)*, 45(3), 293–306.

24   Simpson, L.S. (2006). Enhancing food promotion in the supermarket industry: a framework for sales promotion success. *International Journal of Advertising*, 25(2), 223–45.

25   Lindblom, A., and Olkkonen, R. (2006). Category management tactics: an analysis of manufacturers' control. *International Journal of Retail & Distribution Management*, 34(6), 482–96.

26   Ailawadi, K.L., Beauchamp, J.P., Donthu, N., Gauri, D.K., and Shankar, V. (2009). Communication and promotion decisions in retailing: a review and directions for future research. *Journal of Retailing*, 85(1), 42–55.

27   Srinivasan, S., Pauwels, K., Hanssens, D.M., and Dekimpe, M.G. (2004). Do promotions benefit manufacturers, retailers, or both? *Management Science*, 50(5), 617–29.

28   Van Heerde, H.J., and Bijmolt, T.H.A. (2005). Decomposing the promotional revenue bump for loyalty program members versus non-members. *Journal of Marketing Research (JMR)*, 42(4), 443–57.

29   Kumar, N., Rajiv, S., and Jeuland, A. (2001). Effectiveness of trade promotions: analyzing the determinants of retail pass through. *Marketing Science*, 20(4), 382–404.

30   Steenkamp, J.-B.E.M., Nijs, V.R., Hanssens, D.M., and Dekimpe, M.G. (2005). Competitive reactions to advertising and promotion attacks. *Marketing Science*, 24(1), 35–54.

31   Moorthy, S. (2005). A general theory of pass-through in channels with category management and retail competition. *Marketing Science*, 24(1), 110–22.

32   Shannon, R., and Mandhachitara, R. (2005). Private-label grocery shopping attitudes and behaviour: a cross-cultural study. *Brand Management*, 12(6), 461–74.

13 Integrated campaign development

Direct and database marketing, outdoor and point of purchase

LEARNING OUTCOMES

After studying this chapter, you will be able to:

- Discuss the scope of direct and database marketing (D&DBM) and its role within marketing communication

- Critically evaluate the advantages and disadvantages of D&DBM activity both in the short and long term

- Debate the impact of growing moves towards permission models on the potential effectiveness of direct and database marketing

- Discuss ways of measuring the effectiveness of different forms of direct and database marketing

- Discuss ethical considerations and how these might be resolved

Introduction

Direct and database marketing (hereafter referred to as D&DBM) evolved from direct mail advertising and mail order catalogues.[1] Despite it being widely used, there is no well defined definition of what 'direct marketing' is. This may be in part because direct marketing is often a combination of tools and techniques, rather than a tool or technique in its own right. The Direct Marketing Association definition defines it as:

> an interactive system of marketing which uses one or more advertising media to effect a measurable response and or transaction at any location.

This definition suggests that it is a collection of techniques aimed at delivering marketing messages directly to the consumer and mostly trying to directly link a response to a message (i.e. measure the response). The focus is therefore on having a measurable and attributable response to a specific message, rather than on an overall campaign for which the return on investment from individual components may be difficult to separate out.

Direct and database marketers use a variety of tools, including interactive media advertising, **direct mail**, **telemarketing** and personal selling,[2] with new ways of communicating direct to current and prospective customers evolving rapidly as communication technology itself evolves. D&DBM itself is often, though by far not always, a database driven process, i.e., messages are sent directly to consumers or business customers based on data held on a computer database which may include information on past purchase behaviour as well as contact details.[3] This may be either in the form of letters or leaflets, telephone calls, visits from sales people, email messages or similar. Its foundation is on the capture of customer information at the point of first contact or sale.[4]

D&DBM is increasingly popular as the trend data in Chapter 1 showed and is frequently described in terms of building a relationship with customers, or potential customer, often linked to database information and data mining driven marketing[5] and enabling different communications to be tailored to different sectors of customers – or completely personalized.[6]

For example, many airlines use customer data obtained from customer bookings and past flights as a way to interact with customers. They may email customers before their flight departs, offering them added-value services, such as parking and flight up-grades, and after the flight, welcoming them back home as well as providing regular updates on special offers, or complementary products or services such as special deals on hotel rooms or rental cars. In addition, they use customer data to email special offers at a later date. Large retailers such as Tesco use previous purchase data as the basis for special offers to those customers holding a Tesco Clubcard.[7]

MINI CASE: LOYALTY SCHEMES

Analyse the way that the Tesco Clubcard operates by visiting their website: <www.tesco.com/clubcard/clubcard/> and then compare this to competitor schemes such as Sainsbury's Nectar card: <www2.sainsburys.co.uk/nectar/nectar_homepage.htm>.[8]

- How do you think people respond to price discount coupons allocated on the basis of past spending with a store?
- Do these cards attract new customers, persuade existing customers to remain with one supermarket as their principal grocery outlet – or do they simply cancel each other out? Justify your answer.

- Can manufacturer grocery brands leverage off these cards? If so, how?
- What can small independent grocery stores do to maintain or build customer loyalty?
- Now consider airline loyalty schemes (points based on air miles travelled which can be used for free flights, upgrades etc.). How do these differ from grocery loyalty schemes?
- What impact do you believe they have on loyalty compared to price discounting or specific promotional campaigns?
- How might behaviours differ by air traveller type such as young holiday makers versus frequent business travellers?
- Compare and contrast these schemes with other retail-based schemes such as Boots Advantage Cards or vouchers given at point-of-sale by large retailers such as WHSmith.
- What do all of these schemes have in common? In what ways are they different? What can marketers learn from them?

Direct marketing can be used within a company in one of three ways. The vast majority of companies use direct marketing techniques as part of an overall marketing mix, for example by providing after sales follow-ups, informing previous customers of new offers etc. as part of ongoing **customer relationship management**.[9] It is also commonly used for cross-selling additional products or services a company may offer to those who have at least one product or service purchased from the company. For example, a bank may use cross selling to offer home contents and vehicle insurance to account holders.[10]

ETHICAL ISSUE TO CONSIDER

What ethical issues may arise from cross-selling? How should these be dealt with?

How would you recommend evaluation of the ethical implications of different cross selling options?

Some companies have a more limited use of D&DBM techniques, often because they don't specifically capture customer data or use any data given by the customers to them. They may use direct marketing as part of the communication mix, but often in a non strategic, non-relationship forming way. For example by distributing flyers or leaflets in the area in which they are operating, sometimes adding specific calls to action, such as

THINK BOX

Direct mail

- How many generic and personally addressed direct mail items do you receive in an average week? Which ones do you pay attention to and which ones do you ignore?
- Check with 5 or 6 other people and compare your impressions. What lessons can be learned from your combined responses?
- What advice would you give marketers on the basis of your findings?

'money off coupons' to flyers. This is commonly seen in operation by local restaurants or retailers. On the other extreme, some companies use exclusively direct marketing techniques, and direct marketing forms the basis of a company (such as the direct to consumer company TimeLife[11]).

It is not just commercial markers that use D&DBM techniques; non-profit organizations such as charities and the performing arts frequently use D&DBM to communicate with current or prospective patrons.[12] Local and central government organizations and individual political parties also use D&DBM techniques to canvas voter opinion, communicate key policies and encourage voter turnout.[13]

Strengths and weaknesses of direct and database marketing

D&DBM has a number of distinct advantages (and weaknesses) when compared to other marketing tools and techniques.

Strengths

One of the main advantages is that it can be easily targeted,[5] or in some cases even personalized. For example, in the previous example about airlines, the email messages can be personalized in terms of departure time, name of passengers, destination etc. – and can therefore be made significantly more relevant to the needs of the individual customers. Equally, follow-up emails can be personalized in a similar fashion.

The same holds true for most other forms of D&DBM, from personalized letters to sales calls with relevant offers based on the previous purchase history of customers. Especially with advancements in technology, many previously fairly expensive direct marketing tools can now be easily personalized, and in the case of email, may cost very little to send, unlike bulk postings of material through the normal mail system.

Most direct marketing tools can also be easily measured and the response attributed to the specific communication. For example, 'click through' links embedded in an email can be easily measured, sales persons either in person or over the phone can show how many customers they recruited, etc.[14]

D&DBM is also comparatively easy to test in a live setting. While other marketing tools, such as advertising, will have to go through extensive pre-testing before being launched in order to ensure that they are received by the target audience in the way they were intended (and lead to the desired results), D&DBM can be much easier tested.[15] For example, a leaflet or brochure can be distributed to a limited number of prospects to test how they will respond and how responses differ by customer characteristics. If the response is universally good, then the same material can be sent to all of the prospective customers.[16] Equally, if the response is not as desired, the leaflet can be easily adapted and a similar test carried out again.

Interlinked with the above point is that many of the tools are extremely well controllable when compared to other marketing tools. For example, television advertising does not allow the level of precision targeting D&DBM offers, with considerable wastage in exposure of the advertising to those who are not and never will be customers of an organization.

It is relatively difficult to make amendments quickly to a television campaign once it has begun to appear. With D&DBM this can be easily controlled: it can be precisely targeted (provided, of course, a well maintained database), and it can be fully cost controlled, including the possibilities of taking a break in the promotional activity if a

THINK BOX

Direct and database marketing

How might D&DBM be used as part of an integrated marketing communication campaign for:

1. a new model of car
2. domestic or international holidays
3. insurance.

What should be avoided in the D&DBM approach for each of these?

certain target threshold of expected responses is reached – or conversely stepping up activity easily if targets are not met.

Finally, another major advantage of D&DBM is the ability to actively increase customer **loyalty**, which is linked to increased customer retention and increased revenue generation.[17] However, some scholars have cautioned that the impact some loyalty programmes have on actual revenue generation has often been overstated.[18]

Weaknesses

On the negative side, D&DBM is often associated with unsophisticated marketing.[19] While this is not universally true, the association with junk mail and email spam[20] certainly does not help the general perception of D&DBM.

Another potentially negative aspect of D&DBM is that many campaigns focus on direct calls to action, rather than trying to build up a brand image long term, which in turn may result in less customer loyalty. However, as with the previous point, this disadvantage may be more because of poorly designed D&DBM campaigns, rather than D&DBM itself as there is ample evidence of customized programmes enhancing brand equity and loyalty.[21]

Another potential disadvantage of D&DBM is that it is reliant on an accurate database, which in itself is potentially expensive and time-consuming. This is largely because consumers tend to only rarely update their details in databases used for commercial purposes, thus resulting in duplicate data or old entries. A challenge for many companies is in developing ways to manage and effectively utilize the information they may have in (often large) databases.[22] Some marketing sectors such as the tobacco and alcohol industries are restricted in many countries in terms of what marketing of any form they are able to do. Direct marketing to current or potential smokers is totally prohibited in many countries.

ETHICAL ISSUE TO CONSIDER

What ethical issues arise when personal selling techniques such as telephone selling is used?

How should these be resolved?

Table 13.1 Strengths and weaknesses of direct and database marketing

Strengths	Weaknesses
Can be easily targeted, even personalized	Cheap image
Measurable and attributable response	Does not build a brand image/ message (focus on call to action)
Easy to test (e.g. small sample) at little cost	Reliant on accurate database
Easy to control	Expensive per customer (but frequently effective)
Can be used to increase loyalty (e.g. after sales/add-ons etc.)	

Finally, when compared to most other marketing techniques, some D&DBM tools can be very resource intensive. However, this point is heavily reliant on the D&DBM tool being used. For example, personal selling, including phone selling, is fairly expensive per customer, while on the other side, direct emails are fairly cheap. However, conversely, it can be argued that a phone call or even personal visit may be more persuasive and therefore yield much better results than an email or text message.

Table 13.1 summarizes the main strengths and weaknesses of D&DBM, however remember that the precise combination of tools and techniques used will depend on the resources and expertise available and the specific objectives set.

MINI CASE: UNDER-UTILIZED RESOURCES

Assume you are the marketing manager for a large hotel that also offers facilities for conferences, weddings and special events. However, these facilities are rarely used. Customer satisfaction feedback from those who have used the facilities do not show any problems or concerns regarding the facilities or services provided. Most of the bookings have come from word of mouth from people who have seen the facilities.

1. How might D&DBM be used as part of your marketing activity to increase the use of these facilities?
2. From what sources might you obtain details of potential contacts?
3. What ethical issues might arise and how should these be resolved?
4. How might you measure the effectiveness of your D&DBM activity?

Tools used

Direct and database marketing uses a number of specific tools and channels in addition to the tools/channels used by general marketing communications. Broadly, these can be categorized as personal media type tools, where there is an element of personalized communication and general media types, where the initial communication is not directly personalized.

Personal media types

Direct mail and email

Direct mail, and the related direct email, means the delivery of the D&DBM material by either postal or electronic mail. These materials can easily be personalized, for example by adding the name on a covering letter, or by using mass email programmes which insert the name of the recipient or other information into the email.

Many people enjoy receiving relevant marketing material, for example from organizations they are interested in or from companies they like to purchase from, this form of D&DBM is also the most controversial, as it is immediately associated with receiving irrelevant, irritating and often unsolicited marketing material, also referred to as **junk mail** for traditional mail and **spam** in the case of email.

Increasingly, consumers who do not want to receive unsolicited direct mail can use services that limited the amount of direct mail they receive, such as the Mailing Preference Service in the UK. However, as these organizations are usually voluntary on the behalf of the sender, registering with a mailing preference service may not totally stop all unsolicited mail.

In the case of unsolicited junk email, or spam, discussed earlier[20] this has now been outlawed in most countries, including all of the European Union, Australia, New Zealand, the US and Canada. However, sending spam is still legal in many countries, and spam email originating from these countries is not covered by the various legislations, even if received in a country where sending spam is illegal. This has led to many attempts to design software to specifically block spam.[23] However, most serious users of direct mail and email marketing are likely to take privacy concerns seriously and will not send out unsolicited advertising mail or email.

A final cause for concern in relation to advertising/direct mail is the environmental impact it has.[24] In the UK, the total amount of paper used for junk mail is estimated to be between 500,000 and 600,000 tons.[25] Much of this mail is currently not recycled, however, the Direct Marketing Association has agreed to increase the amount of recycling to 70 per cent in 2013.[25]

Telemarketing/telesales

Telemarketing is a direct marketing technique where a sales person calls either prospective or current customers by phone, trying to sell them a product or service.[26] In some cases, the sales person can be replaced by an automated voice recording; this is particularly popular in case of political campaigning, but has been severely restricted in the USA.[27]

Modern telemarketing operations can be highly advanced, with automatic dialling machines that cold call numbers, and in the case of a person answering the phone transfer the call to a sales person. However, if all sales persons are busy, then the call may result in a silent call, i.e. calls generated by the marketer which do not directly connect to a sales person or telephone operator. This is a practice banned under Ofcom rules in the UK, and which may result in fines of up to £50,000.[28]

Similar to direct mail, there are telephone preference services operating in many countries, such as the British Telephone Preference Service, where consumers can register their number for free, resulting in organizations not being permitted to call prospects at home unsolicited.

Door-to-door sales

In the case of **door-to-door** sales, a sales person walks from door to door and tries to solicit business. This can either be done after a sales visit was agreed, for example by telemarketing, or it can be done as a form of 'cold calling'. If the sales person is cold calling, the prospective client does not expect a visit. The sales person does often have a list of names or addresses that they are trying to reach, as a result of data mining. However, it was common up to the 1950s for a range of sales people to simply go literally from door-to-door selling household products.[29] As this type of business is considerably more labour intensive than for example telemarketing, and other forms of direct marketing, it has seen a fairly sharp decline in recent years[30] While it is still popular for organizations such as Avon Cosmetics,[31] for political campaigns and some local events, the cost:benefit ratio in comparison to other D&DBM tools has increased the decline.

THINK BOX

Avon and Tupperware

Contrast the door-to-door approach of Avon Cosmetics with the type of in-home hosted parties used by other companies such as Tupperware.[32] Which do you believe has the more effective long-term strategy? Justify your response.

ETHICAL ISSUE TO CONSIDER

- What are the main ethical issues involved in door-to-door selling?
- How should a marketing organization plan to avoid ethical problems?
- What are the consequences if they do not?

Public/general media types

Door-to-door leaflets

Leaflets (also called flyers or pamphlets) are usually small printed adverts for a product or service, used as a direct marketing tool often on a small, community-based scale (i.e. for example in one neighbourhood). Typical examples of this include leaflets for a local take away, a flyer advertising cleaning services available locally or a post card advertising a local night club. Often these leaflets are distributed door to door, via the standard mail service, or they may be handed out at locations where lots of people pass by, such as shopping malls, underground stations etc.

The main advantage of leaflets is that they are easy and cheap to produce, and they can also be easily designed on home computer systems, reducing design cost. They are also extremely useful if a business has a limited geographic reach, for example a few streets or a neighbourhood, as the business can target households in the specific area they are interested in.

Similarly to direct mail, there are however environmental concerns because of the large volume of paper being distributed, sometimes indiscriminately so.

THINK BOX

Leaflets

Collect examples of leaflets in your home area and critique their effectiveness. What would you advise small retailers with only one or two outlets to do or not do regarding direct marketing activity?

Direct response advertising and television

Strictly speaking, **direct response advertising** is a hybrid between traditional advertising (or television programming) and direct sales, where either printed advertising, or television advertising time is 'replacing' the sales person visit.[33] Direct response advertising can be in the form of single page advertising in a newspaper, or it can be in the form of a infomercial, which typically lasts more than five minutes and is often shown late at night when advertising time is relatively cheap to buy when compared to prime time. A website, email address or telephone number is provided, enabling people to make contact immediately, get queries answered, place orders, make payments and arrange delivery of products.

Some companies use direct response advertising almost exclusively to distribute their products, for example the record company K-Tel and the media company TimeLife Music. However, unfortunately, direct response advertising is also often associated with substandard products, due to the large amount of dubious products using direct response advertising, such as weight loss products and other health food, with often extremely exaggerated claims and testimonials.[34]

ETHICAL ISSUE TO CONSIDER

What are the ethical issues involved in direct response television?

How should marketers try to overcome them?

Inserts

Inserts are similar to direct response advertising within a magazine or newspaper. They are separate from the actual magazine, sometimes just a loose leaf of paper inserted into a magazine or newspaper, or sometimes can take the form of a small booklet or catalogue. Traditionally, Sunday newspapers have a relatively large amount of inserts, though they can also be found in all types of other newspapers.

The main advantage over advertising inside a newspaper is that inserts are more easily seen, especially in the case of a typically large Sunday newspaper, which may consist of several sections. And while they are also easier to keep than a traditional advert in a newspaper or magazine, conversely they are also easier discarded, or even discarded without being looked at.

New media, hybrid media and mobile direct marketing

There is also a lot of direct marketing activity taking place in **new media** environments, such as the world wide web, or using hybrid media forms, combining television and the Internet. For example, a direct response advert on digital television can be used to call for the viewer to press a specific button on their remote control, in order for the television programme to be paused, while the viewer can look at a website or watch additional information or more extensive infomercial for an advertised product. Also, the viewer can then directly order the product using the remote control if he or she wishes to do so.[35]

Similarly, the mobile phone has emerged as a major potential tool for direct marketing activity in recent years. Again, much of the activity is based on hybrid media usage, for example, combining traditional text messages with Internet-based information.[36] As a typical example, customers can be sent a text message when they are entering a specific cell of the network, alerting them to a special offer available at a local retailer if such services are available. Or, more traditionally, customers may receive a SMS text where they can order a particular product or service by simply responding to the text. Some of the more advanced services are also including location-based services.[37]

One of the overarching characteristics of direct marketing campaigns using any of the tools described above is that they tend to combine communication with incentives to respond: For example a special free gift, extended warranty etc. In other words, often D&DBM tends to make extensive use of sales promotion techniques to position the offer, and to entice consumers to act promptly.

Permission marketing

Consider how you would respond to a range of direct marketing offers from insurance or finance companies with which you have had no dealings. You may, however, have purchased a totally unrelated product such as a washing machine and your contact details may have then been sold to these other companies who may send you frequent offers – unless you tell them to stop (i.e. opt out).

In response to widespread concerns about unsolicited direct marketing, the industry has increasingly moved towards a permission-based system of direct marketing.[38] In other words, rather than opting out after being included without their consent, consumers give consent to be contacted with product or service offers (opt in). In email marketing, **permission marketing** has actually been made compulsory in the EU in order to avoid spam.[39]

The main advantage of permission-based marketing is that it's response rate is considerably higher than 'cold calling'. This is largely because it is anticipated, personal and relevant.[40] However, as permission is first sought, the development of a robust list of contacts can be fairly time consuming, as it, for example first requires the potential client to visit a website, then sign up, then confirm the registration (i.e. opt in) before contact can be made.

Measuring effectiveness of direct and database marketing

In order to measure effectiveness of direct marketing communications, D&DBM uses a number of specific performance measures. As previously argued, D&DBM in contrast to other forms of marketing communications is mostly outcome oriented, rather than taking into account the broader picture, such as brand image. Therefore, D&DBM measures tend to be more metric in nature. At the same time, many outcome measures are significantly easier to measure for D&DBM campaigns than for other types of marketing campaigns. For example, if a local take away distributes 500 leaflets, and has 20 orders from the leaflet, then these orders can easily be attributed to the leaflet. If however there is a positive article in the local press, for example as a result of a PR campaign, it will be more difficult to measure the impact, as the impact is more indirect, less attributable and may not be as immediate as would be expected with a leaflet distribution.

Returns/response levels/conversion ratios

Returns, response rates and conversion ratios measure how successful a campaign is in getting people to react after exposure to a campaign. Returns, for example, measure how often a leaflet with a special offer code is 'returned' with requests for more information or actual sales requests, thus giving an indication of the impact a campaign makes.

Response rates show how many people respond to a particular offer, whereas the conversion rate indicates how many people actually take the desired action, for example what is the ratio of people seeing a leaflet for a local take away food outlet compared to the actual amount of people ordering from the takeaway.

Cost per enquiry (CPE)

The cost per enquiry is the average cost it takes to generate a potential customer enquiry. In order to calculate the CPE for a given campaign, it is necessary to add up all the costs for the campaign and then divide this by the total number of enquiries generated. This measure will give a good measure to compare different D&DBM tools, or can be used to compare different messages sent via different D&DBM channels.

Cost per order (CPO)

Similarly to the CPE, the cost per order measures the average amount spent generating one order. Like the CPE it is calculated by adding all the costs for a given campaign, and then dividing this total by the number of orders received.

Average order value (AOV)

The average order value can be used to determine which tool generates the most valuable orders, or together with the CPO can give a good picture about the profitability of a given campaign. In the latter case, if the AVO is greater than the CPO plus the cost of the goods, then the campaign is profitable on a first order basis. However, such a calculation does not take into account the lifetime value of a customer gained, and therefore the original cost may be intentionally negative.

Repeat order values/renewal rates

In order to give a more accurate picture about how valuable on average a customer is, it is important to not only focus on the average first order value, but also to take into account how much the customer will then spend once he or she is ordering again – and how many customers order again, or renew their contract. For example, if a telesales campaign generates new customers for a mobile phone company, then it is important to know how many of these customers will renew their contract once it has expired, or how many customers will go to another company (which then is known as a churn or attrition rate).

Ethical considerations

As previously mentioned in this chapter, there are three major areas of concern in regards to D&DBM: the potentially intrusive nature of the communication, privacy and data protection concerns and finally the amount of waste generated by some D&DBM tools.

Intrusive communication/unsolicited communication

Much of the information and material used in D&DBM is not solicited by the recipients, but rather sent out 'cold'. Therefore it can easily disturb the recipient and may even have a negative impact, for example by receiving too much irrelevant information or even an information overload, which in turn may lead to a negative attitude towards purchasing.[41]

Privacy

Also there are considerable concerns on privacy of data, especially if user data is used for consumer profiling or data mining. These concerns may either be because of the type of data held, or also about accuracy of data held, and possible interpretation of the data. For example, past purchasing history may be attributed towards the purchaser, not taking into account if the purchase was made for the purchaser him or herself, or as a gift. Another example could be 'linked financial profiles' generated by credit agency reports of two male flatmates, which may be seen as indicative of sexual orientation.

Waste and environmental impact

According to a recent report by the British Department for Environment, Food and Rural Affairs, 4.4 per cent of all the paper consumed in the UK is used for direct mail, door drops and inserts,[42] not counting other direct marketing techniques, such as catalogues etc. Of this only about a third was recycled in 2007. This is a potentially considerable waste of resources, and a considerable creation of waste, especially as many direct mail items may never be read and are directly discarded if they are unsolicited.

Outdoor advertising as a direct contact point

We have discussed some of the principles of outdoor advertising in previous chapters. We now focus on it in the context of direct communication with potential target groups at locations close to or actual at **point-of-purchase**.

As noted earlier, outdoor (also called out-of-home) refers to a large, continually changing range of media, from hoardings or posters and roadside signage, or signs on bus shelters or at sports grounds, through to advertising on vehicles (often called transit advertising), and aerial media such as large balloons. The quality also varies enormously. Hoardings with advertisements pasted on them may get dirty or defaced; 3D electronic signs allow more sophisticated changing messages.

When outdoor advertising is used as a supporting medium, imagery transfer is often important. The signs will reproduce a key image used in television or print media. Remember that for many outdoor forms, exposure to potential targets may be fleeting; there may be little opportunity to communicate detailed information.

With some forms of signage, such as at sporting grounds or concerts, the message may be static or repeated at regular intervals. The amount of attention paid to the signage is debatable, given that the focus will be on the activity taking place at the event.

THINK BOX

Outdoor signage

Visit your local high street or shopping centre. Note the range of outdoor displays (and also point-of-purchase displays as discussed in the next section). Do you believe that this activity actually makes people contact the marketer for more information or draw them in store to make a purchase? For what products or services is this most likely to occur?

For what types of products and services is it likely that outdoor signage reinforces messages seen in other media or reinforces decisions that may have already been made regarding a possible purchase?

Consider the particular situation of political parties – what is the role of outdoor signage?

ETHICAL ISSUE TO CONSIDER

Schools may be used as the location for posters, hoardings or other forms of signage. Allowing this practice can bring needed revenue in to the schools to be used for educational resources.

What are the ethics involved with this type of activity?

THINK BOX

Outdoor – visual pollution

Outdoor is often criticized as visual pollution – how would you respond to this criticism? What should marketers do to avoid this perception?

Normally signs may attract attention, but there is a danger that the novelty value of some signage forms may detract from the brand activity being featured. Another problem with some forms of outdoor advertising is the challenge of controlling the advertisements that appear adjacent to each other.

Point-of-purchase advertising

Closely linked to outdoor advertising is the specific category of point-of-purchase. This involves all marketing communications activity that occurs at the point at which sales are likely to occur. Examples include displays in store, product demonstrations including tasting of foods or free sample distribution. Point-of-purchase is important as it is the last point at which an advertising message can reach potential purchasers before they make the decision to purchase one brand rather than another. Displays therefore use many of the same characteristics as outdoor: repeating key images or messages from advertising in other media.

Summary

This chapter has discussed the strengths and weaknesses of direct and database marketing across the range of forms that it may take. A number of methods for evaluating the effectiveness of direct marketing techniques were also reviewed, along with ethical issues associated with some forms of activity. Outdoor and point-of-purchase activities were also briefly described, with the emphasis on the valuable supporting role they may fill in a wider integrated campaign.

Review questions

1. Why do you think D&DBM has become increasingly popular with many marketers?
2. What are the relative strengths and weaknesses of D&DBM compared to:

   - public relations
   - traditional media advertising
   - outdoor advertising
   - point of sales promotions.

3. Discuss which D&DBM tools may be effective or ineffective for the following:

   - a bank
   - a car manufacturer
   - a mobile telephone company
   - a fashion mail order business
   - a record production company
   - a political party.

4. How is D&DBM measured differently from other forms of marketing communications?
5. Discuss the implications of your answer to question 4 for a comparison of the effectiveness of D&DBM against other forms of marketing communication.
6. Discuss the long-term effects of unsolicited marketing communication. What do you think can be done to reduce the impact?
7. How would you respond to criticism that outdoor advertising is visual pollution and ineffective?

Recommended reading

Bird, D. (2007). *Commonsense Direct and Digital Marketing*, 5th edition, London: Kogan Page Ltd.
Godin, S. (2007). *Permission Marketing: Turning Strangers into Friends and Friends into Customers*, London: Simon & Schuster UK Ltd.

Using outdoor advertising to change perceptions of the National Trust in Northern Ireland

Source: Institute of Practitioners in Advertizing: IPA Effectiveness Awards, 2007. Authors: Sam McIlveen, Mike Fleming and Maurica Lavery. Case material provided by the World Advertizing Research Centre (WARC) www.warc.com.

The following case shows how outdoor activity was used as the central advertising contact point with potential customers.

Founded in 1895, the National Trust is currently the largest conservation organization in Europe. Its mission remains constant: to 'promote the permanent preservation for the benefit of the nation of lands and tenements (including buildings) of beauty or historic interest'. It is responsible for 709 miles of coastline, 254,000 hectares of land and 350 historic houses, gardens, ancient monuments, nature reserves and parks across England, Wales and Northern Ireland.

The maintenance of such an extensive portfolio of property is an extremely costly business. The National Trust is a charitable trust and therefore independent of any direct Government funding. It relies instead on the support of members, volunteers, benefactors and tenants and, most particularly, visitors to fund the management and maintenance of its properties.

At the turn of the millennium, the National Trust found that the number of people visiting their properties in Northern Ireland appeared to be in serious decline. Between 2001 and 2002 alone they fell by 12.5 per cent. They were facing major competition from a wide variety of other attractions such as Belfast Zoo, Armagh Planetarium, Ulster Museum, Derry Walls, Giants Causeway and Carrick-a-Rede Rope Bridge. Competing visitor attractions had become increasingly sophisticated and had improved the entertainment value of their offering with the use of greater levels of interactivity. When it came to choosing what they could do with their free time, consumers had a wide variety of options and the popularity of leisure centres, gyms and entertainment complexes also appeared on the rise. This, together with the growth of 'destination' shopping malls, meant that the National Trust was facing a serious challenge.

In an attempt to understand what people thought of the organization, the National Trust commissioned a programme of research and the results were scathing. In Northern Ireland, whilst levels of brand awareness were high, the organization was perceived as arrogant, elitist, thoroughly 'British' and lacking in relevance.

In response to these results, the National Trust commissioned a programme of advertising supported by tactical public relations activity. The objectives of the campaign focussed upon changing public perceptions of the National Trust in Northern Ireland, increasing visitor numbers and raising the level of revenue generated by the attractions themselves. As a charitable trust, the amount of money that the National Trust had to achieve their objectives was limited. With limited resources, it is essential to maximize the effectiveness of every component of a programme and, in such cases, simplicity is often the key.

It was decided that the campaign would be based upon the creative platform of inclusivity and fun. The proposition that underpinned the communication strategy was based upon two words: 'Go Enjoy'. It was hoped that this simple, straightforward call to action could be easily translated across a variety of media if required. It was hoped that it would convey a sense of openness and freedom whilst at the same time dispelling the rather fusty image

Photo 13.1

it had acquired until recently. An example of the 'Go Enjoy' posters to be found in town centre sites in Northern Ireland is shown in Photo 13.1.

In the first instance the majority of the promotional spend was channelled into single media, large-format posters, to ensure the greatest presence. The aim was to target potential consumers when they were 'out and about' at weekends so geographical targeting was employed with key sites identified in city centres.

In an attempt to stretch the limited budget, a media partnership was struck with Propertynews.com, Northern Ireland's foremost property website. Propertynews.com agreed to support the campaign for a period of three years, which gave the National Trust an increased media presence that proved to be extremely cost effective. On the Property news.com website alone, the National Trust achieved over ten million ad views, resulting in approximately 2,500 'click throughs' over the course of the three year period.

This strategy appears to have been very effective. Between the years 2002–2003 and 2005, the number of visitors to National Trust properties in Northern Ireland rose to from 275,000 to just under 510,000. Membership of the organization (i.e. those who pay an annual sub-scription) rose from 34,000 to 50,000 and revenue through on-site cafes and shops also increased.

CASE STUDY QUESTIONS

1. In this case, the National Trust chose to primarily focus upon the use of a single media, posters, to achieve maximum impact. Do you agree with their decision?
2. Compare the value of the use of a single medium versus the use of multiple media in an advertising campaign.
3. What other media might have been used in this case? List your 'top five' and justify your choice.
4. Looking at the 'Go Enjoy' poster, discuss how its creative execution might have helped to overcome consumers' prejudice against the National Trust.
5. What are the relative benefits and pitfalls in media partnerships such as that which existed between the National Trust and Propertynews.com?

CASE STUDY 13.2

Hastings Hotels Group

Source: This case has been condensed from Owens, S. (2007). 'Hastings Hotels Group – Battle of Hastings 2005–06: how email marketing overcame heightened competition to generate increased room occupancy and return on advertising investment for Hastings Hotels', Case Study Institute of Practitioners in Advertising Effectiveness Awards. Case material provided by the World Advertising Research Centre (WARC) www.warc.com.

This case study shows how the Hastings Hotels Group used a tactical strategy of low budget email marketing to increase turnover at a time:

- when the majority of its marketing budget was invested in an extensive rebranding project; and
- when the growth in the number of visitors to Northern Ireland was struggling to keep up with the growth in the number of hotel rooms.

It shows how a planned campaign of direct response email marketing overcame obstacles such as low budget and increased competition to generate online bookings and therefore increased turnover for the hotel group over a two-year period (2005 and 2006).

The Hastings Hotels Group is a locally owned hotel chain in Northern Ireland. Their hotels include the Culloden Estate & Spa, the Europa and the Stormont Hotels in Belfast, the Slieve Donard Resort and Spa in Co. Down, the Ballygally Castle on the Antrim Coast Road and the Everglades Hotel in Londonderry. The Hastings Hotels Group is an indigenous hotel brand in Northern Ireland, having grown out of and survived the years of the 'troubles'.

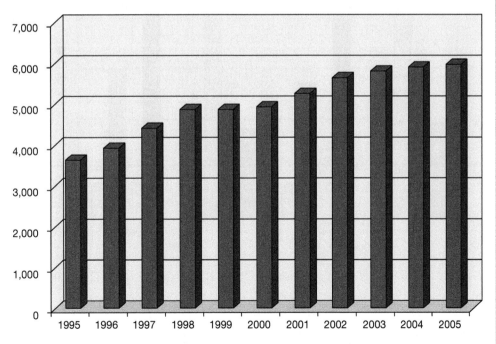

Figure 13.1 Number of hotel bedrooms in Northern Ireland (1995–2005)

With the cessation of violence and consequential recent investment, Northern Ireland has witnessed a dramatic increase in the number of hotels in the past 10 years including the Hilton Hotel (August 1998, Belfast), Radisson SAS (August 2004) and Malmaison (December 2004). As demonstrated by Figure 13.1, the number of hotel rooms in Northern Ireland has rocketed from 3,678 in 1995 to 6,021 in 2005 – a 64 per cent increase according to Northern Ireland Tourist Board (2006) figures. What had been a relatively stable and safe market for the Northern Ireland established hotel group has become increasingly competitive.

In comparison to its neighbours, Northern Ireland has a long way to go to fulfil its tourism potential, with tourism only contributing 2 per cent to its GDP, compared to 7 per cent in the Republic of Ireland (source: Central Statistics Office) and 5 per cent in Scotland (source: Scottish Parliament).

Furthermore, the lack of visiting pure holidaymakers is important to the Northern Ireland hotel industry, as traditionally those visiting friends and relatives (VFRs) do not stay in hotels. Figure 13.2 shows that in 2004 VFRs accounted for 43 per cent of tourists to Northern Ireland, and 49 per cent in 2005, a much higher proportion than the Republic of Ireland. Moreover, in 2004, only 19 per cent and in 2005 only 18 per cent of tourists to Northern Ireland cited a 'holiday' as the reason for their trip, compared with 52 per cent and 49 per cent of tourists to the Republic of Ireland.

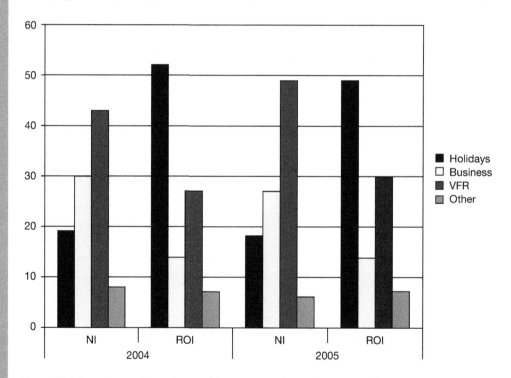

Figure 13.2 Percentage of out-of-state visitors to NI and ROI by purpose of visit (2004–2005)

2005 also saw a 7 per cent decline in the number of visitors to Northern Ireland from its previously reliable market in Great Britain as a consequence of reduced shipping routes and the greater choice of short breaks destinations and low cost access to other destinations (source: Northern Ireland Tourist Board).

Marketing objectives

- To increase sales and contribute towards a 10 per cent increase in turnover for the Group by the end of 2006.
- To make effective and efficient use of the small budget available for tactical sales generating activity and ensure at least a 300 per cent return on investment.

By 2005, the Hastings Hotels Group began to invest in a complete rebranding process for each of its six hotels. The project was extensive and most of the marketing budget for 2005 and 2006 was invested in it, leaving a limited budget for tactical sales driving activity.

By 2001, Hastings Hotels had optimized their website to enable them to receive online bookings. It spent the next three years using a variety of methods to grow a customer database of 8,166 people who were interested in receiving regular updates from the Group.

Customer data was acquired:

- at the moment of offline and online bookings;
- by advertising on Hastings Hotels' website;
- by advertising registration to its customer database in Crown, Hastings' bi-annual magazine; and
- by working with partners.

By 2005, Hastings had access to 8,166 inboxes, an uncluttered place, where people look nearly every day. Therefore, a campaign of email marketing was recognized as the most cost efficient and effective method to generate bookings and contribute towards increased turnover for the Group at a time:

- when Hastings Hotels marketing budget for tactical sales activity was limited due to an extensive rebranding process; and
- when Hastings were faced with increased competition and a slow to grow tourism industry.

Over a two-year period, Hastings Hotels sent 12 regular emails to their customer database. Each email was a direct response vehicle that communicated special bed and breakfast rates with a strong call to action, to encourage the receiver to avail of the offers, by booking online.

Hastings Hotels also used a tactical pricing strategy in order to stimulate demand at times of projected low occupancy levels. The offers communicated in these emails would be better than at times of projected higher levels of occupancy. Each email was distributed to the Hastings customer database at the end of the month, when the receiver had more disposable income available to spend.

The key to converting these emails into actual sales was to make the message relevant and beneficial to the receiver. Different themes were chosen for the regular emails, which captured the mood of the receiver for the time of year and encouraged them to treat themselves to a well-earned break. The focus of each e-shot was seasonal, with emails themed on St Valentine's, Winter, Spring, Summer, Autumn and Christmas breaks.

The following straplines used in the e-shots are some examples of how each email's message tried to capture the mood of the receiver for the time of year:

- January 2006: *Make this Valentine's special and escape to a world of luxury and romance.*
- September 2006: *Ward off the Winter Blues with some Red Hot Autumn Offers!*
- November 2006: *Treat Someone Special This Christmas . . . Or Treat Yourself!*

It was also important to communicate the quality of the Hastings Hotels' offering and not cause stress to the brand through these regular special offers. If the proposition for Hastings Hotels was solely based on price, they could have risked being beaten by the cheaper prices its competitors were offering.

The creative concept in each of the following examples of Hastings' emails conveyed these key messages:

1. Hastings Hotels is a luxurious accommodation choice.
2. Booking with Hastings Hotels is more affordable with special offers available.
3. You can avail of these offers now.
4. You can also buy gift vouchers, refer these special offers to a friend or visit Hastings' website for further information.

The interactivity and insightfulness of each email's call to action buttons (book now, refer a friend, gift vouchers, other offers and contact us) coupled with the relevant seasonality of each email's message, aimed to present Hastings as an intuitive and user-friendly brand, which was providing something of benefit to the receiver's life.

Database acquisition cost Hastings Hotels £19,000. This included the cost to:

*   set up and manage an online booking facility on the website in 2001;
*   set up and manage an online subscription facility to the Hastings' database in 2001; and
*   advertise subscription to the Hastings' database in Crown, Hastings' bi-annual magazine between 2001 and 2005.

Each e-shot incurred costs for design in html and dispatch by a third party database manager:

*   design of e-shot in html: £480.00
*   dispatch by a third party database manager: £200.00
*   total cost per e-shot: £680.00.

As Hastings sent twelve emails to their customer database in 2005 and 2006, the total implementation costs for email marketing was £27,160.

The benefit of email marketing is that it is a direct response tool and conversion into online bookings may be easily tracked. The short-term success of Hastings' email marketing in 2005 and 2006 was measured in the following ways:

1. Number of room nights booked by people on customer database.
2. Amount of revenue and profit generated from these room nights, on a bed and breakfast basis.

Hastings Hotels successfully maximized use of a small budget to ensure sales generation and a **424 per cent** return on investment, thus exceeding their original objective by 124 per cent.

In 2005, Hastings Hotels needed an interim low cost measure to respond to heightened competition and generate sales, at a time when marketing spend was being allocated to an extensive rebranding project for the Group. The additional turnover generated by email marketing has been reinvested into Hastings Hotels' 2007 marketing strategy. With the rebranding process almost complete, Hastings Hotels is now in a position to allocate marketing spend to offline advertising to promote its new brand. Nevertheless, Hastings recognizes the value of online communications as a cost-effective tactical income generator and email marketing continues to be an integral part of its 2007 marketing strategy.

CASE STUDY QUESTIONS

1. Critique this case study – what do you believe were the key factors that lead to the success of the campaign?
2. What do you advise the Hastings Hotel Group to do to keep the campaign fresh and avoid people getting bored with it?
3. How would you expect competitors to react to the campaign – and how should the Hastings Hotel Group counter competitor activity?

Notes

1   Patterson, M., and O'Malley, L. (2000). The evolution of the direct marketing consumer. *The Marketing Review*, 1(1), 89–101.
2   Vriens, M., van der Scheer, H. R., Hoekstra, J.C., and Bult, J.R. (1998). Conjoint experiments for direct mail response optimization. *European Journal of Marketing*, 32(3/4), 323.
3   Bean, R.B. (1997). Business-to-business database marketing: the future is now! *Direct Marketing*, 60(8), 43.
4   Tapp, A. (2008). *Principles of Direct and Database Marketing: A Digital Orientation*, London: FT Prentice Hall.
5   Shankar, V., and Winer, R.S. (2006). When customer relationship management meets data mining. *Journal of Direct Marketing*, 20(3–4), 2–4.
6   Kaelble, S. (2009). Direct mail done right. *Indiana Business Magazine*, 53(2), 34–6.
7   Phillips, T. (2007). Tesco knows loyalty like no other. *Retailing Today*, 46(10), 11–73.
8   Clews, L.M. (2009). Nectar brand campaign bids to increase loyalty card use. *Marketing Week*, 32(24), 11.
9   O'Leary, C., Rao, S., and Perry, C. (2004). Improving customer relationship management through database/Internet marketing: a theory-building action research project. *European Journal of Marketing*, 38(3/4), 338–54.
10 Kamakura, W.A., Wedel, M., de Rosa, F., and Mazzon, J.A. (2003). Cross-selling through data-base marketing: a mixed data factor analyzer for data augmentation and prediction. *International Journal of Research in Marketing*, 20(1), 45–65.
11 Kimberley, S. (2006). Time-Life data deal to slash marketing waste. *Precision Marketing*, 18(40), 1.
12 Kirchner, T.A., Markowski, E.P., and Ford, J.B. (2007). Relationships among levels of government support, marketing activities, and financial health of nonprofit performing arts organizations. *International Journal of Nonprofit & Voluntary Sector Marketing*, 12(2), 95–116.
13 Gerber, A.S., and Green, D.P. (2000). The effects of canvassing, telephone calls, and direct mail on voter turnout: a field experiment. *American Political Science Review*, 94(3), 653.
14 Hollis, N. (2005). Ten years of learning on how online advertising builds brands. *Journal of Advertising Research*, 45(2), 255–68.
15 Michaels, M. (2005). Ignore at your peril the 95 per cent who don't reply. *Precision Marketing*, 18(4), 14.
16 Reed, D. (2008). The secret of customizing. *Precision Marketing*, 20(18), 16–18.
17 Reinartz, W., Thomas, J.S., and Bascoul, G. (2008). Investigating cross-buying and customer loyalty. *Journal of Interactive Marketing*, 22(1), 5–20.
18 Jorna Leenheer, J., van Heerde, H., Bijmolt, T.H.A., and Smidts, A. (2007). Do loyalty programs really enhance behavioral loyalty? An empirical analysis accounting for self-selecting members. *International Journal of Research in Marketing*, 24(1), 31–47.
19 Lewis, H.G. (2008). Back to the future. *Direct*, 20(4), 56.
20 Hedley, S. (2006). A brief history of spam. *Information & Communications Technology Law*, 15(3), 223–38.

21 Merisavo, M., and Raulas, M. (2004). The impact of e-mail marketing on brand loyalty. *Journal of Product & Brand Management*, 13(7), 498–505.

22 Shaw, M.J., Subramaniam, C., Tan, G.W., and Welge, M.E. (2001). Knowledge management and data mining for marketing. *Decision Support Systems*, 31(1), 127–37.

23 Pera, M.S., and Ng, Y.-K. (2009). SpamED: a spam e-mail detection approach based on phrase similarity. *Journal of the American Society for Information Science & Technology*, 60(2), 393–409.

24 Mitchell, A., Hendersoj, I., and Searle, D. (2008). Reinventing direct marketing – with VRM inside. *Journal of Direct, Data and Digital Marketing Practice (formerly Interactive Marketing)*, 10(1), 3–15.

25 The Secretary of State for Environment, Food and Rural Affairs (2003). House of Commons Hansard, Written Answers, 16 October 2003.

26 Hasouneh, A.B.I.M. (2005). Telemarketing: an undertapped opportunity. *International Information, Communication & Education*, 24(1), 67–72.

27 Cooney, M. (2008). FTC bans prerecorded telemarketing drivel. *Network World*, 25(33), 50.

28 BBC (2005). Fines May Rise for Silent Calls. Online. Available HTTP: <http://news.bbc.co.uk/1/hi/business/4395624.stm> (accessed 20 April 2009).

29 Scott, P. (2008). Managing door-to-door sales of vacuum cleaners in interwar Britain. *Business History Review*, 82(4), 761–88.

30 Reed, D. (2008). Doors of perception. *Precision Marketing*, 20(13), 34–5.

31 Campbell, O. (2008). Forecasting in direct selling business: Tupperware's experience. *Journal of Business Forecasting*, 27(2), 18–19.

32 Campbell, O. (2008). Forecasting in Direct Selling Business. *Journal of Business Forecasting*, 27(2), 18–19.

33 Haire, T., and Renfrow, J. (2008). DR spending outdistances general and market growth. *Response*, 16(8), 8.

34 Atkinson, T.W., and Knowles, J.D. (2005). The 'perfect storm' – increasingly aggressive government and private actions. *Response*, 13(8), 51.

35 Jones, G. (2005). Switching TV advertisers on to interactive. *New Media Age*, 10.

36 McPherson, D. (2005). Salkes on cells. *Response*, 13(6), 42–46.

37 Dickinger, A., and Kleijnen, M. (2008). Coupons going wireless: determinants of consumer intentions to redeem mobile coupons. *Journal of Interactive Marketing (Formerly Journal of Direct Marketing)*, 22(3), 23–39.

38 Tezinde, T., Smith, B., and Murphy, J. (2002). Getting permission: exploring factors affecting permission marketing. *Journal of Interactive Marketing* (formerly *Journal of Direct Marketing*), 16(4), 28–36.

39 Commission of the European Communities (2003). The Privacy and Electronic Communications Directive.

40 Godin, S. (1999). *Permission Marketing*, New York: Simon & Schuster

41 Chen, Y.C., Shang, R.A., and Kaoa, C.Y. (2009). The effects of information overload on consumers' subjective state towards buying decision in the Internet shopping environment, *Electronic Commerce Research and Applications*, 8(1), 48–58.

42 DEFRA (2007). Waste Strategy Factsheets – Direct Mail. Online. Available HTTP: <http://defra.gov.uk/ENVIRONMENT/waste/strategy/factsheets/directmail.htm> (accessed 21 April 2009).

14 Integrated campaign development

Marketing PR and sponsorship

LEARNING OUTCOMES

After studying this chapter, you will be able to:

- Understand the difference between general public relations and marketing public relations and their relative contribution to marketing campaigns

- Identify the difference between proactive and reactive public relations

- Analyse the role of lobbying, astro-turfing and word of mouth as a potential component of a marketing PR campaign

- Analyse the contribution of sponsorship activity to both short- and long-term marketing activity

- Discuss ethical issues that may arise in both public relations and sponsorship activity – understand the complexities of evaluating PR campaigns

Introduction

In its broadest sense, **public relations** (PR) is aimed at building positive relations between a company and a wide range of publics or stakeholders who may be impacted by the organization's activity. Publics may include current or potential employees, trade unions, shareholders and investment advisors, lobby groups and government agencies. There is some debate about the scope of public relations, i.e. if PR is limited to immediate stakeholders of an organization – or if it should target a much wider audience or publics. However, in any case, the scope of PR is understood to be much wider than only the immediate customers or users of an organization. Some of the debate is connected to the wording of stakeholders and publics: while in general management terms, stakeholders are usually understood to be those audiences that have an immediate influence on an organization's success or failure, which include for example customers, suppliers and employees. Publics tend to refer to a wider audience: including, for example, people living nearby manufacturing sites, competitors and so on.

Many aspects of a company's operation do not directly involve marketing activity, but rather wider organization and management issues. For example, current employees, trade unions and government agencies may be concerned about the impact of possible relocation of part or all of a company's operation, particularly if the move involves potential loss of jobs.

Lobby groups may be concerned about depletion of natural resources or pollution during the production of the company's products, or the 'carbon footprint' generated by shipping ingredients or finished products from off-shore facilities.

All these activities do however have a long-term effect on the company's performance, especially on the way the affected audiences will relate to a given company or organization, and the way the organization is perceived. That in turn is very likely to influence long-term behaviour, such as making purchase decisions in future etc. It is therefore important to manage these relationships and wherever possible maintain a positive relationship with the audiences concerned.

General PR and marketing PR

Historically, there has been resistance from some members of the PR community to public relations coming within the scope of IMC. This has been partially philosophical opposition to the perceived threat of PR being subsumed within a marketing function.[1] Concerns that the focus may move from the broad range of PR activity to a more restricted focus on marketing-related issues have been valid and are now reflected in a distinction between broad, general PR issues and what is now termed **marketing PR (MPR)**.[2]

MPR focuses on the company's interactions with consumers of the company's products or services,[3] and thus takes a more focussed approach under the umbrella function of general public relations. Some authors[1] argue that such integrated programmes should in fact combine advertising and marketing PR.

A main function of such an integrated programme might be to integrate the messages conveyed to potential consumers, by optimizing and combining different traditional strategies to achieve a synergistic effect. For example, the MPR aspect of such an integrated programme could focus on achieving positive press coverage and word of mouth of a newly launched product, while advertising could be used to remind potential customers of the main product features. Equally, for some products such a combined approach is more sensible, as it can potentially combine the different strengths of the two tools. For example, The Bodyshop used effective MPR to support its Hemp range product launch in Canada in 1998,[4] where the Canadian government was threatening to seize the products. Public relations was particularly useful to explain the more complex arguments centring on the differences between hemp-based products and marijuana as a drug, which involved complex arguments that would have been nearly impossible to convey in a normal advertising campaign.

The ability to deal fairly successfully with complex situations is a major strength of an integrated communication campaign involving public relations. However, conversely it can be argued, that effective PR campaigns take a lot longer to convey messages than advertising campaigns, and that PR campaigns tend not to work particularly well when used in an ad-hoc (and often reactive) way rather than as part of an overall strategy, and in a proactive way.

THINK BOX

Corporate PR

Corporate PR focusses on activities such as a company's overall profile, financial performance or major strategic decisions such as where to locate manufacturing plants.

- How should corporate PR and MPR be aligned to reinforce each other?
- What problems for both PR activities may occur if a company decides to:

    a) relocate a major manufacturing plant to another country, or
    b) the company is required to recall a high profile range of products due to a serious defect?

MINI CASE: EUROSTAR

The Eurostar has had some significant positives and negatives in recent years. Considerable positive publicity was gained when the UK operation moved from Waterloo Station to the newly refurbished St Pancras International Station in 2007.

Confidence in the cross channel service was dented when a fire broke out in the tunnel in September 2008 (there was also a fire in 1996). Not only were services halted on the day of the 2008 fire, but were restricted for some time afterwards while the affected part of the tunnel was repaired, leading to delays and longer travelling times. Further problems occurred during the 2009–2010 winter, with several trains breaking down in the channel tunnel due to snow penetrating engines during the above-ground leg of the journey. Passengers had to wait several hours in uncomfortable conditions for rescue: see, for example: http://guardian.co.uk/world/2010/feb/22/eurostar-breaks-down-london.

A fatal train collision in Belgium in February 2010, while not involving Eurostar, led to cancellations and reduced services for several weeks as the Eurostar service ran over the track on which the accident occurred – see http://news.bbc.co.uk/1/hi/uk/8539336.stm.

Assume you are advising Eurostar.

1. What ongoing PR and publicity do you recommend and why?
2. What contingency plans for PR and publicity should be in place in the event of future disruptions to the service?

3. Review past PR activity such as the St Pancras opening and recommend whether/ what types of special events might be considered for the next 12 months.

Justify your answers to all questions.

Reactive versus proactive MPR

Reactive MPR is usually defensive, responding to pressures and influences originating outside the company, such as competitive activity, changes in government policy or legislation, or changing consumer attitudes. The most high-profile reactive public relations involves crisis management, such as may occur in the event of product recalls or consumers being harmed while using a company's products. The following provides an overview of some of the major product recalls and their impact on the companies concerned.

The action of Johnson & Johnson in the USA recalling its Tylenol product in response to a cyanide-poisoning crisis in 1982 has long been held as the exemplar of crisis management. Three years prior to the crisis, the then CEO had ensured that there was active commitment to the company philosophy statement and the principles it implied, that would be required in a crisis situation. This made the subsequent swift and effective product withdrawal, coupled with full, honest discussion of the company's actions in the media an uncontested course of action,[5] which, while it cost the company some $US100 million in lost earnings in the short term, allowed the company to rebuild and increase market share in the long term and also 'reinforce the company's reputation for integrity and trustworthiness'[6] p. 61.

This case stands in marked contrast to the more recent Ford/Bridgestone,[7,8] which erupted in 2000, although first reports of problems with Bridgestone tyres had surfaced in 1996. In 2000, Ford unilaterally recalled 13 million tyres, at a cost of US$ 2.1 billion, after pressure mounted on the company to investigate increasing reports of faulty tyres. The affair lasted for more than five years after the product recall, and resulted in both sides blaming each other publicly for the faulty tyres, which resulted in more than 270 deaths and over 800 injuries.[9] The affair finally came to an end in 2005, but not until after a massive loss in confidence in both companies.

In early 2010, Toyota announced a number of recalls, totalling over 8.5 million cars due to several mechanical problems that were linked to road accidents, some of which were fatal. See, for example: http://news.bbc.co.uk/1/hi/business/8505402.stm It remains to be seen as to what the long-term impact on the company will be.

Apart from the direct costs in the product recall, there are also substantial direct and indirect costs associated with such a crisis.[10] Jarrel and Peltzman[10] suggest that these indirect costs will be substantially higher than the direct costs of a product recall, particularly as a result of the negative impact on a firm's goodwill, to the extent that negative externalities for competitors may be larger than those of the company producing the recalled product. These financial strains can be so severe, that many companies need to seek bankruptcy protection when faced both direct recall costs, and also resulting fines and product-liability claims and/or lawsuits as a result of faulty products.[11]

Often, consumers react to a product recall with total product avoidance, often beyond the affected products. This product avoidance may well last substantially longer than the crisis itself, and therefore remains a major obstacle long after the recall is finished. As a result, after a recall, a company may well struggle to recover lost market share.[12] However, despite these potentially devastating effects of reactive crisis communication, most firms remain ill-prepared to handle a potential crisis effectively – and some argue if most companies face a crisis they react at best ambivalently.[13]

The example of effective handling of crisis communications, which requires much more than only traditional advertising and other marketing communication activities, especially a proactive engagement with the press and consumer groups highlights the major difference between traditional marketing communication tools and the broader and more long-term nature of public relations. For example, consumers' interpretations of a firm's response to a product recall crisis is heavily dependent on their prior expectations about the firm,[13] which in turn are at the centre of proactive PR efforts. Firms or brands with strong, positive consumer perceptions and expectations are likely to be more resilient to negative publicity resulting from a crisis, for example as a result of a product recall.

Equally, a company that is regarded as generally a 'good' company, may well find it easier to communicate their point in a crisis situation, than a company that is perceived as deceptive or has a poor rapport with its publics. Firms with weaker consumer expectations may also have to undertake more brand support either during the crisis or after the immediate crisis is over, for example with extensive advertising and sales promotions, in order to maintain or restore consumer brand equity and trust.[12] Recovery rates are an indicator of the success of strategies and tactics put into place to deal with a crisis,[14] as seen via Tylenol.

While an in-depth discussion on effective crisis management is well beyond the scope of this book, a proactive handling of communication in a crisis situation is usually the most important aspect for a successful handling of such a situation.[15] Being prepared, expecting and effectively handling an increased media attention as a result of an issue or immediate crisis erupting is a major component of effective crisis communication, which leaves little room for speculation and tries to ensure that the company's position is communicated effectively and clearly.

THINK BOX

Public relations crises

Consider fast moving consumer goods such as foods sold in supermarkets, service companies such as tour operators and the health sector. What sorts of public relations crises might occur in each sector and how can a company anticipate possible problems and prepare to deal with them?

Conversely, **proactive MPR** originates within a company and is planned as part of the overall marketing strategy. It is offensive rather than defensive, with the focus being on enhancing a brand's credibility, image or reputation at all times (i.e. building rather than defending brand equity), rather than just trying to handle negative publicity after it has occurred. As a broad form of marketing-related communication activity, it often complements other marketing, and particularly marketing communications activities, and traditionally is closely aligned with sponsorship and sales promotion activity.[16]

The three primary tools used in MPR are publicity, especially in the form of media relations, events related PR and PR activities to support product launches, although some other activities are also employed, which will be touched upon later in the chapter.

MINI CASE: PRODUCT WITHDRAWALS

Draw on the literature around the withdrawal of Tylenol and the more recent Ford/Bridgestone tyre crisis[17] and the major recall of Toyota vehicles in 2009.[18]

Compare and contrast the way the companies involved handled the problems, the withdrawals and the accompanying publicity.

1. What lessons can be learned from these situations?
2. What are the three most important things a company in a similar situation should not do?
3. How would you propose monitoring the impact of the negative publicity for a company involved in product recalls in the future?

In 2010, a US organization specifically recommended against the purchase of a Lexus (Toyota's luxury brand) 4 wheel drive model, the GX460, due to concerns regarding its safety.[19]

What impact would you expect this to have had on the brand image and reputation of Toyota and Lexus?

Review the academic and consumer literature relating to both the Toyota recalls and the subsequent problem with the Lexus GX460. Draw on the material in the preceding chapters, including the material relating to ethics and brand image/brand equity.

1. Critique the way that Toyota responded to both issues. What do you believe they could have done differently and why?
2. Make recommendations for the management of brand image in the future.
3. What particular role could MPR play in this?

Publicity and media relations

Informing the relevant media about newsworthy stories is a major activity within a public relations context. Some newsworthy stories can be directly related to marketing activities, for example by providing information about new products to relevant media, while other activities are less directly connected to marketing. For example, informing the financial press about an increase in earnings is unlikely to contribute directly to sales, however, coverage of the increased earnings is likely to increase trust and consequently brand equity. However, providing information does not guarantee coverage by the media, nor does it guarantee how the media uses the information: while PR activity may be perceived as being more credible than paid advertising, it is also difficult to control. There is no guarantee that the media will use material supplied, or that they will present it in the form intended.[2,3]

In order to provide the media with relevant information, the company may choose to use publicity such as press briefings, **press releases**, press kits, containing background information and relevant materials, feature stories, videos, photos, pre-recorded interviews and of course Internet-based communications, such as the company's website as the main tools. However, public relations goes well beyond simply managing media relations, although many organizations equate effective public relations with good media relations,[20] and often underestimate the time and effort it takes to build positive relationships with the news media. This is especially true if **media relations** are to be used to create coverage of products and services, and therefore complementing other marketing efforts, as these kinds of stories often only have a limited amount of newsworthiness, especially for mainstream media outlets.

This does not mean that there is no newsworthiness in such stories. For example, product launches are often interesting for the specialist press, such as the launch of a new laptop computer for a computer magazine, as a computer magazine may be interested in reviewing the product. Also, the story may be of interest for the local press where the organization is based, or manufactures the laptop, as the new product is likely to create employment in the region, and so forth. Thus, in MPR it is often important to have a good knowledge of the media related to the company as well as providing often personalized stories with different angles to different media to ensure newsworthiness. The Stanley Tools case at the end of this chapter illustrates effective use of MPR as part of an integrated campaign.

Large companies often accompany product launches or 'newsworthy' events with a large media event, to make it attractive for the media to cover such stories. Examples include movies being released with great fanfare in the West End of London, with the main movie stars attending the premiere of the movie, giving autographs and being available for interviews. Sometimes, these events can also involve giving prizes, for example Apple gave computer items to the 1,000,000th visitor of its flagship Fifth Avenue store.

MINI CASE: MAKING MOVIES GO PUBLIC

Follow the launch of the next major movie to be released and analyse the public relations/ publicity activity around it.

1. What are the three most important things that should be done – or avoided?
2. Assume your launch activity for a new movie or major new product has gone as planned, but subsequent reviews of it are negative. What should you do?
3. How would you recommend monitoring the amount and impact of media coverage (positive or negative)?
4. What are the ethical issues involved in deciding which organizations are suitable and effective partners for merchandise distribution or other forms of co-promotion?

Lobbying

As part of the wider remit of public relations in comparison to traditional marketing communications, PR is often concerned with creating goodwill and understanding for an organization's or company's position, policies or plans with a wide range of audiences not traditionally part of the remit of marketing. For example, liaising with local environmental groups or policy makers is unlikely to have an immediate effect on sales, though in the long run, proactive engagement with these stakeholders may be to the advantage for company organizational strategy.

Lobbying in particular is an activity where an organization builds and maintains relations with local, national and international public and government bodies and uses these relationships to influence legislation and regulation. For some companies engaging in public consultations and lobbying governmental organizations can be crucial, especially if these companies are faced with increasing calls for regulation or legislation in their core business areas. Examples of this include the tobacco industry, which faces significant intervention from governments, or manufacturers of high-sugar or high-fat foods, who again face increasing calls for legislation and regulation, mostly of their marketing related activities, especially in relation to children.[21]

However, the question as to whether or not an organization should engage in lobbying and the extent to which it fully engages can be controversial. On the one hand, lawmakers usually encourage engagement with stakeholders in public consultations, and often the law requires such consultations. In fact, in a recent British government report on lobbying, the practice was described as 'a legitimate and necessary part of the democratic process'[22] p. 5. On the other hand however, lobbying has been criticized as providing privileged access to a selected group of organizations to lawmakers. This criticism is particularly evident in cases where there have often been substantial monetary contributions to political parties or causes either directly or indirectly via lobbying agencies to politicians. Examples of this include the £1 million donation of Formula One entrepreneur Bernie Ecclestone to the Labour party in 1997, and the subsequent exemption of Formula One events from the ban of tobacco advertising.[23]

There is often a fine line between lawful and desired representation and consultation, and unlawful or at least dubious practices, especially in the case of misrepresentation of public concern, for example by using techniques such as **astro-turfing**, discussed later in this chapter, or by implicitly or explicitly linking donations to certain privileges. For example the recent cash for honours scandal, in which several people were found to have donated large amounts of money to the Labour party. Although the final findings of the criminal investigation did not charge any individuals, the final report did conclude that cash *may* have been given in return for peerages.

THINK BOX

Lobbying

Discuss the pros and cons of lobbying.

- At what point do you believe that lobbying activity might be unethical?
- What role do the media play in lobbying?
- What role should they play and who should decide?

Should the public be made aware of specific lobbying activity? If so, how should this be achieved and what impact would it have on the lobbying activity itself?

Word of mouth (WOM) and astro-turfing

Creating positive word of mouth, or a positive 'vibe' or 'buzz' is ultimately about a new product or service, or just an organization in general is a major objective of many public relations campaigns, and can either precede or be the result of a successful publicity campaign. Either way, the goal is to get people to talk from person to person about an organization or product, which is often seen as the most persuasive of all communication forms.

WOM, or sometimes called word of mouth marketing (WOMM), relies on the principle that each social network (or group of friends) has certain individuals that influence decision making within that network. If these individuals can be identified and can positively talk about products or services, then they can influence their 'followers' both to try out these products or services, and then in turn potentially speak to others about their experience with these products or services. The effect is a multiplication of the message through social networks, which has the potential to replicate rapidly. If enough people are talking for example about a newly launched product, then in turn it may be that the media may pick up on the perceived 'trend' and report on about the new product, thus again helping to create more buzz and potentially more word of mouth.

Accessing, replicating and measuring the effectiveness of word of mouth is however notoriously difficult, as the conversations are usually private. However despite these difficulties a number of advertising and PR agencies have recently launched their own WOM agencies to capture this increasingly important market, alongside specialist agencies, such as the British BzzAgent Agency.

As with lobbying, the problem is the grey area between legitimate talk about brands, ideas, products and services between friends, and the commercially driven influencing of other people, who may, or may not, be aware that the conversation is for commercial profit. While the Word of Mouth Marketing Association makes it very clear in its ethics code, that anyone who is being paid or receives benefits (such as free product samples) by agreeing to create word of mouth must identify themselves, such honesty may not always be the case.

An example of a frequently dubious word of mouth related activity is the case of astro-turfing, or an attempt to create the impression of positive word of mouth and public support for a particular cause. This tactic is being seen as unethical by most public relations professional bodies, however it is not necessarily illegal. In fact, in at least one well-publicized case, the case of the People's Republic of China, astro-turfing using blogs on the Internet is actually used by a government to create the impression of positive word of mouth. Reputedly, there are now more than 10,000 regular Internet commentators in China receiving 50 Chinese cents per positive comment,[23] and therefore dubbed the 50-Cent-Party.

Another example of potential astro-turfing includes the American Center for Consumer Freedom, a non-profit organization, that often appears to support industry causes, such as the choice of smoking in restaurants, and is widely regarded as being funded by the industry, such as Philip Morris. Similarly, in the UK, the FOREST organization is funded largely by tobacco companies and campaigns on behalf of smokers' rights.[24]

ETHICAL ISSUE TO CONSIDER

Do you believe that astro-turfing is ethical?

Should organizations behind the activity be forced to declare their interest in the organizations that are the public face of the astro-turfing activity?

What actions, if any, do you recommend regulators take? Justify your response.

Sponsorship

Sponsorship shares many of the characteristics of proactive MPR, being aimed at generating awareness and promoting a positive image of the company and/or its products and services. It involves sponsoring, usually financially, events, organizations (such as charities or sporting organizations or specific causes). While it isn't usually considered part of PR, which is generally seen as not paying for publicity and not being in control of a message, sponsoring an event or service usually involves payment of a fee in return for a predetermined message.

Sponsorship often combines and supports a message by aligning the message with a desirable event, trying to benefit from the values associated with the event. For example, the London Marathon with its immediate connotations of sporty and healthy was sponsored by the margarine brand Flora, and branded itself the Flora London Marathon. Thus, by sponsoring such an event, Flora attempted to become associated in the mind of consumers as healthy. From 2010, the Marathon's sponsor became Virgin Money and it remains to be seen how this association benefits both parties.

MINI CASE: SPONSORSHIP BY ASSOCIATION?

Use the Flora/Virgin sponsorship as a base and consider:

1. What the implications are for a brand that has sponsored an event for several years when the association is terminated and what challenges a new sponsor faces if:

    a) the new sponsor is totally unrelated to the old sponsor (as with Flora/Virgin)
    b) the new sponsor is a competitor of the old sponsor.

2. Assume you have tracking research that shows 12 months after you have taken over a sponsorship that most people still associate the event with the old sponsor. What should you do?
3. Assume you are sponsoring a major sporting event and significant negative publicity is given to illegal drug taking among competitors. What are the implications for you as the sponsor and what should you do?
4. Assume that you are the major sponsor of a high profile event but a large competitor is placing advertising as close as possible to the coverage of the official event (a tactic known as '**ambush marketing**'). How can you counter their activity?

In terms of effective marketing, a match between event values and corporate values is the most desirable type of sponsorship, in some cases such a link may not be immediately present. An example of such a sponsorship is the International University of Bremen in Germany, a private university, which renamed itself Jacobs University after receiving a substantial sponsorship from a charitable foundation associated to a local and leading coffee company in Germany. Several well known and highly regarded business schools in the USA carry the name of their major sponsors.

THINK BOX

Sponsorship

If you worked for an educational institution and you were approached with the offer of a major sponsorship arrangement that would require a name change to that of the sponsor, how would you assess the pros and cons of the change?

Ethics in PR and sponsorship

There is a considerable debate about PR and sponsorship. In the case of public relations, the case of **spin doctoring**, or the attempt to heavily bias public opinion in the organization's favour, sometimes against the common good, or in a deceptive or dishonest way is a particular concern.

While all professional organizations have strict codes of conduct, there is a widespread distrust against many of the activities related to PR. Such mistrust is not surprising given some high-profile cases of spin doctoring. For example the case of Jo Moore, the former press officer for the Transport, Local Government and Regions Secretary, who emailed the press office on 9/11 that it would be 'a good day to bury bad news'.[25]

Equally in the case of sponsorship, there are often considerable ethical concerns of what happens in the case of a potential mis-match between the sponsored organization and the sponsor, and to what extent there is any influence of the sponsor on what the organization says or does. For example, would Jacobs University conduct or even agree to research potential negative effects of coffee?

Measuring results

Many of the benefits of PR campaigns are often seen as being intangible, and therefore difficult to measure, however, measuring and researching the effect a PR or sponsorship campaign had is a vital part of the marketing planning process. Traditionally, public relations tended to rely mostly on output measures rather than impact measures, arguing that especially the long-term impact was difficult to quantify.

While there is some truth in that statement, some of the output measures can be quantified, and often are quantified in a similar way to other marketing communication tools. For example, a popular measure is to 'count' the space an article devotes to discussing a company's new product (favourably) and then converting this into a measurable output by calculating how much it would have cost to buy this space as an advert. Looking at the space mentioning the product as a defacto advert makes it also possible to calculate other measures, such as how many readers have potentially been exposed to the message.

However, the main criticism with this approach is that such an approach does not take into account the source credibility, and in fact may not necessarily track how much the message was favourable, very favourable etc. Such measurements can be particularly 'fuzzy', i.e. difficult to measure precisely in the case of word of mouth campaigns, where there is little or no evidence of the conversation taking place. Sometimes, measures are available, but must be interpreted within the context in which they are likely to have occurred. For example it is relatively easy to measure mentions of a particular brand name in the blogsphere via service like Nielson's Buzzmetrics, however, such measures will not indicate if the name was used in a positive or negative context.

Summary

Over the course of this chapter, we have discussed the various roles public relations can play to support marketing efforts. It can create long-term goodwill and positive brand perception, as well as be a useful tool for creating publicity around an organization or company, its goals or its products or services. There are two distinct types of PR: proactive and reactive public relations. Proactive public relations is part of an overall communication strategy and focusses on the establishment of positive relations with stakeholders or publics in the long term. Reactive PR, on the other hand, is defensive and often unplanned. Sponsorship can provide significant opportunities to enhance brand equity and positive brand associations, but should be approached and managed with care.

Review questions

1. You are planning the launch of a new range of low fat snack foods:

   a. what public relations activity would you recommend and why?
   b. in assessing potential sponsorship opportunities, what types of events might be compatible with your product range. Justify your answer.

2. You are the Brand Manager for a range of electronic goods. You receive a phone call from the media querying whether it is true that some customers have received minor electric shocks from the products. What action should you take?

3. Review the media coverage relating to sun protection advice. You should find considerable confusion and conflicting advice, particularly in relation to Vitamin D production from sun exposure versus increased risk of skin cancer from excessive sun exposure. Outline a media strategy aimed at improving balanced coverage of the issues.

4. Discuss the ethics and acceptability of generating positive word of mouth for five different types of products (one toy aimed at children, one food product, one fashion, one electronics, and one car). Give real world examples to illustrate your answer.

5. Outline a proposed strategy for measuring the impact of public relations activity:

   a) for the new product launch in question 1
   b) for the potential product crisis situation in question 2.

6. You have been asked to assess the merits of sponsoring television coverage of a forthcoming international tour by a national sports team. Prepare a list of the various factors that should be taken into account in deciding whether or not to sponsor the coverage and include recommendations as to how each factor should be assessed or measured.

7. The practice of lobbying within the world of politics is long established yet highly controversial. What are the benefits and pitfalls of lobbying to brand owners and their consumers and also politicians and the electorate?

8. In the UK, individual football clubs in the Premiership League regularly sign sponsorship deals worth millions of pounds whilst clubs for sports like rugby and rowing struggle to obtain a fraction of this figure. Explain why you believe that this is the case and consider the benefits and potential pitfalls for both the sponsors and the clubs themselves.

9. 'Public relations is just soft selling under another name.' Discuss this statement and illustrate your answer with examples.

10. Search in the press or on the Internet for a recent 'product recall' notice. Explain how a Marketing Manager might employ PR to counter any negative publicity generated by the recall notice.

Recommended reading

Davis, A. (2007). *Mastering Public Relations*, 2nd edition, London: Palgrave.
Lattimore, D. *et al.* (2004). *Public Relations: The Profession and the Practice*, New York: McGraw Hill.

L'Etang, J. (2006). *Public Relations: Critical Debates and Contemporary Practice*, New Jersey: Lawrence Erlbaum Associates Publishers.

McClaren, N. (2013). The personal selling and sales management ethics research: managerial implications and research directions from a comprehensive review of the empirical literature. *Journal of Business Ethics*, 112(1), 101–25.

Theaker, A. (2008). *The Public Relations Handbook*, Abingdon: Routledge.

CASE STUDY 14.1

Stanley Tools

Source: Institute of Practitioners in Advertising: IPA Effectiveness Awards 2009. The case has been condensed from 'Stanley Tools – Stanley "Judgement Day": The Case for Turning Communications Inside-Out'. Principal authors: Charlotte Turland, Jacqui Power, Tony Holmes (McCann Erickson Communications House, Birmingham). Contributing authors: Andy Aston, Duncan Nealon, Nicola Sutton (McCann Erickson Communications House, Birmingham). Case material provided by the World Advertising Research Centre (WARC) www.warc.com.

This case study illustrates what can be achieved with a well planned, targeted and executed small budget campaign. It also illustrates the effective use of often overlooked traditional forms of advertising.

The background

Stanley is the largest global manufacturer of hand tools, with nearly 170 years of history in tool innovations and manufacturing excellence. The name is synonymous with construction and DIY hand tool icons such as the Stanley Knife and Stanley PowerLock(r) tape.

Throughout the years, Stanley has continued to be an industry leader, creator and manufacturer of toolbox essentials. It has maintained competitive advantage through continued investment in its team of industrial designers, process engineers and material scientists – a.k.a. 'The Discovery Team'. This investment in continual observation and constant investigation by The Discovery Team into how professional tradesmen use their tools on-site provides Stanley with unique insights into their changing behaviours and needs. This insight is then built into new product development which is tested 'in field' with professional tradesmen and then refined accordingly before being launched to market. in this respect, Stanley's new product innovation is designed from the 'inside' out.

The problem

Although firmly rooted historically in the professional trades and the sales channels that support the professional tradesmen channel (independent hardware stores, trade merchants and industrial tool distributors), the 1990s proliferation of home-makeover TV programmes and the subsequent consumer interest in DIY, prompted Stanley to shift its focus and to place its sales and product development emphasis in the fast growing and lucrative DIY sector, in which consumer spending grew by 76 per cent from 1996–2006.

This dilution of focus and reduction in emphasis on professional tradesmen was successful in terms of opening up new sales opportunities, but proved to be to the detriment of relationships with the professional sales channels – where accounts and sales started to decline. Pro Users too felt a distancing from Stanley with very little new product or promotion discrete to them over this period of time.

This change of focus also coincided with the rise in own-label hand tools commoditizing hand tool categories such as tape measures and utility knives in which Stanley traditionally dominated. It also allowed competitor brands, namely Irwin and Draper, to encroach into Stanley's previously solid professional tradesmen channel territory with new products and promotions (Figures 14.1, 14.2 and 14.3).

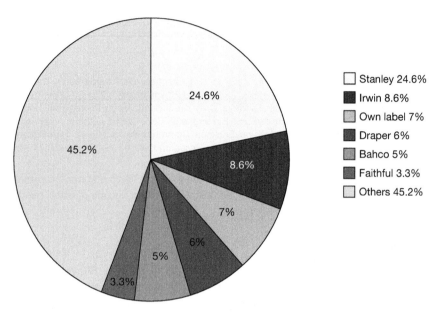

Figure 14.1 2007 hand tool professional tradesmen market share showing dominance of Stanley and the share of Irwin, Draper and own labels

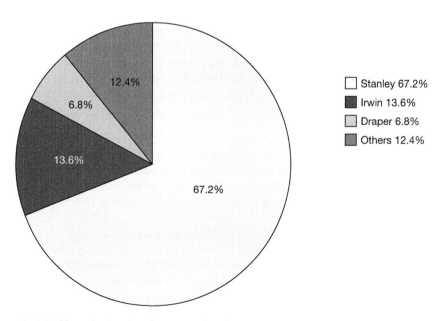

Figure 14.2 Knife professional tradesmen market share

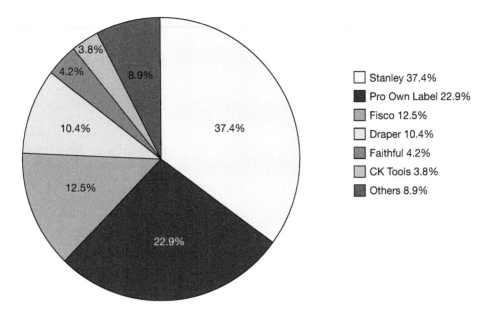

Stanley 37.4%
Pro Own Label 22.9%
Fisco 12.5%
Draper 10.4%
Faithful 4.2%
CK Tools 3.8%
Others 8.9%

Figure 14.3 Tapes professional tradesmen market share

The mission

In 2006, the erosion of its position within the professional tradesmen channel and the consumer market shift back away from DIY to DFY (Done For You) led Stanley to take stock of its situation and it engaged McCann Erickson Communications House (MECH) on the following mission:

- Regain Stanley's position from a brand for 'DIY-ers' back to a brand that champions the needs of professional tradesmen users.
- Reverse its declining sales into the Pro Channel and regain confidence amongst trade buyers.
- Defend its brand leading position within core product categories of tapes and knives.
- Attack categories 'owned' by competitor brands of hammers (Estwing) and levels (Stabila).
- Shift Stanley from an outdated brand of yesterday's professional tradesman to a dynamic brand of today's.

Key to the mission

Stanley believed success in achieving this mission would come through the successful launch of a new product line – 'Stanley FatMax XL'.

Introducing Stanley's new range

The new range of Stanley FatMax XL products (Photo 14.1) was the vehicle through which Stanley believed it could reawaken its brand with professional tradesmen. This product range was the toughest, meanest, sharpest and strongest set of tools that Stanley had created. It was developed using the unique insights gained by The Discovery Team – to

Photo 14.1

defend knife and tape categories and attack hammer and level categories. It even created two new products (the 'DemoDriver' – cross between a chisel and a screwdriver – and the 'FuBar' – the first all-in-one demolition tool). The range was not only built '**with** the Professional Tradesmen, **for** the Professional Tradesmen' – but most critically would only be available to the professional tradesmen via an exclusive distribution agreement with professional sales channels.

At the same time as launching FatMax XL, Stanley took the opportunity to realign the distribution policy on its existing product lines. Stanley branded products would be available through all channels and form its 'good' product offer, Stanley FatMax (a range of products that had been released in a staggered roll-out over a period of two years between 2004 and 2006) would become its 'better' offer available through DIY and professional tradesmen channels whilst FatMax XL would be its 'best' proposition . . . available exclusively through professional tradesmen channels.

The planning

By integrating seven channel specialists within one agency site – with brand and channel planning at the centre – McCann Erickson Communications House Birmingham is able to take a neutral approach to communications.

The team started by building their understanding of the size of the professional trades audience and their media touch points and then by understanding their psyche – what makes them tick and, more importantly, what barriers would our communications programme need to overcome to get them to buy into the Stanley FatMax XL range.

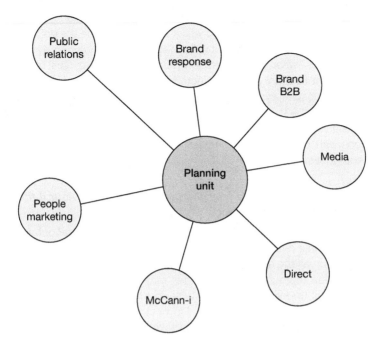

Figure 14.4 Channel specialities structure

The Pro – the primary audience

The professional tradesmen is not only difficult to reach, but because traditional media planning tools do not cover trade press, even more difficult to measure. To understand the size of the audience, National Readership Survey occupation codes were used which revealed that with 3.5 per cent of UK adults falling under these occupation codes, there was a potential target audience of around 1.7m. To understand their media touch points, the team created 'A Day in the Life of . . . ' schematic following one-on-one interviews with a cross section of professional tradesmen.

The insight – we started getting to know professional tradesmen from the 'outside in'

Getting into the world of the pro is something the team was passionate about from day one, and early focus groups defined how valuable this would prove to be.

Focus groups with professional tradesmen from different trades highlighted vital insight that would shape the programme in terms of message, creative style and tone and channel selection.

Key learnings:

- *Professional tradesmen want respect* – and they like to receive acknowledgement from their **peers** and customers for their knowledge, experience, accuracy and speed in doing a job well.
- *There's an on-site hierarchy* – younger professional tradesmen look to the more experienced and more mature professional tradesmen for guidance on what are the 'approved' tools. Turn up on site with the wrong tools and you won't be taken seriously.

- *There are unwritten 'tool rules'* – due to passed-down attitudes and default behaviours on which tools are best for the job. So whilst Stanley might be the default in tapes and knives, it is not in hammers (owned by Estwing) and levels (owned by Stabila).
- *Try before you buy* – when it comes to new products they are cynical of manufacturer's claims. They want to see/try new products for themselves before they'll believe.
- *Tool passions* – despite cynicism about manufacturer's claims – it doesn't stop them looking at new tools – looking at tool catalogues was described as 'tool porn'!
- *Barriers to Stanley* – seen to be a brand of the past, but not of the present. Still strong associations with product quality, especially in knives and tapes, but not across all product categories.

The critical intelligence – we could only change purchase behaviour if the campaign worked from the 'inside out'

One critical insight became clear: for professional tradesmen it's all about advocacy! Vital if we were to change their default tool buying behaviour and switch to Stanley's new FatMax XL range. You can run all the ads you like telling them your hammer is the best – but if the guy working alongside them doesn't use it, then they won't listen. But, they will listen to seasoned professional tradesmen that they look up to and . . . every site has these key influencers. They're the guys whose work is the best, whose opinion counts most – and who the younger professional tradesmen want to emulate. And, because of the level of passion that surrounds tools – anything new will be talked about.

Introducing 'Tooled-Up Top-Dogs'

The team called these key influencers 'Tooled-Up Top-Dogs' and knew that getting them on-side was critical to the mission to regain Stanley's credibility amongst professional tradesmen. The team needed to get inside their hearts and minds, and then get them working inside their own circle of influence on Stanley's behalf. Hence working from the 'inside out'.

The channel plan

The team recognized that creating an advocacy network needed three core components and the campaign would therefore need a channel plan for the launch of Stanley FatMax XL that mirrored this:

- advocacy sourcers (the opinion formers – our 'tooled-up top-dogs')
- advocacy seeders (those who spread the word, looking to emulate our 'Tooled-Up Top-Dogs' and engender respect and status)
- advocacy support (high profile communications activity, that gives both sourcers and seeders the confidence and justification to endorse Stanley).

They knew that advocacy sourcers – the 'Tooled-Up Top-Dogs' – have a sceptical view of advertising in isolation . . . with them it's 'don't tell me, show me'. So, to get their attention it was determined that the Stanley FatMax XL tools should be taken directly to them.

The campaign sell-out

The campaign team visited some of the UK's biggest building sites as well as professional tradesmen-only events such as Interbuild and ToolFair with an initiative called 'Judgement Day' (Photo 14.2) – where they invited professional tradesmen to trial the new Stanley FatMax XL range against leading competitors' products. This was no ordinary 'show-and-

Photo 14.2

tell' but an event with a real sense of occasion and competition designed to have a lasting impact and create the advocacy we needed.

> Judgement Day: A touring event to encourage hands-on re-discovery and advocacy of Stanley.

> A 'Wrestle-Mania' theme enabled them to run extreme tool challenges. The team encouraged bout winners to become advocates – publicly crowning them as 'Site Champions' and awarding them a 'Champions Belt' of Stanley tools to use and talk about.

Judgement Day was supported with activities that kick-started the organic trialling and seeding of Stanley FatMax XL tools: free product sample bags, discount vouchers and friend-get-friend discount vouchers for every challenge entrant; online forums where professional tradesmen could post and discover these new tool views; memento-style posters and downloads for bout winners enabling them to show off to their mates; long lasting ambient activity and ambient gifts were left on-site following our event to keep the buzz we generated front-of-mind.

It was also important to win over the trade press journalists and radio and TV presenters who have a regular dialogue with our professional tradesmen. Because they too are seen as trusted 'sourcers'. They were approached via a proactive PR campaign and invited to take part in the same Judgement Day events. They then seeded their personal experiences and endorsements of Stanley through the magazines, websites and radio stations they presented.

Photo 14.3a

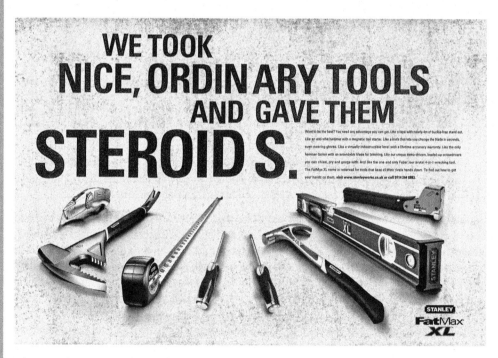

Photo 14.3b

This activity was supported by tightly targeted sport programming on multi-channel TV, sporting content in popular print titles, plus key trade titles. Research discovered that advocates need the reassurance advertising gives them, in order to support the cause they are championing. This learning was an important part of the strategy, because sourcers and seeders will only feel comfortable making a recommendation if the brand is seen to be 'credible' (in our professional tradesmen's mind, this was about being on the telly, in the press (Photo 14.3a–b) and being talked about by others who they respected).

The channel planning model – sourcing, seeding and supporting advocacy

The pre-campaign sell in

The team were mindful of the fact that the campaign would not be effective without the support of buyers within the professional tradesmen channel – and due to several years of relative neglect from Stanley they were somewhat cynical. The introduction of the FatMax XL range, designed to be sold exclusively through the professional tradesmen channel, would need to show that Stanley was committed to rebuilding its brand beyond product alone.

The approach was the same as that for 'Judgement Day' . . . the campaign had to 'show' buyers that Stanley had changed and not merely tell them – in a way that they could feel, that would get noticed and be talked about within the industry. Stanley 'XL Boot Camp' was created – a series of exclusive experiential briefings for key buyers at Stanley HQ – where key Stanley personnel talked openly and honestly about the plan to regain Stanley's territory with the professional tradesmen. Followed by hands on trials for the buyers in the XL Boot Camp tool assault course.

The effectiveness results

Advocacy and creation of advocates: post event qualitative research advocacy conversations generated

Table 14.1 illustrates the number of pros reached by Judgement Day activity. This also shows potential magnification, if WOMMA ratio is used, of 1 unit of advocacy creating 62 conversations.

Table 14.1 Creating advocates and generating conversations

Judgement day events	Total days activity	Number of pros	Number of conversations
Exeter building site	2	1,500	93,000
Bristol building site	3	1,200	74,400
Sheffield	2	1,200	74,400
Strathclyde	1	800	49,600
Newcastle	2	650	40,300
Reading	1	900	55,800
High Wycombe	2	1,350	83,700
Interbuild 2007	5	19,793	1,227,166
Interbuild 2008	5	13,120	813,440
Tool Fair (2008)	4	2,894	179,428
Total		43,407	2,691,234

PR RESULTS

Combined 2007 and 2008 estimated advertising value = £509,009
Combined circulation 2007 and 2008 = 57,381,487
Against combined 2007 and 2008 PR budget = £140,000

BRAND AWARENESS 2007–2008

Research showed that in addition to an increase in unprompted brand awareness from 53 per cent to 58 per cent, Stanley also had highest prompted awareness (from 94 per cent in 2007 to 95.5 per cent in 2008).

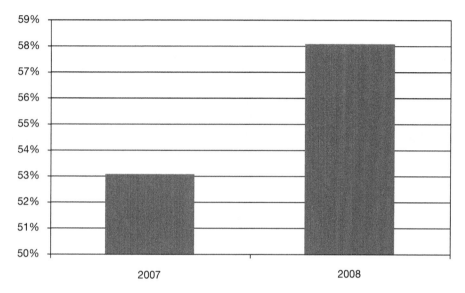

Figure 14.5 Stanley unprompted brand awareness

This statistic is supported by unprompted advertising recall of 23 per cent with the professional tradesmen audience, with 26 per cent of those stating the communications received prompted them to go and buy a Stanley product.

STANLEY WERE THE ONLY BRAND TO GROW THEIR SHARE IN THE PROFESSIONAL TRADESMEN MARKET

Stanley achieved 1.1 per cent growth in volume share of the professional tradesmen market between 2006–2007. With 'Other' and 'Pro Own Label' commoditized brands losing 1.9 per cent and other competitors, such as Irwin and Stabila maintaining – but not growing – theirs. This is certainly an achievement.

SUPERBRANDS RECOGNITION

This is the sixth year that Stanley has been awarded Superbrands status, but particularly impressive is the fact that they soared up the rankings by almost 150 places, from 403 in 2007–2008 to 255 this year – testament to the use of innovative marketing techniques.

Superbrands also gave Stanley 'special recognition' for its efforts in experiential and advocacy work.

PRO CHANNEL GROSS SALES

Thinking back to two of the campaign missions, it needed to:

- defend and protect market leadership position for knives and tapes
- attack and grow market position for levels and hammers.

Setting the benchmark – Stanley FatMax vs Stanley FatMax XL

The campaign developers have compared the launch of a knife, tape, level and hammer from the Stanley FatMax range with an equivalent knife, tape, level and hammer from the Stanley FatMax XL range. Why?

- Stanley FatMax products had minimal marketing support, with in-store literature and POS only.
- Whereas Stanley FatMax XL had an integrated budget and market support, as illustrated in this document.
- Both products, in their launch times, represented Stanley's premium offering to the professional tradesmen. They had similar comparative advantages and positioning against competitors.
- This therefore allows us to compare similar products, with and without integrated budget and marketing support.

Knives and tapes

Figure 14.6 shows the real GSV totals for knives and tapes comparing FatMax with FatMax XL. Using the FatMax figures to show sales within these two product categories where Stanley did not support products with pro engagement, this activity was then projected onto FatMax XL to predict performance without any sell-out support. The difference here is £454,555.

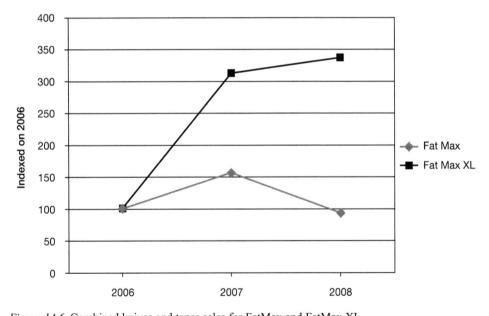

Figure 14.6 Combined knives and tapes sales for FatMax and FatMax XL

Levels and hammers

Figure 14.7 shows the real GSV totals for levels and hammers comparing FatMax with FatMax XL. Using the FatMax figures to show sales within these two product categories where Stanley did not support products with pro engagement, this activity was then projected onto FatMax XL to predict performance without any sell-out support. The difference here is £872,883.

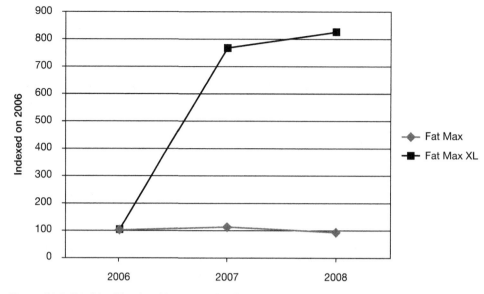

Figure 14.7 Combined level and hammer sales for FatMax and FatMax XL

Rebuilding confidence and sales through the professional tradesmen channel

A decline between 2004 and 2006 was turned around to continuous growth between 2006 and 2008 with campaign activities to rebuild confidence and sales within the professional tradesmen channel, starting with 'Stanley XL BootCamp' as detailed earlier in this document.

Return on marketing investment (ROMI)

Incremental Stanley FatMax XL sales margin – marginal contribution

This has been calculated by taking an average of profit in months where there was no activity and using this as a base, the team then took the profit in months that were supported by FatMax XL activity and took the difference to calculate the incremental profit (marginal contribution).

Based on that and the corresponding spend, using the ROMI calculation provided by Les Binet, European Director DDB Matrix.

Net profit generated = marginal contribution (£332,104.50) – cost of campaign (£196,700)

Net profit = £135,404.50

ROMI = (net profit £135,404.50/cost of campaign £196,700) × 100

ROMI for 2007–2008 = 68.94 per cent

Summary

Uncovering the insight that led to the 'inside-out' strategy was both exciting and quite daunting for the team. How exactly did you source advocates and ensure that they not only talked to others but talked in a positive way? They found an absence of previous models

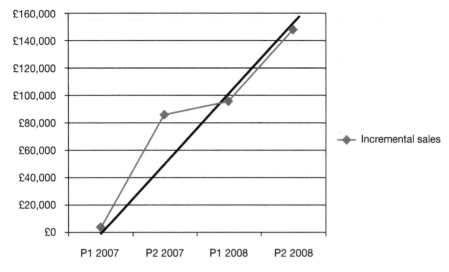

Figure 14.8 Incremental profit (marginal contribution) over the campaign key periods

to help and therefore built this campaign through listening, learning and understanding the behaviours of the professional trades. In essence, this insight directed the structure of the channel plan and the messaging and tonality of the campaign.

The fact that the campaign stimulated 2.7 million endorsement conversations amongst professional tradesmen, achieved ROMI of 69 per cent and became the only hand tool brand to increase its market share in a static category is testament to the success of the campaign.

Through this case, the team has shown how they created a strong model for building a campaign around advocacy, one that they have learnt from and will continue to build for Stanley in the future.

The success of the launch of Stanley FatMax XL through the 'Judgement Day' initiative was summed up by Jeff Ansell, Global CEO and President for Commercialization, Stanley Tools:

> Without doubt, this has been the best launch that Stanley has ever pulled together – globally

and . . . Scott Bannell, Director Corporate Brand Marketing, Stanley Tools:

> We brag about your work all the time amongst the global managers. Sales have been the best in years.

CASE STUDY QUESTIONS

1. Critique the case study. What factors do you believe were central to the campaign's success?
2. What specific challenges did on-site hierarchy of trades people approval of tools present?
3. Given that there are small but increasing numbers of females entering trade areas that have been traditionally male dominated in the past, what impact do you believe that the 'Judgement Day' events would have had on female trades people? What do you recommend be done in the future to target females?

4. Drawing on the discussion of publicity and media relations in the chapter, what role do you believe the trade press played in the campaign success?
5. Had the trade press not been prepared to endorse the campaign, what impact might this have had on the campaign's success?
6. How would you expect competitors to react to the campaign and what would you advise Stanley to do in anticipation of competitor activity?
7. How would you advise Stanley to track satisfaction with product quality and performance and to react to any possible problems encountered? Justify your response.

Notes

1   Grunig, J.E., and Grunig, L.A. (1998). The relationship between public relations and marketing in excellent organizations: evidence from the IABC study. *Journal of Marketing Communications*, 4, 131–62.
2   De Pelsmacker, P., Geuens, M., and Van den Bergh, J. (2001). *Marketing Communications*, Harlow: Pearson Education.
3   Shimp, T.E. (2003). *Advertising, Promotion and Supplemental Aspects of IMC*, 6th edition, Independence, KY: Thompson South-Western.
4   Oliver, S. (2001). *Public Relations Strategy*, London, England: Institute of Public Relations.
5   *Fortune* (2003). James Burke acted before crisis hit. 138(3), 11 August, 69.
6   Pearson, C.M. and Clair, J.A. (1998). Reframing crisis management. *Academy of Management Review*, 23(1), 59–76.
7   Govindaraj, S., and Jaggi, B. (2004). Market overreaction to product recall revisited – the case of firestone tires and the ford explorer. *Review of Quantitative Finance & Accounting*, 23(1), 31–54.
8   O'Rourke, J. (2001). Bridgestone/Firestone, Inc. and Ford Motor Company: how a product safety crisis ended a hundred-year relationship. *Corporate Reputation Review*, 4(3), 255.
9   BBC News (2005). Bridgestone Ends Ford Recall Row, BBC News. Online. Available HTTP: <http://news.bbc.co.uk/1/hi/business/4335324.stm>.
10   Jarrell, G., and Peltzman, S. (1985). The impact of product recalls on the wealth of sellers. *Journal of Political Economy*, 93(3), 512–36.
11   Kwon, B. (2000). When bad things happen to good companies. *FSB: Fortune Small Business*, 10(8: November), 104–7.
12   Siomkos, G.J., and Kurzbard, G. (1994). The hidden crisis in product-harm crisis management. *European Journal of Marketing*, 28(2), 30–41.
13   Dawar, N., and Pillutla, M.M. (2000). Impact of product-harm crises on brand equity: the moderating role of consumer expectations. *Journal of Marketing Research (JMR)*, 37(2), 215–26.
14   Kabak, I.W., and Siomkos, G.J. (1992). Monitoring recovery of a product harm crisis. *Industrial Management*, 34(3), 11–12.
15   Glaesser, D. (2006). *Crisis Management in the Tourism Industry*, Oxford: Butterworth-Heinemann.
16   Kitchen, P.J. (1993). Public relations: a rationale for its development and usage within UK fast-moving consumer goods firms. *European Journal of Marketing*, 27(7), 53–75.
17   Sosa, M.E., Eppinger, S.D., and Rowles, C.M. (2007). Are your engineers talking to one another when they should? *Harvard Business Review*, 85(11), 133–42.
18   BBC News (2010). Q&A: Toyota Recalls. Online. Available HTTP: <http://news.bbc.co.uk/1/hi/business/8496902.stm>.
19   BBC News (2010). Toyota Suspends Sales of Lexus GX 460 Worldwide. Online. Available HTTP: <http://newsvote.bbc.co.uk/mpapps/pagetools/print/news.bbc.co.uk/1/hi/business/8621402.stm?ad=1>.
20   Hon, L.C. (1997). What have you done for me lately? Exploring effectiveness in public relations. *Journal of Public Relations Research*, 9(1), 1–30.

21 Eagle, L. and Brennan, R. (2007). Beyond advertising: in-home promotion of 'fast food'. *Young Consumers*, 8(4), 278–88.

22 Public Administration Select Committee (2009). *Lobbying: Access and influence in Whitehall*, London: House of Commons.

23 Bristow, M. (2008). China's Internet 'Spin Doctors'. BBC News. Online. Available HTTP: <http://news.bbc.co.uk/1/hi/world/asia-pacific/7783640.stm> (accessed 4 January 2009).

24 Forest FAQ: Who Funds Us? Online. Available HTTP: <http://forestonline.org/output/faqs-1-2.aspx> (accessed 4 January 2009).

25 BBC News Online (2002). Spin Memo Row Duo Quit. Online. Available HTTP: <http://news.bbc.co.uk/1/hi/uk_politics/1823120.stm> (accessed 4 January 2009).

15 Integrated campaign development

Personal selling and sales management, retail key account liaison, exhibitions and shows

LEARNING OUTCOMES

After studying this chapter, you will be able to:

- Describe the role of personal selling within the marketing communication mix

- Analyse the specific challenges selling and sales management face across a range of sales sectors, including large retail organizations and the business-to-business sector

- Debate the strengths and weaknesses of key account management

- Analyse the sales support function of in-store merchandisers

- Analyse the role of exhibitions and shows in sales support

Introduction

This chapter brings together a number of disparate 'threads' that need to be considered in planning both strategic and tactical marketing communications activity. While many of the functions described here are not regarded as mainstream marketing communications, they play a significant role in contact between an organization and the purchaser and/or end user of products and services. They therefore can provide reinforcement of key messages sent via traditional media, new electronic media or other marketing communications activity.

What comes to mind when you think of a sales situation? Your ideal may be a sales person who:

* is knowledgeable about the products or services on offer
* is prepared to listen to your ideas and specific preferences
* is able to recommend product or service options that are most likely to meet your needs
* does not try to force a decision on you
* you would be happy to contact again in the future.

However, the reality may be, based on your own personal encounters, more like the following:

* someone who appears to have very little knowledge about, or interest in, product or service options, features or benefits
* someone who has no interest in finding out what your preferences are
* someone who just wants to sell you something as quickly as possible.

The 'ideal' is an example of a relationship-based sales encounter, the latter situation an example of transaction-based sales. In transaction-based sales situation, the emphasis is on completing a specific transaction with no consideration of the implications for future sales opportunities.[1] You have probably encountered both types of situations – and possibly also have encountered good service, knowledgeable staff at a retail outlet on one occasion but at a later visit to the outlet find that the staff have changed and the service no longer as good as in the past.

A bad encounter at a retail outlet or via phone, Internet or email contact may lead to negative perceptions about the organization and the brands on offer, coupled with an increased likelihood of considering other brands or outlets. This may be particularly important when other promotional activity such as advertising and sales promotions promise much

THINK BOX

Shopping experience

Reflect back on recent purchases you have made.

* When did a sales person really impress you and why?
* When have sales staff irritated you or left you feeling disappointed with your purchase?
* What lessons might be learned from this?

– but there is a failure to live up to expectations at the final sales point. From the perspective of the brand itself, this may impact on brand equity – and on consumer loyalty.[2] However, in spite of the obvious importance of the **personal selling** (i.e. a direct contact sales encounter), often the actual face-to-face encounter between a potential customer and a salesperson is outside the control of the Brand Manager or the sales manager.

Personal selling/sales management

Sales and **sales management** are often neglected in strategic planning, resulting in the link between marketing communication and sales being seen as an afterthought,[3] potentially hindering synergies and, at the extreme, resulting in reluctance by sales staff to actively use marketing communications material that has been created without their input. Conversely, sales-created material may be viewed by marketing communications staff as not reflecting the desired image of products or services.[4] There is, however, considerable evidence that integration of sales and advertising activity not only provides motivation for the sales staff in knowing that their efforts are supported, but also have been shown to help make their own selling activity more productive.[5,6,7]

This raises another often-neglected area – internal marketing or communicating with sale within an organization whose activities may in any way impact on sales. There has long been evidence of the positive impact of effective and timely internal marketing on the implementation and integration of marketing communications activity.[8] Conversely, failure to consult and inform staff and to gain their support for marketing communication strategies and tactics may hamper support for the activity, possibly resulting in negative publicity if activity does not occur efficiently, such as dealing with product queries or complaints.[9]

What makes a good sales person has been debated for decades[10] without a single 'formula' being decided. Generally, a sound knowledge of the products or services being sold is essential. Obviously, in retail situations such as supermarket checkouts, sales training and product knowledge expectations will be limited. Contrast this with sales staff working in stores selling expensive electronic equipment – product knowledge and the ability to demonstrate product operations and key features will be important and regular training will be needed as new models are introduced. Those working in complex areas such as business-to-business, pharmaceuticals etc. may need extensive training in the product range they are selling.

THINK BOX

Sales staff training

What type of educational background, experience and training would you expect for the following sales staff?

- A sales representative for a pharmaceutical company who calls mainly on general practitioners or veterinary surgeons.
- A sales representative working for a company that makes customized electronic components for aircraft.
- A sales representative working for an electronics retailer when there has been a major technological change in the industry.

THINK BOX

Sales person's behaviour

Consider how a sales person's behaviour may change in their dealings with customers and the ethical issues that might arise from different forms of payments.

- How might unethical behaviour impact on brand image or brand equity?
- Would their behaviour change if customers were made aware of the basis for their remuneration?
- What should marketers do to ensure that ethical issues do not arise?

Sales representatives or sales staff will be trained in sales techniques and methods of planning sales strategies and will be familiarized with marketing communication activity planned for the products in order to be able to respond to queries. Additionally, sales staff should be trained in dealing with complaints, but this may be a separate function in large companies.

Depending on the nature of the sales situation, some knowledge of the customer and their needs may be important. Each sales person in non-retail environments will generally be allocated a territory – a geographical area or a specific number of current or potential customers who are to be the focus of their activity.

A key decision in motivating and managing sales staff is remuneration or 'compensation'. Sales staff in many retail environments are simply paid wages or salary, with little recognition of relative performance. For sales representatives where greater complexity and levels of sophistication are needed, different forms of remuneration may be considered. These may include any of the following, or combinations of these:

- Incentives (monetary or other forms of reward such as travel or products) to reach specific sales targets.
- Bonuses for exceeding sales targets (paid either to individuals or paid as a collective reward for overall sales results).
- A base salary which is then added to according to the level of sales achieved.
- Payment made purely on the basis of commission for each successful sale completed.

The advent of increasingly sophisticated electronic **sales force automation (SFA)** packages in which products or services are evaluated online and orders placed with minimal (if any) contact with actual sales staff has also changed the role of sales staff and methods of developing and maintaining positive relationships with their customers. There is evidence that SFA adoption does improve sales staff performance;[11] the impact on long-term job satisfaction is not known.

Various forms of sales force control and measurement scales have been developed and tested but tend to show inconsistent results across studies.[12] While some of the variation in findings has been due to the use of differing measurement scales and techniques, hindering comparability across studies, some of the variation is also due to the selling function taking many forms, only some of which are under the direct control of the organization producing the products or services, such as a sales force responsible for liaising with retail outlets or clients who incorporate components or ingredients into their own products.

MINI CASE: DIFFERENT SKILLS FOR DIFFERENT SITUATIONS

Consider the sales force used by Coca-Cola versus a manufacturer of industrial goods. Also visit the websites of companies in different categories to look at the sales support and product/service information offered to retailers and end customers.

- What are the differences in knowledge and skills expected of members of a sales force for a company such as Coca-Cola and an industrial (business-to-business) company?
- How do their likely customer expectations of the sales force differ?
- How would you expect representatives from the two types of organization to be rewarded for sales activity?

Where a **manufacturer**'s products are provided to a **wholesaler** who then on-sells them to retailers, the manufacturer loses control of the relationship with the retailer[13] and may be dependent on the wholesaler's sales force to represent the products in the way the manufacturer would prefer – but cannot enforce. However, remember that behind every visible sales person, there are a large number of sales people who have been instrumental in getting the range of products in store. For every product seen in a retail store, a sales team (unseen to the general public) will have dealt with either the individual retail outlet or via a central purchasing office for an entire retail chain to negotiate the initial stocking of the products, to arrange for replenishment of stocks as necessary and to deal with product returns.

Where a manufacturer's products are sold via a retailer, such as in the fast moving consumer goods (FMCG) sector, such as in supermarkets, pharmacies, bookstores etc., the manufacturer has little influence over the way the products are presented to the eventual purchaser. The next time you are in a supermarket, observe any requests for product information or advice from the supermarket staff. With a huge range of products in any one store, retail staff cannot acquire more than a basic level of knowledge about any product.

Different levels of expertise can be expected for other forms of retail sales. Think about the level of product knowledge a potential purchaser might expect from a bookshop, a pharmacy or a mobile phone retailer. In business-to-business sales, considerable expertise and customer knowledge should be expected of sales staff as the emphasis is very much on building and maintaining long-term relationships as the marketing mix will generally de-emphasize advertising and rely more heavily on personal selling as a key ingredient in the overall marketing communications mix.[14]

THINK BOX

Adding value

Assume you are giving advice to a local independent bookshop who has just found out that a major national bookstore chain is about to open a shop nearby. Your client is worried about retaining customers as the buying power of the national chain will enable them to undercut the local independent stores' retail prices.

You have been asked whether adding value by enhanced customer service is a viable option. What do you advise?

It is not unreasonable to expect some staff in bookshops, usually full time experienced staff, to be familiar with the majority of the frequently purchased items. Even when staff members are part time, familiarity should be expected with electronic databases to check for stock availability and/or to order specific items not in stock.

For retailers such as pharmacies, different levels of training are provided to staff involved in sales of medication versus cosmetics and toiletries and staff may be trained both as part of their overall job requirements and/or certification or registration, but also by the major companies whose brands are sold in store. Staff training can therefore be the responsibility of several different people or organizations, often with quite different priorities. However, in some areas, such as fast moving consumer goods (FMCG) sold via major supermarkets and food stores, training is likely to be much more limited. However, as we will show in the next section, the influence of the retailer may be far stronger.

MINI CASE: FASHION SHOWS – CHALLENGES AND OPPORTUNITIES

Fashion shows are extremely popular, but the show itself is rarely the sole activity. Involvement in a 'catwalk' show may be part of a much wider integrated promotion including extensive publicity, media coverage, special editions of magazines and sometimes specially themed television programmes. On site at the shows, a company may have sales staff demonstrating products, giving away free samples or gathering sales leads to be followed up at a later date.

Fashion shows are also invariably controversial, not just for the new fashions featured, but also for brands themselves. Two main issues may arise. Firstly, a brand may manufacturer in countries with poor labour records, leading to allegations of 'sweatshops' and massive profits being made because of underpaid labour (see the protest website www.nosweat. org.uk/).

Secondly, the entire industry frequently comes in for criticism for the use of 'skinny'/'underweight'/'size zero' models. Note: size zero is an American term – a UK size 8 is a size 4 in the US). This issue became very high profile after the death of a young model.[15]

A part of this debate is the accusation that the fashion industry promotes unrealistic body images which are unachievable for the majority of the population. Most clothes are modelled by UK size 8 models, whereas the average woman is a size 14. Some fashion shows have banned the use of underweight models, but others refuse to do so. Some non-fashion brands have ignored the controversy and used fashion shows to raise awareness and generate trial of their products among trendsetters. For example, McDonalds organized a sales promotion around the 2009 Mercedes-Benz Fashion Week in New York.[16] The latter organization sponsors a number of high profile fashion shows around the world. While their involvement is primarily related to image promotion, displaying their cars and generating possible sales leads is also important.

1. Do you believe that the fashion industry has a responsibility to ensure underweight models are not used? Why or why not?
2. If the average woman is a UK size 14, why are size 14 models not routinely used for fashion shows?
3. Why do brands as diverse as McDonalds and Mercedes-Benz associate themselves with fashion events?

4. How should these organizations respond to criticisms of involvement in events such as this?
5. How should they measure the impact of their involvement on brand image and on sales?

Retailer dominance

The shift in the balance of power between manufacturers and retailers, particularly within the supermarket sector, is well documented in the literature.[17,18] Through a combination of customer loyalty schemes and electronic data systems, retailers are able to access more detailed and sophisticated customer purchasing profile data than is obtained by manufacturers themselves,[19,20,21] thus allowing retailers to make strategic decisions regarding the optimum composition of a particular category. Such decisions include, increasingly, decisions regarding retailer house brands.

As noted earlier, in the UK, as in many other countries, a small number of major organizations control the bulk of grocery retailing. Review the latest statistics regarding the size and power of retailers such as Tesco, Boots and other large retail chains. What are the positive and negative implications of retailer power for customers?

Now think about the implications for marketing communication activity – and for sales-related activity in particular – for a relatively small manufacturer whose major sales volume comes from the supermarket sector. What level of control are they likely to have over the way a product is positioned or priced relative to competitors? What is the impact of this on marketing communications activity aimed at positioning a manufacturer's brand with a desired image?

The role of retailers in developing and maintaining a brand's image or consumer-based brand equity is under-researched. It is retailers who, through the provision of the environment in which a brand is displayed and through their own pricing and promotional strategies, have the ability to enhance or detract from the manufacturer's own promotional efforts.[20] Small amounts of research relating to store image and perceived personality have been conducted,[22] however the interaction between store equity, i.e. customer-based brand equity relating to a retail outlet or chain as opposed to the individual brands that organization may carry, and manufacturer brand equity has not been studied in detail.

Additional complexity is provided by the growth in retailer house brands and by retailer co-branding or identification of the source of ingredients for their house brands.[23] While a manufacturer may desire that their brands are given priority, they cannot expect that staff within the grocery retail environment will share this view, particularly in view of the increased number of products sold under retailer's own branding (house brands).

Growth of retailer house brands

As noted in earlier chapters, retailer influence impacts on all areas of marketing communication. We focus here specifically on the impact of retailer power on manufacturer sales force activity. Remember that house brands are presented alongside retailer-branded products and effectively compete with them for shelf space and customers, presenting a number of challenges to manufacturer sales activity. Given that house brands are significant contributors to overall retail sales and are often brand leaders in some product categories,[24] their importance as brand competitors cannot be ignored.

House brands raise the level of competition within a category, with the possible outcome being more intense price competition,[25] particularly when the store brand is positioned close to leading manufacturer brands. There is evidence that a store brand can shield manufacturer brands from direct price competition from other brands.[26] A more negative perspective suggests that house brands reduce loyalty towards manufacturer brands, potentially reducing competition within the product category if manufacturer brands are withdrawn and thus ultimately negatively impacting on consumer choice – and possibly also driving up prices.[27] Furthermore, it is suggested that retailers deliberately advertise national brands to attract customers – but then provide preferential shelf placement to house brands in order to attract price-sensitive shoppers;[28,29] it is not clear whether there is evidence to generalize this claim across all product categories.

Why then would a manufacturer enter into an agreement to sell its products to a large retailer to be sold under the retailer's own brand? The reality is often that, if one manufacturer does not provide the product, its main competitors may very well do so, potentially jeopardizing their own long-term access to sales via the retailer. Even with some cannibalization of a manufacturer-brand's sales by a house brand which is produced by the affected manufacturer, the additional sales generated by such a de-facto brand extension may make the combination of the two profitable, thus it may make economic sense for a manufacturer to produce a retailer's house brand to compete against its own brands.[30]

THINK BOX

Key account management

You have reviewed the last two quarters sales figures and there has been a marked drop in sales for one particular retail chain. Your sales staff report no problems.

- What possible causes might there be for the sales decline and how should you investigate?
- If your investigation indicates that there is a clash of personality between the retail chain's buyer and your key account manager assigned to the chain, but the problems appear to emanate from the retailer, what courses of action are open to you?
- If your investigation indicates that there has been an apparent deterioration in the amount of shelf space given to your products compared to a major competitor, what courses of action are open to you?
- If house brands appear to be receiving preferential shelf space or are being offered at a significantly lower price than all other manufacturer brands in the category, what courses of action are open to you?

Key account management

As noted earlier, sales within the business-to-business sector usually require sales representatives who are knowledgeable about their own offerings and the specific current and likely future needs of their clients. Even within end-consumer oriented sales situations, some large customer organizations will exist that are extremely important to manufacturers. Generally, experienced sales staff will be assigned to a small number of these key accounts, working closely with the retailer staff to ensure that the retailer's requirements are met, including joint sales promotional activity, pricing agreements etc., and that ongoing relationships between manufacturer and retailer remain profitable for both parties,[31] often drawing on the support of other staff within the manufacturer's own organization to support activity in stores.

Role of in-store merchandisers

A key sales support role is that of in-store **merchandisers** who ensure that point of sales material is correctly displayed and the product is presented as negotiated in terms of location in store and shelf position, together with the number of units on shelves at any one time,[32,33,34] and ensuring that products are never out of stock. Sales volume increases of more than 400 per cent have been attributed to effective merchandizing[35] and eye-level displays positively impact on unplanned purchases.[31] Out-of-stock situations and product proliferation may lead to product substitution, reducing brand loyalty and the chance of future sales.[36]

Internet sales

The amount of sales made over the Internet continues to grow, however often Internet-based sales operate alongside traditional retail ('bricks and mortar') outlets. This may be

THINK BOX

Start-ups

Previous chapters have discussed aspects of the Internet as a marketing tool. How would you advise a new start-up company to assess the various options available to market their goods? What implications are there in terms of sales force and supporting staff?

Visit the Internet and do a search for organizations across a range of categories. What types of organizations rely solely on the Internet rather than selling products or services via retail outlets, catalogues and other means? Why do you believe they have made their decisions?

a deliberate choice, or a strategic necessity in order to counter competitor's activity.[37] Remember that it is now possible to order groceries and many other items online and have them delivered to your home without actually setting foot in an actual store (see the earlier discussion re sales force automation).

How potential customers use Internet sites to search for products and services varies enormously, however it is obviously in the interests of the manufacturer or retailer to ensure that Internet and traditional retail outlet activity is integrated, particularly when customers may search for information on the Internet and then contact manufacturers or visit retail stores armed with information not only about their own products but also competitors' offerings as well.[38] Even for Internet-based sales, there is a need for the sales support staff to be knowledgeable about the offerings and to be able to deal effectively and efficiently with customer queries – and complaints.

Exhibitions and shows

This is a very diverse category of sales-linked activity. Exhibitions have a long history, originating in Roman times.[39] They may focus on narrow or broad areas, such as bridal shows, home furnishings, agricultural shows, outdoor activities, and a range of food and wine shows, to name just a few. They may be aimed at the general public, members of the trade or both.

The objective for visitors is to be able to view, sample, try out or discuss whichever of the featured range of products and services interests them. From the exhibitors' perspectives, direct sales may be an objective, or the generation of sales leads to be followed up by members of the sales force after the event. Sales leads may be passed on to a specific retailer to follow up.

Organizers of these events, and the companies sponsoring them, or having some involvement as exhibitors, may run advertising to raise awareness of, and interest in, the event. They will also try to maximize PR and publicity opportunities, including activities such as celebrity appearances, or sweepstakes and prizes for those visiting particular displays. Key customers and/or retailers may receive special invitations to attend, usually at special times when hospitality will be provided and senior company management will be present.

Exhibitions and shows are thus closely linked with overall sales management, public relations and sales promotional activity. They can be extremely useful for introducing new products or new models, particularly when demonstrating features or giving potential customers the chance to 'try before they buy' – such as somewhat daunting new electronic products.

MINI CASE: STANLEY TOOLS REVISITED

Revisit the Stanley Tools case study at the end of the previous chapter. Examine in particular the use of exhibitions as a part of an integrated campaign.

1. What role do you believe exhibitions at events such as Interbuild and ToolFair played in the campaign's success? Critique their ROI measurement for this activity.
2. How would you assess what other exhibitions or fairs might be effective for professional trades people and also for the DIY sector?
3. Use the Internet to research forthcoming events and evaluate their potential suitability for Stanley Tools. Justify your selection.
4. What type of exhibition (product demonstration/video demonstrations etc.) or promotional activity would you recommend be undertaken at each of these events and why?
5. Now contrast the decision processes that would be undertaken by potential exhibitors and the type of activity that might be undertaken by them at exhibitions for:
    a. travel
    b. cars
    c. electronic goods
    d. gardening (consider events such as the Chelsea Flower Show – see the following link: www.rhs.org.uk/Shows-Events/).
6. How would you measure return on investment of each of these types of activity?

Summary

The activities discussed in this chapter rarely occur in isolation, but function as part of integrated marketing activity. Sales and sales management activity is often not considered as part of mainstream marketing communication activity, but they are an essential component of integrated campaigns and a key area of interface between marketers and their customers. Large retail organizations offer both challenges and opportunities to manufacturers in terms of product stocking and presentation decisions, as does the Internet and exhibitions and show events. These latter activities rely heavily on sales force and sales promotional activity as an integral part of involvement.

Review questions

1. A manufacturer of a range of electronic products receives a complaint from a customer who has purchased a product from a retail store and who now wishes to complain that the product does not have the features the sales person promised. On checking, you find that the specific product does not have these features and that the model of the product that does have the features is more expensive. What do you do?
2. You have been alerted to several situations where your leading brands appear to have been out of stock in major retail outlets for several days.
    a. What might have happened and what can be done to rectify the situation?
    b. What are the implications for the brand if the situation is not resolved?

3. You are half way through a major sales promotion programme that involves mass media advertising and retail-based sales promotional activity based on a sweepstake. You become aware that your major competitor has reduced their pricing substantially. What action should you take?

4. One of your major retail clients complains that the new key account manager assigned to them is not sufficiently knowledgeable and asks for them to be replaced. What action should you take?

5. A customer who has attempted to make a purchase via your website complains that the site does not provide sufficient information and, when they emailed the sales support section, no response was received. What action should you take?

6. You are planning the marketing communication programme for the next financial year. Outline a strategy for ensuring that your marketing communication specialists and your sales management team work together to develop integrated programmes. How would you measure the success of your strategy?

7. Outline a strategy for a manufacturer to evaluate the knowledge and enthusiasm of retail sales staff for the manufacturer's products.

8. Consider the following scenario:

   You are the Brand Manager of a market-leading brand of breakfast cereal. One of your clients, a major supermarket chain, has asked you to produce a 'look-alike' house brand to be sold through their outlets.

   What would be the consequences (both positive and negative) of agreeing to this request? What would be the consequences of refusing it?

9. 'The advent of the Internet has made the practice of personal selling obsolete'. Discuss this statement and use examples to illustrate any points that you make.

10. For a product or service of your choice, discuss the extent to which the use of personal selling techniques might be perceived to add value to a brand. Are there any products or services for which personal selling techniques might be unsuitable?

Recommended reading

Anderson R. (1995). *Essentials of Personal Selling*, London: Prentice Hall.

Anderson, R., and Dubinsky, A.J. (2006). *Personal Selling*, 2nd edition, London: Houghton Mifflin.

Smith, T.M., Gopalakrishna, S., and Smith, P.M. (2004). The complementary effect of trade shows on personal selling. *International Journal of Research in Marketing*, March, 21f(1), 61–77.

CASE STUDY 15.1

Hiho Silver

Source: Design Business Association: Bronze, Design Effectiveness Awards, 2009. The case has been condensed from 'Hiho – Corporate/ Brand Identity'. Case material provided by the World Advertising Research Centre (WARC) www.warc.com.

This case study illustrates what can be achieved to support small retail chains through revitalizing the retail environment itself and focusses on some of the the specific challenges faced by small retailers. It is somewhat unusual in that mainstream advertising was not used, however exhibitions and shows were an integral marketing communications tool.

Executive summary

Let's face it: retail is not exactly the category anyone is clamouring to get behind at the moment. The figures are grim – almost continuous negative like-for-like sales growth in the past year.

This case study illustrates how Hiho, a family owned jewellery, giftware and home-ware retailer, is bucking that trend, thanks to its new identity. Hiho recognized that to sustain retail and show sales growth amidst some of the worst trading conditions this country has seen in a generation, it needed to invest in a strong positioning and a powerful brand identity.

Five months later, with one shop refit and a new show stand at two events, the results speak for themselves:

- 21.4 per cent like-for-like sales increase for first refitted shop
- entire retail estate like-for-likes up 2.7 per cent since the brand re-launch in a retail market that is declining by 1.6 per cent
- refitted shop doubles overall estate like-for-likes
- 11 per cent like-for-like growth at refitted shop versus spiraling declines at competitors H. Samuel and Ernest Jones
- first refitted shop outperforms the rest of the Hiho estate by 20 per cent
- best ever sales at shows and events with up to 31 per cent like-for-like uplift
- return on design investment in just five months.

These results are all the more significant because four months prior to the first shop refit like-for-like sales of that shop were down 0.8 per cent, while the rest of the estate was up 11.5 per cent. The first refit's success means that at a time when many retailers are stream-lining and cutting back on investments, Hiho is now fast-tracking all its stores to the new look and feel by the end of 2009.

And all this, with virtually no other influencing factors.

Project overview

Outline of project brief

Hiho Silver, retail silver jewellery specialist, had introduced many new lines and extended their range into giftware and houseware products so the name and brand identity no longer fully represented who they were and what they were doing to existing and new customers.

They came to Blue Marlin Brand Design for a full review of their positioning, name, brand identity and look and feel to:

- increase sales in their retail shops
- increase sales at shows and events.

Description

Hiho Silver, based in Somerset, consists of 14 retail units, a stand presence at shows and events across the UK, and a web shop. They source and design beautiful, unique silver jewellery, gifts and housewares.

Formed in 1995 as a partnership by brother and sister Andrew and Caroline Ransford, it has maintained a steady growth curve. Initially the business retailed at UK shows and events. It developed a loyal customer base, but in 2001 its schedule was affected by the first foot-and-mouth outbreak, leading to the cancellation of many key shows. That was when they started opening shops. The first shop's success in Lyme Regis led to expansion into high streets in South Somerset, and later nationwide. A transactional website (www. hihosilver.co.uk) launched in May 2007.

The directors of the business have been working on a two-year strategic growth plan since 2007, yielding 49 per cent growth in the first year. By 2008, customer and employee research showed that the Hiho Silver brand had become disparate and confusing. In order to continue growing, Hiho Silver decided to redefine its brand positioning, name (now Hiho), identity, and look and feel.

Overview of market

Hiho's success since the rebrand is all the more telling given the current state of the UK retail market which is seeing some of the most challenging conditions in its history. In April 2009 the British Retail Consortium (BRC) director general said retail sales from June 2008 – March 2009 had reported negative like-for-like sales growth in 9 of those 10 months (Source: brc.org.uk).

In the jewellery sector, like-for-like sales at Signet, which trades as H. Samuel and Ernest Jones in the UK, spiralled in its fourth quarter, with sales falling 9.2 per cent in the 13 weeks to 31 January 2009. Like-for-like sales dropped 7.8 per cent at H. Samuel and 11 per cent at Ernest Jones in the same period (Source: retail-jeweller.com).

More locally, Hiho has anecdotal evidence that over the two quarters since its Sherborne shop was refitted, nearby High Street retailers have seen a fall in trade (Source: local Sherborne High Street shop owners).

Project launch date

The new brand launched at Hiho's Sherborne shop in November 2008, with a redesigned show stand appearing at Cheltenham Racing Festival and Badminton Horse Trials in Spring 2009.

Sherborne's success means Hiho is fast-tracking all its stores to the new look and feel by the end of 2009. Additional shops were refitted in April 2009, with more underway. The redesigned website with the new look and feel launched 7 May 2009.

Size of design budget

< £50,000 design fees paid to Blue Marlin.

Outline of design solution

Blue Marlin Brand Design helped the directors encapsulate the brand vision for the company as an 'English, Eclectic and Eccentric' retailer of jewellery, gifts and homeware. This brand vision is now the driving force for everything Hiho says and does, from employee training through to marketing communications.

Blue Marlin's work also included a name change to Hiho, a new identity and brand look and feel. As Hiho has limited funds for implementation, it was also important that Blue Marlin provided a kit of parts and guidelines for the identity and look and feel, allowing Hiho to implement the identity itself in a cost and time efficient way.

The identity captures all that is 'English, Eclectic and Eccentric'. It echoes Hiho's aspiration to be the only stylish, contemporary and accessible jewellery retailer that places uniqueness at the heart of everything it does.

Summary of results

Increase in sales

Sales: retail – 21.3 per cent like-for-like sales increase versus 1.6 per cent decline in retail market

Hiho's Sherborne shop relaunched November 2008. In an overall UK retail market that has seen like-for-like declining sales of 1.6 per cent from November 2008 – March 2009, Hiho's Sherborne shop has significantly bucked this downward trend with a like-for-like sales rise of an astonishing 21.4 per cent. This is almost solely due to a significant increase in the number of customers as the amount spent per customer has not risen.

Not only this, but Hiho's entire estate, including Sherborne, is up 2.7 per cent like-for-like since the brand relaunch, compared to a declining retail market of 1.6 per cent (see Table 15.1).

Table 15.1 Hiho Sherborne like-for-like versus retail market

	UK retail market like-for-like %	Hiho Sherborne like-for-like %	Entire Hiho Estate like-for-like %
Nov 2008	–2.6	–5.6	–2.3
Dec 2008	–3.3	+16.2	–5.9
Jan 2009	+1.1	+22.4	–7.3
Feb 2009	–1.8	+49.8	+19.5
Mar 2009	–1.2	+24.3	+9.3
5 month average	–1.6	+21.4	+2.7

Source: British Retail Consortium-KPMG Retail Sales Monitor and Hiho internal sales data.

Beating the competition: 11 per cent like-for-like growth versus declines for H. Samuel and Ernest Jones

Not only is Hiho bucking the overall retail market, the Sherborne shop saw 11 per cent like-for-like sales growth in the 13 weeks to 31 January 2009 versus spiraling drops for High Street jewellery chain powerhouses H. Samuel (–7.8 per cent) and Ernest Jones (–11 per cent).

Hiho Sherborne is significantly outperforming the rest of its retail estate by 20 per cent. In the five months post refit, like-for-like sales were up 21.4 per cent compared to the rest of the estate which was up 1.3 per cent (Table 15.2). Sherborne's success was responsible for doubling the entire estate's like-for-like sales from 1.3 per cent to 2.7 per cent since relaunch.

These results are all the more significant because in the four months prior to Sherborne's refit, like-for-like sales of that shop were down 0.8 per cent, while the rest of the estate was up 11.5 per cent. While it's true that Sherborne was closed for one week in October for the refit, the shop was still underperforming against the rest of the estate in the three weeks that it was trading in October.

Hiho has also totally rebranded its shows stand, with record-breaking results in its first two shows with the new stand:

* Best ever sales achieved in 10 years of trading at Cheltenham Racing Festival, up 31 per cent like-for-like over 2008 (Source: Hiho internal sales data).
* Best ever sales achieved at Badminton Horse Trials, up 20 per cent like-for-like over 2008 (Source: Hiho internal sales data).

Table 15.2 Hiho Sherborne like-for-like versus the rest of the estate pre and post relaunch

	Hiho Sherborne like-for-like %	Hiho total estate like-for-like (excl. Sherborne) %	Hiho total estate like-for-like (incl. Sherborne) %
Prior to Sherborne launch			
Jul 2008	+12.2	+14.5	+14.3
Aug 2008	+3.7	+13.7	+12.9
Sep 2008	+0.7	−1.4	−1.3
Oct 2008	−19.6	+19.5	+16.2
4 month average	−0.8	+11.5	+10.5
Post Sherborne relaunch			
Nov 2008	−5.6	−2.0	−2.3
Dec 2008	+16.2	−7.5	−5.9
Jan 2009	+22.5	−9.7	−7.3
Feb 2009	+49.8	+17.5	+19.5
Mar 2009	+24.3	+8.0	+9.3
5 month average	+21.4	+1.3	+2.7

Source: Hiho internal sales data.

In many ways achieving these results was much more difficult to achieve than in retail shops. For anyone who understands what doing a show entails: the logistics and difficulties in setting up a stand to look like a newly rebranded shop in the middle of a field; this really demonstrates what an impressive performance this is.

Returns on design investment

Hiho's design investment was repaid within just five months. This is just accounting for like-for-like sales increases at the Sherborne shop, Cheltenham Racing Festival and Badminton Horse Trials. With more shop refits and events planned over 2009 Hiho estimates that by end of this year their investment will have repaid itself at least ten times over, not a mean feat in retail where margins are notoriously low.

Customer feedback

The following feedback is from shoppers at the Sherborne store in February 2009:

> I love Hiho because your shop [in Sherborne] is so beautifully displayed. Your staff are always really friendly and just before Christmas we were given a free glass of champers!

> I love Hiho because of the friendly staff, the beautiful shop layout and for the fabulous range of unusual and fantastic gifts and products.

> Every time I enter the shop I don't want to leave.

> After a visit I leave feeling happy, inspired and with hundreds of ideas for original gifts.

Other testimonials

> The re-branding of Hiho has had an extremely positive impact on PR and marketing activity: it has completely re-energized and updated the brand and made it far more media-relevant and consumer friendly. This has meant we have been able to expand

the type and number of publications we approach and has therefore created a huge number of new opportunities for showcasing the brand and its unique collections within mainstream, high fashion consumer media.

Jonathan Kirkby PR Account Director, Hiho EdenCancan

I have no doubt whatsoever that our new identity is the single largest contributing factor to the remarkable success of our Sherborne shop, shows at Cheltenham and Badminton, and to the business overall.

Andrew Ransford Managing Director, Hiho

Awards

- Fast Growth Business Awards 2009: finalist for Retailer of the Year.
- UK Jewellery Awards 2009 (the pre-eminent jewellery industry awards in the UK): finalist Multiple Retailer of the Year (winners to be announced 16 July 2009).
- UK Jewellery Awards 2009: finalist Employer of the Year (winners to be announced 16 July 2009).

Research resources

- Hiho internal sales data
- Hiho customer feedback forms
- British Retail Consortium-KPMG Retail Sales Monitor
- brc.org.uk
- Retail-jeweller.com
- local Sherborne High Street shop owners.

Other influencing factors

Was it advertising?

Hiho did not undertake any advertising, so it's not that.

Was it new product ranges?

There were some new products specific to Sherborne but they made a very small impact on the gross sales figures and they were mainly there to show off the new branding. Hiho has now introduced these new products in all refitted shops, stands and the web shop. The overwhelming success of the Sherborne shop versus all other Hiho shops cannot be attributable to this.

Was it employee training?

Prior to the brand relaunch, employees at the Sherborne store received training but this was entirely around the brand positioning, its design and how employees should use the look and feel in store.

Was it email marketing?

A Valentine's Day email marketing campaign was done in February 2009. Hiho used this as an opportunity to focus on the new identity and look and feel in the communications and to drive footfall to Sherborne. This resulted in a 49.8 per cent like-for-like increase at Sherborne that month, compared to 17.5 per cent for the rest of the estate.

Was it sales/promotions?

Hiho had a January sale, but this happens in all stores every year so the increased sales at Sherborne cannot be attributable to this. They also had a promotion leading up to Christmas. Again, this was in all stores and has happened for the past two years.

Was it changes in marketing communications at the shows?

Marketing communications at shows has changed, with Hiho much more aware of the fact that they have to tell their customers what is happening at Hiho. However, all the communications echo the brand's look and feel developed by Blue Marlin.

Was it PR?

Hiho works with a PR agency and there has been an increase in coverage since the rebrand. However, per the testimonial from their PR agency noted earlier in this entry, they believe it is the new identity that has helped them reach a wider fashion audience.

Was it the website?

The website with the new look and feel didn't relaunch until 7 May 2009 so the success of Sherborne and the show stands were not affected by this.

CASE STUDY QUESTIONS

1. Critically review this case. What were the main factors that you believe led to Hiho's success? Justify your response.
2. Refer back to earlier chapters such as branding. What impact do you believe the name change to Hiho had?
3. Given that advertising was not a central marketing communications tool, explain the success of the branding activity.
4. What role do you believe sales staff played in Hiho's success? How would you expect them to have been involved in the redesign process?
5. What do you believe the role of special shows and events was in their success? How would you measure this?
6. How would you track the link between event activity and subsequent retail sales?
7. How can HiHo maintain the momentum gained from rebranding and refitting of its retail outlets? What role should sales staff play in this and how do you recommend they be rewarded?
8. Visit your local shopping centre or high street and evaluate the impact of the retail environment on staff activity and on customer experiences. List three outlets that you believe are very good and three that you believe could be improved. Justify your responses.

Notes

1 Sharma, A. (2007). The metrics of relationships. *Journal of Relationship Marketing*, 6(2), 33–50.
2 Taylor, S.A., Celuch, K., and Goodwin, S. (2004). The importance of brand equity to customer loyalty. *Journal of Product & Brand Management*, 13(4), 217–27.
3 Clemente, M.N. (2008). The forgotten element. *Sales & Marketing Management*, 160(3), 9.

4   Maddox, K. (2008). Moving past the culture of blame. *B to B*, 93(12), 1–38.

5   Murthy, P., and Mantrala, M. (2005). Allocating a promotion budget between advertising and sales contest prizes: an integrated marketing communications perspective. *Marketing Letters*, 16(1), 19–35.

6   Naik, P.A., and Raman, K. (2003). Understanding the impact of synergy in multimedia communications. *Journal of Marketing Research (JMR)*, 40(4), 375–88.

7   Naik, P.A., Raman, K., and Winer, R.S. (2005). Planning marketing-mix strategies in the presence of interaction effects. *Marketing Science*, 24(1), 25–34.

8   Greene, W.E., Walls, G.D., and Schrest, L.J. (1994). Internal marketing: the key to external marketing success. *Journal of Services Marketing*, 8(4), 5–13.

9   Asif, S., and Sargeant, A. (2000). Modelling internal communications in the financial services sector. *European Journal of Marketing*, 34(3/4), 299–317.

10 Webster, F.E. (1968). Interpersonal communication and salesman effectiveness. *Journal of Marketing*, 32(3), 7–13.

11 Rapp, A., Agnihotri, R., and Forbes, L.P. (2008). The sales force technology-performance chain: the role of adaptive selling and effort. *Journal of Personal Selling & Sales Management*, 28(4), 335–50.

12 Panagopoulos, N.G., and Avlonitis, G.J. (2008). Sales force control systems: a review of measurement practices and proposed scale refinements. *Journal of Personal Selling & Sales Management*, 28(4), 365–85.

13 Hogarth-Scott, S. (1999). Retailer–supplier partnerships: hostages to fortune or the way forward for the millenium. *British Food Journal*, 101(9), 668–82.

14 Garber Jr, L.L., and Dotson, M.J. (2002). A method for the selection of appropriate business-to-business integrated marketing communications mixes. *Journal of Marketing Communications*, 8(1), 1–17.

15 *Daily Mail*. (2006). This is the Model Who Sparked Size Zero Debate. Online. Available HTTP: <http://dailymail.co.uk/news/article-406316/This-model-sparked-size-zero-debate.html>.

16 York E.B., Zmuda N., and Sterrett D. (2009). McDonalds sends McCafe onto Fashion Week catwalks. *Advertising Age*, 80(5), 2.

17 Dapiran, G.P., and Hogarth-Scott, S. (2003). Are cooperation and trust being confused with power? An analysis of food retailing in Australia and the UK. *International Journal of Retail & Distribution Management*, 31(5), 256.

18 Tarzijan, J. (2004). Strategic effects of private labels and horizontal integration. *International Review of Retail, Distribution and Consumer Research*, 14(3), 321–35.

19 Burt, S.L., and Sparks, L. (2003). Power and competition in the UK retail grocery market. *British Journal of Management*, 14(3), 237–54.

20 Burt, S.L., and Sparks, L. (2002). Corporate branding, retailing, and retail internationalization. *Corporate Reputation Review*, 5(2/3), 194–212.

21 Buchanan, L., Simmons, C.J., and Bickart, B.A. (1999). Brand equity dilution: retailer display and context brand effects. *Journal of Marketing Research*, 36(3), 345–55.

22 Hartman, K.B., and Spiro, R.L. (2005). Recapturing store image in customer-based store equity: a construct conceptualization. *Journal of Business Research*, 58(8), 1112–20.

23 McCarthy, M.S., and Norris, D.G. (1999). Improving competitive position using branded ingredients. *Journal of Product & Brand Management*, 8(4), 267.

24 Sayman, S., and Raju, J.S. (2004). Investigating the cross-category effects of store brands. *Review of Industrial Organization*, 24(2), 129–41.

25 Bonfrer, A., and Chintagunta, P.K. (2004). Store brands: who buys them and what happens to retail prices when they are introduced? *Review of Industrial Organization*, 24, 195–218.

26 Shannon, R., and Mandhachitara, R. (2005). Private-label grocery shopping attitudes and behaviour: a cross-cultural study. *Brand Management*, 12(6), 461–74.

27 Olbrich, R., and Buhr, C.-C. (2004). Impact of private labels on competition: why European competition law should permit resale price maintenance. *European Retail Digest*, 41(Spring), 1–6.

28 Corstjens, M., and Lal, R. (2000). Building store loyalty through store brands. *Journal of Marketing Research (JMR)*, 37(3), 281–91.

29 Oubina, J., Rubio, N., and Yague, M.J. (2006). Strategic management of store brands: an analysis from the manufacturer's perspective. *International Journal of Retail & Distribution Management*, 34(10), 742–60.

30 Reddy, S.K., Holak, S.L., and Bhat, S. (1994). To extend or not to extend: success determinants of line extensions. *Journal of Marketing Research*, 31(2), 243–62.

31 Ryals, L.J., and Holt, S. (2007). Creating and capturing value in KAM relationships. *Journal of Strategic Marketing*, 14(5), 403–20.

32 Abratt, R., and Goodey, S.D. (1990). Unplanned buying and in-store stimuli in supermarkets. *Managerial and Decision Economics*, 11(2), 111–21.

33 Dhar, S.K., Hoch, S.J., and Kumar, N. (2001). Effective category management depends on the role of the category. *Journal of Retailing*, 77(2), 165–84.

34 Mishra, B.K., and Raghunathan, S. (2004). Retailer- vs. vendor-managed inventory and brand competition. *Management Science*, 50(4), 445–57.

35 Buttle, F. (1984). Merchandizing. *European Journal of Marketing*, 18(6/7), 104.

36 Rajaram, K., and Tang, C. S. (2001). The impact of product substitution on retail merchandizing. *European Journal of Operational Research*, 135(3), 582–601.

37 Bernstein, F., Song, J.-S., and Zheng, X. (2008). Bricks-and-mortar vs. clicks-and-mortar: an equilibrium analysis. *European Journal of Operational Research*, 187(3), 671–90.

38 Thompson, D. (2008). Embracing the future. *Sales & Marketing Management*, 160(4), 21–2.

39 De Pelsmacker, P., Geuens, M., and Van den Bergh, J. (2001). *Marketing Communications*, Harlow: Pearson Education.

16 Evaluation and control

Evidence of effectiveness and the challenge of measuring return on investment

LEARNING OUTCOMES

After studying this chapter, you will be able to:

- Understand the reasons why organizations increasingly seek to measure the impact that marketing activity has upon their overall business

- Recognize the benefits of developing and managing systems to measure and analyse the effect of marketing activity

- Appreciate the limitations and challenges associated with the measurement and analysis of IMC activity

- Recognize and understand the different methods of measuring effectiveness and return on investment (ROI)

Introduction

Whatever the state of the business environment, getting value for money, or at least covering costs, should always be a priority for marketing professionals. However in order to do this it is important to understand what managers are actually getting for their money but also how to measure its value. Not only does it make good business sense, but it helps managers identify the most effective communication vehicles and strategies for future activity. In economically strident times, it becomes increasingly imperative that organizations employ their resources as prudently as possible to ensure that they get the maximum return for every penny spent.

Yet while there is no doubt that an understanding of the relative **effectiveness** of business actions can yield huge benefits and is an important tool when seeking to achieve competitive success, marketing professionals encounter unique challenges in their endeavour to measure the value of their work. This chapter examines both the benefits and the challenges faced by marketers. It discusses the relative value of the various methods used to analyse marketing effectiveness and return on investment and concludes with some recommendations as to how to formulate a basic business case.

Defining marketing effectiveness and return on investment

It is a common mistake that some Brand Managers and marketing executives use the terms 'marketing effectiveness' and 'return on investment' interchangeably. 'Return on investment' is an accounting-based term that relates to the percentage profit achieved on the basis of a given amount of expenditure before taxes and other deductions. For instance, if a cola company spent £100,000 on an IMC campaign and achieved an uplift in sales of £130,000, then they would have achieved a return on investment of 30 per cent,

> i.e. £130,000 sales minus £100,000 investment = £30,000 return. This is then expressed as a percentage of the investment:

> 30,000/100,000 = 30 per cent

By contrast, the analysis of the effectiveness of an integrated marketing campaign focusses primarily upon the degree to which the objectives of that campaign have been achieved. These objectives are not necessarily related specifically to increases in sales and can take a variety of forms that do not necessarily relate directly to quantifiable sales figures. Such objectives might include:

- improved levels of prompted/unprompted brand recognition
- increased positivity towards a brand
- clearer understanding of the brand values
- effective repositioning of a brand within a given market.

In social marketing, 'sales' are not a target. Factors that may be used to measure effectiveness of marketing communications include any or all of the following:

- improved levels of awareness of messages (however, while awareness is necessary, it is not of itself sufficient to generate behaviour change)
- improved levels of understanding of the consequences of specific behaviours for health or well-being

- positive change in attitudes towards changing behaviours
- measurement of actual behaviour change
- consequences of this behaviour change (such as reduction in road accidents as a result of drinking and driving).

Think of three specific areas of social marketing – recycling, road safety and skin cancer prevention. The first is relatively easy to evaluate at all stages from awareness through understanding of the benefits of recycling through to changes in actual recycling rates. For road safety, ultimately, the measure is of accidents, injuries or deaths that did not occur and which can be attributed to the impact of social marketing communications activity.

For skin cancer prevention, while protective behaviours can be measured, the actual impact on skin cancer rates will only become evident after several years due to the time between skin damage and the development of observable skin cancer.

The following three tables have been drawn from one of the few papers that specifically focusses on the evaluation of the effectiveness of social marketing interventions.[1] It shows a hierarchy of effects, progressing from awareness through to, ultimately, an improvement in overall societal or environmental wellbeing.

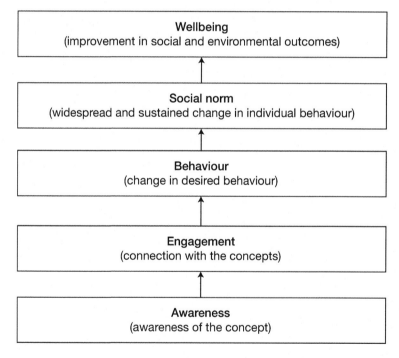

Figure 16.1 Levels of social marketing effectiveness

Tables 16.1 and 16.2 provide possible types of changes that could be sought at each of the preceding levels – and provides a selection of techniques and data sources by which these changes can be measured.

Now think about the very different area of political marketing, such as the marketing communications activity undertaken by political parties and/or individual candidates before an election. What measures of ROI are likely to be used here?

Table 16.1 Changes sought at each level of effectiveness

Level	Key changes sought	Result level
Awareness	Increase in awareness of issue	Individual changes in awareness
Engagement	A change of attitude and contemplation of behaviour change	Individual changes in attitude and responses to programmes
	Behavioural responses to individual programmes	
Behaviour	Individual behaviour change	Individual changes in behaviour
Social norm	The desired behaviour change has permeated widely and sustainably and is therefore maintained	Normative changes in attitude and behaviour
Well being	The desired behaviour change has resulted in an improvement in quality of life for individuals and society	Changes in social and environmental outcomes

Table 16.2 Possible indicators of success at each level of effectiveness

	Indicators	Means of measurement
Awareness	X% aware of issue	Surveys (formal/informal – think about how to administer questionnaires/who, where, when)
Engagement	X% contemplating behaviour change X% discussing/responding/participating	Surveys Behavioural data (e.g. website hits, requests for brochures, calls to helplines etc.)
Behaviour	X% self report behaviour X% behaviour changes recorded	Self report (think of methods) Behavioural data (e.g. participating in sports clubs, road speed data)
Social norms	X% positive attitudes/ positive media coverage Anecdotal feedback/observation Political environment	Surveys Media and political tracking Anecdotal feedback Observation
Well being	X% increase in social outcome X% increase in environmental outcome	Social reports (annual complications of indicators of wellbeing) Epidemiological data Environmental data

THINK BOX

What is 'value'?

It was noted that it might be difficult to assign a monetary value to the list of potential objectives listed in this section. However, does this mean that they are without 'value'? Consider what we mean by 'value' when generating and then seeking to measure marketing communications objectives such as these.

The value of evaluation

There are a number of benefits attached to evaluating the contribution that marketing activity makes to a business:

1. Knowing what works and what doesn't allows Brand Managers and marketing executives to make best use of the limited resources of a marketing budget by choosing the most effective tools for the job.
2. Effective **evaluation** is a continuous process. Therefore, managers are able to monitor the progress of their IMC programmes on an ongoing basis and make changes to rectify poorly performing aspects of any project.
3. The possession of a clear understanding of the potential impact that marketing communications tools, either individually or in concert, can have upon a business is hugely important both in terms of sales forecasting and resource planning.
4. A good grasp of how to measure return on investment can be positively career enhancing. A lack of measurement and accountability has been blamed for the rather limited presence of marketing executives at Board level. Whilst this has yet to be empirically proven, there can be no doubt that, when seeking promotion, individuals who can point to tangible and measureable contributions to the business are likely to be more successful than those who cannot.
5. Evidence-based bids for increased levels of resourcing are likely to be more successful than those that are poorly supported as, increasingly, managers find themselves having to compete for slices of finite marketing budgets to support their brands.
6. Within the context of a pitch, those agencies who can communicate the value of their proposition and support it with a clear business case are likely to be more persuasive and therefore more successful than those who cannot.

The process of evaluation

There are four key stages in the evaluation process: objective setting, benchmarking, tracking and post-testing (Figure 16.2). Ideally, evaluation should be treated as a cyclical process in that once post-testing is complete, the results should then be used to inform any further formulation of objectives.

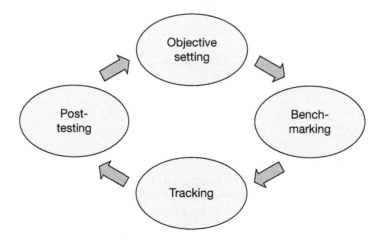

Figure 16.2 The four key stages in the evaluation of an IMC campaign

Objective setting

The importance of effective objective setting has been a recurring theme in management literature over recent years. On the face of it, this makes perfect sense – after all, how do managers know their actions are successful unless they have some criteria to measure them by?

It is the nature of an IMC campaign that it comprises multiple elements and thus any objectives can and should encompass both specific elements and broader outcomes; in effect there should be 'micro' and 'macro' objectives. The 'micro' objectives relate to individual elements of the campaign and most often focus upon short-term phenomena, for example, the 'reach' of a television advertisement or the redemption level of a money-off coupon. By contrast, 'macro' objectives relate to the broader and often more long-term elements of a campaign such as increased market size and improved levels of brand equity.

At both a micro and a macro level, there must be a clear and universal understanding of the objectives of the campaign amongst all of those involved – from the most junior account executive to the members of the Board of Directors. If there is any question as to the clarity of the objectives, the SMART acronym should be employed:

S   Specific
M   Measureable
A   Achievable
R   Relevant
T   Time-framed

Without clear and universally agreed objectives, there is the potential for time and money to be wasted if the marketing team are not working to the same end. Therefore, if the objectives of a project are not clearly and specifically stated, are not relevant to both the aim of the campaign and the wider marketing and corporate objectives of the organization, are not achievable within the given time-frame and are not measureable against a given set of criteria, then they should be reformulated until they meet all five requirements identified within the SMART acronym.

Benchmarking

Having established a set of objectives, **benchmarking** is a form of research that effectively establishes 'marks' or baseline measurements from which any changes in consumer behaviour or market characteristics induced by an IMC campaign might be measured. When constructing a 'benchmark', the following criteria must be satisfied:

- The research sample tested must offer an adequate reflection population to be targeted with the IMC campaign. Therefore, if the target audience for the IMC campaign is male students attending university in the north east of England then the research sample should reflect this.
- In order to ensure that the benchmarks are meaningful ones, the metrics used must reflect the stated objectives of the IMC campaign. For example, if one of the objectives of an IMC campaign is to raise awareness of a brand of toothpaste amongst a target audience, the pre-test must establish the levels of awareness amongst them prior to the start of the campaign. Only then are they in a position to gauge any change of awareness levels after the campaign has concluded.

- Certain objectives can be stated easily in terms of numbers, for example, a certain percentage uplift in sales in a specific geographical area or a percentage redemption level of coupons. However, where an objective relates to 'intangibles' such as attitude or purchase consideration, responses should be measured upon some form of scales, for example Likert or semantic differential scales,[2] to establish a benchmark from which outcomes of IMC campaigns can be gauged.

Pre-testing of all marketing communications material should also be done as part of the initial evaluation phase. This ensures that the message that is intended to be sent is what the target group is receiving. Thus it gives the marketer the opportunity to test the effectiveness of various components of the IMC campaign for impact, message delivery and 'ad liking'[3] before the full launch of a campaign and make changes in any areas of perceived weakness. For example, if a message fails to persuade or confuses the target, pre-testing enables changes to be made before the material is actually used. There is always a balance between testing rough, unfinished creative material – and asking people to imagine the finished version – and testing the finished version – with costly implications if the messages are not effective.

Tracking

Having launched an IMC campaign, tracking is the process by which marketers monitor its ongoing effectiveness. Tracking is a form of longitudinal research and can be under-taken on either a continuous basis (i.e. daily or weekly) or regularly but at longer intervals throughout the course of a campaign (i.e. monthly, bi-monthly, quarterly) until its com-pletion. Remember that no marketing communication message will appear in isolation – there will be a range of possible competitive messages as well as the types of noise and distraction discussed in Chapter 2. Tracking helps determine how effective your com-munications are relative to competing messages.

At its simplest, for some elements of the IMC mix, tracking simply involves counting, for example, levels of coupon redemption or 'clicks' on a particular web link.

Heath cites a number of areas that are commonly covered by tracking studies for commercial products or services[4]:

- spontaneous (unprompted) and prompted brand awareness
- brand usage and availability
- brand image
- prompted advertising awareness
- detailed recall of key advertising messages
- executional diagnostics – for example ad liking and wearout
- purchase consideration
- purchase intention.

Tracking studies can take a variety of forms such as questionnaires and omnibus surveys but one of the most common is that of a consumer panel. A consumer panel is comprised of a group of consumers considered to be representative of the target population. They agree to take part in research into their attitudes, purchasing and consumption habits on a regular basis, usually in exchange for some reward (i.e. money, store vouchers, free products). Both throughout the course of a campaign and also at the point of its completion, marketers monitor and measure tracking studies against the campaign objectives in order to gauge its relative success.

Post-testing

Post-testing is the process by which a marketer, using the pre-campaign benchmark measures as a base, analyses key metrics to identify any changes that might have occurred as a result of the IMC campaign. For those elements of a campaign that are easily quantifiable, determination of short-term effectiveness and return on investment is relatively simple to calculate using accounting-based methods. It is simply a matter of off-setting the cost of the promotional element against the value of the uplift in sales.

EXAMPLE

Effectiveness = results of promotion/target set by promotional objectives

Therefore, where the stated promotional objective is a sales uplift of 100 units and an uplift of 120 units is achieved, then the promotion may be deemed to be 120 per cent effective. However, if only an uplift of 97 units is achieved then the promotion was deemed to be only 97 per cent effective.

Return on investment = net profit value of uplift in sales – cost of promotion

If an IMC campaign that cost £50,000 yielded an uplift in sales to a net profit value of £75,000, then the return on investment would be £25,000 or 50 per cent.

MINI CASE: CUTTING THE COST OF CRIME

When we think of measuring the 'return on investment' (ROI) of a campaign, too often we focus purely upon its monetary impact. However, it is important to remember that campaign objectives can take many forms and the measure by which ROI is assessed should reflect this.

Take for example a crime prevention campaign launched by the UK's Home Office in 2009. The 'Don't Advertise Your Stuff to Thieves' campaign was designed to prevent burglary, car crime and identity theft. In spite of sensationalist headlines and scare-stories regarding knife attacks and terrorism, the most commonly experienced crime in Britain is theft or 'acquisitive crime'; theft of or from vehicles, burglary or mugging/pick-pocketing. With the objective of reducing levels of such crime, the Home Office commissioned a campaign that sought to empower individuals by raising awareness of how easily such crimes might be avoided. Using a primary medium of television but supported by ambient media in car parks and on parking meters, it portrayed crime from the perspective of the thief and highlighted the many careless things that people did that made them easy prey.

As a result of the campaign, levels of awareness, recall and feelings of empowerment all increased. The resulting behaviour change was clearly evidenced in a fall in theft or 'acquisitive crime' of 19 per cent – equivalent to 698,000 fewer crimes. However, whilst the primary objective might have been empowerment and behaviour change, it is still possible to put a monetary value on the ROI in this case. Every crime costs the taxpayer money and therefore this campaign had potentially saved a minimum of £189 million that would otherwise have been spent on the detection and prosecution of offences.

- What are the pitfalls in measuring the return on investment (ROI) in anything other than monetary value?
- In the context of this campaign, is measurement of the monetary impact of any real value?
- To whom do you think it would be of most value?

Reference: 'Don't Advertise Your Stuff to Thieves' campaign. Online. Available HTTP: <http://westlothian.org.uk/armadaleacademy/documents/Crime per cent20Prevention per cent20advice.pdf> (accessed 29 March 2013).

Taking the long-term view

However, measurement of the value of long-term effects of IMC campaigns and the relative value of the more intangible objectives such as brand equity as opposed to actual sales are much more difficult to quantify accurately. Therefore, the way organizations measure long-term effects together with the broader contribution that IMC campaigns make to business success need to be appraised in other ways.

According to McDonald, there are three levels at which marketing evaluation and analysis should take place within an organization (see Figure 16.2).

Level 1   The focus of analysis at Level 1 is upon the long-term contribution to shareholder value. It relates to the extent to which marketing activity and integrated marketing communications programmes contribute to the long-term growth objectives of an organization. The metrics used at this level can be many and varied and will relate to the cumulative effect of combined and multiple layers of marketing activity. Good examples of these metrics include measures of brand equity and brand value.

Level 2   At Level 2, the focus of analysis is upon the assessment of achievement of critical success factors and involves the identification of factors and conditions that need to be satisfied in order for the long-term objectives at Level 1 to be achieved. These 'critical success factors' can take many forms and it is often the case that a tangible return may take many months or years to materialize, particularly in the case where the attainment of specific technical expertise, knowledge of a new geographical market or the development of a new product is required.

Level 3   Analysis at Level 3 is a relatively simple affair in that it relates specifically to those elements that can be easily measured, monitored and quantified and relates specifically to the short-term, tactical activity managed on a day-to-day basis by marketers. However, evaluation and analysis at Levels 2 and 1 differ in that they require greater acknowledgement of the strategic role that marketing plays within an organization and should take into consideration the contribution it can make to its success in the medium and long term.

Concerns and challenges associated with measuring IMC effectiveness and return on investment (ROI)

There are concerns and challenges associated with the measurement of effectiveness and return on investment at each of the three levels identified by McDonald.[5] At all stages,

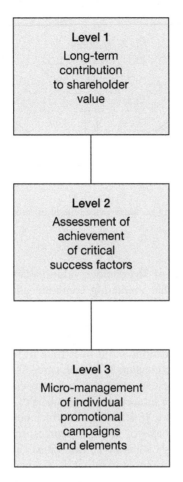

Figure 16.3 McDonalds' three levels of marketing evaluation and analysis[7]

challenges emanate from three key factors: a lack of isolation, multiple synergies and the effect of competitor activity (Figure 16.4).

The first of these factors, a lack of isolation, reflects the fact that, in the main, growth of shareholder value or the achievement of critical success factors are usually the cumulative result of a number of factors and it is difficult to isolate the contribution of a single constituent. For example, for a company like Cadbury's, the successful launch of a new range of boxed chocolates may increase the value of the company to its shareholders.

The success of the launch may be the result of the correct identification and achievement of a number of critical success factors which, in turn, may be the result of the cumulative effect of insightful market analysis, effective new product development processes, high quality production systems, creative and effective marketing campaigns, persuasive sales force initiatives and well-managed distribution channels. On this basis, the isolation and measurement of the contribution that a single department, let alone a single piece of marketing communications, might make to a growth in shareholder value becomes highly problematic.

The second of these factors, the impact of 'multiple synergies', develops the concept of the lack of isolation a stage further. It builds upon the acknowledged fact that marketing

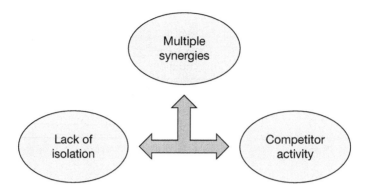

Figure 16.4 Three factors impeding accurate measurement of effectiveness or return on investment of IMC Activity

contributes to the generation of shareholder value in tandem with a number of other departments and recognizes that marketing communications do not exist in isolation. However, it also notes that potential synergies exist between layers of corporate and brand communication that might be transmitted at any one time.

In addition the potential existence of a temporal form of synergy is acknowledged as layer upon layer of communications build over time to reinforce brand awareness and brand values in the mind of the consumer. In such cases, isolating the incremental impact of a single medium or message can prove difficult, particularly in light of the fact noted in Chapter 2, that consumers are subject to large numbers of messages and communications from multiple sources every day. In situations in which consumers' formulate brand perceptions and attitudes on the basis of multiple sources, many of which do not emanate from brand owners themselves[6], isolating contributions can be difficult.

The final factor is that of 'competitor activity'. 'Competitor activity' may be defined as any activity that has the potential to draw attention away from an organization's marketing efforts and can take many forms. For example, United Biscuits recently redesigned and relaunched their 'Phileas Fogg' range of crisps in the UK accompanied by a major burst of television advertising. In response, competitors implemented a variety of price-based sales promotions (for example, 'buy one get one free') within supermarkets in an apparent attempt to deflect attention away from the brand at the point of purchase. These short-term 'spoiling' tactics make it very difficult to gauge the impact of a marketing campaign both in the short and the long term.

In addition, concerns even exist with regard to the metrics mentioned earlier that appear so easily measured:

1. Conventional tools whose roots are in the field of accounting generally regard marketing as an expense rather than an investment.[7] The effect of this is a focus upon short-term performance with the result that the time frames involved do not always capture the long-term impact of a piece of marketing activity.[8]
2. The tendency to focus upon historical information is often inappropriate within dynamic markets where past performance is not necessarily an accurate predictor of future.
3. Accounting tools often struggle to fully appreciate the value of intangible assets such as brand equity.[9]

Ultimately, concern exists not only as to the extent to which these accounting-based methods can accurately value the important contributions of marketing activity, but whether it is possible to ever accurately measure the value and contribution of marketing and, specifically, integrated marketing communications.

MINI CASE: 'BOM CHICKA WAH WAH' – THE CHALLENGE OF MEASURING THE IMPACT OF A CATCHPHRASE

Source: Mintel (2009) Teen and Tween Beauty and Personal Care Consumer – US – August 2013. Report purchased online. Available HTTP: <http://oxygen.mintel.com/display/637821/> (accessed 21 November 2009); Warc Word of Mouth Marketing Awards (2008) Axe/Lynx – UK dinner party: a real-time approach to measuring buzz. Available online. HTTP: <www.warc.com> (accessed 21 November 2009).

According to Mintel (2009), in the UK, the £459 million market for personal care products had reached a point of stagnation in value terms having experienced several years of growth. As a result, the 'personal care' sector largely consisting of cosmetics, toiletries, deodorants and body sprays has become increasingly more competitive.

One of the most high-profile brands in the sector is owned by Unilever. In 2007 it sought to run an IMC campaign that focussed upon the catchphrase 'Bom Chicka Wah Wah' for their Lynx brand. The primary aim was to use the catchphrase to create a 'buzz' around the brand and generate positive associations by linking it to 'cool' people, places and events. This apparently nonsensical catchphrase is, in fact, an onomatopoeic representation of the guitar riff often used in pornographic films in the 1970s. The campaign used a combination of new and traditional media and was targeted at young, single males aged 14 to 35 years of age.

However, measuring the effectiveness of such a campaign is not an easy task. In response to the challenge, an innovative solution was adopted that used 'real-time' data. Four hundred research participants, recruited from online panels, were asked to send a text every time they saw, heard or experienced anything to do with one of a number of 'cool' brands. In their text they were asked to send a code that indicated what the brand was, where they saw it and how it made them feel. The participants' responses were then uploaded onto their own online diary where they could add photos and additional comments to further illustrate their experiences. In particular, managers were sought to analyse the extent and context in which the catchphrase was used and measure the linkage with the Lynx brand name.

This approach had many benefits. It allowed the marketers to track the most effective elements within their media mix and communication strategy and make changes to areas of weakness almost immediately. It also enabled marketers to probe the associations and usage occasions of Lynx and identify the extent to which the catchphrase was linked to the brand.

- Is it possible to assign 'value' to the measurement of this campaign?
- If so, in what way?
- What is the potential short-, medium- and long-term return on investment for this campaign?

Summary

There can be no doubt that measurement of return on investment within the context of marketing can be challenging. However, it is arguable that measurement of integrated marketing communication programmes is probably one of the most difficult aspects to quantify – if it is possible at all. Not only is the marketer faced with issues of measuring the value of 'intangibles' such as attitude change, there is also the issue of separating and measuring the impact of individual media. Finally, there is some recognition that some aspects of ROI take longer to materialize than others and generating a precise measurement of their impact is problematic.

That said, there can be no doubt that the benefits of monitoring and measuring levels of return have the potential to yield huge benefits. An understanding of the relative levels of potential return can be used to maximize the value obtained from limited marketing budgets. It can be a persuasive tool when bidding for funding and, on an individual level, can be used as evidence of success when seeking career advancement.

Yet in order for ROI systems to be effective, marketers must first have a definitive vision of what they are trying to achieve and how it might best be measured. This requires an organization to have a clear understanding of their current position and an effective process of objective-setting at all levels. Only then are marketers in a position to measure the relative effect of their actions.

Review questions

1. Define what is meant by the term 'return on investment' within a marketing context.
2. Distinguish between the terms 'return on investment' and 'marketing effectiveness'. Why do you think these terms are sometimes, if mistakenly, used interchangeably?
3. What are the benefits of measuring return on investment and/or marketing effectiveness? What are the challenges?
4. Discuss the importance of 'objectives' within the context of an IMC campaign. Why are they so essential to the measurement of ROI and marketing effectiveness?
5. Distinguish between the following concepts and explain their value within the measurement process:

   - pre-testing
   - tracking
   - post-testing.

6. The objective of an IMC campaign is to increase the sales of sun hats from 120,000 to 160,000 per annum. However, it is very successful and actually generates sales of 180,000. What is the percentage effectiveness of the promotion?
7. A chocolate manufacturer funds an IMC campaign for its new range of bars called 'ChewyChocs'. The campaign has two primary objectives: to encourage trial of the product and to generate sales of 400,000 units in the first year. The campaign costs £50,000. Each chocolate bar costs 50 pence of which 40 pence is net profit.

   - If the campaign is successful and generates sales of 440,000 units, what is the percentage effectiveness of the promotion?
   - Calculate the return on investment for sales of 440,000 units.

8. McDonald identifies three levels at which marketing analysis and evaluation should take place. Describe each level and explain why analysis and evaluation is required at each.

9. Explain the potential difficulties that might be encountered in isolating the contribution of a single element of an IMC campaign.

10. 'If you can't measure the return on investment by a piece of marketing activity, the return doesn't exist.' Discuss this statement and use examples to illustrate your answer.

Recommended reading

Dunn, M., and Halsall, C. (2009). *The Marketing Accountability Imperative*, San Francisco, CA: John Wiley and Sons Inc.

Fisher, T. (2009). ROI in social media: a look at the arguments. *Journal of Database Marketing and Customer Strategy Management*, 16, 189–95.

Hoffman, D., and Fodor, M. (2010). Can you measure the ROI of your social media marketing? *MIT Sloan Management Review*, 52(1), 40–9.

Moeller, L., and Landry, E. (2009). *The Four Pillars of Profit-Driven Marketing: How to Maximize Creativity, Accountability, and ROI*, London: McGraw-Hill Professional.

Wallace, R. (2001). Proving our value: measuring package design's return on investment. *Design Management Journal (Former Series)*, 12(3), 20–7.

CASE STUDY 16.1

Californication

Source: Institute of Practitioners in Advertising: Entrant, IPA Effectiveness Awards 2011. The case has been condensed from 'California Travel and Tourism Commission – Californication of the UK'. Principal author: Jonah Whitaker, Black Diamond. Contributing author: David Heggarty, Feather Brooksbank. Case material provided by the World Advertising Research Centre (WARC) www.warc.com.

Background

The California Travel & Tourism Commission (CTTC) is 'dedicated to persuading the travelling public to visit California by promoting the state's recreational, cultural, entertainment and scenic attractions with the goal of attracting visitors who would otherwise not visit California'.

Following a prolonged period of growth in the 1990s, the September 11th terrorist attacks in New York hit USA visitor numbers hard during 2001. The next six years had seen a return to growth in visitor numbers.

During the preceding few years there had been no above the line communication activity by California Travel and Tourism Commission (CTTC); visitor numbers were being generated by latent desire for the destination. The state has a huge influence on TV programmes, films and newspaper reports ensuring the California brand is being continuously refreshed in customer's minds. However, competitor 'longhaul' (i.e. long distance as opposed to 'short haul' – such as UK to France, Germany or Spain) destinations were advertising continuously across all media to generate visitors.

California's inactivity had given Florida an opening which they seized; this state had become the first choice family holiday destination in the US for UK travellers. Simultaneously, low cost air travel made New York a weekend city break and Las Vegas cemented its status as the party capital of the world. Comparatively California's tourism was seen to be struggling.

The final nail in the coffin was the growth of budget airlines like Ryanair and Easy Jet making the lure of European city breaks much stronger. California's share of travel was decreasing. In 2007 the CTTC decided to expand advertising efforts in the UK to re-build tourism to the pre-September 11th levels. With a huge state tourist industry this would have a dramatic effect on the local economy.

Research and insight

Earlier research in the USA had developed a set of TV scripts and associated commercials. Our first job was to use these as stimulus to test the UK consumer base to define perceptions, and understand why people weren't visiting. The universal prevalence of the California brand actually gave a fairly uniform perspective on both sides of the Atlantic.

Abundance

California is seen as having the biggest and the best of everything, whether it's beaches, shopping, sun or money. Hollywood has cemented the universal perception of the destination as a star.

Lifestyle

The public believe that the casual Californian lifestyle of surfing, beach living and tolerance is worthy of aspiration. Both groups of perceptions are extremely positive. People knew what to expect from California; as a concept it's wonderful. In fact, they wanted to visit California, someday. And herein lay the problem for our client. People liked the idea of California as a destination for a holiday, they just weren't prioritizing it for their long-haul trip.

Objective

Given that people loved the idea of California, and as a destination it appealed, our challenge was to reinforce the existing perceptions and make visiting an option for now. In summary: **Make California a destination for today, not someday**.

The visitor

Visitor profiles for California were studied, looking for high spending segments to ensure that we maximized revenues.

Two clear demographic segments stood out:

- 'Baby Boomers': age 45–65 **AND** spent at least £2,500 on last/last but one holiday.
- 'Good Lifers': age 35+ **AND** AB **AND** agree with TGI statement 'I go for premium rather than standard goods/services'.

However, it's easy to slip into demographics when targeting, and whilst this gave the team an idea of where to point our communications activity, in truth, air travel has become democratized over the last 10 years. Budget airlines have grown, the British public have started to take more weekends away in Europe; Barcelona and Rome have replaced Blackpool and Caernarfon. A shrinking Europe has pulled world travel behind it, with pricing pressure on long haul flights.

In 2007, the economy was still growing, as were disposable incomes and the ability to max out your credit cards, and exchange rates were on the side of British travellers to the

USA. A trip to California was affordable to the masses, it wasn't just the preserve of the wealthy. Thus, marketing communication efforts were focussed on crafting a proposition from the attitudes and perceptions brought out in research.

Developing the strategy

Most long haul destinations suffer from the same challenges as California; positive implanted perceptions made visiting an interesting, but distant concept.

Also, many competitor destinations could claim similar options for visitors:

- amazing scenery
- beaches
- activities and adventure.

The activity had to showcase the breadth of the California offer showing repeat visitors what they missed the first time – and providing a justification for making the long flight for new customers. It also needed to confirm subconscious positive emotional perceptions about California and raise them to the surface – the marketing communication needed to deliver California soul.

The decision was made to use California's undoubted star quality, featuring famous Californian residents to provide a point of difference for the destination over other long haul options.

Making a difference with communications

The team had to understand how people went about booking a long haul holiday and deploy marketing communications to lead them to California. Research into the decision making process for purchasing long haul holidays saw the team identify a three step process: inspiration, information, action.

Inspiration

People planning a long haul journey have a lengthy mental shopping list and, as they move closer to booking, this is slimmed down by a series of softer, emotional factors and harder, practical factors: money, holiday availability etc. The consumer ranks these destinations, and starts to sort them based upon things that are going to happen in the next few years – such as grandchildren or work commitments.

Information

Late in the year before, or early in the year of travel, consumers who are planning to travel long haul consider how much money and time they're willing to put into holidays. These practicalities further reduce the list of places to visit. There may be an initial foray onto the web or the back pages of the holiday supplements to refine this list by cost.

Action

The use of the Internet means that people can compare prices easily and in their own time. Using search engines and comparison sites, they can tailor a journey to deliver what they need at the right price.

Deploying communications

As the team developed their understanding of the customer journey, they realized that competitors were delivering communications at various points within it, but they weren't providing a series of interactions to help customers reach the end.

Therefore, the team built a marketing communications plan that would engage customers throughout their consideration process, providing what they needed at every stage. It was designed to get their attention early on, provide information to pull them in further and finally, help them book. California would become the obvious choice of destination.

The Visit California website would sit at the core of the customer journey, providing extra information about holidays and, vitally, linking customers to travel providers for bookings after we had convinced them! The digital elements of our plan would be tracked and optimized in real time, to ensure that every opportunity to engage was maximized.

Inspiration

Inspiration would come when the team confirmed all of the latent positive perceptions customers have about California. By showing the breadth of experiences we would make sure that as customers shortened their holiday shopping lists to cope with medium-term emotion and practicality, California was still on there. This would also provide new reasons to repeat visit by broadening the Californian offer.

We needed to get people's attention in the inspiration phase, and the most obvious way of engaging the masses was through TV. Television reaches more of the core demographic audience than any other media, but the California Soul of the ad allowed the campaign to engage based upon attitude, delivering a deep emotional impact.

The first phase of the TV activity saw the team launching with a heavyweight campaign. Here they drove awareness of the creative as quickly as possible. The launch took place during the week between Christmas and New Year when programming is of a high quality and there are plenty of relaxed viewing opportunities to provide the right context for our offer. The intention was that the advertisement would be given maximum exposure as people were planning for the year and building their mental shortlist of holiday destination.

The quick build of awareness was central to re-introducing California to people and therefore after one week, the advertising had reached 60 per cent of all 35–54s in the UK, 1+ coverage (i.e. those within the target group who had seen at least one advertisement) at 84 per cent and 4+ coverage (i.e. those within the target group who had seen four or more advertisements) at 44 per cent.

After the initial launch burst, a more traditional TV buying strategy was adopted for this sector. As awareness amongst the audience was now high it was crucial for the CTTC brand to remain 'top of mind'. This phase required the team to take a more refined approach by being highly selective in the selection of programmes in which the advertisements were placed to ensure that the creative would have maximum effect amongst those who already were familiar with it. The team aimed to use frequency to drive people's awareness by booking regularly into specific programming.

Information

The team knew that the target audiences looked to the quality press for travel information. However it was felt that it would not be possible to deliver a robust and impactful national campaign across key titles within budget so they decided to look at a partnership with a single title. This would be a cost effective way to deliver core objectives and also leverage brand awareness.

A partnership was formed with *The Times* newspaper. This centred around a series of in-paper advertorials which would highlight the breadth and depth of the Californian offering – driving the information part of our strategy. The activity included co-branded ads that acted as inspiration providers to get consumers onto the microsite for further information, support of classified adverts which would direct readers to visitcalifornia.co.uk and provide the booking mechanism.

Press activity was also supported by a microsite and a number of different traffic drivers to the microsite including a major competition allowing readers to win a trip to California. This combination of advertorials, microsite and standard ads allowed the team to provide a high quality, trusted source of information for customers who had been inspired. The

Photo 16.1

partnership also gave consumers more reasons to visit as opposed to the reliable LA and San Francisco. What this messaging did was make the communications more relevant to more people, as the campaign helped people discover the winelands (wine growing regions), the national parks and the classic drives of California.

The intention was that the high profile TV and press partnerships would result in more customers undertaking their own information searches online. The team needed to ensure that Visit California was in front of customers at this stage, to steer customers along the purchasing journey.

With the majority of web sessions starting on a search engine, the team ensured paid search ran across the campaign. This provided a cost effective route in which to drive high volumes of traffic to visitcalifornia.co.uk and convert interest created by the other media activity. Paid search acted as a harvester of customer attention, ensuring that all points of contact were maximized and that the most possible time was gained with every customer.

Allowing action

Putting the website at the core of the activity, and maximizing chances of getting every customer to visit gave the campaign an opportunity to prompt action. Partnerships were arranged with travel organizations and a constant source of links for customers were provided to progress to booking. The website functionality also gave customers the opportunity to download or order the Official State Visitor Map and Guide, reducing the effort of organizing a trip to California and guiding customers through the booking journey. This was also further facilitated by the extensive listing of Tour Operators on the visitcalifornia.co.uk site.

Costs

The costs below are based on actual media spends in pounds, as well as production costs in US dollars that was converted into UK pounds at the average conversion rate through the period of $1 to £0.49.

The production of the TV ad cost $1.8m, and the ad was played out in three territories (the USA, Canada and the UK) over two years, which gives us a cost of $300,000. This then converts into UK pounds as £147,000.

Table 16.3 Campaign costs

Media	Client cost
TV	£1,498,945.25
Press	£123,865.40
Online PPC	£114,198.35
Total media	£1,737,009.00

Production	Client cost
TV	£147,000.00
Print	£4,000.00
Online PPC	£1,000.00
Total production	£152,000.00
Combined agency fees	£288,665.79
Total	£2,177,674.79

Results

The campaign exceeded all expectations. Eschewing the standard industry broadcast models and using media to drive people through a customer journey differentiated California from other tourist destinations. This innovative planning saw the campaign outperform other territories throughout the world.

Awareness

The UK industry recognized the TV ad as both a highly impactful piece of creative, and a very well planned piece of media buying as the campaign made it into the top 20 of Marketing Magazine's adwatch with a modest budget compared to the other advertisers in the top 20.

While the TNS Adwatch data indicated a 37 per cent awareness level, BARB data indicated that by the end of the TV campaign 83 per cent of ABC1 35–54-year-old target audience had seen the ad (7.52m people) on an average of 5.1 occasions showing a strong TV campaign that efficiently reached huge numbers of our target. However, CTTC's research agency (SMARI) saw 63 per cent of respondents claiming that they were aware of the TV ad, while 21 per cent were aware of one or more print ads and 13 per cent were aware of both TV and print.

The research vindicated the team's proposals to move some of the TV budget away to press, as the addition of the print ads helped to boost the California UK campaign awareness to 71 per cent, up from 63 per cent during the tracking wave.

While the print ads reached fewer households than the TV ads, significantly lower print spending ultimately yielded a cost per aware notably lower than that realized for television advertising – print cost $0.12 (£0.06) to reach a household, while TV cost $0.38 (£0.19).

This shows that by adding a relatively inexpensive medium such as print is a cost-efficient way to boost awareness. Not only did this differentiate the campaign from others in the market it was a cost effective solution.

Incremental travel

The key measure of this campaign's effectiveness was to generate incremental travel, or the amount of travel directly attributable to the advertising efforts. The assessment of incremental travel is determined as follows:

- The level of travel of those unaware of the advertising is the rate of California visitation that would have occurred without any marketing efforts.
- The extra travel generated from those aware of the advertising represents incremental travel that the advertising generated.

The base rate of California travel by those unaware of the advertising was 1.8 per cent. Considering 3.1 per cent of those aware of the advertising visited California, the incremental travel generated is 1.3 per cent. This is the more conservative incremental travel measure, as it accounts for only those who have already visited California, not those who plan to visit in the future.

Another way to assess incremental travel is to include those who indicated that they are already planning a trip to California. While they had not travelled at the time of the study, they plan to and thus should be included when assessing the economic impact of the campaign. Consideration from this standpoint reveals an incremental travel rate of 1.8 per cent.

Table 16.4 Average trip expenditure of a California visitor from the UK

	2008	2009	2010
Nights spent in California	8.3	7.6	9.1
Used paid accommodations	82%	82%	82%
Visited other states	61%	70%	60%
People in party	2.3	3.0	2.8
Children in party	17%	21%	38%
Expenditure type	*2008*	*2009*	*2010*
Lodging/accommodations	$995	$989	$1,047
Meals/food/groceries	$582	$484	$567
Attractions	$317	$375	$465
Shopping	$571	$479	$570
Entertainment	$134	$198	$173
Other	$60	$103	$210
Total	$2,659	£2,628	$3,032

Economic impact

Average trip expenditures must be considered before assessing the economic impact of the campaign. Table 16.4 reveals that on average, a California visitor from the UK spent $3,775 – with the bulk of spending on transportation, lodging, food and shopping.

The quantity of incremental trips resulting from advertising efforts can be calculated by applying the rate of incremental travel to the number of aware households. Then, economic impact, or the amount of travel revenue that is directly attributable to the advertising campaign, is determined by applying average trip expenditures.

Like with incremental travel, economic impact is analysed in two ways: the first includes only those who have already travelled and the second includes those who are planning a trip to California but have not visited yet in addition to those who already travelled. Only 80 per cent of these 'already planned' trips are counted, as some are likely to not follow through with plans.

Of those who already visited California, over $500 million (£250m) in travel revenue is directly attributable to the advertising. When including those who are planning to travel to California, the advertising is responsible for $670 million (£335m) in travel revenue for the state.

Return on investment

Finally looking at return on investment, this campaign outperformed all other worldwide territories according to SMARI. The California Travel & Tourism Commission spent $4,444,234 on the UK advertising campaign, resulting in an ROI of $115 when including only those who already visited and an ROI of $151 when considering those who are planning a trip. CTTC's research agency estimated the average ROI for a travel campaign at $50, so in this consideration the California UK campaign produced a very strong return on investment.

Taxes generated are also an important consideration for the CTTC. Every dollar spent on advertising returned $8 in tax revenue for the state from those who already visited. Including those planning to visit, the campaign generated $11 in tax revenue for every dollar spent.

Summary

The success of the campaign was clear and has been attributed to the opportunity the marketing communications team saw within the market to reach people at different stages within their decision making process. The team carefully selected media to drive people through the customer journey and use them in ways that differentiated California from other tourist destinations. This innovative planning saw the campaign outperform other territories throughout the world, delivering an increase of 4.3 per cent in visitation, and an increase in market share of circa 1 per cent, all as the economy began to slip into a recessionary decline.

CASE STUDY QUESTIONS

1. Critique the campaign. What marketing communication factors do you believe led to the success of the campaign? Justify your response.
2. How can you determine the individual monetary and non-monetary contribution of television, print and the website to the success of the campaign? What contribution do you believe each made to the decision process? How would you recommend evaluating this in the future?
3. What role might travel agents have played in supporting activity and how would you measure this? Discuss the implications of their playing a significant versus a minor role.
4. Critique the ROI measures used. Drawing on the methods discussed in the chapter, what other tools might they have considered? Justify your answer.
5. The case study provides an overview of advertising schedule weights. Refer back to earlier chapters that discussed aspects such as effective frequency, wearin and wearout. How would you recommend that these factors be assessed for this marketer and for others in the same sector?
6. Assume that you are one of California's destination competitors (e.g. Florida, Australia, New Zealand, South America, the Pacific Islands or Japan). How would you evaluate the impact of the Californication campaign on your destination's visitor numbers? How would you recommend countering the impact of their activity?
7. Visit the California website given in the case study and those of three of its competitors. Drawing on the concepts discussed in earlier chapters how would you determine the relative strengths of:

   - branding
   - effectiveness of segmentation strategies
   - communication strategies.

8. How would you recommend ROI be compared for different destinations within the industry? What non-marketing or marketing communications factors might impact on ROI rates?

CASE STUDY 16.2

Measuring Mastercard's ROI . . . priceless?

Source: Institute of Practitioners in Advertizing. Case material provided by the World Advertising Research Centre (WARC) www.warc.com.

In recent times, low levels of financial regulation and over-extension of resources by the banks have resulted in the term 'credit' becoming almost a dirty word. However, the use of a credit facility has become part of day-to-day life, not just for banks and businesses but also for ordinary people who use credit cards to manage fluctuations in expenditure.

In the UK, both debit and credit cards allow customers to undertake 'cashless' transactions in the purchase of goods and services. In recent years they have shown themselves to be particularly useful in the face of the growing trend towards online shopping as they facilitate instant payment. However, whilst debit cards deduct the value of the purchase directly from a customer's bank account, credit cards possess the additional benefit that they also extend a line of credit to customers on a short- to medium-term basis. Credit card customers are expected to repay a minimum monthly amount and then pay interest on the remaining balance until it is repaid.

The credit card market is a highly lucrative one. Despite the recession, which has seen customers reduce their overall levels of spending, gross credit card lending totalled £131 billion in 2008, an increase of 2 per cent on the 2007 total of £128 billion. In the UK alone, gross lending on credit cards amounted to £32.3 billion in 2012.

The credit card industry is dominated by three main brands: Visa, Amex (American Express) and MasterCard. In the late 1990s, Visa and Amex had very clear and distinct brand positionings; Visa, the market leader was the 'status' card whilst Amex was the card of business. By comparison, the image of the MasterCard brand seemed rather muddled. Five different campaigns over 12 and 15 different agency partners resulting in a level of inconsistency appeared to have undermined the clarity of the MasterCard brand.

In light of the strength of their competition, the time had come for MasterCard International to take action. The formulation of effective marketing communications within the credit card sector is a challenging brief for any agency. Consumers are increasingly cynical and there are ethical issues relating to any marketing communication that might encourage customers to get into debt. However, in response to these challenges, McCann-Erickson New York broke the 'Priceless' campaign in 1997.

The 'Priceless' campaign employed a variety of scenarios to illustrate the intangible rewards that might be obtained following the purchase of a 'shopping list' of items. For instance, one of the first executions in the US depicted a father and son at a baseball game. The 'shopping list' included 'two tickets, $28; two hot dogs, two popcorns and two sodas, $18; one autographed baseball, $45' and then finished with 'real conversation with 11-year-old son, priceless.'

A variety of media, including television, radio, billboards, print and the Internet were employed over the course of the campaign with billings estimated to have cost between $85 and $100 million. The major strength of the campaign was that it had the benefit of both consistency and flexibility. Using the same underlying 'Priceless' theme, MasterCard were able to tailor their message to resonate with separate target audiences without undermining its basic proposition. As a result it was able to adapt the campaign to suit geographic, cultural and demographic differences in their target populations.

The campaign was rolled out globally and, by 2006, it had aired in 106 countries and had been translated into 48 different languages. They were also able to target key demographic segments identified as particularly important: wealthy 40–50-year-olds and potential customers in their twenties. Whilst the 40–50-year-olds that comprise the baby-boomer generation were seen to be particularly attractive because of their high levels of income, those in their twenties were also seen as good prospects because the sector was characterized by low levels of brand switching. As a result, once customers selected a brand of credit card to use, they rarely changed.

The 'Priceless' campaign was measurably successful on a number of levels. In its first 18 months, it garnered an increase in advertising awareness of 13 percentage points and between 1997 and 2002, MasterCard's sales increased from $1.08 billion to $1.89 billion. In the UK alone, an estimated 11 million new MasterCards were issued between 2002 and 2005. Furthermore, of the turnover of credit, (measured in Gross Pound Volume (GPV)), £17.6 billion was directly attributable to the 'Priceless' campaign between 2002 and 2005.

It also became clear that the 'Priceless' format had become engrained in popular culture, evidenced by the fact that it had been publicly parodied at least 50 times. In the US, parodies were found on such high profile shows as *The Simpsons* and *Saturday Night Live* whilst in the UK, the broadsheet newspaper *The Daily Telegraph* reported that, on the death of the

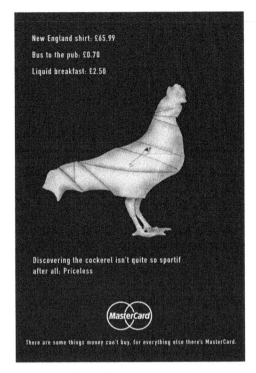

Photo 16.2 Examples of 'Priceless' campaign advertisements from the UK

legendary footballer George Best, a banner was seen to read 'Shevechenko: £30m. Ronaldino: £50m. George Best: Priceless'.

Unfortunately not all parodies were so welcome. In 1999, MasterCard International sued US cable channel Home Box Office (HBO) for $15 million over a trailer to promote one of its shows: *Arliss*. The show's central character, Arliss, an unpleasant, rather corrupt sports agent, is depicted engaging in a variety of shady transactions. The commercial concludes with the line 'There are some men money can't buy. Arliss isn't one of them.' A year later, MasterCard threatened legal action when Ralph Nader, a Green Party candidate in the US Presidential election, parodied the format of the 'Priceless' in his 'Priceless Truth' commercials. Using footage of both Democratic and Republican candidates with such captions as 'Promises to special interest groups: $10 billion' and 'Finding out the truth: Priceless', he sought to focus attention on the nature of financial contributions to political campaigns. Issuing an injunction to halt the broadcasting of the offending spots, MasterCard also demanded $5 million in damages. According to Larry Flanagan, Senior Vice President – Marketing at MasterCard: '"Priceless" is a very valuable asset . . . We're concerned about consumer confusion'.

However, the parodies both welcome and unwelcome do not appear to have harmed the brand significantly. By 2006, the 'Priceless' campaign won more than 100 awards, including two gold EFFIE awards in the Sustained Success category and it grew revenues by 42 per cent (2002–2005) which enabled them not only to out-perform key competitors Visa and Amex, but also to out-perform the market as a whole. In addition, the campaign has been recognized by Wall Street as having asset value and is therefore included in the valuation of the MasterCard organization as a whole. On a number of levels, for MasterCard International, this campaign was truly 'priceless'.

CASE STUDY QUESTIONS

1. Having analysed the 'Priceless' case, what additional information would you require in order to calculate a monetary value for the ROI for the campaign?
2. Discuss the challenges of measuring ROI when a campaign such as 'Priceless' runs for such a long period of time.
3. What are the main issues to be considered when measuring the ROI of a campaign when it is run across such a large number of countries?
4. Are there any intangible benefits that might have been accrued as a result of the campaign? How might they be measured?
5. Discuss the benefits and pitfalls of parody in this case when seeking to measure ROI.

Notes

1   Varcoe, J. (2004). Assessing the Effectiveness of Social Marketing. Paper presented at the ESOMAR Conference, Berlin.
2   Dillon, W.R., Madden, T.J., and Firtle, N.H. (1990). *Marketing Research in a Marketing Research Environment*, Ill: Irwin Inc.
3   CIM Study Text (2006). *Marketing Research and Information*, London: BPP Professional Education.
4   Heath, R. (1999). Can tracking studies tell lies? *International Journal of Advertising*, 18(2), 169–90.
5   McDonald, M. (2005). Let us drop, once and for all, the nonsense about marketing return on investment. *Journal of Medical Marketing*, 5(3): 256–60.
6   Lloyd, J. (2009). Keeping Both the Baby and the Bathwater: Scoping a New Model of Political Marketing Communication. Paper presented at the eighth IAPNM Congress, University of Valencia.
7   McDonald, M. (2005). Let us drop, once and for all, the nonsense about marketing return on investment. *Journal of Medical Marketing*, 5(3): 256–60.
8   Ittner, C.D., and Larcker, D.F. (1998). Cited in Seggie, S.H., Cavusgil, E., and Phelan, S.E. (2007). Measurement of return on marketing investment: a conceptual framework and the future of marketing metrics. *Industrial Marketing Management*, 36, 834–41.
9   Sawhney, N., and Zabin, J. (2002). Managing and measuring relational equity in the network economy. *Journal of the Academy of Marketing Science*, 30(4) 313–32.

Glossary and key terms

Above the line: (see also **Below the line** and **Through the line**): A historical term originally used to describe advertising in mass media, for which commission was paid by the media, compared to activities such as public relations or direct mail for which a fee was charged to the client – a line being drawn on invoices to separate out commission-bearing activity from fee-based activity.

Account management: (see also **Retail account management**): In a marketing communications agency, a role focussed on liaison with a client or number of clients on behalf of specialist sections such as creative, media and research. Responsible for ensuring that marketing communications activity is developed in accordance with clients' overall objectives and that budgets and deadlines are met.

ACORN: A geodemographic profiling system using postcodes as the basis for analysis. ACORN is an acronym for A Classification of Residential Neighbourhoods.

Actual self: The way individuals actually see themselves within society.

Adapting: (see also **Standardization**): Taking a marketing communications concept and amending it for specific countries or population segments on the basis of cultural preferences.

Adoption: (see also **Diffusion**): Consumer decision to try, or to continue to use, a new product or service. Populations usually can be divided into discrete groups on the basis of how quickly adoption occurs relative to others in the population.

Advergames: Electronic (computer or video) games which contain advertising embedded within the games. This may include signage or the use of products or services by the characters within a specific game.

Advertainment: Blend between advertising and entertainment in which persuasive messages for a product, service or concept may be included within the scripted entertainment, for example, a website which includes games or competitions may also feature promotional material regarding products or services, or feature them as part of the game (see also **Product placement**).

Advertising: Communication of persuasive messages regarding goods, services or concepts via channels such as mass media (e.g. television, magazines etc.) with the source (advertiser) identified and paying for the placement of the messages within the medium.

Advertising Standards Authority (ASA): Independent regulator of the content of advertisements, sales promotions and direct marketing in the UK. May require advertisements deemed to be in breach of the Advertising Codes of Practice to be amended or withdrawn.

Affective: Component of attitudes based on feelings or emotions regarding a specific product, service or idea.

Agency (marketing communications): An organization that specialises in the development, management and evaluation of any or all forms of marketing communications on behalf of clients such as manufacturers or retailers.

Agency compensation: (see also **Commission**): Payment ('compensation') to a marketing communications agency in the form of commission from media for advertising placed with them and/or fees for work undertaken on a client's behalf such as development of creative material.

AIDA model: A model that proposes a consumer passes through distinct stages in response to a promotional message such as an advertisement: Awareness, Interest, Desire and Action (purchase). Originated more than 100 years ago when a small number of mass media dominated; of limited use in the increasingly complex and fragmented communications environment.

AIO: A form of lifestyle segmentation based on the Attitudes, Interests and Opinions of a particular population.

Ambush marketing: A term usually used in connection with sponsorship, when one brand is an official sponsor of an event and pays for this right but another competing brand attempts to connect itself with the event, without paying a fee. Also called guerrilla marketing.

Applets: A small programme that can be sent along to a user of a web page. Java applets can perform tasks such as providing simple animations, calculations etc. without having to exit the page or open another computer programme.

Artistic value: Value of communications for its sensory (e.g. visual or auditory) appeal rather than for its ability to be persuasive.

Aspirational group: A group an individual may desire to join or copy in terms of dress, behaviour or products used.

Astro-turfing: Public relations activity that attempts to portray itself as originating not from the sponsoring organization, but from the population at whom it is targeted.

Attitude: A learned tendency to respond or behave in a consistent (favourable or unfavourable) manner towards a product, service or idea (e.g. liking, preference). Consists of three components: affective (feelings), cognitive (knowledge) and behavioural (buying intentions).

Audit: A systematic review of the performance of a marketing communications programme against objectives set, identifying factors (both within the control of a marketer and those which are beyond direct influence such as economic factors and competitive activity) that enhanced or inhibited achievement of objectives. Used as part of an ongoing planning, implementation and review cycle with results of the review/audit phase being used as inputs into the planning of the next cycle of activity.

Awareness: A measure of the percentage of a specific target group who are able to spontaneously (unprompted) or with prompting recall aspects of a specific communication programme.

Bastion brand: A stable and profitable brand.

Behaviour: Response to marketing activity such as purchase of a product or service or adoption of a particular behaviour.

Below the line: (see also **Above the line**): promotional activity via channels other than traditional mass media (from which commission would be paid to the advertising agency). Includes public relations, sales promotions, direct mail, packaging, point-of-sale material, Internet activity and new, hybrid forms of promotion such as product placements.

Benchmark: Measurements made to establish attitudes, brand preferences, actual buying behaviours or the extent of social marketing problems or political part preferences prior to a campaign starting. The difference between the pre-campaign benchmarks and subsequent measurements is used to determine the effects of a campaign and competitive activity.

Bespoke websites: A website that is custom-built to suit the needs of a business or organization. The site may include client-specified layouts, custom database integration, and other extra features developed to suit the client's specific needs.

Blog: A web log where entries are made in chronological order and displayed in reverse order (i.e. most recent first). Commonly used to provide comment on specific issues or subjects, but also used as personal diaries.

Bluetooth: Is a way of exchanging data wirelessly, i.e. replacing traditional cables, over short distances, often just a few metres. It can be used to send files between two or more devices, for example exchange pictures, send ringtones to a mobile phone, synchronise a mobile phone and a computer or it can be used to exchange sound data between a phone and a Bluetooth enabled handsfree kit or headset.

Brand: A company's product or service that is clearly identifiable via words or symbols and differentiated from other products for services, for example, Coca-Cola or Nescafé (a brand owned by Nestlé).

Brand architecture: Organizational structure of brands within an organization or business unit which shows the role or position of each brand relative to others.

Brand equity: A term with multiple meanings according to different disciplines. For example, financial-based brand equity may reflect the difference between balance-sheet valuations and the specific value of tangible assets. Marketing-based brand equity refers to consumers' perceived strength of a brand relative to its competitors. It is thus a factor in brand loyalty and the willingness of consumers to pay a premium compared to other brands in the category.

Brand identity: Combination of product attributes, organizational attributes, personality and symbolic factors. Ideally, the identity desired by the marketer should match what is perceived by potential purchasers.

Brand loyalty: Consumers' consistent purchase of a specific brand in a product or service category. Few brands achieve absolute loyalty many are part of a consumer 'portfolio' of acceptable brands that may be purchased.

Brand Manager: Person within an organization who is responsible for the management of the marketing and marketing communications of a specific brand or group of brands, for example, Brand Manager of Nestlé's beverages or soups ranges.

Brand personality: Artificial personality created for a brand as if it was a person or animal (e.g. friendly, caring, smart, stylish).

Brand portfolio: In a retail context, the range of brands within a specific category stocked by the retailer. Portfolio managers will decide on relative pricing, shelf positions, and promotional strategy and tactics, including price discounting.

Brand strength: A term related to brand equity, but specifically focussed on relation to market share, price relating to other brands, loyalty and ability to withstand short-term competitive activity such as price discounting.

Branded entertainment: Entertainment such as sponsored programmes or websites in which the brands of the sponsoring organization are clearly featured.

Broadband: Transmission technology using a range of frequencies (such as for television channel) that enables multiple messages to be transmitted simultaneously, making use of increased data throughput, for example by combining traditional voice, data and other services on a single line.

Budget: A specific amount of money allocated for a finite period – a client may allocate an overall budget, with a marketing communications agency then recommending how the budget should be split across different marketing communications activity, including allocations for production of material as well as its placement in media, and for material associated with PR, publicity, sales promotions and event sponsorship.

Business-to-business advertising: Advertising directed at organizations who may use a manufacturer's products as ingredients or components in their own products (as opposed to advertising directed at end purchasers or consumers of finished products).

Business-to-business marketing: Sector of marketing involving production and marketing of goods for other manufacturers rather than being aimed at end consumers (see also **Business-to-business advertising**).

Buzz creation: Efforts to encourage target groups to talk about and recommend a specific product or service to others. Appears spontaneous but often underpinned by highly orchestrated/organized efforts by marketers to generate 'buzz'.

Campaign: Coordinated marketing communications activity for a specific product or service over a designated time period and with specific objectives set for the activity such as awareness, sales, attitude or behavioural change.

Category management: A system originally developed by Procter & Gamble to assign responsibility for all aspects of marketing activity (and responsibility for profit generation) for a group of products to a specific manager. Now also used to describe the way in which retail organizations, such as large supermarkets, manage the brands stocked within a specific product category, the pricing of individual brands relative to each other and other promotional activity within the category.

Cause-related marketing: Cooperative marketing between a commercial (for profit) organization and a not-for-profit organization such as a charity. It does not involve direct donation of funds.

Celebrity: A well known (famous, popular, or at times notorious) public figure such as an actor, musician etc.

Celebrity endorsement: (see also **Spokesperson**): Endorsement of a product or service by a celebrity, either by directly promoting it or indirectly by being shown using it in marketing communications material such as advertisements, leaflets, videos etc.

Central route of persuasion: (see also **Elaboration likelihood model** and **Peripheral route of persuasion**): One of two routes by which a message is received and processed by a person 'exposed to' (i.e. seeing, hearing, reading) the message. The central route involved direct consideration of the message and previous knowledge, counter arguments etc. It is most common when involvement or interest in the subject area is high.

Chavs: People from a lower socio-economic background, showing loutish behaviour and frequently wearing either real or counterfeit/imitation designer label clothes.

Channel: In marketing communication, the means by which a persuasive message is sent to the intended target group. For example, television, radio, public relations activity. Note: the term can also refer to distribution channels.

Client: Manufacturer, retailer or other organization who contracts a marketing communication agency to provide a range of services for the products or services controlled by the client organization.

Code: Symbols by which information can be communicated and meaning understood (e.g. colours of a traffic light).

Codes of Practice: Set of guidelines or rules, such as those relating to advertising, sales promotion and public relations spelling out the standards of conduct and practice expected of members (see also **Advertising Standards Authority**).

Cognitive dissonance: Inconsistency between current attitudes, knowledge and beliefs and the 'ideal' situation as perceived by a potential customer. Discomfort generated by dissonance may lead people to seek out products or services to reduce the dissonance.

Commission: Historically, media organizations paid commission to advertising agencies based on a set percentage (as high as 15–20 per cent) of the value of the television or radio time/newspaper or magazine space purchased on behalf of the agency's clients. Now usually considerably lower and based on estimates of or actual services provided by a marketing communications agency to a specific client for a finite period.

Communication: All forms of contact between a marketer and their target groups, including intermediaries such as wholesalers or retailers as well as other 'publics'. Includes traditional advertising, new media forms and PR, publicity, sales promotions and personal selling.

Communication models: Diagrams of how persuasive communication such as marketing communication activity is believed to operate. Models incorporate the sender of persuasive messages, the channel through which messages are sent, noise or other distractions that may hamper the message being sent, and the way in which the message is received and understood by its intended receiver. Closely related to communication theory.

Communication theory: Hypotheses regarding the way that persuasive messages are sent through channels and received and processed by the intended target groups.

Competitive analysis: Analysis of all aspects of competing organizations' marketing activity, including product range, pricing decisions, promotional strategy and distribution strategy, used as part of communications audits and as part of planning future activity.

Complementary products: Products or services that add value to the purchase of a different product or service, such as conditioner with hair shampoo or special offers on hotel rooms and rental cars for airline passengers.

Comprehension: Understanding (or otherwise) of a marketing communication message, including words, signs and symbols and the meaning taken from the message by its receiver.

Concept: Initial idea for a creative strategy based on client briefing, competitive analysis and an understanding of the target market. The concept will use this information to design a way in which a product or service can be differentiated from competitors in the minds of the target market.

Concept testing: Research undertaken to determine whether an initial concept is acceptable to a target market, including whether the message intended to be sent is actually what is received by the target group and whether the impact on the way a product or services is regarded by the target is positive.

Context effects: (see also **Message context effects**): The effects of the medium itself, such as a television programme, on the way an advertisement is perceived. For example, if there is a marked contrast between an advertisement and the programme in which it appears (such as an advertisement stressing warmth and caring placed in a violent movie), the advertisement may not be perceived as positively as when it appears in a programme that is compatible with the values being portrayed in the advertisement.

Contingency: Planning for unlikely but possible future events such as product recalls, major competitor activity or disruption to a market or the supply of ingredients etc.

Continuity: Media activity that focusses on maintaining opportunities to see advertising over the duration of a campaign.

Cookies: A small file placed on a user's computer by a website they visit. Designed to track the use of the website and to provide information about possible future preferences.

Cooperative advertising: Advertising run by a manufacturer in conjunction with smaller or local advertisers (usually retailers) in which the creative material is developed by the manufacturer to ensure consistent brand presentation. Local retail addresses and other details, including specific promotional activity are then inserted into the material before it appears in local media.

Conventions: Customs or commonly accepted values and behaviours.

Convergent thinking: Logical consideration of current ideas in order to solve a problem.

Cost efficiency: A measure of the amount of persuasive messages sent to specific target groups balanced against the cost of the messages. Usually used to compare different strategies and tactics, with the option that provides the lowest cost per number/ percentage of the target group reached or rating points achieved being selected.

Coupons: Promotional activity providing price-off or value-added benefits through vouchers that can be 'redeemed' (cashed-in) at point-of-sale. Often used as part of loyalty schemes.

Creative brief: Verbal or written information and instructions used to discuss the development of creative material such as copywriting and advertisement design for a specific campaign. Developed by an account manager in conjunction with the client.

Creative strategy: Use of material from the creative brief to develop a recommended communication 'position' that will meet the client's objectives and differentiate a brand, product or service from it's competitors.

Creative tactics/execution: The development of a creative strategy into recommended specific marketing communication elements such as advertisements for different media prior to final production of the material. For example, print ads, scripts for radio commercials, 'story boards' for television commercials showing how the agreed strategy will be communicated via individual media.

Creativity: Ability to look at an issue from different, often new perspectives and to develop new connections or relationships between concepts, ideas and factors in people's lives that may hinder or help purchase or behaviour change.

Cross-cultural considerations: Decisions regarding how persuasive communication strategy and tactics may need to be modified for individual cultural groups to conform to their norms, preferences and beliefs.

Culture: Set of learned beliefs, customs and values within a particular society. Culture may impact on the acceptability of particular products and on the way promotional activity is perceived.

Customer relationship management (CRM): Management of communication with customers, including dealing with complaints and concerns as well as specific product or service requirements or preferences.

Decoding: The mental (thought) processes by which a target for marketing communications activity interprets and understands the message, including signs and symbols being sent, drawing on past knowledge, attitudes and beliefs and on communication from a range of other sources about both the advertised product or service and its competitors.

Demographics: Profile of a specific population on the basis of any combinations of: gender, age, marital status, social class, education, occupation, ethnic background etc.

Deontology: Ethical reasoning focussed on aims or objectives – with a presumed intention of trying to do good, but accepting that some negative consequences may occur (see also **Teleology**).

Design: Plan or layout of an advertisement, brochure etc. – including written material (copy) and illustrations/photographs/graphics.

Differentiated medium: (see also **Undifferentiated medium**): A media channel that has a very specific target either in terms of a narrow demographic group or special interest.

Differentiated message: (see also **Undifferentiated message**): A communications message targeting a specific segment of the population, defined by demographics, psychographics, product usage, interests etc. as opposed to a message targeting broad segments of the population.

Diffusion: (see also **Adoption**): the way in which acceptance of a product or service spreads through its intended target market.

Diffusion of innovation: The manner and speed at which an innovative product or service spreads through the population (see also **Diffusion**).

Direct and database marketing: Marketing communication directed to a potential target, usually with personally addressed communication and product or service offers specifically tailored to the known or assumed needs of the target.

Direct mail: Direct marketing using personally addressed letters or other material sent to targets via the standard commercial mail system.

Direct response advertising: Marketing communication carried through media where a website, email address or telephone number is given to encourage people to make contact immediately.

Disassociative group: A group whose behaviour or product use mark them as NOT what appeals to an individual or group of individuals. Products purchased or displayed by the group will be avoided.

Distribution channel: Means by which a potential purchaser can obtain a product or service, ranging from conventional retail outlets or service providers, to Internet-based purchases.

Divergent thinking: Drawing together previously unconnected elements to create unusual, novel or different solutions to a problem.

Door-to-door sales: Sales strategy based on sales personnel literally going form household to household or from business to business, often unannounced and with no previous communication, to try to gain sales.

eCommerce/electronic commerce: Is the way of buying or selling products or services electronically, or more specifically usually online, for example by using the Internet or other data networks. With the rise of the Internet, this has become a much more lively field, and the usage of the term now often refers to any business transaction, whether business-to-business (B2B) or business-to-consumer (B2C) done online.

Editorial: Non-advertising content of a publication, such as news stories, articles etc.

Edutainment: Activity that blends both educational and entertainment activity. May be overtly sponsored by an advertiser or feature products or services ('product place-ment') within the content.

Effectiveness: Measurement of how well a campaign achieved the objectives set for it. Often used to compare different strategy or tactical options.

Efficiency: (see also **Cost-efficiency**): Measurement of how well individual elements of a campaign achieved their objectives in relation to the cost of using them. Often used to compare the relative costs of one medium to another or the cost of advertising in a specific medium such as a television programme or magazine relative to the viewership or readership likely to have the opportunity to see the advertisement.

Elaboration: Thought about a message received, involving prior experience with the advertised product or service, existing thoughts or beliefs about it in relation to competitors.

Elaboration likelihood model: Model of persuasion developed by Petty & Cacioppo which suggests that two different routes may be taken when processing a message. A central route operates when individuals are highly interested or motivated to pay attention to the message. A peripheral route operates when interest and motivation is low.

Electronic technology: The technology behind Internet, eCommerce and mCommerce applications and devices as opposed to conventional mass media technologies.

Endorser: (see also **Spokesperson**): A person contracted to publicly promote a product or service, either in advertising/publicity or via direct appearances at events.

Entropic: A measure of uncertainty in message content.

Environmental factors: Features within the environment in which people live, work or interact with others that may positively or negatively influence lifestyle, product or service use, health or well-being. For marketers, environmental factors may also disrupt normal activity (see also **Environmental turbulence**).

Environmental turbulence: Disruption to normal marketing or marketing activity; may be caused by economic factors such as a recession, a significant change to competitor activity, introduction of new technology, or a significant change to the available marketing communication channels.

Ethics: Moral (as opposed to legal) rules, principles and expectations or codes of behaviour (written or unwritten). There are substantial differences between cultures as to what types of behaviours are considered to be ethical and therefore acceptable.

eWOM: Electronic word of mouth, see also buzz – spreading the word about a product or service using electronic means, for example Twitter updates or Facebook status updates.

Evaluation: Assessment of the effects and effectiveness of all individual elements of a marketing communications campaign and of the campaign overall. Both performance against objectives and against competitors are generally included.

Event: A specific function, exhibition, competition, concert etc. which may be the focus of public relations, publicity and or sponsorship activity.

Execution: (see **Creative execution**).

Exhibition: A specific display, such as at a museum or art gallery which may be sponsored or a show targeting the general public and/or retailers at which marketers display and demonstrate their products or services.

Experiential marketing: Marketing communications activity whereby direct contact is made between the marketer and the customer, with the intention being that a positive experience is provided, leading to some form of emotional connection for the customer, leading to purchase and/or increased brand loyalty.

Extended self: The way individuals relate to anything external to themselves upon which they might base their self concept.

Facebook: The world's largest social networking site, which allows users to easily set up a profile and interact with other users. This interaction can be by exchanging messages, broadcasting status information, online gaming etc. The site also allows users to set up fan pages for commercial products and services and to become friends/ fans of such pages.

Fast moving consumer goods (FMCG): Frequently purchased products, especially those sold via supermarkets or other stores.

Fear appeals: Communication based on generating distress, alarm or apprehension in order to draw attention to a specific message and to generate action from the message recipient such as behaviour change.

Fighter brand: A brand used to protect a bastion brand by directly competing with competitive brands.

Flanker brand: A brand offering similar quality to a bastion brand but catering to slightly different needs and offering the bastion brand some protection from actual or potential competitors.

Flash: A multi-media development platform extensively used for developing rich media Internet applications, such as interactive graphics, embedded videos and sounds and website animation.

Flickr: The world's largest photo sharing website, which combines posting of pictures with various social networking functions, in particular so called 'photostreams', which allow users to share their pictures real-time via RSS technology.

Flights: Scheduled marketing communication messages for specific periods of time, followed by a period in which no messages appear, then a further period during which the messages reappear. It is a common strategy for advertisers who cannot fund continuous messages throughout the campaign period.

Four Ps (4Ps): Decisions made by a marketer regarding the **P**roduct to be offered, the **P**rice at which it should be sold, how it is to be **P**romoted and distributed, i.e. the **P**lace at which it is to be made available to potential purchasers. Marketers of services usually add several additional Ps including **P**eople providing the service.

Fragment: The breakdown of mass media into smaller entities, generally each focussing on a more specific (and therefore smaller) target group.

Frequency: The average number of times a population or specific target group had the opportunity to see any of a specific schedule of marketing communication messages. Usually used in conjunction with other measures of advertising weight, particularly rating points and reach. For example, a schedule may achieve 210 rating points, with 70 per cent of the target group having seen the messages at all; the average number of times the messages were seen (frequency) would be 3 (reach x frequency = total rating points.

Froogle: A comparison shopping search engine operated by Google that allows buyers to compare prices for various items.

Full service agency: A marketing communications agency that provides services relating to traditional advertising, including creative and media placement services, newer electronic media such as Internet-based activity, and also public relations, sales promotion services.

Global advertising: Advertising that is run in multiple countries, with our without adaptation to meet the preferences of specific cultures (see also **Cross-cultural considerations**).

Gray marketing: Also referred to as parallel importing, it involves the selling of trademarked goods through channels of distribution that are not authorized by the trademark holders. It is legal in some countries and totally banned in others.

Guerrilla marketing: (see **Ambush marketing**).

HABBO (also called HABBO Hotel): A social networking site aimed at teenagers.

Hedonistic appeals: Appeals to pleasure, enjoyment, reward or aspects of a lifestyle valued by a target market.

Hierarchy of effects model: A model that proposes that people move through clearly defined stages from being initially unaware of a product or service, through interest in it, to a final stage of actually purchasing it.

High involvement: (see also **Low involvement**): A product, service or marketing communication which is seen as being particularly relevant or interesting to a target group. High levels of attention will therefore be paid to marketing communications and the central route of persuasion is likely to be active.

Homeostasis: Maintenance of equilibrium or balance within an individual or group of individuals such as a family or social group.

House brand: A product that is branded with the retailer's name rather than that of the manufacturer who produced the product for the retailer. For example, Tesco has a wide range of brands that carry only the Tesco name. These products will be placed on shelves next to other products in the category, often including the manufacturer-branded products of the company who produced the house brands.

HTML (Hyper Text Markup Language): Is a way of structuring and laying out ('coding') web pages, by using a defined set of codes.

Humour appeals: Communications based on generating amusement in order to draw attention to a specific message. Humour is culturally situated and what is seen as amusing to one group may be offensive to another.

Hybrid media: Media forms that combine elements of two distinct forms of activity such as advertising and computer games ('advergames').

Ideal self: The way individuals would like to see themselves and to be seen by others.

Identity: The way an individual sees themselves both physically and in social settings and interactions with others.

i-mode: A largely Japanese Internet standard for mobile phones, being made obsolete by more modern mobile phones using the same standard as traditional Internet communications for data exchange and mobile browsing.

Impact: Result of a persuasive message. Positive impact should move people from awareness, through interest, to desire and actual purchase or behaviour change.

Industry analysis: Analysis of trends within a specific industry, identifying both potential threats to, and opportunities for, a marketer. Also considers external factors such as changes to legislation, economic factors and technological advancements.

Ingredient brand: A brand that is a component of a product or combination of products marketed under a different name, but featured within the latter's marketing communication activity. For example, 'Intel Inside' is frequently used by computer brands to suggest that the Intel processors are high quality, thereby offering an indirect assurance regarding the quality of the overall computer package.

Innovation: A major change to a product or service, such as significant advancement in technology. Likely to cause environmental turbulence if competitive offerings cannot match the technical superiority. Marketing communications will focus on stressing the advantage the innovation offers and issues such as ease of use etc.

Integrated marketing communication: Management of marketing communication activity to ensure synergy and consistency of messages sent via different channels.

Integration: (see also **Integrated marketing communication**): The management practices involved in ensuring that all elements of marketing and marketing communications activity work together to achieve overall objectives.

Interactive media: Media forms, usually electronic that responds to user choices by offering different content choices or which allows two-way communication.

Internal marketing: Marketing, and especially marketing communication (promotion), aimed at an organization's own staff in order to gain support and enthusiasm for a campaign or acceptance of a major change to the way an organization operates.

Internal promotion: (see **Internal marketing**).

Internet (traditional): A network of internationally interconnected networks in order to exchange data amongst users in different networks or localities on a global basis using a specifically designed standard for data exchange and data addressing (TCP/IP).

Interstitials: Web pages that are displayed before another (destination) webpage. This can be, for example, an advert which needs to be looked at by the user before he/she can proceed to the originally intended page.

Involvement: (see **High involvement** and **Low involvement**).

JavaScript: Is an object oriented script langue often used to enhance web pages. Used for applets.

Joint promotion: Promotional activity undertaken jointly by two organizations such as two manufacturers of complementary products, or by a manufacturer and a retailer.

Junk mail: Unrequested and unwanted letters or other printed material sent via commercial mail.

Key account management: Sales management whereby large customers such as major retail chains are given high levels of sales force attention and service, usually with a dedicated team of sales people or a single, highly experienced sales person assigned just to look after the needs of a single client.

Lag effect: Delays in sales after marketing communication activity is run – may be due to customers using up old stock before making purchases of new products, or the actions of intermediaries such as advice from pharmacists for a new medication.

Layout: The design of print material showing where headings and other copy are to be placed in relation to illustrations and the relative size of each component.

Legislation: Laws covering a specific country or group of countries such as the European Union.

Lifestyle: Literally how people live their lives including activities, interests, attitudes, opinions, consumption of products or services, living conditions and behaviours that may enhance or damage health and well-being (e.g. smoking) or excess alcohol consumption.

Line extension: Development of a new product under the same brand name as existing products and complementary to the existing offerings.

Literacy: Ability of people to read and understand material. Some 20 per cent of the population of most developed countries are functionally illiterate and a further 20 per cent have limited literacy abilities. Marketers must therefore ensure that written material caters for the specific challenges faced by these groups.

Lobbying: Public relations led activity designed to influence decisions such as government policy, planning decisions etc.

Location-based services: Is a location specific product or service accessed usually through a mobile device, for example special offers displayed on a mobile phone depending on where the phone is located.

Looking glass self: The way individuals would ideally like others to see them.

Low involvement: (see also **High involvement**): A product, service or marketing communication which is seen as NOT being particularly relevant or interesting to a target group. Minimal attention will therefore be paid to marketing communications and the peripheral route of persuasion is likely to be active.

Loyalty: (see also **Brand loyalty**): Degree to which consumers will include a brand in a group of brands they will buy regularly. Rarely does loyalty extend to only one brand being purchased exclusively.

Loyalty schemes: Activities (such as Tesco Clubcard) designed to encourage repeat purchase of a product or shopping at a specific retail chain. May include price discount coupons or vouchers for products or services in addition to those normally purchased.

Manufacturer: (In marketing communication, also termed the marketer; for communications agencies, the client.) The organization producing products, usually branded for sale to other producers, as in business-to-business activity, or to end consumers.

Manufacturer brand: A brand produced and marketed by a specific manufacturer (for example, Procter & Gamble or Coca-Cola) rather than being marketed under the name of a retail chain such as Sainsbury's.

Market disruption: A major event that leads to significant changes to the way marketing activity is conducted, including such factors such as availability (or lack) of credit, the impact of industrial disputes that may affect distribution or to the strengths of a specific product or service relative to its competitors.

Market share: Relative percentage of sales in a specific category achieved by a brand compared to sales for all brands within the category.

Market stability: The extent to which a specific market shows no significant changes to structure, size or any other factor likely to influence supply of or demand for products or services (see also **Market disruption**).

Marketing: Activity designed to plan products or services, decide on pricing and distribution strategies and communication activity by which persuasive messages will be directed at target groups (see also **4Ps** and **Marketing mix**).

Marketing communications: All elements in an organization's marketing mix that focus on communication with specific target groups. Includes advertising, PR/publicity, sales promotion and personal selling.

Marketing mix: Decisions about the strategies and tactics to be used with regard to what is referred to as the 4Ps: products, pricing, promotion and place (or distribution). In services marketing, other elements such as the people involved in delivering the service are also included in the mix decision process.

Marketing PR (MPR): Public relations activity specifically focussed on supporting the marketing communications activities undertaken in a campaign, as opposed to public relations activity that is focussed on activity supporting the organization as a whole.

Mass media: (see also **Traditional media**): Television, radio, newspapers and magazines (as compared to newer, primarily electronic forms of communication such as social networks which may have appeal to a narrow specific population segment only.

mCommerce: Business transactions carried out using a mobile device, such as a mobile phone. This can range from small items, like purchasing public transport tickets via mobile phones to shopping online using a mobile phone.

Media convergence: Changes to technology that result in formerly specific media forms being able to offer services formerly found only on other media, for example, television viewing via computers or mobile phones.

Media literacy: Ability to understand the intentions behind media and persuasive communications such as advertising.

Media relations: PR activity designed to build communication between an organization and the media. Intended to share news and ideas of potential interest to the users of the media, such as new technology, new product models or design features, or corporate activity such as charity or community support designed to portray the organization in a favourable light.

Medium (plural: media, sometimes mediums): A channel of communication (e.g. television, Internet) through which a marketer endeavours to communicate, using an advertisement or other form of persuasive communication, with a specific target audience.

Membership group: A group, such as a sporting or social group, of which an individual is a member. Products and services used and displayed will be influenced to at least some extent by the perceived norms and expectations of the group; some products or services may be actively avoided, even if the individual would like them, in order to conform to the group's perceived norms.

Merchandiser: A member of a sales team whose specific responsibilities include either ensuring effective stock allocation and distribution (to wholesalers, retailers etc.) or for ensuring that products are displayed as intended within retail environments, and that out-of-stock situations are rectified as quickly as possible.

Merchandising: (see **Premiums**).

Message: The meaning, such as product image, benefits or positioning relative to competitors intended to be taken from a specific marketing communication programme.

Message context effects: (see **Context effects**).

Message framing: (see **Positive framing** and **Negative framing**).

Message relevance: How personally important and relevant a message is seen to be by the intended target. Relevance will affect the amount of attention paid to messages and whether the central or peripheral route of persuasion is activated.

Microblogging: Smaller version of traditional blogging, for example using brief text updates or sending small links to other multi-media content without a large description.

Microsite: An individual web page or a group of related pages embedded within a larger website. They are used to provide specialized information relating to a specific topic.

MMS (multi-media messaging service): Or a standard for delivering multi-media or mixed content, such as images and sounds, in a message to a mobile device (usually a phone).

Mobile advertising: A form of advertising via mobile (wireless) phones or other wireless devices, usually involving banners at the top or bottom of a page, or an 'interstitial' page between two content pages.

Mobile Internet: Internet on a mobile device, for example on an iPhone.

MOSAIC: A demographic profiling system. MOSAIC is an acronym for modelling, optimisation, scheduling and intelligent control.

Multiples: Retail outlets owned by the same parent company (i.e. multiple outlets).

MySpace: A social networking site.

Negative framing: Presentation of a message in terms of threats, potential losses or other negative events rather than stressing the benefits of an action (see also **Positive framing**).

Negative self: Attributes an individual has or believes others perceive them to have but which they do not want to be associated with.

New media: Digital, and often networked media forms, for example websites, video games or DVDs or Bluray delivered media.

NFC (near field communication): Or a technology that allows rapid wireless exchange of data in a very limited range. Used mostly for contactless technology, for example in payment systems for swiping card on payment terminals or for swiping tickets at public transport ticket gates (such as the Oyster Card used on London transport systems).

Noise: (see also **Technical noise** and **Semantic noise**): Any factor external to a message that interferes with its reception by the intended target.

Norms: Types or standards of behaviour expected, required or assumed to be 'normal' within a culture or group.

Objectives: Goals that are to be completed for a specific campaign or event. SMART objectives (credited as having been designed by Peter Drucker) are specific, measurable, achievable, realistic and time specific.

Offline: Marketing activity not involving the Internet, mCommerce or other electronic channels of communication.

On demand: Also known as video on demand (VoD). Electronic systems such as BBC iPlayer and ITV Player which enable people to access television or radio programmes at times convenient to them rather than when the programmes are first broadcast on television or radio.

Online: The opposite of offline.

Online retailing: Sales made using the Internet rather than traditional retail outlets.

Opportunity to see: A measure of the percentage of a population or specific target group who used a particular medium at the time an advertiser's message appeared (e.g. watching a specific television show or reading a specific issue of a magazine). It does not measure those who actually paid attention to the message.

Outdoor: A term that has slightly different meanings across countries. Generally taken to refer to billboards, hoardings, posters or other forms of advertising displays. May also include advertising on buses, in railway carriages etc. (this may also be referred to as transit advertising).

Perception: The way a message is interpreted or understood.

Perceptual defence: Mental processes whereby an individual blocks or screens out obviously or suspected persuasive messages.

Perceptual selectivity: Mental filtering of messages to focus only on those which appear interesting, relevant or worthy of further involvement or study.

Perceptual vigilance: Seeking messages that may be potentially relevant, interesting or important.

Peer: Friends or members of social groups whose opinions may be valued, or whose approval may be sought for behaviours or purchases or whose actual or likely disapproval may inhibit purchases or specific behaviours.

Peripheral route of persuasion: (see also **Elaborate likelihood model** and **Central route of persuasion**): A form of message processing when interest in the topic is low and there is therefore minimal motivation to pay attention to the message. Background music, scenery or attractive models/presenters might produce an attitude towards the advertised product rather than the central message itself.

Permission marketing: Permission for persuasive messages to be sent to an individual or groups of individuals.

Personal selling: Direct contact between a member of a sales force, from either a manufacturer or retailer, and potential purchasers.

Persuasion knowledge: A concept suggesting that people's behaviour changes when they become aware that they are the target of attempts to persuade them to make a purchase or change behaviours (see also **Persuasion resistance**).

Persuasion resistance: Defensive behaviour aimed at combating attempts to persuade people to make a purchase or change behaviours. Often behaviour will be resisted as a result of the persuasion attempt, even if an individual may agree with the message that is being attempted. Resistance is particularly high when personal freedoms, including choice or actions are seen to be threatened or when the persuasion is seen as coercive.

PEST analysis: Market analysis undertaken at the early stages of a planning cycle involving analysis of trends and possible future changes to the **P**olitical, **E**conomic, **S**ocial and **T**echnological environment.

Planning cycle: A management cycle which commences with initial objective setting, campaign briefings and development, followed by actual implementation and evaluation of the campaign effects. Results and lessons learned from one cycle are used in the next planning cycle.

Podcast: A digital media file distributed via the Internet, which can be updated or subscribed to using a specific version of RSS. Often these files can be downloaded periodically and made available for playing while on the move on an iPod (hence the name).

Point-of-purchase: Marketing communication activity within retail outlets aimed at reminding potential purchasers of recent advertising and helping to reinforce positioning and differentiation from competing products or services. Activity may include demonstrations, displays, visuals from television commercials etc.

Pop-up ads: Advertisements that appear without being requested when accessing Internet pages.

Positioning: Marketing communication activity aimed at developing a specific image or 'position' in the mind of the consumer for a brand in relation to competing brands or an overall product category.

Positive framing: Presentation of a message in terms potential gains or benefits of an action rather than stressing the potential negative consequences of an action (see also **Negative framing**).

Post-testing: Research carried out on completion of a campaign to measure changes in key factors such as awareness, preference, intentions or actual purchase behaviour – or behaviour change. Usually compared to benchmark measurements taken before the campaign was implemented.

Premiums: Special merchandising such as branded clothing not normally available through conventional retail outlets. Aimed at stimulating interest in a product or service and in stimulating sales or commemorating a specific event (see also **Self-liquidating premiums**).

Press release: News released to the media regarding significant events, activities etc. for a company. Editorial staff may then decide whether or not to use any or all of the material provided as part of their editorial content.

Prestige brand: A brand offering a higher quality (often associated with a higher price) compared to a bastion brand or key competitive brands.

Pre-testing: Evaluation of marketing communication, usually in concept or unfinished form, in order to test whether the message intended to be sent is actually received by the target group and also how persuasive the message is.

Price-based sales promotion: Sales promotion based on price discounting.

Proactive MPR: (see also **Reactive MPR**): Public relations activity carried out by an organization in order to maximise positive aspects of a brand or organization, or to pre-empt possible future negative comments.

Product: (see also **Fast moving consumer goods** and **Services**): A tangible good that can be purchased, as opposed to services which may involve intangible components.

Product placement: The practice of featuring branded products in movies, television programmes etc. as part of the content, either as active placement, with a member of the cast using and/or endorsing the product as part of the scripted activity or as passive placement where the product simply appears as part of the 'background' to a scene.

Promotion: The component of the 4Ps that includes advertising, public relations and publicity, sales promotions and personal selling.

Promotional mix: The specific combination of promotion tools (see above) that are appropriate, affordable and potentially effective for a particular product, service or campaign.

Protection motivation theory: A theory explaining how individuals react to perceived or actual threats in terms of assessing the possible severity of the threat, the likelihood of it occurring, the possible success on alternative actions in preventing the threat from occurring, and how well people are able to take up the alternative actions.

Psychographics: Profile of a specific population on the basis of lifestyle factors such as activities, interests and opinions. Frequently used in conjunction with demographics to identify population segments that should be the primary focus of a campaign.

Public relations: Communication with relevant internal and external publics (see below) aimed at explaining a firm's actions or promoting the benefits of a firm's products or services and developing positive impressions, relationships, understanding or acceptance.

Publicity: Non-paid communication, frequently involving mass media, about a firm or its products or services, for example, press releases (see above) about a new product launch. Most publicity is planned by a company as part of its overall marketing communication strategy. Major environmental changes or problems with a product or service may result in media-generated publicity which may be negative in tone and therefore potentially damaging for a company.

Publics: Groups of individuals with common characteristics who may be the target of public relations or publicity activity. Groups may include shareholders, potential investors, regulators or policy makers, employees, retailers or customers.

PVR (personal video recorder): A device that connects to a television set which allows programme content to be recorded without the use of videotapes or DVDs.

Quality-based image: Projected image or positioning (see above) for a product or service based on superior quality relative to others in the category.

Rating points: The number or percentage of people in a target group who have had the opportunity to see, hear, read or otherwise be exposed to a message. Most current media measurement facilities do not measure actual exposure – only opportunities to see (for example, if someone is reported as having read a particular issue of a magazine, it does not mean that they read every article or advertisement.

Reach: The percentage of a population or target audience that is exposed to at least one message from an advertiser over a specific time period (usually a week or a 4 week period).

Reactance theory: Theory suggesting that actual or potential perceived threats to personal freedom, such as recommended restrictions on consumption of specific products or engaging in particular behaviours, may be resisted as a means to regain control of that freedom. The perceived threat itself, rather than the actual consequences of the threat, may motivate individuals or groups to assert their freedom and regain control of their own decision making and threatened freedom. Engaging in the threatened behaviour is one means of re-establishing this freedom.

Reactive MPR: (see **Proactive MPR**): Public relations activity undertaken in response to external pressures (such as competitive activity, media coverage or regulatory pressures). The objective is to minimise negative impacts on an organization or brand.

Recall: A research measurement technique in which respondents are asked to remember aspects of marketing communication messages they have seen. Usually takes two forms: unprompted recall (also referred to as unaided recall) in which prompting is limited to the product or service category and no clues to the specific marketer are provided. Prompted recall (also referred to as aided recall) involves the researcher giving specific clues as to the specific marketer and/or specific marketing communications (e.g. an advertisement) about which data is sought.

Reference groups: (see also **Aspirational groups**, **Disassociative groups** and **Membership groups**): A group whose behaviours are used as a guide to an individual's own behaviours.

Regulation: In marketing, a level of control below legislation, put in place to ensure conformity to a set of Codes of Practice or rules, such as the codes administered by the Advertising Standards Authority.

Repetition: The number of times a specific marketing communication message (e.g. an advertisement) appears in a specific time period (see also **Wearout**).

Retail account management: (see **Key account management**).

Retailer: A company with multiple outlets, or an individual outlet selling products or services to consumers on behalf of manufacturers or their agents or intermediaries (wholesalers). Sales may also be made direct to consumers by manufacturers or to wholesalers who will buy in large quantities from a manufacturer and then sell them in smaller lots to individual retailers.

Return on investment: For products and services, the calculation of the sales, revenue or profit from a specific marketing communications campaign. For social marketing and some public relations activity, the calculation may be made on the basis of attitude change as a precursor to actual behaviours.

RFID (radio frequency identification): An RFID tag can be attached to or incorporated into a product. Tags can be read via (radio waves) from several metres away, for example determining what percentage of a group are wearing a particular brand of clothing or footwear; the technology is causing some concern regarding privacy issues.

Rich media: Web pages using sophisticated technology such as video streaming or applets which allows content to change as the viewer interacts with it.

Role model: An individual, often a celebrity whose behaviour serves as an inspiration to others who may change their behaviours (and the products/services they use) to imitate the role model.

RSS: Really simple syndication is a type of webfeed for material that is often frequently updated, allowing the material to be distributed across websites and being subscribed to, for example on mobile devices. Thus, when material is updated, the material becomes available to all the subscribers without the need to check the original site for updated material.

Sales force: All sales staff working for an organization or division of an organization. Usually coordinated and controlled by a manager or director working closely with other marketing personnel.

Sales force automation (SFA): Computer-based systems, usually offered via the Internet or mobile phones that allow potential customers to evaluate products and services online and place orders or make purchases with little or no actual contact with the sales force.

Sales management: Coordination and control of a sales force in order to provide effective and efficient service to wholesalers, retailers and, ultimately, end purchasers.

Sales promotion: Incentives such as premiums or price discounts aimed at either or both of consumers and trade (wholesalers, retailers etc.) aimed at encouraging trial and/or purchase of a product.

Salience: Perceived importance or relevance of a persuasive message to its receiver.

Samples: Actual or trial-sized (small packs) products or small portions of food in store or at exhibitions and displays as part of cooking demonstrations or formal 'tasting' opportunities for consumers. Often used during product launches to stimulate interest and trial of the product and sometimes used in association with premiums or coupons.

Scepticism: Doubt about the trustworthiness or truthfulness of persuasive communication. May occur when the message conflicts with existing beliefs or perceived norms, when the source of the message is not trusted, or when overtly persuasive messages trigger persuasion resistance.

Scheduling: Decisions regarding the timing of marketing communication, such as whether to maintain continuity of exposure across a campaign period or whether to concentrate activity in a smaller number of weeks.

Second life: Internet-based virtual world in which users (residents) can interact with each other, participate in activities together – and create/trade items.

Segmentation: Division of a target population into subgroups, where members of each subgroup have significant characteristics in common and each group is different from other groups on dimensions that are central to the product or service being promoted.

Self concept: Beliefs a person holds about themselves and how they are perceived by others, together with how the beliefs are evaluated and expressed.

Self esteem: Extent to which the self concept is positive or negative.

Self-liquidating premiums: Non-standard items not usually available through conventional sales channels. These are normally sold in return for proof of purchase of a product or service that was purchased through conventional outlets. The cost reflects the cost of the product or service, plus a fee to cover costs including postage and packaging.

Semantic noise: Messages, signs or symbols that may disrupt or interfere with intended communications or distort its meaning.

Semantics: Study of the meaning of written and spoken language and associated signs and symbols. The focus is on what they represent to people rather than what they might be intended to represent by the sender of the material.

Semiotics/semiology: Study of signs and symbols as opposed to written or spoken language. Influenced by cultural and context-based factors; different population segments may assign different meanings to signs and symbols.

Services: Commodities such as banking, insurance, travel etc. that are mainly intangible (i.e. cannot be physically touched) as compared to tangible product such as fast moving consumer goods which may be taken away by the consumer after payment. Professional services may include accounting or legal advice and medical expertise.

Sexual appeals: Marketing communication/advertising appeals based on physical attractiveness.

Share of voice: Relative weight of opportunities for an advertisement to be seen (e.g. rating points) compared to other advertisers in a specific category. The higher the share of voice relative to the share of advertising expenditure, the more efficient the campaign will be judged to be.

Signs: Marks, symbols or devices conveying information.

Simultaneous media use: Use of two or more media channels (e.g. Internet and radio) simultaneously. There is little research into the effects of this on attention to, or comprehension of, persuasive messages that may appear on any or all of the media channels.

Skype: A software-based social networking system allowing free phone calls over the Internet to anyone else who has specific Skype software.

SMS (short message service): Technology that allows short messages to be sent via mobile phones

Social grade: Systems of demographic classification based on factors such as income or occupation (see also **ACORN**). The most widely used classification system is that of the National Readership Survey (NRS Ltd), funded by the UK Institute of Practitioners in Advertising (IPA). The classifications are based on the occupation of the head of the household and are as follows:

Grade	Social class	Chief income earner's occupation
A	Upper middle class	Higher managerial, administrative or professional
B	Middle class	Intermediate managerial, administrative or professional
C1	Lower middle class	Supervisory or clerical and junior managerial, administrative or professional
C2	Skilled working class	Skilled manual workers
D	Working class	Semi and unskilled manual workers
E	Those at the lowest levels of subsistence	Casual or lowest grade workers, pensioners and others who depend on the welfare state for their income

The grades are often grouped into ABC1 and C2DE and these are taken to equate to middle class and working class respectively. Approximately 2 per cent of the UK population are identified as upper class. This group is generally not included in this, or other classification schemes. Additional social grade classifications are described at: www.businessballs.com/demographicsclassifications.htm.

Social group: A group of individuals who interact on the basis of friendship, companionship, mutual interests or activities.

Social marketing: The use of commercial marketing tools to improve a population's health or well-being such as for road safety, anti-smoking, sexual health or medical screening interventions.

Social media: Online technologies and practices, such as blogs used to share individual or group opinions, insights, experiences and perspectives with others.

Social networks: Usually refers to online groups or communities that share common interests or activities (see also **Facebook**, **MySpace** or **Twitter**).

Socio-economic: Combination of social and economic factors impacting on lifestyles or purchase behaviours.

Source credibility: Perceived believability, trustworthiness, truthfulness or expertise of the source of a persuasive message.

Spam: Unrequested and unwanted electronic junk mail such as email messages.

Spin doctoring: Provision of a favourable image for an item of news or potentially unpopular policy. Often criticised for providing incomplete information, bias or misleading impressions.

Spokesperson: (see also **Endorser**): Identifiable person who features in advertisements or public relations/publicity activity and who endorses a particular product or service or demonstrates its features.

Sponsorship: Investment in a event, organization, exhibition etc. in order to generate positive links between the sponsor and the event itself and thereby gain a positive image for the sponsor and its products or services.

Standardization: Use of the same marketing communications strategy or materials across population segments, cultures or markets.

Stealth marketing: Marketing activity which is disguised so that recipients are not immediately aware of its persuasive intent. For example, paying people to say positive things about a product or service in a way that appears to be a personal recommendation or endorsement. Perceived by many as unethical.

Stereotyping: A perception or image of the behaviour of all members of a particular group; assumes all members of the group have identical characteristics and predictable behaviours.

Strategy: The selected option in terms of marketing and marketing communications activity that will maximise the chance of overall objectives being met (see also **Tactics**).

Streaming: (see **Video streaming**).

Subliminal advertising: Advertising projected at levels below the conscious thresholds of awareness (e.g. very brief messages that a person may not be conscious of having seen within other content). Subject to considerable debate regarding its impact. In spite of research in the 1950s claiming significant effects having now been discredited; many people believe it is widely used by advertisers.

Superstitials: Pop-up ads that need to be closed or removed by the viewer.

SWOT analysis: Analysis of an organization's strengths, weaknesses, and market opportunities and threats. Undertaken before deciding on appropriate and achievable strategies and tactics for a campaign.

Symbols: A letter, sign, emblem or other distinctive device that, in marketing communication represents a brand, or an organization.

Synergy: In marketing communication, the ability of different components to reinforce each other, achieving a stronger overall impact than any component could achieve on its own.

Synthesis: Combining objects or ideas into a whole, such as all the elements that combine to make a brand's identity or that combine to make an effective marketing communications campaign.

Tactics: The way in which strategy will be carried out (implemented), such as detailed media selection or public relations activity specifying exactly what material will be used where and when.

Target market: The group or groups that are the primary focus of marketing and marketing communications activity. May be defined by demographics, psychographics, product use or highest need (in the case of social marketing).

Technical or mechanical noise: External distractions such as noise from family or friends that interferes with the receipt and processing of a message.

Technology acceptance model: Theory of how users try, use and ultimately accept new technology. Key factors include perceived and actual ease of use and usefulness.

Telemarketing: Selling or attempted selling of products or services via the telephone. Often involves 'cold calling' i.e. without the prior knowledge or permission of the person being contacted.

Teleology: Ethical reasoning that focussed on actual outcome effects rather than what was intended (see also **Deontology**).

Theory: Set of concepts or hypotheses explaining the influences of behaviour. Used to identify key influences on behaviour and to describe past behaviour and predict future behaviour.

Through the line: Range of services provided by a marketing communications agency incorporating traditional media for which some commission is paid by the media for placement of the advertising, and other forms of marketing communication, including new media for which a fee will be negotiated (see also **Above the line** and **Below the line**).

TIVO: (see also **PVR**): The brand name of a type of personal video recorder. In the USA, it has become a generic name for PVRs in the same way that 'Hoover' hs become a generic term for vacuum cleaners.

Touchpoints: The various marketing communication channels through which companies communicate or interact directly with current and potential customers. Two different uses of the term exist. One encompasses media such as television, radio, magazines etc.; the other limits touchpoints to only those forms of communication where there is actual engagement and dialogue. For this second definition, traditional touchpoints include face-to-face contact such as with sales representatives, phone and mail. Electronic media touchpoints include web services, email and potentially mobile phones.

Tracking research: Longitudinal study used to identify trends or changes over time such as attitudes or preferences.

Trade: Wholesalers, retailers and other distribution channel intermediaries between a marketer and the end-user or purchaser.

Trade show: Exhibitions not generally open to the public, but rather limited to wholesalers, retailers or specific groups of customers in the business-to-business sector.

Traditional media: (see **Mass media**).

Tweet: A Twitter update.

Twitter: The most popular microblogging website, allowing people to share short text updates (Tweets) with friends on the Internet, via SMS as well as increasingly other platforms.

Typeface: A design or style for a set of characters within an alphabet, such as Times New Roman, Arial or Courier.

Undifferentiated message: A message sent to a broad target group rather than to a specific segment (see also **Differentiated message**).

Undifferentiated medium: A media channel that aims for or caters to a very broad range of users rather than to specific segments (see also **Differentiated medium**).

Utilitarian appeals: Appeals stressing the functionality of a product (as opposed to hedonistic appeals).

Value-added promotion: Promotional activity providing additional features or bonus products rather than discounting price. For example, recipe books may be offered as part of a sales promotion for baking products.

Values system: Personal aspects such as beliefs and issues held to be important by an individual or social group.

Vblog: a video blog

Video on demand: (see **On demand**).

Video streaming: Video data transmitted via web pages as a continuous 'stream' as opposed to individual pages or segments of material.

Viral marketing: Technique of using existing social networks (either in the real world or online) to spread the word or a marketing message amongst friends, thus replicating the way a virus would spread from person to person.

Virtual word of mouth: (see **eWOM**).

Vodcasting: A video podcast.

WAP (wireless application protocol): Was a way of structuring and laying out ('coding') web pages, similar to HTML, by using a defined set of codes for use on mobile devices. It was much hyped in the early 2000s; however with mobile devices becoming more sophisticated and able to display full HTML the usage has greatly reduced.

Wearin: The need for an advertisement to be seen more than once in order for the full details to be communicated to the target audience.

Wearout: Diminishing effectiveness of an advertisement or other form of marketing communication over time due to repetition.

Web 2.0: Second-generation of Internet-based services – such as social networking sites, which enable information sharing online in ways that were not possible with early Internet activity.

Web feed: Data format allowing information to be frequently updated. Used by news organizations and for podcasts and blogs.

Webisode: A short video or episode of a television show available as an Internet download or stream rather than screening on television.

Weblog: (see **Blog**).

Wholesaler: Organization that purchases products from a manufacturer and then resells them to retailers at increased costs. Often used when retailers want to purchase products in quantities which are uneconomic for a manufacturer to deal with direct.

Wikis: A website which allows users to add and edit content collectively (from the Hawaiian word for 'quick').

Word of mouth (WOM): Conversations regarding products or services, often involving users of the products/services who comment on satisfaction with product performance, service delivery, ease of use etc.

WSP: Wireless session protocol.

YouTube: A free video sharing website which lets users upload, view, and share video clips with other YouTube users. Both registered and unregistered users can also share on other platforms, for example Facebook or on mobile devices videos as part of viral marketing campaigns.

Index

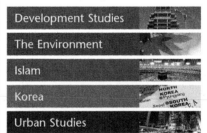
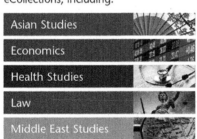